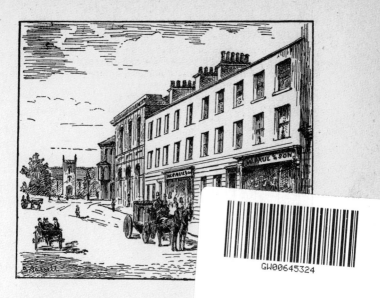

WILLIAM PAUL & SON,

DRAPERS, &c.,

PORTADOWN.

EXCELLENT QUALITY,

LARGE VARIETY,

MODERATE PRICE.

OUR MILLINERY, DRESSMAKING & TAILORING DEPARTMENTS

Are distinguished for Style and Superior Workmanship.

PUBLISHERS' NOTE

This volume contains a reprint of *The Book of County Armagh* by George
Henry Bassett, first published 1888. This new edition has been given the
title *County Armagh 100 years ago: a guide and directory, 1888.*

The Book of County Armagh first published 1888 (Dublin).
This edition, 1989, Friar's Bush Press, 24 College Park Avenue, Belfast.
Cover design and printing by W. & G. Baird Ltd., Antrim.
ISBN 0 946872 16 3

COUNTY ARMAGH
100 YEARS AGO

a guide and directory
1888

by
GEORGE HENRY BASSETT

The Friar's Bush Press

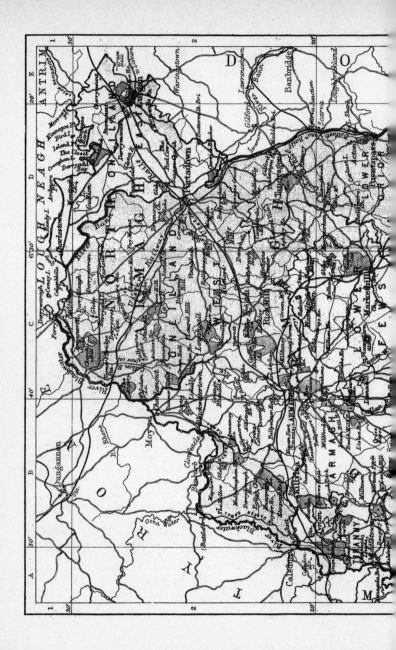

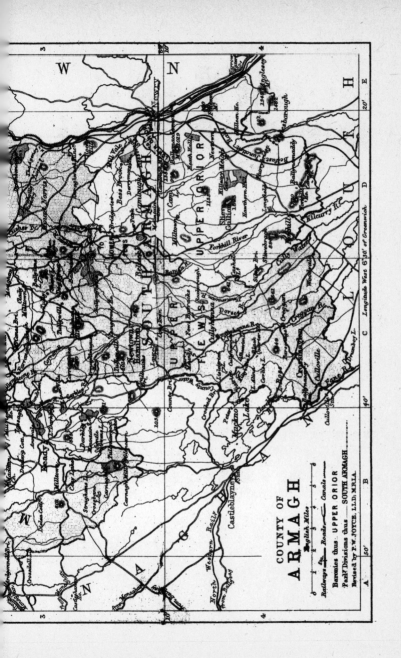

COUNTY OF
ARMAGH

English Miles

Railways ⊢⊢⊢ Roads —— Canals ——
Baronies thus UPPER ORIOR
Par.l Divisions thus ——— SOUTH ARMAGH
Revised by P.W. JOYCE, LL.D. M.R.I.A.

THE

BOOK OF COUNTY ARMAGH.

A MANUAL AND DIRECTORY FOR MANUFACTURERS, MERCHANTS, TRADERS, PROFESSIONAL MEN, LAND-OWNERS, FARMERS, TOURISTS, ANGLERS AND SPORTSMEN GENERALLY.

BY

GEORGE HENRY BASSETT,

Author of similar works for Antrim, Down, Louth, Wexford and Kilkenny.

~~~~~~~~~~

DUBLIN:

SEALY, BRYERS & WALKER,

94, 95 & 96 MIDDLE ABBEY STREET.

LONDON: SIMPKIN, MARSHALL & CO.,
4 STATIONERS' HALL COURT.

NEW YORK: ROBERT J. McMILLAN,

21 PARK ROW.

1888.

COUNTY ARMAGH.

THERE are many reasons why Armagh deserves to rank with the most interesting of Irish Counties. For centuries it contained the palaces of kings and princes. Macha, the only Queen who actually ruled in Ireland, was born within its borders. St. Patrick gave it first place among the centres of religious activity, and founded in it a school of theology and literature which had no superior in Europe.

Armagh is an inland County, bounded on the north by Lough Neagh, south by Louth, east by Down, and west by Monaghan and Tyrone. It is 32 miles from the extreme points north and south, and 20 miles from the extreme points east and west. The area is 328,086 acres. Of this 166,353 are in tillage, 112,655 in pasture, 4,580 in plantations, 27,460 in waste, bog and plantation, and 17,038 under water. In 1881 the valuation of rateable property was £420,718.

The population in 1881 was 163,170, showing a reduction in forty years of 69,223. Of the total number of residents in 1881 2,064 were natives of Leinster, 457 of Munster, and 302 of Connaught; 1,288 of England and Wales, 647 of Scotland, and 430 of foreign countries. Natives of England and Wales increased by 821 since 1841, Scotchmen multiplied their numbers by 420, and foreigners by 354.

From the tourist point of view, Armagh has numerous attractions. The shore of Lough Neagh, which lies between the Counties of Antrim and Tyrone, is exceedingly beautiful. There are two islands to be seen on the way, one of which—Coney—faces Maghery, and is a favorite resort for pic-nic and excursion parties. From Maghery to the old castle at Charlemont, thence through Blackwatertown, via Tynan Abbey and Middletown, to the City of Armagh. On this drive acquaintance may be made with some of the finest examples of inland scenery to be found in the fertile districts of Ireland. The surface is diversified by undulations which, aided by plantations and small lakes, produce effects of the most charming nature. Within a few miles, in every direction, from the City of Armagh, there are

INGLIS'S
BELFAST BREAD
IN
COUNTY ARMAGH.

AGENCIES.

R. Wallace & Co., **Armagh**

Miss Imrie, **Lurgan**

Jno. Walker, **Portadown**

J. Towell, **Richhill**

R. Emerson, **Tandragee**

R. H. Roleston, **Keady**

John Renshaw, } **Newry**
Jas. Anderson,

Jos. Thompson, **Middletown**

NOTE—See that the name " **INGLIS** " is Stamped on each Loaf.

AGENTS WANTED in UNREPRESENTED DISTRICTS.

JAMES INGLIS & CO., LTD.
BELFAST.

combinations of the character indicated. In the south-eastern region mountains of great height, rocky glens, a few lakes of goodly size, and numberless lakelets, are the principal features. Remains of castles and earthen fortifications are not so extensive as in other counties, but are important enough to greatly increase the pleasure of tourists who have a taste for antiquities. In 1586, Sir John Perrott, then Lord Deputy of Ireland, made a division of the greater part of Ulster into seven Counties, to secure a more perfect system of government. Armagh was one of the number. The district from which the lands were taken is said to have been included by Ptolemy, the geographer, in the territories of the *Vinderrii* and *Voluntii*. It also formed part of the independent Principality of Argial, embracing the Counties of Louth and Monaghan, and a portion of Meath. This, it is supposed, was marked out in 332 after a great battle in Fermuighe, part of the present County Monaghan. Colla Uais and his two brothers, at the head of a formidable army, defeated Fergus, last of the Ultonian Kings, who resided at Emania near the city of Armagh. Colla Uais had been proclaimed King of Ireland, in 315, in succession to his uncle Fiachadh, whom he had overthrown and slain in rebellion. After reigning four years, he and his brothers were driven out of the kingdom by Muireadhach, son of Fiachadh. Weary of exile, they returned and surrendered themselves, believing in a prophesy that if put to death by the King of Ireland, their children would come to the throne. Muireadhach, aware of the prophesy, first gave them command in his armies, and afterward, to provide occupation, encouraged the expedition against Fergus, which resulted in the loss of his life and the overthrow of his dynasty.

The line of Kings thus brought to an end, had ruled Ulster for centuries, from their head quarters at Emania. Colla Uais, Colla Da Crioch, and Colla Mean were the progenitors of the most powerful families of Ulster : the O'Neills, MacDonnells of Antrim, the MacMahons, Macguires of Fermanagh, and the O'Hanlons.

St. Patrick began his labors at the city of Armagh, in 445, thirteen years from his arrival at Downpatrick, and it was to Daire, a descendant of Colla Da Crioch, he was indebted for a grant of the lands upon which the first buildings were erected there under his direction.

In 830 the Danes entered the district of Argial, which became the County Armagh. This was 36 years after they had made their first descent upon the country at the Island of Rathlin, County Antrim. Newry was the port at which they debarked, and having arrived at the city of Armagh, in 836, they burned it to the ground. Turgesius, famous as a leader among

them, marched through the County from Meath to Lough Neagh, burning and plundering as he went. In 852, he burned Armagh city, in spite of the combined efforts of the princes and chieftains of Ireland. All through the 10th century the Danes continued to burn and plunder in Armagh, their operations being chiefly directed against the city. During that period Brian Boru, king of Ireland, visited Armagh, and was so much impressed that he chose it as his burial place. His remains, with those of his son Murchard, were borne hither from the battle field at Clontarf, where the Danes were defeated in 1014.

Sir John De Courcy laid the foundation of the British connection with Armagh, in 1179. He had received from Henry II. an authority to possess himself of all the lands of Ulster that he might succeed in wresting from the native chiefs. At the head of 22 men-at-arms, and 300 soldiers, he marched to Downpatrick in 1177. In two years he had built a castle there, and so firmly established himself as to warrant further developments. He visited Armagh, and plundered the city in 1179. The Conquest of Argial was completed in 1183. Philip of Worcester, Governor of Ireland, during a tour of inspection to the various British garrisons, passed through Armagh, and permitted his soldiers to pillage the city and its churches. King John, in 1210, among other parts of Ireland, visited Ulster, and colonies were planted under his direction. Armagh appears to have been to a large extent, if not entirely, subject to the authority of England in 1236, for the record shows that the king at that time directed his writs to the Archbishop. Edward Bruce, brother of the King of Scotland, in 1315, made many incursions into Armagh while resident at Dundalk. It was due to the representations of the descendants of De Lacy, successor of De Courcy in Ulster, backed by the native Irish chiefs, that Bruce was induced to embark for Ireland, where he was proclaimed King, and within three years, defeated and slain near Dundalk, by the English, commanded by Gen. De Bermingham.

Of the efforts to maintain the English connection, the most eventful from the Armagh point of view were those which were made during the rebellion of Hugh Roe O'Neill, Earl of Tyrone, 1594-1603. O'Neill had been at the Court of Elizabeth, and made use of his time by mastering the English system of military organization. Although a favourite of the Queen, on his return home, he began to mature plans for throwing off the yoke of allegiance. He caused the young men of his territory to be instructed in the tactics of the English, and prepared a store of bullets from sheet lead, which he was permitted to import in the belief that it was to be employed in the building of a castle at Dungannon. A great battle was fought in 1598

between the forces of O'Neill, strengthened by those of O'Donnell and other chiefs, and the English, commanded by Sir Henry Bagnall. The scene of the conflict was within two miles of the city of Armagh, on the way to Blackwatertown. Bagnall was slain, and the arms of O'Neill were victorious. The war was waged also in other parts of the county, notably in the parish of Killeavy, at the foot of Slieve Gullion, including the Moyre Pass, separating the counties of Louth and Armagh. O'Neill made submission to Queen Elizabeth in 1602, and to James I. in 1603. It is estimated that the rebellion cost the English, "exclusive of extraordinaries," £1,198,718. O'Neill and O'Donnell, having failed to organize a new rising in 1607, fled to the Continent. A year afterward, O'Donnell died at Rome; O'Neill, who had become blind, survived him eight years, dying also in the same city.

By the departure of O'Neill and O'Donnell an opportunity was offered for carrying into operation a scheme of plantation which had been for some time cherished by James I. The chief part of the property available for this purpose had been forfeited by the O'Neills, MacCahons and O'Hanlons. A commission, issued by the King in 1618, enquired regarding the occupation of 22 proportions of 2,000, 1,500 and 1,000 acres each. Of these, 11 in the barony of O'Neilland, were found in possession of English undertakers, and 7 in Orior had been allotted to servitors and natives.

In the rebellion of 1641 Armagh was again a battle-ground. This was the period of the Catholic Confederation, distinguished by the maintenance of a Parliament in the City of Kilkenny. Sir Phelim O'Neill, commander of the rebels, was educated in England, and inherited the place at Caledon, which had been given to his ancestor, Turlough O'Neill, by the English, in 1498. He took Charlemont Castle by stratagem. In the course of the campaign the town of Lurgan and the Castles at Markethill and Tandragee were destroyed. Col. Owen Roe O'Neill succeeded Sir Phelim in command of "the Catholic Army of the North," and in June, 1646, met and defeated Gen. Monroe at Benburb, on the border of Armagh. Owen Roe O'Neill died in 1649, it is said, from the effects of poison, administered through the medium of slippers, given to him at a ball in Derry. Cromwell had then arrived in Ireland, and was in the third month of the campaign which in less than ten months brought Ireland into complete subjection to the English Commonwealth. After the death of his kinsman, Sir Phelim O'Neill took the field again, but he was compelled to surrender, and was hanged at Dublin. During the Revolution, 1688-90, in which James II. and William

B

of Orange contended for the mastery, an attempt was made to hold the County for James. The people rose for William in the City of Armagh. Charlemont Castle was garrisoned for James, but surrendered to Duke Schomberg. Lurgan was destroyed by the troops of James, and Mr. Brownlow, owner of the town, declared an outlaw.

Armagh was prominently identified with the volunteer movement. A troop of cavalry was raised in the city, 1769, to oppose Admiral Thurot, who had seized Carrickfergus. In 1778 a company was formed, under command of Lord Charlemont. A French invasion and civil disturbances were feared at that time. A troop of volunteer cavalry, also under Lord Charlemont, was formed in 1782. On the 25th of February of that year, a Convention of Volunteers, representing 143 corps, called at Dungannon, consulted at Charlemont House, and unanimously adopted resolutions in favor of the Legislative and Judicial independence of Ireland. Toward the end of the following May, it was announced that the demand had been granted by the British administration. Sir Capel Molyneux, of Castle Dillon, Armagh, erected an obelisk, 60 feet high, in honour of the event. The hill upon which this monument stands belongs to Mr. Alexander D. Allen. The Retreat, Armagh.

Many of the disaffected inhabitants of Armagh were enrolled for service during the Rebellion of the United Irishmen, in 1798, but there was no battle in the County like those fought at Antrim, Ballinahinch and Saintfield, County Down.

Before the Legislative Union with England—1801—the County of Armagh returned six members of Parliament. Now it sends three members to the Imperial Parliament. For the convenience of local government it is divided into the baronies of Armagh, O'Neilland East and West, Upper and Lower Fews, Upper and Lower Orior, and Turanny.

LEAD MINES, COAL INDICATIONS, LIMESTONE, MARBLE, GRANITE, &c. SLATE QUARRIES, MOUNTAINS, RAILWAYS, TRAMWAYS AND ROADS, NAVIGABLE WATERWAYS.

WHEN lead-mining again becomes a profitable speculation in Ireland, several mines may be opened in the County Armagh. Ore has been found in many districts, including Keady, Newtownhamilton, Crossmaglen, Forkhill, Markethill, Ballymoyre, and Middletown. A mine was worked, not far from Keady, more than fifty years since, but the expenditure for development purposes was so greatly in excess of the yield that the enterprise was not

persevered in. The mine at Cregganduff, in the neighbourhood of Crossmaglen, has not been worked for more than fifteen years. Mining was discontinued at Tullydonnell, also within a short distance of Crossmaglen, about the same time. While wood lasted for smelting, mining was carried on near Newtown-hamilton. That was a long time ago.

Thin veins of coal, said to be of fair quality, have been discovered in the parish of Mullaghbrack, district of Markethill, in the vicinity of Charlemont, and in the parishes of Tynan and Killylea. Some indications of iron have been noticed, but they are not regarded as of much consequence.

Limestone of good quality is extensively quarried close to the city of Armagh, near Loughgall and Tynan. The Armagh limestone has a pink tinge which is improved in weathering. Red marble is also quarried in the vicinity of Armagh. It polishes prettily, and at one period was used very much for mantel-pieces. In the south-eastern part of the county there is an abundance of excellent granite. It is quarried profitably at the works of the Bessbrook Spinning Company, Limited, between Bessbrook and Camlough, and by another firm at Goraghwood. Slieve Gullion, which rises to a height of 1,893 feet above the level of the sea, at the south-eastern point, is an offset of the granite district of county Down. The top is flat, and contains a lake. During the successful days of milling, the Slieve Gullion granite was highly esteemed for grinding purposes. Its composition includes feldspar, mica, quartz, and hornblende. Veins of pink quartz, in the granite, are of frequent occurrence. A hard stone, approaching to dark blue in color, called whin in this county, is found in various places. Several slate quarries have been opened, but none are worked.

All the mountains of the county are named on the map, in the front of the book and their heights given. The railways are also marked on the map. For some time the several lines have been under the control of the Great Northern Company. The northern, middle, and south-eastern districts are fairly well supplied with broad gauge roads, but there is still room for narrow gauge enterprises like those which have rescued much of the county Antrim from isolation. A narrow gauge road enters the county at Caledon, and ends at Tynan, one mile from the border. It is called the Clogher Valley steam tramway. A line of this kind from Blackwatertown to Keady, via Armagh city, would be a great convenience to farmers and others. Some time ago the Grand Jury gave a baronial guarantee for twenty years to a Company organized for the purpose of building the tramway, but would go no further. The shareholders were desirous of doing all they

DO NOT

Buy 2s. 8d. TEA until you have tried my unparalleled 2s. TEA—Makes fast friends for itself.

DO NOT

Buy 1s. 4d. FLOUR elsewhere until you have tried my wonderful new Flour at 11½d. per stone. Deserves special notice.

DO NOT

Buy Groceries, Meal, Flour, and Provisions at high prices when you can get best quality of goods so wonderfully cheap.

This is a Genuine all-round Reduction. Quality Guaranteed.

W. J. CULLEY,

The Golden Canister, North St., Newry.

could in the matter without incurring the risk of loss. They could not, however, be convinced that a guarantee for such a short period would be sufficient, and the project remains in abeyance. An electric tramway, three miles in length, connects Bessbrook with Newry. It was built as a private enterprise by shareholders of the Bessbrook Spinning Company, Limited, and opened for traffic in October, 1885. In 1886 it carried 97,668 passengers. The gates on the public road over which it passes are opened and closed automatically by an invention of Mr. Henry Barcroft's. In this manner a saving in wages is effected, which would be a very serious item in the working expenses.

For the year 1887 it cost the county £19,130 16s. for repairing a little over 1,575 miles of roads.

Two navigable water-ways facilitate the carrying trade of the county. The more important separates the County Down from Armagh. It runs from the tidal basin at Fathom, below Newry, to Lough Neagh, and is served by the Bann and the Newry river. The depth of water is sufficient to float lighters 70 tons burden. Direct communication with Belfast is secured by means of the Lagan Canal, *via* Lough Neagh. Coal, grain, timber and general merchandise form the cargoes. The Newry Canal was the first of the kind completed in Ireland. About fifty years ago connection was effected between Lough Erne and Lough Neagh, by means of the Ulster Canal. This passes for a considerable distance along the western and north-western borders of Armagh. It is being largely taken advantage of at present by some of the leading merchants of the City of Armagh. The shipping place is at Blackwatertown, distant four miles. It is expected that the Ulster Canal system will be soon very much improved by the Ulster Canal Company who receive possession of it this year—1888—under special Act of Parliament.

MANUFACTURING AND OTHER INDUSTRIES.

THE manufacturing interests of Armagh, considering its area in statute acres, are more important than those of any other Irish county with, perhaps, a single exception. Twenty-seven out of the thirty-two, are larger. Four are more than twice the size, and six more than three times the size. Down to the close of the seventeenth century the woollen industry maintained a substantial footing. It was then destroyed by legislation in favor of the English manufacturers. Some attempts have been made at revival, but it has now no representation. Cotton spinning and weaving were carried on in the first half of the century. Until 1856 there were extensive mills at Glenanne. At present

JAMES THOMPSON,

Wholesale and Family

GROCER, GRAIN, SEED AND PROVISION

MERCHANT,

4 and 5 Kildare Street,

NEWRY.

there is not a mill within the limits of the county devoted exclusively to cotton manufacture. The linen industry, in all its branches, absorbs the bulk of the capital possessed by residents, and a large part of that belonging to Belfast.

During the past fifty years a great deal has been done in the way of development, particularly at Lurgan. The weaving, hemstitching and finishing of cambric and linen handkerchiefs give employment to a large number of the inhabitants. The first machine hemstitching factory in the United Kingdom, on Mr. Jos. B. Robertson's patents, was erected here. Linens of every description, damasks and cambrics are sent from Lurgan all over the world. Until a comparatively recent period the weaving was nearly all done by handlooms. Lurgan is a centre from which yarns are given out to be woven by cottage weavers. Thousands of these men live in the adjoining County of Down, and thousands in Armagh and other Counties. There are three power loom weaving factories in Lurgan, about a dozen machine hemstitching factories, print works and several finishing works.

Portadown has four linen weaving factories, one flax spinning mill, and several hemstitching factories. It is also a centre for the manufacture of linen, and linen and cambric handkerchiefs by handlooms.

In the City of Armagh and vicinity there are four power loom linen weaving factories, and two power loom coarse linen weaving factories, one at Allistragh, and the other at Lislea. There is also a large flax spinning mill at Armagh. On the Armagh side of the Blackwater, at Benburb, there is a power loom factory for weaving coarse linens, and one also of a similar kind at Dundrum, Tassagh.

Extensive power loom linen weaving factories are situated at Bessbrook, Annvale and Darkley, near Keady, at Glenanne, and Laurelvale, Tandragee. There are large flax spinning mills at Bessbrook, Darkley, Tandragee, and on the Armagh side of Newry. Bleaching and finishing are done at Annvale, Portadown, Glenanne, Bessbrook and Milford. Whiskey distillation, at one period carried on with large capital, has ceased. The only brewery in the County is at Lurgan. There are three mineral water factories, all at Lurgan. Two tanneries at Richhill represent the County. Coach-building is done at Armagh, Portadown and Lurgan. Bacon-curing for exportation is a new industry. Two firms are engaged in it at Portadown. There are flour and corn mills at Armagh, Portadown, and Tandragee, and a large number of small corn and scutch mills are scattered through the rural districts. One mill, on the Callan, represents paper manufacture. In the description of the towns and villages, the manufactures are referred to separately.

The general trade of the County is conducted on lines indi-
cating spirit, ability, and enterprise. In the chief towns the
competition is very keen, and the methods of the leading business
men are admirable.

ANTIQUITIES, GOLD, SILVER, BRASS & BRONZE, BELLS, RATH DWELLINGS, CAIRNS, CAVES, DRUIDIC CIRCLES, &c.

MANY specimens illustrating the artistic taste and skill
of the ancient Irish workers in gold, silver and bronze
have been dug up in the County Armagh. They
have gone to enrich private and public collections to
the loss of the city of Armagh, where they might have accumulated as a most interesting feature of the Library. The late
Primate Marcus Jervis Beresford evidently appreciated this
deficiency, and probably to encourage others, presented some
flint arrow-heads, bronze swords, celts, &c. These are on exhibition, and it is to be hoped may have the effect suggested.
Some of the golden torques, collars, amulets and rings, brought
to light, there is good reason to believe, went to the melting pot.
A massive finger-ring was found in 1781 on the site of Emania,
residence of the Ulster Kings. It was said to have been richly
engraved, and weighed 20 ounces. Sale was made of it in
Dublin at the rate of £4 per ounce. The Museum of the Royal
Irish Academy is rich in gold ornaments from other Irish
counties, but has only one belonging to Armagh. This is an
unclosed ring ⅝ths of an inch in external diameter. It was
purchased in 1884. In the strong room of the Academy, highly
prized, is an ecclesiastical bell bearing the inscription, in Irish,
"Pray for Cumuscach, the son of Ailill." Cumuscach was
economist of the Cathedral of Armagh, and died in the year 904.
His mother was Gormlaith, daughter of Muireadach, King of
Ulster. This bell was obtained for the Academy by the Dean
of St. Patrick's in 1840. It had been for many generations in
possession of an Armagh family named O'Hanan. The Bell of
St. Patrick, 6 inches high, 4¾ inches at the shoulder, and 5
inches at the foot, is preserved in Trinity College, Dublin. It
was made by joining two pieces of sheet iron with rivets, and
coating them with brass. A bronze trumpet in a good state of
preservation, found in Armagh, 1794, is included in the Royal
Irish Academy collection. This may be one of four discovered
in boggy land close to Loughnashade, near Armagh, about the
time mentioned. One of the most imperfect is described as
having two joints, the whole length of the sweep being six feet,
and almost semi-circular. The diameter of the tube at the small
end was one inch, and that of the large end 3¾ inches. The

plate forming each joint was rivetted to a thin strip of brass, and made perfectly air-tight without the use of solder.

The Belfast Museum contains a few valuable objects belonging to Armagh. Among the number are four sculptured marble panels, each about 5½ inches in height, and 4½ inches in breadth. They were found in the ruins of the Abbey of Armagh, within the primate's demesne, and presented by Mr. James Gibson, who also presented some good specimens of stone hatchets from Armagh. In the fine collection of fossils at the same Museum there is a very perfect fish spine in carboniferous limestone, found at Armagh. It was the gift of Mr. W. Swanston, F.G.S.

Remains of earthen fortifications are numerous. Those of Emania, residence of the Kings of Ulster for 700 years, are situated at a distance of two miles from the city of Armagh. Next in interest is the Dane's Cast. It is supposed to have originally extended from Lough Neagh, via Scarva, through the County Down to the sea. A section of the "cast," in the demesne of Scarva House, residence of Mr. Reilly, is carefully preserved, and freely open to the inspection of tourists and excursionists. Lisnagade, or "the fort of a hundred," is also in the parish of Scarva, and, although in Down, is worthy of notice here for the reason that many of the hundred forts seen from it were in Armagh, then called Argial. Rathtrillick, in the barony of Turanny, near Middletown, forms the centre of a district in which there are many others of the same description. By reference to the list of farmers and residents, following the directory to each town and village, the names of the townlands will indicate those in which such fortifications once existed, and in some of which they still exist. Whenever the first syllable of the townland begins with *Rath, Lis,* or *Dun,* meaning fort, identification may easily be made. Lisbanoe is well preserved and picturesquely situated on the estate of Col. Thomas Simpson, J.P., Ballyards House, Armagh. A fine view of it is obtained from Millford House, residence of Mr. Rt. G. McCrum, J.P. In ancient times raths and mounts were entrenched villages, where during the winter months the people lived in community as a protection from wild beasts and from hostile tribes. In summer they removed to the mountains and tended their flocks. Down to the 16th century this practice was common. Excavations in forts have revealed secret passages and chambers. These were used as places of refuge for women and children, and for the storage of food supplies and valuables. Within the circle of each fort huts were erected of wood and sometimes of stone. The forts which clustered in the same neighbourhood usually had underground connections to facilitate the massing of the fighting forces, as well as the removal of non-combatants to

The ONLY Food that will keep good in TROPICAL CLIMATES.

TRADE MARK.

ORX ET LABORA

For the Healthful Rearing of Hand-Fed Children, and the Preservation of Infant Life.

∴ MELLIN'S FOOD ∴

(NOT FARINACEOUS)

Is the only Infants' Food correctly prepared in accordance with the well-known laws of Physiology as regards Digestion and Nutrition. Is not farinaceous, the insoluble starchy components which cannot pass into the blood stream having been changed into soluble bodies, which are ready to supply immediately material for nutrition and growth.

∴ FOR INFANTS ∴

Has saved thousands of infant lives, many cases apparently hopeless, and is prescribed by the majority of medical men. Is supported by unsolicited testimonials from all great medical authorities, and from immense numbers received from the public.

∴ AND INVALIDS. ∴

THE FOOD OF THE PRESENT AND FUTURE.

Apply for Pamphlet and Sample to the Inventor and Manufacturer,

G. MELLIN,

Marlboro' Works, PECKHAM, LONDON, S.E.

places of greater security. Kings, princes and soldiers occupied the larger raths, and the petty chiefs, with their families and dependents, the smaller ones. The Danes built raths in Armagh for use as places of habitation and defence. Before the plantation of the country, 1609, by English and Scotch undertakers, raths were more numerous. Since then a great many have been removed to give greater scope for farming operations. Even within the last fifty years the leveling has been carried on, and the levelers have reached a good old age in spite of the superstitious fears of their neighbours. One of the number whom I met in Scotchstreet, Mr. Robert Love, removed a rath an acre in extent, in the townland of Timakeel, over 40 years ago. There are several Danish forts in Lord Gosford's demesne at Markethill.

Cairns still exist in different parts of the county. Many have been reduced in size and some carried away altogether to enable thrifty farmers to increase the number of their out offices, and for fencing and other purposes. What is left of the Vicar's Cairn occupies the top of a hill 819 feet high, to the west of Markethill. A large cairn on the summit of Slieve Gullion, about the year 1834, underwent a very careful examination by archælogists. It is supposed to have been the burial place of Cualgue, a Milesian chieftain, who fell in battle at the foot of the mountain. A poem, ascribed to Ossian, refers to this matter, and also to the cairn, and the lake beside it. By comparison with Antrim, the known caves in Armagh are very few. In the parish of Killeavy, at the foot of Slieve Gullion, there is one which has attracted a great deal of attention. In the townland of Drummond, on the Castle Dillon estate, there is one, built of field stones. It consisted of two chambers; one about 7½ feet in height still exists ; the other was destroyed 30 or 40 years ago. There are two natural caves at the Sheepwalk, close to the City of Armagh. There is no perfect Druidic circles now in the County. About three-fourths of one, originally 23 yards in diameter, may be seen upon the farm of Mr. Thomas Knipe, townland of Ballybrawley, 2½ miles north by west from Armagh. A second circle occupied a site within 150 yards of the first. The last stone of this was removed about 12 years ago.

At the foot of the stairs, in the Public Library of Armagh, there is an Ogham stone, 5 feet 2 inches long, and 15 inches broad at the inscribed face. It was discovered in 1879 by Mr. Robert Pillow, of Armagh. The search was suggested by reading a passage in the Annals of the Four Masters, brought under his notice by Mr. Edward Rogers, Deputy Librarian. This refers to a battle at Aenach Macha, where King Conmael was

defeated and slain, 3579 A.M. He was supposed to have been buried in the townland of Drumconwell, within 3½ miles of Armagh. Mr. Pillow, by bearing this fact in mind, came upon the stone in a field, 150 yards from the dwelling-house of Mr. Samuel Ireland. Only a few inches were above ground. Mr. Ireland kindly allowed it to be taken up, and it was placed in the Library by desire of Dr. Reeves, present Bishop of Down and Connor and Dromore. The stone bears an inscription in Ogham characters signifying " Dinigal, son of Cueta."

ANCIENT CASTLES: ARMAGH, CHARLEMONT, TANDRAGEE, MOYRE PASS, CRIFCAIRN, ARDGONNELL, ROE, JOHNSTON FEWS & BLACK BANK.

ASTLES, formidable in proportions, of which nothing now remains, once served important military purposes in various parts of the county. One of this number was in Armagh. Obscure references are made to the existence of a castle here at an early period, but it cannot have been very strong, considering that it was so easily wiped out and rebuilt. The Castle of Armagh, referred to in *Lodge's Peerage* as the work of Maurice Fitzgerald, second Baron of Offally, bore date 1236. Mention is made of it in the account of the Rebellion of Hugh O'Neill, Earl of Tyrone. In 1596 the garrison surrendered to him.

Charlemont Castle still continues in a fair state of preservation, but the approaches don't seem to be maintained in as good condition as they used to be some years ago. This castle was built by Lord Mountjoy in 1602. He was then Lord Deputy of Ireland. The name Charlemont was derived from Charles Mountjoy. A wooden bridge then afforded a passage across the Blackwater into Tyrone, and the castle was specially intended to guard it against the attacks of the O'Neills. At the beginning of the war of 1641, Sir Phelim O'Neill captured the Castle. He invited himself to dine with the Commander, Lord Caulfield, and at a certain signal his followers rose, seized and made prisoners of the host and his family. The successor of Sir Phelim, Col. Owen Roe O'Neill, on arrival in Ireland to take command of the " Catholic Army of the North," was introduced to his leading officers at this place. It was ultimately captured by Sir Charles Coote, and was sold to Charles II. in 1665 for £3,500. Sir Teague O' Regan held possession for James II. in 1690, but was compelled to surrender to Duke Schomberg. Lord Charlemont owns the castle at present, and has an ex-military sergeant in charge.

JOHN THOMPSON,

Ornamental Painter, Decorator, &c.,

10 SUGAR ISLAND, **NEWRY**.

PAPER HANGING, GLAZING, &c.

PICTURES FRAMED ON MODERATE TERMS.

CROWN AND ROLLED PLATE GLASS, &c.

Agent for Newry and district for M'Caw, Stephenson and Orr's

Patent "Glacier" Window Decoration.

S. FLEMING,

Plumbing, Gas Fitting, Copper, Iron and Tin Plate Works,

46 NORTH STREET, NEWRY.

Pumps, Baths, Water Closets, Gasaliers, Brackets, Sheet Lead, Lead
and Composition Pipe, Iron and Steam Tubes, Steam and Water
Cocks, Bell Fittings, &c., &c.

Buildings Fitted with Hot Water Apparatus, &c.

Competent Workmen sent to any part of the country.

Tandragee Castle belongs to the Duke of Manchester. It is the finest structure in the County, and commands a very strong position at the head of the town. The site was originally occupied by a castle belonging to the O'Hanlons, descendants of one of the Collas, who, in 332 A.D., dethroned Fergus, last of the Kings of Ulster. They owned a large territory which was forfeited to the Crown through connection with the rebellion of the Earl of Tyrone, 1594-1603. On the Plantation of Ulster by James I., 1609, Sir Oliver St. John was given the property. He rebuilt the castle, but it was completely destroyed by the O'Hanlons in the war of 1641. Viscount Mandeville built the present castle over fifty years ago.

The ruin of Moyre Castle is in the parish of Killeavy, near the boundary of Louth and Armagh. It stands upon a rock commanding the narrow pass between the hills, and was built by Lord Mountjoy in 1601. He and the Earl of Tyrone had fought a battle at this point during the previous year, ending in the repulse of Tyrone.

Crifcairn Castle appears to have suffered severely from the "tooth of time." The ruin, which might now be better described as a fragment of the western wall, 9 feet thick, occupies a most picturesque situation overlooking a small sheet of water called Hanslough. It is about 2¾ miles from Middletown, off the direct road to Armagh. The highest part of the ruin is about 60 feet, and is partly ivy-covered. Lord Caledon, who owns the property of the district, some time ago had the ruin enclosed by a wire fence, and some yews planted around it. Crifcairn belonged to the O'Neills. The road now passing in front was part of the moat. Some remains of Ardgonnell Castle also exist. They are situated in the townland of the same name, within a short distance from Middletown. Ardgonnell was a stronghold of the O'Neills. The last of the race who used it was Sir Phelim.

The ruin of Castle Roe occupies a commanding position. It is in sight of the village of Kilmore, within a mile of Loughgall 2 miles of Richhill, 5 miles of Portadown, and 5 miles of Armagh Rory O'Neill is said to have been the builder in the 16th century The structure is cruciform, 37 feet each way, and the walls 4 feet thick, and about 40 feet at the highest point. The grounds were surrounded by a circular intrenchment, the castle being in the centre, at a distance of nearly 350 feet. About one-third of this remains. Castle Roe, also called Castle Raw, is on the estate of Mr. F. R. Cope, in the tenancy of Mrs. Williamson. John Cooke, a handloom weaver, rents a small house close to the castle, and takes pleasure in showing it to visitors. The view from here includes Slieve Gullion, the Mourne Range, Co.

Down, Black Mountain, County Antrim, and the spires of Dungannon.

There are insignificant remains of the castles of Johnston Fews and Blackbank, built after the Plantation of Ulster to protect settlers. In both places efforts were made to establish towns, but without success, and after the removal of the troops to Newtownhamilton the castles went to ruin.

FARMING, FRUIT GROWING, HORSES, CATTLE, SHEEP, PIGS & POULTRY, MARKETS & FAIRS.

IN the greater part of the county the soil is fertile, and may be worked profitably when fair prices can be obtained for produce. The formation affords facilities for drainage, and there is an abundance of limestone. By a system of treatment called heating, the boggy districts are capable of yielding good crops. This consists of lighting peat fires around a spot about to be planted with potatoes or oats. The surface is also sprinkled with hot ashes, and when warmed thoroughly, so forces vegetation that results are achieved equal, if not superior, to those secured from the richest loam lands. When this process is not applied, the oat crop hardly pays for the labor. The Southern section, including the baronies of Upper Fews and Upper Orior, has much rocky and barren land. Granite boulders are plentifully distributed over the surface, and there are other obstacles of a discouraging nature. The northern, eastern, western and middle sections of the county are thickly populated, and the farms are small, particularly in the districts where handloom weaving is done in almost every cottage.

But for the help given by "the bit of land" this industry would very speedily come to an end. Many of the weavers have apple orchards, and between the various modest sources of income contrive to live comfortably. Fruit growing is an extensive feature in the districts of Portadown, Loughgall and Richhill. Representatives of the Scotch and English preserve manufacturers come over every season and purchase apples, damsons, plums, gooseberries and currants, in large quantities, direct from the farmers. Preserving is also done by growers and merchants in the county.

Owing to the great number of small farmers, there are few large dairies or stock masters. Butter making is chiefly done in lump, and the merchants pack for exportation to suit their own requirements.

At the flower, dog and poultry show, held at Armagh City in July of this year, there was a department for butter, in which

several prizes were offered. It gave an opportunity for a lecture to the farmers and their wives and daughters, by Canon Bagot, whose work in this field has proved valuable in Munster and Leinster.

There is no regular farming society existing in Armagh, but the county is represented in the North-East Agricultural Association of Ireland, by four vice-presidents and a large array of committee men. At the annual shows of this excellent organization many residents of Armagh are exhibitors in the live stock, poultry and honey departments.

Two ornithological societies flourish in the county, one at Lurgan since 1880 ; and the other at Armagh, since 1883. Both societies hold annual shows for poultry, pigeons and cage-birds, and, thus far, have been most successful in their objects.

In 1887 the total area under tillage was 107,640 acres, exactly 17 acres more than in the previous year. Meadow and clover represented 51,964 acres, an increase of 3,904 acres over the previous year. The largest area was under oats, 54,231, an increase of 1,610 acres. Potatoes, 26,871 acres, showed a decrease of 640 acres. There were 12,738 acres of flax, compared with 13,346 in 1886. In a few localities where the land is very heavy, the farmers still stick to wheat, but they seem to be losing faith in it every year. Last year the acreage was 2,552, a reduction of nearly 1.000 acres, compared with that of 1886. There was a considerable increase in the area devoted to turnips, mangel wurzel, carrots and parsnips. The turnip acreage was 7,998. The calculation in regard to the amount of cabbage required for the entire county has evidently been brought down to a very fine point. In 1886 there were 332 acres devoted to it, and 336 acres in 1887.

Live stock statistics show a striking difference between the years 1886 and 1887. The total number of horses in the former year was 13,239, and in the latter year 13,710. Of these 10,724 were used for agricultural purposes in 1887, and 10,746 in 1886. There were 468 mules in 1886, and only 318 in 1887. Donkeys seem to have suffered in popularity also. There were 2,268 in 1887, a decrease of 332 in twelve months. Milch cows numbered 31,852 in 1886, and 30,601 in 1887, a decrease of 1,251. The total number of cattle was 85,328 in 1886, and 82,428 in 1887, a decrease of 2,900. Sheep numbered 12,441 in 1886, and 13,817 in 1887, an increase of 1,376. Pigs increased from 28,696 in 1886 to 30.243 in 1887. and goats decreased from 8,902 in 1886, to 8,892 in 1887. There was an increase in poultry from 403,289 to 411,581. The decrease in the number of milch cows seems to have caused an increase in sheep and a decrease in mules and donkeys.

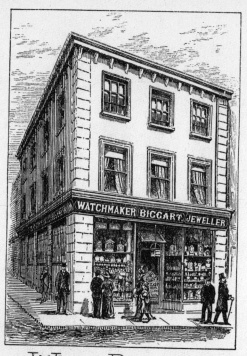

Wm. Biggart,

Watchmaker, Jeweller, Silversmith & Optician,

Corner of Market Square and English Street,

ARMAGH.

Watches, Clocks and Jewellery.
Tea and Coffee Services, Salvers, &c. &c.

REPAIRS EFFICIENTLY EXECUTED.

*Fancy Goods of the choicest description in great
variety.*

The market places of the county, fifty years ago, included most of the villages. Now the large towns seem to monopolize nearly all the advantages derived from the great weekly gatherings of farmers. Armagh city, Portadown and Lurgan are the great centres for the sale of produce, live stock, &c. Markethill, Keady, Newtownhamilton, Crossmaglen, and Poyntspass, have also weekly markets. To these points, with some exceptions, the fairs are also confined. The exceptions are Hamiltonsbawn, Killylea, Ballybot, Camlough, Ballsmill, and Forkhill.

ANGLING, NET-FISHING, FOWLING, THE MANDE-VILLE GUN CLUB, RIFLE SHOOTING.

THE rivers and lakes of the County Armagh are, with very few exceptions, open to the public, and afford good sport for anglers. At the mouths of the Bann and Blackwater, both of which rivers discharge into Lough Neagh, salmon-trout of excellent quality, and brown trout are obtainable. Neither the Bann nor the Blackwater amount to much for trout on the way through the county, but have plenty of eels, pike, bream and roach. The Blackwater improves for trout just beyond the limits, in the vicinity of Benburb. Some parts of the Callan are good for trout, notably in the vicinity of Armagh city and Milford. It rises in the barony of Armagh, near Keady, and flows through the barony of O'Neilland west until it joins the Blackwater. Between Allistragh, site of the battle of Yellow Ford, and the paper mill, at the road from Armagh to Keady, it is fairly good, but not further up. The Butterwater, a small tributary joining at Milford, is said to be much better for trout than the Callan. It is within three miles of Armagh. Brown trout are pretty numerous in the Cusher, above and below Tandragee. Anglers can make a beginning at a point near Madden, a station on the Great Northern Railway, between Goraghwood Junction and Portadown. Culloville, a small station on the North-Western Railway, between Dundalk and Castleblayney, is near the Fane, a first-rate salmon and trout river, at that point bordering the counties of Armagh and Monaghan. Crossmaglen, a splendid centre for a few weeks' trout-fishing, is within three miles. See reference to Crossmaglen at index. At a distance of less than a mile from Crossmaglen, the Creggan is very good for trout, and continues good until it becomes the Cullyhanna. Forkhill river, and the Flurry water are good. Forkhill is four miles, Irish, from Dundalk, the nearest railway station. Flurrybridge is about eight miles, English, from Dundalk. The county water is good for trout. It divides Armagh from Monaghan, and may be fished

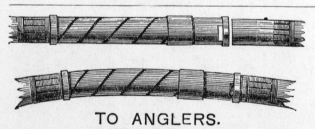

from Altnamachan Bridge, about three miles, Irish, from New-townhamilton. The Monaghan river, two miles from Markethill Railway Station, is sometimes fair for trout. For those who desire to enjoy beautiful scenery as well as good trout-fishing, I recommend the lake region of Crossmaglen. It begins at a distance of about a mile from the village. A chain of small lakes, over eighteen in number, winds between cultivated hills for several miles. Most of these are well stocked, and are open to the public. The shortest way from Armagh city is by Tassagh, and Altnamachan, turning to the left at The County Bridge. The road runs from here along the top of a ravine, for a mile or more, gradually descending toward Kiltybane, one of the lakes containing a small wooded island, in view of the remains of an extensive rath.

County Armagh abounds in small lakes, but with a few exceptions, those in the Crossmaglen district only have trout. A lake in Forkhill demesne is fairly well supplied, and is open to the public. There are some trout in Loughgall, Manor House demesne, but leave to fish has to be obtained. The troutless lakes, including Marlacoo and Ballynewry, between Tandragee and Armagh, and Dartrey, near Blackwatertown, have plenty of pike and eels. Net fishing is confined to Lough Neagh, of which 15,554 acres belong to the County Armagh. In the village of Milltown, postal district of The Birches, many fishermen live. They catch pollen, eels, trout, pike, perch and salmon, but pollen are their main reliance for profit. Several resident dealers ship to England at the Annaghmore railway station, 3½ miles from the Lough.

Opportunities for fowling are fair. Nearly all the bogs and marshes afford snipe and plover, and the lakes have widgeon, duck and teal. Lough Neagh is particularly good, and there are several places near the shore which can be relied upon to provide comfortable quarters. Maghery is one of the number. This is in view of Coney Island, an attractive wooded spot for wild birds. The bogs between Blackwatertown and Armagh are good for snipe. Duck and snipe are found at Dartrey Lake, near Blackwatertown, and at Marlacoo and Ballynewry lakes toward Tandragee. In the lake region of Crossmaglen plenty of duck, teal widgeon and snipe are to be had. There are many preserved places, including Brownlow House demesne, Lurgan, Lord Gosford's demesne, Markethill, and the demesnes of Tynan Abbey, Castle Dillon, Forkhill, and the Manor House, Loughgall.

The Mandeville Gun Club, for Pigeon Shooting, flourishes at Tandragee. Lord Mandeville is President, Mr. Thomas Dickson, of Hazelbank, Laurencetown, Secretary, and Mr. Wesley Watson, Belfast, Treasurer. It has about fifty members, sub-

scribing annually two guineas each. Meetings are held once a fortnight in the Counties of Armagh, Down and Antrim.

Rifle shooting, by civilians, is confined to Lurgan, where there is a well-organized club of about 30 members. Mr. Geo. Greer, B.L., J.P., is President, and the range, a good one, is within his demesne at Woodville.

HUNTING : COUNTY HARRIERS, COURSING DOG BREEDING, THE WOLF PERIOD, HORSE-RACING, JUMPING, TROTTING, DRIVING, "FEEDING" AND FINISHING.

HUNTING has been successfully carried on in this county from a very early period. At present there are two first-rate packs of harriers maintained by subscription. There are no fox coverts. An effort was made to provide them in the Tynan country many years since by Sir James Stronge, Bart., but it failed. At that time trapped foxes were imported from Donegal. The Tynan Harriers were established by Sir James between 45 and 50 years ago. He maintained the pack at his own expense until failing health compelled him to give up the sport. His love of it was intense all through life. A committee was formed to carry on the pack, and Sir James gave over hounds, horses, kennels, etc., rent free, and a subscription of £50 a year. The nominal mastership he retained ; the field masters being Dr. T. Huston and Mr. W. Upton Moutray, of Fort Singleton, Emyvale, Co. Monaghan. This arrangement continued until the death of Sir James about three years ago. The kennels are now at Killylea. Mr. Moutray is secretary and treasurer, and the huntsman is George McAree. The pack consists of 22 couples, averaging 18 inches in height. Monday and Thursday and Monday and Friday alternately, are the days of meeting. The hunting country includes parts of Armagh and Tyrone, within a six-mile radius of the town of Caledon. It is fair on the whole, cramped in some districts, and in others there is a great deal of grass land. Subscriptions from 50 members range from £10 down to £1, producing a total of about £230 per annum. A pretty good stock of hares is kept up, and, as a rule, the farmers are very friendly. The members of the Hunt—at present numbering about 50—usually dined together in the second week of April. This practice was given up, and a race or two for ponies of local farmers substituted.

The Armagh Harriers existed as a pack in the last century, but the records available, deal only with its management from about the year 1835. Lord Waterford was then Master. The hounds were next taken by Mr. M. R. Bell, and he kept

them until 1849. Captain Hutchinson was his successor. A committee took charge in 1875, and continued until 1881, when Mr. Joseph Atkinson became master. Mr. George D. Beresford succeeded him in 1886, and Mr. Thomas Lonsdale became master the following year, and is still in office. Twenty inches is the average height of the dogs, and there are eighteen couples. The kennels are at the Pavilion, Armagh, the residence of the master. Mr. William G. Robinson, Beechhill, Armagh, is secretary and treasurer. Seth Lowe and Thomas Gillespie, respectively, fill the posts of huntsman and whip. There are twenty-five members. Hunting members pay an annual subscription of from £5 to £10, and non-hunting members from £1 to £5. Wednesday and Saturday are the days of meeting. The country consists principally of tillage land, with some good grass districts, small fields, with banks, ditches, hedges, and drains, Hares are proverbial for their stoutness in the several districts, and are not seriously diminished in numbers, save in one or two, notwithstanding the fact that they are constantly harassed by small local packs.

The late Captain Atkinson, of Crow Hill, forty years ago, had a private pack of harriers. About the same time, a private pack was also maintained by the late Sir George Molyneux, of Castle Dillon. Apropos of this subject, it is interesting to know that there were 403 horses kept for "amusement or recreation" in the county in 1886, and 439 in 1887, an increase of 36.

Wolf hunting was one of the exciting sports of the county shortly after the plantation of Ulster. Armagh, as well as the rest of the Irish counties, was so overrun with wolves, that the attention of James I. was attracted to the matter. In 1614 he granted a patent to an adventurous Englishman, named Tuttesham, under which he was to receive from the public treasury four nobles sterling for the head of every wolf, young or old, delivered by him to the public officers. A noble was a gold coin of the value of six shilling and eight pence sterling. Although he was permitted to keep twelve couples of hounds and four huntsmen in each county for seven years, he did not succeed in effecting extermination, for it is recorded that Sir John Ponsonby in 1662, promoted a Bill in Parliament to finish the work. The last wolf seen in Ireland was killed in Kerry in 1710.

Coursing, down to a short time ago, was a prominent feature in the sports of Armagh. The great event of each year came off in the Raughlan meadows, near Lurgan and Lough Neagh, under the auspices of Lord Lurgan. Three days in October were devoted to the meeting. There was a splendid stock of hares kept up, and the stakes were large. Lord Lurgan owned the famous Master McGrath. There is no regular meeting now held in the county, but many of the residents of Lurgan still

have greyhounds. Mr. Frank Watson of Lake View, and Mr. John Parkes, of William St., are among the owners. Private coursing is done in various parts of the country. At Crossmaglen, several of the merchants have greyhounds. Hares are plenty in the neighbourhood, and the practice is to take out four dogs, and slip off two at a hare.

The fancy for keeping well-bred dogs is indulged by quite a number of people in the county. As the direct result of the growth of popular taste in this respect, a department for the exhibition of dogs was added to the Armagh Flower Show this year, under the Kennel Club rules, and it proved most successful. The first prize for collies was won by Mr. Samuel T. Mercier, Drumlin House, Gilford. Ten years ago Mr. Mercier made a special feature of breeding collies, and during that period he has won over 100 prizes, at the leading shows in the United Kingdom. At present he has about twenty grown dogs, beautiful in color and marking, and a large lot of puppies. He ships extensively to America. In 1887 he was invited to be a judge at the New York and Boston shows. Among the other owners of good collies are Mr. John Moir, V.S., Mr. Frank Adams, and Mr. Josiah Peel, Armagh ; Mr. Thomas McClure. Rose Cottage, Killylea; and Mr. G. M. Running, Woodview ; Mrs. West, of Glenall, has some splendid mastiffs, and Blenheim spaniels ; Mr. Wm. Bright, and Mr. William Couser, Armagh, have mastiffs, and Mr. John Kindness, and Mr. Moir, V.S. Armagh, Irish terriers. Mr. H. G. MacGeagh, Derry Lodge, Lurgan, also has some fine dogs.

Horse racing is favored by a great many of the natives, but there is now no regular course within the county. The Maze, County Down, near Lisburn, and Hillsborough, in the same county, are so accessible that they prevent attempts to revive the good old days of Armagh. Seventy-five years ago the farm attached to Course Lodge, near Richhill, had a celebrated racecourse. It was then owned by Mr. James Orr, grand-uncle of Messrs. J. & W. Orr, the present proprietors. The high field at the back of the recreation ground, is called the " Tower hill," for the reason that it was the site of the grand stand. Remains of the water cuts are still visible. Races are held annually by the Tynan Hunt Club on the borders of the county at Caledon. Horse jumping, trotting, and driving were features at the sports organized twice this year at the Brownlow House demesne at Lurgan, by Mr. William White, editor of the *Times* of that town. Horse jumping, trotting, and driving were also features of the Armagh Flower, Dog and Poultry Show.

Horse finishing, known chiefly as "feeding," is an important industry. Ragged colts, recognized to be good, are purchased in Southern fairs. After having undergone a course of treat-

D

ment in the Armagh stables, they are shipped to the English markets, and bring splendid prices. Dealers at Armagh, Middletown, Keady, Forkhill, and elsewhere, have achieved wonders in this line, and some of them have made a great deal of money.

LAWN TENNIS, ARCHERY, CRICKET, FOOTBALL, BICYCLING AND TRICYCLING.

LAWN Tennis is exceedingly popular throughout the county. The city of Armagh is the greatest stronghold of the game. A large society there makes it a medium for much social enjoyment. The paying members number over 100, one subscription being sufficient for an entire family. The club is able to muster from 250 to 300 people. Archery is a feature of its attractions. At the annual meeting this year, 1888, it was arranged to hold two tennis tournaments, and two archery prize meetings. The committee consists of Messrs. George D. Beresford, St. John Blacker-Douglas, J. A. M. Cope, Capt. Mark Synnott, Rev. W. M. Morgan, Acheson St. George, Hugh Boyle, Wm. G. Robinson, T. A. Prentice, Col. Hopton, Hy. J. Harris, J. G. Sharkey, T. Gordon, H. Babington, E. R. Johnston, Wm. C. Hobson, treasurer, and George W. Bowen, secretary. The ground and courts are at the back of the Pavilion Park, College Street, and are entered from there by courtesy of Mr. James Lonsdale, J.P. Members pay a subscription of 25s. per year, and the entrance fee is £1. The Archery Club was established in 1862, and has enjoyed considerable fame, several English archers having come over to compete at its tournaments. About ten years ago, the Lawn Tennis Club was established. There are five grass courts. One subscription covers the archery and the lawn tennis departments.

Lurgan has had a successful tennis club of 40 members for eight years. The subscription is 10s. for gentlemen, and 5s. for ladies. It has ground in the demesne of Brownlow House, where there are three grass courts. Some good club tournaments are on record. Mr. Thomas Watson is secretary, and Mr. Courtney Johnston, treasurer. A first-rate club was established in Portadown 7 years ago, through the instrumentality of Messrs. Charles Johnston, James McFadden, J. B. Atkinson, W. H. Atkinson, and William Jones. Mr. W. H. Atkinson is secretary, and Mr. James McFadden, treasurer. There are 40 members. Gentlemen pay 10s., and ladies 5s. each. The grounds of the club, at Tavanagh, contain at present four grass courts.

There is a well-equipped tennis club of 30 members at Tan-

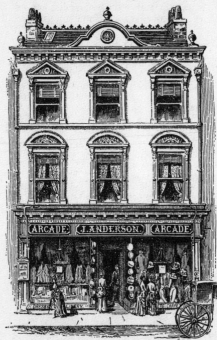

dragee. It was established eight or ten years ago. The subscription is 7s. 6d. per annum. Lord Mandeville permits the club to use the castle demesne for practice. Two grass courts are found to be sufficient to meet all demands.

Cricket and football clubs are numerous in the County. Reference is made to them under the headings of the different towns and villages. There are boat clubs at Portadown and Lurgan, described in each department with the other sports and pastimes.

No regular bicycle club exists, but bicycling and tricycling are becoming very popular recreations. At Armagh the ladies have taken to the tricycle with a show of enthusiasm which promises well for success in the immediate future.

ARMAGH COUNTY DIRECTORY.

[*See also Towns and Villages.*]

Arranged Alphabetically.

ASSIZES.

North-Eastern Circuit, held at Armagh
Crown Counsel—James Orr, Q.C. ; W. P. Ball
Crown Solicitor—John Kilkelly, 46 Upper Mount street, Dublin

BARONY CESS COLLECTORS.

Armagh—John Atkinson, Broomfield, Clare, Tandragee
Upper Fews—John King, Lurgana, Whitecross
Lower Fews—Thomas E. Reid, Dobbin street, Armagh
O'Neilland East—Leonard Calvert, Lurgan
O'Neilland West—Thos. W. Sinclair, Tullyrone, Moy
Upper Orier—James Best, Latt, Jerrettspass, Newry
Lower Orier—Wm. B. Bennett, Poyntzpass
Tureny—Wm. Gamble, Derryhaw, Tynan

CHURCH OF IRELAND.

Diocese of Armagh, includes portions of Armagh, Louth, Meath, Derry, and Tyrone
Archbishop—Most Rev Robert Bent Knox, D.D., Primate of all Ireland, The Palace, Armagh
Chancellor Diocesan Court—Right Hon. John T. Ball, LL.D.
Prov. Registrar—Charles Wood
Marriage Licenses — District Officers for issue of : Chas. Wood, Armagh ; Rev. Paul L. Jameson, Loughgilly ; Rev. Robert J. Ballard, Newtownhamilton ; Rev. Dr. A. Fitzgerald, Portadown
COMMISSIONERS
for administering Oaths in the Supreme Court of Judicature in Ireland
Armagh—Ephraim Fullerton, English street ; D. P. Walker Martin, English street : John Mulholland, Lower English street ; Hugh Porter, Court House; S. M. Steel, Abbey street

Crossmaglen—Hugh Morris
Forkhill—James Smith
Keady—Robert Thompson
Lurgan—Thomas Lutton, James Ussher, sol
Newry—Ml. Denvir, Rt. H. Doherty, Edward Greer, Rt. G. O. Johnston, J. H. Moore
Portadown—Thomas Shilling-ton, William Langtry
Tandragee—Robert Trotter

COMMISSIONERS

perpetual, for taking Acknowledgments of Deeds by Married Women in Ireland

Armagh—Andw. W. M'Creight, Barrack hill
Lurgan—James Ussher, sol., William street
Newry—Michael Denvir, sol., Hill street
Portadown—Wm. H. Atkinson, sol., Magharee

CORONERS, DISTRICTS.

Armagh—Thomas George Peel, Oulart villa, Armagh
Newry—John F. Small, sol., Hill street, Newry
Portadown—Wm. H. Atkinson, sol., Magharee, Portadown

COUNTY COURT.

Judge—W. H. Kisbey, Q.C., 59 Lower Mount street, Dublin
Registrar—Arthur F. Moffet, 24 South Frederick street, Dublin
Sessions held quarterly at Armagh, Ballybot, Lurgan, Markethill, Newtownhamilton
Sessional Crown Solicitor—Saml. H. Monroe, sol., Russell street, Armagh

COUNTY INFIRMARY.

See Armagh City Directory.

COUNTY SURVEYOR.

R. H. Dorman, office County Court House, Armagh
Clerk—Wm. Clarke
Assistant County Surveyors—
Samuel Greer, Tandragee; John Henderson, Derryhaw, Tynan;

James Atkinson, Teague, Portadown ; James Anderson, Mullurg, Markethill

COUNTY TREASURER.

Acheson St. George, Woodpark, Tynan

CRIMES DEPARTMENT
(Ulster).

Headquarters, College street, Armagh
Inspector—F. N. Cullen
District Inspectors —W. W. B. Faussett, Wm. Reeves
Head Constable—Robt. B. Hatch

CROWN AND PEACE.

Clerk—George Gerald Tyrrell, M.R.I.A., 30 Upper Pembroke street, Dublin
Deputy—Hugh Porter
Office, Court House, Armagh

DEPUTY LIEUTENANTS.

See also magistrates marked thus[*]
Cope, Francis R., The Manor, Loughgall
Harris, Hugh, 65 Harcourt st., Dublin, and Ashfort, Tynan
Wilson, Joseph, Clonmore, Stillorgan, Co. Dublin

GRAND JURY.

Secretary—John G. Winder, Armagh
Secretary's Clerk—Wm. Clarke
Office, Court House, Armagh

H. M. LIEUTENANT AND CUSTOS ROTULORUM.

The Earl of Gosford, Gosford Castle, Markethill

H. M. PRISON.

See Armagh City Directory.

LUNATIC ASYLUM.

See Armagh City Directory.

MAGISTRATES.

Marked thus [*] are Deputy Lieutenants.
Acheson, Joseph, Derryvolgie av., Belfast
Adams, Wm., Brackagh House, Portadown
Adamson, Dr. J. G., High-street, Lurgan

*Alexander, Capt. Granville, Forkhill House, Forkhill

Anderson, Joseph, Winder terrace, Armagh

*Armstrong, Henry Bruce-Wright, Dean's Hill, Armagh

Armstrong, Thos. Edenhall, Portadown

*Atkinson, Jos., Crowhill, Loughgall

Atkinson, Joseph, junior, Summer Island, Loughgall

Babington, Hume, Ballinahone House, Armagh

Barcroft, John, Ennislare House, Armagh

Barcroft, Thos. M., Dundrum House, Tassagh, Armagh

Bell, Samuel A., Belle Vue, Lurgan

Beresford, George de la Poer, Castledillon, Armagh

Best, W., Melbourne ter., Armagh

Best, W. J., Hartford pl,, Armagh

Biggar, John, Falmore Hall, Dundalk

*Bond, Joshua W. M., Drumsill House, Armagh

Bond, R. S. M., The Argory, Moy

Bowen, George E., Portaferry

Boyle, Hugh, Charlemont place, Armagh

Bradford, Samuel, Carnbeg, Dundalk

Brooke, Henry G., Glenburn, Rockcorry

Brownlow, Claude, Manor House, Lurgan

Brush, Richard C., Howard ter., Dungannon

Burke, Matthew, Middletown

Byers, Samuel, Mowhan, Armagh

Carvill, Pat G., Moygannon, Rostrevor

Charlemont, the Earl of, Roxborough Castle, Moy

Clarke, Robert, Charlemont, Moy

Close, Max C., Drumbanagher, Newry

Collen, John, Killicomain House, Portadown

Compton, John, Richmond terrace, Armagh

Cope, John A. M., Drummilly, Loughgall

Cross, Wm, P. Dartan, Killylea

Davies, William, Bessbrook

Dempster, Robert, Newry

Dobbin, Lieut.-Col. George Miller, Armagh

Douglas, John, Mountain Lodge, Keady

Douglas, St. John Thomas Blacker, Elm Park, Killylea

Edwards, Geo. A., Prospect House, Armagh

Ensor, Charles, Ardress, Loughgall

Erskine, James, The Yews, Newry

Fforde, James, Raughlan, Lurgan

Fulton, Jno. Chisholm, Church street, Portadown

Garland, Richard, Whitecross

Gillespie, Robt., English st, Armagh

Goodlatte, Alfred R., Salem Lodge, Moy

Gray, George, Glenanne House, Glenanne

Gray, Joseph Henry, Maytone House, Glenanne

Greer, George, Woodville, Lurgan

Hall, Major William J., Narrow Water Castle, Warrenpoint

Hall, Thomas, Eden Cottage, Loughgall

Hanratty, James, Crossmaglen

Harpur, Robert, Divernagh House, Newry

*Harden, Richard, Harrybrook, Tandragee

Henry, J., Mourne Abbey, Kilkeel

Hobson, Wm. C., Scotch street, Armagh

Horner, Francis, Strathmore, Rostrevor

Hughes, John, Glenview terrace, Keady

Irwin, Henry, Mount Irwin, Tynan

Irwin, Capt. Wm. Arthur, Carnagh House, Castleblayney

Johnston, Charles, Milbank, Portadown

Johnston, James, Carrickbreda House, Forkhill, Dundalk

Johnston, John, Woodvale, Ball's Mill, Dundalk

Johnston, John, Lurgan

Kaye, Sir Wm. S. B., Q.C., 62 Fitzwilliam square, N., Dublin

Kelly, Peter J., Heath Hall, Newry

Kilmorey, Earl of, Mourne Park, Rostrevor

Lavery, Dr. Philip, English street, Armagh

Leeper, Dr. Wm. W., Loughgall

Liddell, Wm., Banoge House, Lurgan

Lochrane, Ferdinand, 36 College green, Dublin

Lonsdale, James, The Pavilion, Armagh

*Lurgan, Lord, Brownlow House, Lurgan

M'Bride, Samuel W., Tannaghmore Lodge, Lurgan

M'Clure, Wm. W., Windsor ter., Lurgan

M'Clure, Sir Thomas, Bart., Strandtown, Belfast

M'Crum, Robert G., Milford, Armagh

M'Ferran, Henry, Newtownhamilton

MacGeough, Robert J., Silverbridge House, Silverbridge, Dundalk

M'Glynn, Bernard, Market street, Lurgan

M'Kean, Wm., Millmount, Keady

M'Mahon, James, Bellevue, Newry

M'Master, H. Dunbar, Dunbarton, Gilford

*Malcolm, James, High street, Lurgan

Maginnis, Dr. E., Lurgan

M'Nally, John, Avenue road, Lurgan

M'Parland, John, English street, Armagh

Manchester, the Duke of, Tandragee Castle, Tandragee ; Kimbolton Castle, St. Neot's

*Mandeville, Viscount, Tandragee Castle, Tandragee

Mathers, Robert, Market st., Lurgan

Meade, Francis (Q.C.), 22 Mountjoy sq., east, Dublin

Moorhead, Edward, English st., Armagh

Moorhead, Herc. B., Belmont, Newry

Murphy, Edmund, St. Patrick's, Dunfanaghy

Murphy, Joseph, William st., Lurgan

O'Brien, Charles W., Parkview, Tandragee

O'Hagan, John James, Newry

O'Hanlon, Frank I., Market st., Portadown

Orr, Jacob, Cranagill, Loughgall

Orr, James, Cranagill, Loughgall

Pratt, Dr. Joseph, Markethill

Paul, William J., High st., Portadown

Palmer, Dr. Benjamin A., Crossmaglen

Quinn, Peter, The Agency, Newry

Quinn, John T. Campbell, Tower Hill, Newry

Reed, James T. K., Rahans, Carrickmacross

Reilly, John T., Scarva House, Loughbrickland

Shelton, Ralf B., The Argory, Moy

Shillington, Averell, Alta Villa, Portadown

Shillington, Thomas, Tavanagh House, Portadown

Simpson, Colonel Thomas, Ballyards House, Armagh

Simpson, Major Thomas, Armagh

Sinclair, Abraham W., Sugar Island, Newry

Small, Alex., Lattery, Markethill

Small, Thos., The Hermitage, Keady

Stanley, Charles, Roughan Park, Newmills, Dungannon

Stewart, Dr. Wm. Alten Place, Portadown

Stronge, James H., Hockley Lodge, Armagh
Stronge, Sir John Calvert, The Abbey, Tynan
*Synnot, Mark Seton, Ballymoyer, Newtownhamilton
Synnot, Parker G., Lurganah, Newtownhamilton
Tenison, Major Wm., Portneligan, Tynan
Thompson, Henry, Altnaveigh House, Newry
Todd, John K., Sugar Island, Newry
Wade, Dr. Jas., Middletown
Wann, James C., Markethill
*Waring, Col. Thomas, Waringstown House, Lurgan
White, Thos. H., Orange Hill, Tandragee
Wilson, Abraham, Newry
Winder, John G., Seven Houses, Armagh

MAGISTRATES. RESIDENT.

Captain John Preston, Charlemont pl., Armagh
Wyse, Major A., Ballybot, Newry
Mayne, Charles E. B., Windsor terrace, Portadown

MARRIAGES—DISTRICT REGISTRARS,

7th and 8th Vic., cap. 81 (1844).
Armagh—Robt. Turner
Lurgan—Wm. Mahaffy
Newry—James Burns

MEMBERS OF PARLIAMENT.

North—Lt.-Col. Edward J. Saunderson (C.)
Mid.—Sir James P. Corry, Bart., Dunraven, Belfast (C.)
South—Alex. Blane, Scotch st., Armagh (N.)

MILITARY.

Head-quarters, Belfast.
87th Regimental District Barracks, Armagh city
Colonel—Edward Hopton (C.B.);
Majors—C. A. Barker, A. J. Roberts; *Captain*—H. C. Adams;

Deputy Surgeon General—W. T. Harding (A.M.D.)

MILITIA.

3rd Batt. Royal Irish Fusiliers, Barracks, Armagh city
Hon. Colonel—E. Brownlow ;
Col. Commanding—T. Simpson ;
Lieut-Col.—R. Cuming ; *Major and Adjutant*—C. Packenham :
Quarter-Master—N. J. Drewin

PETTY SESSIONS.

See Directory, Towns & Villages.

POLLING PLACES.

Armagh, Ballybot, Charlemont (Moy), Cladymilltown, Clonmacate (The Birches), Crossmaglen, Forkhill, Keady, Loughgall, Lurgan, Markethill, Middletown, Newtownhamilton, Portadown, Poyntzpass, Richhill, Tandragee, Tynan.

POOR-LAW UNIONS.

Armagh, Lurgan, and Newry.
See Directory to Armagh City and Lurgan, and " BOOK OF COUNTY DOWN," by George Henry Bassett.

POPULATION OF CO.

1841 ..	..	232,393
1851 ..	..	196,084
1861 ..	..	190,086
1871 ..	..	179,240
1881 ..	..	163,170

PROBATE REGISTRY.

Armagh district embraces Counties of Armagh, Louth, Monaghan & Fermanagh, and Baronies of Clogher, and Dungannon, Co. Tyrone.
Office, College Hill, Armagh
Registrar—Arthur Nelson; *Clerks*—Thomas W. Cowan (chief), Leonard D. Ray ; *Office Keeper*—Michael Rafferty.

RAILWAY—GT. NORTHERN CO.

Head Office, Amiens, st., Dublin.
Chairman—Jas.W. Murland, J.P.
Deputy Chairman—James Gray.
Secretary—J. P. Culverwell.
Asst. Secretary—Foster Coates
Engineer-in-Chief—W. H. Mills

Locomotive and Carriage Superintendent· James C. Park.

ROMAN CATHOLIC CHURCH

Diocese of Armagh, including Louth, greater parts of Armagh, and parts of Tyrone, and Derry.

Archbishop—Most Rev. Michael Logue, D.D., Primate of all Ireland, The Palace, Armagh

R. I. CONSTABULARY.

(See also Towns and Villages.)

County Inspector—George H. W. Dobbin, Woodford House, Armagh

SESSIONAL CROWN SOLICITOR.

See County Court.

SHERIFFS.

Sheriff—Lieut.-Col. John M. A. C. Richardson, Rossfad, Ballycassidy, Co. Fermanagh

Sub-Sheriff—Wm. H. D. Moore, Solicitor, High street, Lurgan

UNIONS.

See Poor-Law Unions.

THE CITY OF ARMAGH.

Population 10,070 *in* 1881.

NO person of taste, who had travelled much, would consider it exaggeration to give the City of Armagh a leading place among the most delightfully situated inland towns of the United Kingdom. A cluster of hills, rising gently out of a beautiful valley, form the site upon which striking architectural effects have been produced. Three of the hills are crowned by imposing Church edifices, including the ancient and modern Cathedrals of St. Patrick, and the Church of St. Mark. A fourth hill bears upon its summit an Observatory, the green domes of which contrast most agreeably with the neighbouring towers and spires. The Royal School occupies the fifth hill, the military barracks the sixth, the Catholic Convent the seventh, and the eighth is divided between the Union Workhouse and Sheil's Institution for persons of reduced income. The hill upon which the ancient Cathedral stands originally formed the centre of the chief quarter of the city, and is still so regarded. It is encircled by streets and places, and a large part of one side is embraced in the Market Square.

The thoroughfares of greatest importance, from the business point of view, have the narrowness that is so suggestive of sociability and good feeling between the occupants of the houses at both sides.

In the fittings of the shops, and in the general arrangement of mei handise, effect are produced that indicate artistic instinct and good sense.

Armagh is a thriving city. As a market for farm produce,

GEORGE A. EDWARDS,

STEAM
Sawing, Planing and Moulding Mills,
RAILWAY STATION,
ARMAGH.

Departments:

Timber—Foreign and Native.
Slates, Tiles and Drain Pipes.
Cement, Alabaster, and Whiting.

Foreign and English Sheet Glass.
Paints, Oils and Colors.
Iron—Bar, Rod, and Hoop.

Patent Roofing and other Felts.
Galvanized Roofing Iron.
Coal—House, Steam and Smiths'.

Marble Mantel-pieces in all Shades.
Enameled and Plain Slate, in all Shades.
Ranges—Close and Open.

Stoves—Cooking and Church.
Registered Tile Grates in Variety.
Portable and Fixed Farm Boilers.

Turnip and Hay-Cutters
Fencing Wire.

considering the population, it is one of the best in Ulster. Manufacturing and other industries give extensive employment, and numerous advantages are derived from being the capital of the County. The Assizes are held twice a year; its gaol receives prisoners from all the towns and villages, and from Cavan, Monaghan, and portions of Down and Fermanagh. It is also a regimental district and militia head-quarters, and has the County Lunatic Asylum and County Infirmary.

The religious, educational and other attractions make Armagh a favorite place of residence for cultivated people, and the salubrity of the climate has caused the return to its hospitality of many of the families of ex-military men and ex-civil servants who had been stationed there for short or long periods while in active service. To accommodate the demand for private dwellings, several of the wealthier merchants have expended a large amount of money in bricks and mortar. A great part of the high ground has been devoted to this purpose, and in recent years entire streets have been added to encourage the settlement of families of the kind mentioned. The only low ground almost entirely monopolized by private houses is generally known as The Mall, although the various sections of it have separate names. The Mall proper is really the city park, a well-planted and handsomely enclosed green vale of eight acres. It is surrounded by a broad foot-way, well shaded and amply provided with seats. All classes of the inhabitants freely use this breathing space, and it is a perfect paradise for children.

Armagh is well provided with places for recreation. Within a short distance of The Mall, a foot-path runs along the bank of a winding stream, through a wooded region known as The Folly. By the kindness of Mr. Dobbin, this is open to the public every day in the year but one. The roads and lanes leading in every direction from the city bring into view scenic charms of the most varied character.

Armagh is a railway junction. It has direct communication with Newry, and connects with the Great Northern main line at Goraghwood, and by another *route* at Portadown. Dublin is 89¼ miles from Armagh, Belfast 35½ miles, Newry 21 miles, Goraghwood 17½ miles, Portadown 10¼ miles, and Lurgan 15½ miles.

BEFORE AND SINCE THE ENGLISH CONNECTION.

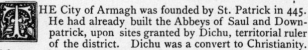

THE City of Armagh was founded by St. Patrick in 445. He had already built the Abbeys of Saul and Downpatrick, upon sites granted by Dichu, territorial ruler of the district. Dichu was a convert to Christianity. After a residence of twelve years in his country, St. Patrick

"BERESFORD ARMS" HOTEL,

ARMAGH.

IN order to meet the greatly increasing business, the Proprietor has just completed an additional Wing, containing a large number of Bed-rooms.

Commercial gentlemen have both Sitting and Dining-rooms.

'Bus attends all Trains.

Two Billiard Rooms.   Posting.

WM. CAMPBELL,

PROPRIETOR.

started for Argial, an independent principality, of which the present County of Armagh formed part. The beautiful hills at Armagh must have captivated him, for they resembled those at Downpatrick. He speedily found favor in the eyes of the owner, Daire, a lineal descendant of one of the three Collas, who, in 332, had dethroned the last of the Kings of Ulster, and divided his possessions between them. Daire gave him the site of an abbey in the lowland, and afterward the hill upon which he built his first cathedral. This was called the Hill of Sallows, and ultimately became *Ardmacha* (Armagh), very likely in order to perpetuate the name of Macha, whose queenly rule is referred to in the chapter on Emania. Around Macha's hill the city grew and became famous all over Europe for piety, learning and wisdom. With the exception of the Cathedral and Abbey the houses were doubtless constructed of wattles or boards. At that time such materials were easily obtained from the surrounding woods. Stones were also to be had, but the idea of solidity in connection with habitations evidently had not then been carried into effect to any great extent, if at all. Having been destroyed by fire many times, and rapidly rebuilt, suggests a degree of combustibility hardly to be associated with stone and brick. Two fires originating by accident wiped out the city twice in the seventh century ; and toward the close of the eighth century a flash of lightning almost brought about a similar result.

Acquaintance with the inhabitants by the Danes was begun in the first half of the ninth century, and continued at various periods through the tenth century. They had the utmost contempt for Christianity, and seemed to delight in plundering the churches, and heaping indignities upon the bishops and priests. In 836 Turgesius captured the city, and initiated his work of plunder and sacrilege by driving out Bishop Faranan, his clergy and the students of the school established by St. Patrick. He laid the city in ashes, destroying the Cathedral with the rest. The people returned to their ruined homes and were permitted to remain unmolested until 852. The Danes then re-appeared, and carried off the most desirable of the treasures that had accumulated in sixteen years. In 873 the Danes, under Amlave, made a descent upon Armagh, and committed shocking atrocities. The city was burned to the ground, and of the inhabitants over a thousand were either severely wounded or killed outright. In 890 the Danes of Dublin plundered Armagh, and took away 710 of the inhabitants. Plundering and burning, with brief intervals of rest, were frequent during the remainder of the Danish period. They destroyed everything of value in the way of records, and carried away relics of antiquity in the precious

metals, the value of which in our day would be beyond the power of estimation. In the tenth century the Danes, commanded by Sitric, were driven out of Armagh, and fled to their ships in the Bay of Dundalk. This happy event was brought about by the united forces of the Munster Chiefs, who came hither to rescue King Callaghan, of Cashel, taken prisoner by the Danes.

Brian Boru, King of Ireland, celebrated for the vigor of his opposition to the Danes, visited Armagh in 1002, at the head of his army, and, in obedience to a last request, his remains were interred in the Cathedral after the great battle of Clontarf, which resulted in the defeat of the Danes, 1014, and the death of Brian.

During the eleventh century Armagh was frequently laid in ashes, churches, public buildings, and fortifications going with the rest. The frequency of the fires was attributed to the flimsiness of the dwellings.

A synod was held in Armagh about the year 1172, in which the then sad condition of the country was taken into consideration. It was common in the twelfth century to purchase and make slaves of Englishmen. The bishops had long set their faces against this cruel proceeding, but now believing that the wrath of Heaven had been excited by it, decreed the immediate release of all who were held in bondage.

Sir John de Courcy, whose patent from Henry II. empowered him to hold all he could seize in Ulster, following the example of the Danes, burned and plundered Armagh in 1179 and in 1206, making no reservation in favor of the churches and religious houses. His successor, Hugh de Lacy, was guilty of even greater sacrilege, having permitted his followers to spend ten days in plunder.

In the war waged to establish the authority of Edward Bruce, 1315, as King of Ireland, Armagh suffered considerably from the incursions of his Scotch and Irish adherents.

Shane O'Neill, also known as John the Proud, from the beginning of his career until his death, kept the people of Armagh in a constant state of misery. In 1542 an effort was made by the English to secure a lasting friendship with the O'Neills, by creating Con, father of Shane, Earl of Tyrone. This might have secured peace for an extended period if Shane had been induced also to accept an earldom. Instead of this it was decreed that the title should descend to Con's illegitimate son, Matthew, and his lineal descendants. Shane, in the course of events, assumed the title of The O'Neill, and maintained that this, being his birthright as a descendant of the Kings of Ulster, was far more important and dignified than any that could be given him by Elizabeth, then Queen of England. He had the peasantry

E

THOS. COLLEN & SON,

Building Contractors,

ARMAGH.

Limestone Quarry Owners,

LIME BURNERS,

THE NAVAN.

EVERY DESCRIPTION OF
ROUGH & DRESSED LIMESTONE.

Steam Joinery, Saw Mill,

Stone Yards and Offices,

RAILWAY STREET.

☞ Estimates free on application.

trained to arms, and his encounters with the English government forces were frequent. When, 1557, Lord Deputy Sussex marched against Shane and his Scotch allies, Armagh was "wasted with fire and sword" by the English, the Cathedral only being exempted. Shane's own doings in the city were referred to by Camden, 1566, as having in his memory, so "foully defaced" the "Church and City of Armagh," that they lost all their ancient beauty and grandeur. Shane contributed to the picturesque features of his reign by, 1562, going to the Court of London, with a numerous following of gallowglasses, richly clothed and brilliantly accoutred, in bare heads and flowing locks. He went through the form of making submission to Elizabeth, and returned to Ireland, loaded with presents. After that it was recorded that his pride and tyranny became intolerable. He endeavoured in 1567 to induce Charles IX., King of France, to send 6,000 soldiers to enable him to drive the English out of Ireland. By that time he had lost much of his power through over indulgence in wine and other causes. At length, in June of 1567, during a visit to the Scotch camp, he was murdered, and his head sent to Dublin, where it was exposed on the top of the Castle. The Scotch had been his faithful allies, and his murder was the result of a fit of anger, excited by his ingratitude.

Hugh Roe O'Neill, Earl of Tyrone, made the period of his rebellion, 1594-1603, an eventful one for the people of Armagh. At the beginning of the war he took possession of the city, but was forced to withdraw. He subsequently tried to compel the surrender of the garrison to escape starvation, but failed. The English, after defeat at the battle of the Yellow Ford, 1598, evacuated the city. This battle was fought within two miles of Armagh, on the way to Blackwatertown. O'Neill having had intimation of the advance of Sir Henry Bagnall, at the head of the English forces, sent word to O'Donnell and other chiefs, by whom he was joined in ample time. Great trenches were dug across the road to intercept the passage of the English. The advance was valiantly made on their part, but the preparations of O'Neill and O'Donnell gave them an advantage, which was assisted by an explosion of powder among the English, and the loss of General Bagnall. He was struck with a musket ball in the head while raising his helmet for a better view of the field The further facts of O'Neill's life are referred to in the chapter giving a synopsis of the history of the county. Lord Mountjoy, in 1601 arrived at Armagh and made it a base of operations against O'Neill.

In the war of 1641, directed by the Confederate Parliament of Kilkenny, Sir Phelim O'Neill secured a foothold in Armagh. He was driven out, but before leaving, the Cathedral was set on

fire, and a number of the inhabitants slain. At the time of the Revolution, 1688-90, an effort was made to hold Armagh for James II., but the people rose in favor of William, Prince of Orange. The garrison was disarmed, and permitted to leave. It was succeeded by Lord Blayney. He, in turn, was driven out, and James passed a few days at Armagh on his way from the siege of Derry. Duke Schomberg was the next occupant, 1690. He made it a base for provisioning his troops. Armagh took a foremost place in the Volunteer Movement. In 1778, 1781, 1782, 1788 and 1796 corps of volunteers were organized to repel invasion, as well as to help the government to quell disturbances among the natives. They did garrison duty during the rebellion of the United Irishmen, 1798, and were disbanded in 1812. The cause was ill-feeling, engendered through the act of one of the Lieutenants, John Barns, who had signed a petition to Parliament in favor of Catholic Emancipation. Lord Charlemont was commander of the first corps.

The appearance of Armagh in 1765 was not calculated to produce a favorable impression upon the stranger. During that year Richard Robinson, D.D., Bishop of Kildare, became Primate, and by the most liberal expenditure of money, succeeded in making the city worthy of the great name it had borne for centuries.

GOVERNMENTAL SYSTEM, GAS, WATER SUPPLY, FIRE BRIGADE, MARKETS AND FAIRS.

 CHARTER was granted by James I. for the government of Armagh, in 1613, the Corporation to consist of a sovereign, twelve free burgesses, an unlimited number of freemen, a town clerk and registrar, and two sergeants-at-mace.

The sovereign was to be chosen from among the burgesses on the 24th of June each year. Two members were to be returned to the Irish Parliament by the sovereign and burgesses. The sovereign and remaining free burgesses filled vacancies in their number, and admitted freemen. James II. set aside the charter of his predecessor, and substituted one conferring larger powers, but the original was restored by William III., and parliamentary representatives were chosen under it until the Union —1801. The borough was represented in the Imperial Parliament by one member until the Act of 1885, when it was disfranchised, not having the requisite population. Capt. George De La Poer Beresford, D.L., Castle Dillon, was the last representative.

The governmental system was reconstructed in 1833, under

HENRY HILLOCK,

The City Steam Saw Mills,

Thomas St. and Dobbin St.,

ARMAGH.

Departments:

Timber and Slates,
General Ironmongery,
Iron and Coal,
Wire Fencing, Hurdles, &c.,
Tiles and Drain Pipes,
Alabaster and Cement,
Ranges and Grates,
Marble and Slate Mantel-Pieces,
Plumbing and Gas-Fitting,
Electric and Crank Bells,
Hot and Cold Water Apparatus,
Bedsteads and Bedding.

FARM IMPLEMENTS OF ALL KINDS.

Improved Laundry Machinery.   Artificial Manures.

the 9th of George IV., chapter 82, and Town Commissionesr elected having powers in regard to lighting, watching, cleansing, etc. These are still exercised. In 1878 the provisions of the Public Health Act were taken advantage of, and there are now three committees of the general body of commissioners, one for "finance and pipe water," one for general purposes, "watching, lighting and cleansing," and one for "urban sanitary."

Primate Robinson, as a public benefactor, devoted attention to improvements under ground as well as over ground, and in his time a good beginning was made in the matter of sewerage. Since the Public Health Act came into operation the work which he initiated has been continued at the expense of property-owners in several districts. From 1881 over £900 has been disbursed for this purpose. The total valuation of property subject to rates in 1887 was £27,981. This does not include churches nor public buildings, some of which—the observatory and library—are exempt by Act of Parliament. The rate struck for the next municipal year, 1888-9, is graded as follows :—2s. in the £ on all houses and tenements valued at £20 and upward, 1s. 6d. in the £ on houses, etc., valued at £10 and under £20, and 1s. in the £ on houses, etc., valued at £5 and under £10. Half the total rate of 4s. 6d. in the £ is to be used for town expenses, and half for sanitary and expenses of construction and maintenance of water works. The cost of lighting and maintaining 247 gas lamps for the year ending 31st December, 1887, was £198 16s. The gas works are owned by a limited liability company, and charge the Town Commissioners 3s. 9d. per 1,000 feet, which is under the rate to private consumers. It cost £83 4s. to watch the city for the year. This amount pays three watchmen. Two receive 10s. per week each, and one, the sergeant, 12s. per week. The cleansing cost £121 18s. 3d.

The history of the water supply began in 1792. Lady Primrose left £1,000 in charge of two trustees, to be applied to "any useful purpose," in their discretion. Lady Primrose was daughter of Charles Drelincourt, D.D., a native of France, who was appointed Dean and Rector of Armagh in 1691. It was considered a "useful purpose" to help to give the city an abundance of pure water. Lowry's Lake was purchased. It is situated at a distance of about two miles from the city, on the way to Tandragee. There was a good spring, and it was impounded by building a bank all around. Between the years 1825 and 1868 over £2,000 was spent in improvements to the piping, etc. The first pipes were wooden, with iron connections. These were replaced by pipes of cast metal, the largest 13 inches, and the smallest 3 inches in diameter. The money was raised by debentures under the Water Acts of 1789 and 1794. In 1878 an additional

MY object in giving the above Drawing is to show the position of my House in Market Square, so that those who have not yet favoured me with a visit may be induced to do so.

My aim is to treat customers well, so that they will not only come back themselves, but bring others with them.

In this I have succeeded so far, my business having increased steadily, and new customers are almost daily coming in on the recommendation of others who have already tried my Goods and found them reliable. This in itself is a proof that the value must be good.

I keep a Large Stock of General Drapery Goods, suitable for the various Seasons as they move round, and will esteem it a favour should you kindly give me a trial.

W. J. LENNOX,
43 MARKET SQUARE, **ARMAGH**.

sum of £1,000 was expended in the purchase and embanking of six acres adjoining the lake. A loan received from the Board of Works was used to pay off the debenture holders and in the purchase and embankment of the six acres, etc. The lake and shore now consist of about 20 acres. In 1884 five and a half acres were added, and a house built for the caretaker. There are two filtering beds, a quarter of a mile from the lake, and a clear water basin with which the mains are connected. According to Sir Charles Cameron's analysis the water has no peculiar odor, or flavor, and is soft and well adapted for washing or cooking purposes—in fact is as good as the Vartry, Dublin. A supply is maintained at 24 public fountains conveniently distributed throughout the city. In July of the present year the depth in the lake was 8 feet 8 inches. A Volunteer Fire Brigade is maintained under the supervision of the Town Commissioners at a cost of £16 a year, of which £10 comes from the Town Commissioners and £6 from the Toll Committee. With three exceptions, all the members of the brigade are volunteers. One of the three is paid £8 a year and the other two £4 each. The pressure from the water plugs is sufficient to send a stream to the top of the highest house in the city. A manual engine is kept for country work, within a radius of ten miles.

At the petition of Hugh Roe O'Neill, Earl of Tyrone, Queen Elizabeth in 1587, granted a patent for a market to be held in Armagh every Tuesday. This was confirmed to the Primate by James I. and Charles II. The great market continues to be held on Tuesday down to the present, for all kinds of produce, with the exception of grain and grass-seed. These are sold in the season on Wednesday and Saturday. Every Tuesday throughout the year the principal thoroughfares are crowded in every part by country people. There is a splendid limestone Market House in Market Square, built by the Hon. William Stuart, D.D., in 1811, eleven years after he became Primate. The market places are, for flax, in Irish-street ; poultry and eggs, Dobbin-street ; butter, Dobbin-street ; grain, grass-seed, pork, hay and straw, the Shambles, Mill-street ; live pigs, Gaol Square. There are two weigh-bridges at the Shambles, and one in Gaol Square.

The Primate for the time being leased the market rights. In 1821 David Beatty was lessee, and sold his interest to a few of the leading inhabitants for £1,700. This amount was raised by the issue of debentures of £25 each. The debenture holders elected a Committee of eight to manage the market, and it was understood that the surplus received from tolls, after paying interest on the debentures at the rate of 6 per cent., was to be used in the improvement of the city and its market places.

By a sinking fund the debentures were reduced from
£25 to £15. In 1829 the Primate, Lord John George
Beresford, renewed the lease to the Toll Committee. In
1874 the title of the Primate to the head rent was acquired
from the Church Temporalities Commissioners at a cost of
£1,000, raised by the issue of 50 debentures. It is claimed
by the Toll Trustees that they have expended in improvements about the City fully £11,000 since 1821. Under the Royal
Commission for inquiring into the management of Markets in
Ireland, Mr. C. W. Black, Assistant Commissioner, sat at
Armagh in June of this year. Evidence was given on behalf of
the Toll Trustees to show that nothing had been left undone to
sustain the reputation of and improve the markets. Evidence
was also offered to support the opinion that the Trustees had not
used their powers to the advantage of the markets, that the
surplus received in Tolls, over expenditure, had not been employed for the improvement of the City, and that the management
of the markets should be given to the Town Commissioners.
Here are a few of the principal tolls levied : bag of meal, oats,
or potatoes, 1d. ; cart of potatoes, 2d.; hamper, bag, or
package of apples or other fruit, 1d.; cart of apples, 4d.; cart
of turnips or carrots, 2d.; bag of grass-seed, 1d.; barrel or box
of fish, 1d. ; cart of fish, 2d. ; nurseryman's cart with flowers,
or plants, 6d.; cart with plants, young trees or brooms, 2d.;
crock, firkin, or butt of butter, including weighing, 2d.; lump of
butter under 10 lb., ½d. ; under 20 lb., 1d. ; 20 lbs. or upward,
2d.; box or package of eggs, 1d.; cart of fowl, 2d.; hand-basket
of eggs or fowl, free ; cart of young pigs, 2d.; shambles market,
carcase of beef or veal, 4d.; pork, per pig, weighed or unweighed,
4d.; hay or straw, if weighed, 2d. per load ; grain, if weighed,
per sack or bag, 1d.

Fairs are held on the first Thursday of every month, for horses,
cattle, sheep, and pigs, and are usually well attended by buyers
and sellers.

THE ANCIENT CATHEDRAL OF ARMAGH.

GOOD authorities agree in the opinion that St. Patrick
did not begin to erect the Cathedral until 458, three
years after his arrival in Armagh. The original walls
beyond doubt, occupied a part of the site of the present
edifice, and must have been within the area now used for burial
purposes. This was the " hill of sallows," granted by Daire, in
addition to the low ground where St. Patrick first made a residence. In the historical sketch of the city, frequent reference
is made to the burning of the Cathedral. The Danes had no

respect for its sacred character, and in the midst of savage warfare Irish chiefs and English adventurers also allowed it to be plundered by their followers. It was destroyed by lightning in 995. Brian Boru, in 1002, some time after he had succeeded Malachy as King of Ireland, made a visit to the Cathedral, and left upon the high altar as alms, twenty-eight ounces of gold. He also made an endowment of gold and cattle. His remains and those of his sons were interred here in 1014, immediately after the battle of Clontarf, which ended in the crushing defeat of the Danes. From the time the Cathedral was destroyed by lightning, 995, it was not fully roofed until 1125, a space of 130 years. Patrick O'Scanlon, who was elevated to the primacy in 1261, and died in nine years afterward, restored and enlarged the Cathedral. In 1405 it was again destroyed by fire. The Lord Deputy, Sussex, in 1561, used it as a storehouse for provisions, and fortified it by the erection of ramparts. He was then engaged in a campaign against Shane O'Neill and his Scotch allies. Shane destroyed the Cathedral and the city five years later, so that it might not afford habitation to his enemies. After the battle of the Yellow Ford, the remains of Marshal Bagnall were interred within the Cathedral. The fortifications of Lord Sussex were used a second time by the English on that occasion, and the Church as a refuge.

Christopher Hampton, who become Primate in 1613, restored the Cathedral. The celebrated James Ussher, D.D., was appointed to the primacy in 1624. During his time the question of precedence, in regard to the Irish bishops, long a cause of extreme annoyance, was settled in favor of Armagh. Sir Phelim O'Neill, in 1641, caused the Cathedral as well as the city to be destroyed by fire. John Bramhall, who was primate for three years, 1660-1663, left £500 to the fund for the restoration of the Cathedral. His successor, Primate Margetson, promoted a subscription with this view, and drew largely on his own private means, so that the work might be accomplished. Thomas Lindsay, D.D., translated to the primacy from Raphoe. 1714, presented an organ and a peal of six bells. Primate Boulter, celebrated for his munificence, contributed toward extensive improvements in the Cathedral, 1739. Richard Robinson, D.D., Baron Rokeby, was spared for 29 years in the office of Primate, 1765-94, to effect a great change in the appearance of the Cathedral as well as in the entire city of Armagh. It was his intention that the Cathedral should have a tower over 100 feet high. The erection of this had been more than half completed when fears began to be entertained regarding its safety. The Primate, to guard against the possibility of a

catastrophe, had most of it removed, and a tower put up so low that its solidity could not be questioned. He intended to have built a much finer tower at the west side, but died before initiating the project. The work of restoration was continued by his successor, Primate Newcombe. The Hon. William Stuart, D.D., who became Primate in 1800, also helped to improve the Cathedral. He was succeeded by Lord John George Beresford in 1822. Primate Beresford lost no time in demonstrating to the people of Armagh what was meant by "a lordly way." He decided that the ancient cathedral should be put into better shape. Mr. Cottingham, a London architect of repute, was engaged for the purpose, and although he at first estimated that everything needful could be accomplished at an expense of £8,000, he was, at a later period, virtually given a *carte blanche*, so that the restoration might be made as perfect as possible. The undertaking was begun in 1834, and the Cathedral was reopened in 1840. It entailed a total expenditure of nearly £36,000. Of this amount Lord John George Beresford contributed about £26,000, and the balance was made up by subscription. An important feature of the new work was the substitution of more solid masonry for the piers of the tower erected by Primate Robinson. A splendid organ, costing £1,200, replaced the instrument which was the gift of Primate Robinson. This was presented by Lord J. G. Beresford. The cathedral walls are of sandstone, and the style of architecture Gothic. Lord J. G. Beresford increased the number of bells in the tower from six to eight. Within a short distance of the ancient cathedral there was a round tower with conical cap, like the perfect specimen in the demesne of Mr. Geo. Clarke, D.L., Antrim. The cap is said to have been thrown down during a storm in 1121, and of the rest of the tower nothing is now visible. At the beginning of the present year, 1888, further alterations and improvements were being effected in the Cathedral. The interior is dignified by clustered columns, and is rich in memorial sculptures by Roubiliac, Rysbrack, Marochetti, Nollekins, and others. Among those who are commemorated are Sir Thomas Molyneux, Bart., M.D., a lineal descendant of Sir Thomas Molyneux, Knt., Chancellor of the Irish Exchequer in the reign of Elizabeth, died 1703; Andrew Craig, LL.D.; Alex. Duke Simpson, Captain 13th Prince Albert's Light Infantry, 1874; Peter Drelincourt, LL.D., Dean of Armagh, 1720; Rev. Alexander Irwin, Precentor of Armagh Cathedral, 1872; Lord John George Beresford, D.D., Primate, died 1862; Turner Macan, Captain 16th Hussars, 1836; Thomas Osborne Kidd, R.N., killed in the attack on the Redan, 1855; Rev. Thomas Carpendale, A.M., 1817; Lt.-Col.

CHARLEMONT ARMS HOTEL,
ARMAGH.

J. H. MANN { LATE OF LONDON AND GLASGOW. } **PROPRIETOR.**

This Hotel is in the best business centre, and has been remodeled and refurnished throughout.

ELEGANT COMMERCIAL AND WRITING ROOMS STRICTLY RESERVED.

'Bus Attends all Trains.

Public Dinners, Suppers, &c., on the shortest notice.

Hot and Cold Luncheons always ready.

TURKISH AND OTHER BATHS.

POSTING IN ALL ITS DEPARTMENTS.

Carriages, Broughams, Waggonettes, Phætons, &c., always ready.

❈ TURKISH BATHS. ❈

LADIES : Monday and Friday, 2 to 6 p.m. ; Wednesday, Thursday and Saturday, 10 to 12 noon.

GENTLEMEN : Monday and Friday, 7 a.m. to 2 p.m., and from 6 to 9 p.m. ; Tuesday, 7 a.m. to 9 p.m. ; Wednesday, Thursday and Saturday, 7 a.m. to 10 a.m. ; 12 noon to 9 p.m.

Sulphur and other Medicated Baths, and full Hydropathic treatment as at any of the famous sanitariums.

Saml. Kelly, of the East India Company, 1840; Colonel Wm. Kelly, C.B., 24th Regt., a brave officer, who served under the Duke of Wellington during the Peninsular War, died 1818; Elizabeth, wife of Primate Marcus Gervais Beresford, died 1870; Rev. James Jones, Chancellor of Armagh Cathedral for 30 years, died 1871; the Hon. Wm. Stuart, D.D., Primate, died 1822; Richard Robinson, D.D., Primate. 1794; Marcus Gervais Beresford, D.D., Primate, died 1886; William Viscount Charlemont, 1671; Baron Caulfield; Joshua MacGeough, 1756; Wm. MacGeough, 1771; Joshua MacGeough, 1817; William MacGeough Bond, 1866. There are several memorial windows in stained glass. One of the finest of the number was erected to the memory of Lord John George Beresford, by the clergy and laity of the Archiepiscopal diocese. Five in the east end were erected by Lord John George Beresford. Of these one specially commemorates J. E. Jackson, M.A., Dean of Armagh. He died in 1841, after the restoration of the cathedral, in the work of which he had given " zealous and effectual assistance." The other windows commemorate Lady Catherine Beresford, 1843; Lady Anne Beresford, 1841; William Blacker, 1850; Rev. Samuel Blacker, LL.D., 1840; Rev. Cosby Stopford Mangan, 1862; Rev. Richard Allott, 1858; Wm. Lodge Kidd, M.D., died 1851.

The monuments in the burial-ground attached to the Cathedral, so far as historic interest is concerned, are a blank. The sponge of time would have been ample for wiping out the inscriptions, even if it were not aided by the batterings and burnings of Danish and other barbarians. Several of the kings and chieftains of Ireland were laid to rest here, but there is nothing legible in the way of record bearing date anterior to 1638. The burial-ground and Cathedral occupy a little over two acres.

ABBEYS FOUNDED BY ST. PATRICK AND HIS SUCCESSORS—CROSSES—THE ANCIENT SCHOOL, THE ROYAL SCHOOL, PUBLIC LIBRARY, "BOOK OF ARMACH."

SOON after the arrival of St. Patrick, he endeavoured to obtain the site of the present Cathedral, with a view to the building of an abbey and church. According to an entry in the *Book of Armagh*, he did not at once succeed in accomplishing this. Daire, owner and chief of the district, instead, gave him the low ground, which Dr. William Reeves, now Bishop of Down and Connor and Dromore, believes

F

to be that in Scotch street, belonging to the Bank of Ireland.
There he built the abbey of Na-Fertae. The other abbeys built
in Armagh included St. Peter and Paul's, The Culdee, St.
Columba, and that for Friars Minor. St. Peter and Paul stood
to the north of the Cathedral, in the vicinity of the Public
library. It was for Canons regular of the order of St. Augustine,
and had attached to it the famous school referred to in another
part of this chapter. The Culdee Priory was in Castle Street.
It was founded in the 7th Century. The Culdees were secular
priests serving in the Cathedral choir, where their superior
officiated as Precentor. Primate O'Scanlain built the abbey for
Friars Minor soon after his elevation to the primacy in 1261.
It is the only one of which there are remains. The ruin is
situated within the Primate's demesne. Time has dealt
severely with the walls, but the ravages are to a great extent
hidden by ivy. Several of the broken arches are wrapped in
mantles of ivy springing from leaders of tree-like proportions.
One of the number, still flourishing, appears to be larger than
the famous ivy in Mucross Abbey, Killarney, said to be over
200 years old. The ruin is about 150 feet long, 30 feet wide,
and between 25 and 30 feet high. Ivy covers the interior and
exterior. An archway in the centre of the main gable is a
curiosity. Although it must have been long in the present
state of delapidation, yet the visitor passes under with a
sense of fear that it may fall and crush him. The picturesque
effect of the immediate surroundings is heightened by several
splendid Irish yews and stately forest trees. Out-offices, which
stood close to the ruin, in the last century, were removed by Lord
John George Beresford. About twelve years ago a portion of one
of the walls fell. The interior of the abbey appears to have been
used for burial purposes. A slab inscribed to the memory of
Terence Nugent, bears date 1741. This is the oldest legible
monument. The Christian character of the people of Armagh
was attested by the presence of many crosses in the thoroughfares. The last one disappeared in 1813. It stood in Market
Square. A portion is preserved in the Cathedral.

The school established by St. Patrick, which made Armagh
famous all over Europe, was attached to the Abbey of SS. Peter
and Paul, and its professors were of the Order of St. Augustine.
The Abbey and its dormitories were rebuilt by Imar O'Hedegan.
Liberal endowments were given for the support of the school by
the native kings. The last of these, Roderick O'Connor, in
1169, decreed that the superior should receive ten cows every
year. Students flocked to Armagh from every Christian country,
until there were assembled at one time 7,000. Its graduates in
theology were preferred to all others. The number of English

[Established over Half a Century.]

FRIZELL'S
Cabinet and Upholstery Warehouse,
THE SEVEN HOUSES,
ARMAGH.

Every description of Cabinet Furniture,
Bedding, &c.

Importer of the latest designs in
Artistic Furnishings from
Paris and London.

A LARGE STOCK TO SELECT FROM.

 Funeral Undertaking—

All Requisites.

students was so large as to give name to the quarter in which they were lodged.

After the Plantation of Ulster, the reputation of Armagh as a seat of learning was maintained by means of a Royal School, established in 1627. The intention was to have it at Mount Norris, then a fortified place, but subsequently an insignificant village. A grant of 1,514 acres in that district, producing an income of £1,377, was made for its maintenance. Armagh was considered to be a more appropriate site, and a transfer was secured. The first building erected was in Abbey Street, opposite the Provincial Bank. In 1772 the present college was completed through the instrumentality of Primate Robinson, restorer of Armagh. It occupies one of the hills of the city, and is capable of accommodating 120 students. At the beginning of this year, 1888, between 65 and 70 were enrolled. Primate Robinson contributed £3,000 toward the total cost of the structure (£5,000) in 1772, and Lord John George Beresford, primate, gave an equal amount to cover the outlay on an extension made in 1849. The buildings and grounds embrace about fifteen acres. The Royal School was founded for the education of Protestants, but after the death or resignation of the head master, Rev. Dr. M. M. Morgan, the Roman Catholics are to have half the revenue. This is in accordance with the Draft Scheme, published this year, objections to which are under consideration by the Commissioners.

Armagh seems to have had a library, or house for the preservation of manuscripts, at a very early period. It was, no doubt, the knowledge of this fact that influenced Primate Robinson to build, north of the Cathedral, the public library which continues to this day one of the chief attractions of the city. It was opened in 1771. He bequeathed to it his private collection of books and engravings, and a revenue of £339 a year. There are at present in it about 17,000 books. A large part deal with theological subjects. Departments are also devoted to classics, archæology, science, and general literature. An interesting feature is a collection of manuscript records of the archbishops since 1361. By an Act passed in the reign of George III., the Primate and Dean and Chapter are trustees. Busts of the late Lord John George Beresford, and Charles R. Elrington, biographer of Ussher, adorn the reading-room. There is also a small collection of antiquities, bequeathed by the late Primate, Marcus Gervais Beresford, D.D. The library is open to the public every day in summer from noon until four o'clock, and in winter from noon until three o'clock. New books are added from time to time. This year, 1888, about £150 was expended in the purchase of books, &c. The Rev.

Benjamin Wade, M.A., Precentor of the Cathedral, is Librarian, and Mr. Edward Rogers, author of a most interesting " Memoir of Armagh Cathedral," is Deputy Librarian. A portion of the libraray building is occupied as a residence by the Librarian.

The famous manuscript, known as *The Book of Armagh*, was presented to the Library of Trinity College, Dublin, in 1858, by Lord John George Beresford. It was purchased by Bishop Reeves, when Dean of Armagh, for £300, from Mr. William Brownlow, in 1853. It had been in the possession of a family named MacMoyre for a very long period. Florence MacMoyre, the last custodian, pledged it for £5 to pay the expenses of a trip to England in 1680 He went there to give evidence against Oliver Plunkett, Roman Catholic Primate, put to death for treason in 1681. MacMoyre did not release the book, and it was secured by the father of William Brownlow, some years afterward. Bishop Reeves says that the *Book of Armagh* "was so called because it was the most precious literary possession of the Church of Armagh." He describes it as

" A small thick quarto, measuring in height, 7¾ inches ; in breadth, 5¾ ; and in thickness, 2¼ ; consisting of 221 vellum leaves, on each side of which the writing appears in double columns. The penmanship is of extreme elegance, and is admirable throughout for its distinctness and uniformity. There is no date entered in the book, but the scribe's name, Ferdomnach, appears in several parts of it ; we know from the Ancient Irish Annals what was the period at which he lived. At the year 845, is recorded 'the death of Ferdomnach, the wise and very admirable scribe of Ardmagh.' Internal evidence proves that part of the volume, viz., that containing the Gospel of St. Matthew, was finished on the 21st September, about 807. * * * The Manuscript, it may be briefly stated, contains the following subjects :—The Acts of St. Patrick by Muirchu and Tirechan, being the earliest memoirs of the Apostle of Ireland which have been preserved, together with some important passages in Irish, which are among the oldest, and are the fullest specimens of the language now in existence. These are followed by the Confession of St. Patrick, purporting to be copied from his autograph. The whole is in writing anterior to the year 807. The entire New Testament in Latin, accompanied by the Prologues of St. Jerom and Pelagius, and here and there illustrated by Irish glosses. The version agrees in the main with the Vulgate, but presents occasional departures from it in cases which may be considered as characterizing the Irish Use. The life of St. Martin of Tours, by Sulpicius Severus."

OBSERVATORY, PALACE, MALL, FOLLY, WALKS AND DRIVES.

IT was due to the wonderful liberality of Primate Robinson that the city became possessed of an Observatory. He founded and endowed it with lands in 1793, making the buildings extensive enough to provide comfortable quarters for the Astronomer. The Observatory stands on one of the hills, north by east from the ancient Cathedral, and by its green domes becomes a most striking feature in the view of Armagh from many points. About twenty acres are included in the grant. Owing to the death of Primate Robinson, in the year following the erection of the Observatory, the necessary instruments were not fully provided for. Lord John George Beresford, who succeeded to the Primacy in 1822, spent about £3,000 in making good the deficiency. In 1884 the Government granted £2,000 to partly repair the loss in revenue occasioned by the Church Disestablishment. Soon afterward a dome was put up in the grounds for an equatorial reflector, ten inches aperture, by Sir Howard Grubb. Hitherto meridian observation had engrossed the attention of the Astronomer and his Assistant. The results were published in two catalogues of stars, 1859, 1886, both of which can be seen at the Armagh Public Library and in the Library of the Armagh Philosophical Society. The Observatory is under the control of a Board of Governors, of which Primate Knox is Chairman. Dr. J. L. E. Dreyer, F.R.A.S., is the present Astronomer, and Rev. Charles Faris, M.A., L.C.E., Assistant Astronomer. The appointment of Astronomer is made by the Primate, subject to the approval of the Astronomer Royal for England.

Until the time of Primate Robinson, the Archbishop of Armagh, was not provided with a place of residence in keeping with the revenues of the office. In the evil times, when nothing was left of either city or churches, a precedent was formed for living elsewhere in the diocese, and for a considerable space the Primates had palaces at Drogheda and Termonfeckin, in the County of Louth. During St. Patrick's time the primatial residence was situated on a part of the hill crowned by the Cathedral. Bishopscourt, in Mullinure, north north-east of the city, was a residence, and it is recorded that there were rooms for the Archbishop in the Culdee Priory. When Dr. Robinson was appointed Primate, the residence was in English Street. He built the present palace in 1770, and shortly afterward a chapel, close to it, in the Grecian style of architecture. Numerous plantations then started in the splendid demesne, are still maintained, adding greatly to the beauty of the scenery sur-

BOYD & CO.,

TIMBER, IRON, SLATE, CEMENT

AND

COAL STORES,

DOBBIN STREET,

ARMAGH.

ALL COALS IMPORTED DIRECT.

GLASS, PAINT, OIL, VARNISH,

AND

HARDWARE MERCHANTS.

☞ FUNERAL UNDERTAKERS:

Requisites of every description kept in Stock.

Drain Pipes, Ranges,
Grates and Stoves,
Wire Fencing,
Farm Boilers (Portable & Fixed),
Metals of all kinds.

rounding the city. Primate Stuart walled the demesne at a cost of £20,000, reserving for his successors in the See the privilege of sharing in this needful expenditure. Lord John George Beresford, appointed to the Primacy in 1822, raised the palace from three to four stories, thereby greatly increasing the dignity of the structure. There are three entrances to the demesne. At the upper end [the ground ascends to a point called Knox's Hill. On this there is an obelisk, erected by Primate Robinson in 1783, to perpetuate the memory of his intimacy with the Duke of Northumberland, through whose instrumentality he had been translated to Armagh from the Bishopric of Kildare. The obelisk is 113 feet in height, and it is due to Dr. Robinson's memory to say that its erection was suggested as a means of honourable employment for the people of Armagh during a time of severe distress. The view from Knox's Hill is not surpassed by any other at Armagh, but a more extensive one is obtained from the Cathedral tower. The lands surrounding the palace became a demesne by Act of Council, dated 1769. Until then the residence of the Archbishop had not been legally transferred from Drogheda. One of the interesting places in the demesne is St. Bride's Well. It is situated on the right side of the avenue from Palace Row, at a distance of about two hundred yards. An arch was built over it and an iron door put up for protection against cattle. The present Primate, Most Rev. Robert Bent Knox, D.D., occupies the Palace, but in order that it may be available for residence by his successors, a fund was being promoted at the beginning of this year, 1888. This was rendered necessary through changes arising out of the Dis- establishment of the Church.

The Mall is really the only park at Armagh always open to the people. It includes eight acres of the valley, at both sides of which are situated the public buildings that give to the city its distinctive character. In the less favored period, before the advent of Primate Robinson, this ground was a swampy common, and the handsome road now surrounding it was a race-course. By an Act of the 13th and 14th George III. it was granted to the Lord Primate for useful purposes. In 1797 Primate Newcombe, successor of Primate Robinson, leased it to the Sovereign and Burgesses, for the purpose of being transformed into " a public walk for the people." This was accomplished by subscription, in a creditable manner. The trees then planted, and some afterward added by a citizen, are now of majestic proportions. Football and cricket matches are played on the green, and the country in town feature is furnished by the presence of grazing cattle. One of the guns captured during the war with Russia, 1854, mounted on its carriage,

City Medical Hall

(Late Dr. Armstrong's),

ENGLISH STREET,
ARMAGH.

ESTABLISHED 1826,

For the correct dispensing of Physicians' and Surgeons' Prescriptions,

AND THE PREPARATION AND SALE OF

GENUINE DRUGS & CHEMICALS

Proprietor—HENRY FRAZER, M.D.

The Compounding Department

Is conducted on the most improved principle, under the personal care of the Proprietor and Manager. Neither trouble nor expense are spared to ensure a first-class article at a moderate price.

The Special Advantages of this Establishment are—

1st—None but the finest possible quality of Drugs and Chemicals are employed. This is of paramount importance, as drugs are to be had in a great variety of qualities, the inferior or lower priced ones being of little or no medicinal value.

2nd.—The directions of the prescriber are faithfully carried out, all Pharmacopœial Preparations being prepared according to the Official Standard.

3rd.—Particular attention is paid to the prompt delivery of Medicines.

4th.—The Assistants are Certificated by Apothecaries' Hall, Dublin.

occupies such a conspicuous place, that while reminding of strife, it also helps thoughtful persons to appreciate the advantages of peace. The Mall trustees are Rev. W. M. Morgan, LL.D.; H. Davidson ; J. G. Winder, J.P. : T. A. Prentice, and Hugh Boyle, J.P.

A beautifully-planted glen, known as The Folly, owned by Col. George Dobbin, is generously given over by him to the use of the public. By the aid of a dozen or more stout fellows he succeeds in preserving his proprietary rights by closing on the 18th of June every year. The Folly is a popular resort in winter as well as in summer. A small stream passing through, in order to supply motive power to two or three mills, serves in its impoundings to form several cascades. These are framed by the spreading branches of giant trees, and with plenty of water and occasional glimpses of sunshine, form exceedingly pretty pictures.

All the roads from Armagh bring into view objects to interest tourists. Look-out points are frequent in every direction, and, either in walking or driving, a great deal may be seen and a few days most agreeably spent.

ST. MARK'S CHURCH. THE PRESBYTERIAN CHURCHES. METHODIST AND CONGREGATIONAL CHURCHES. CHRISTIANS.

ONE of the commanding heights on the eastern side of the city is occupied by the Church of St. Mark. The architecture is in the later English style, emphasized by a battlemented pinnacled roof, resting on buttressed walls, and relieved by a pinnacled tower of good height, bearing date 1811. The interior of the church is spacious, the seating capacity being increased by galleries on three sides. A new chancel, very chaste in design, has four pointed freestone arches, supported on massive freestone pillars, with handsomely-carved capitals. A fine organ is one of the attractive features of the chancel. Among the others are three stained windows, erected by the parishioners to the memory of the Rev. John Young Rutledge, D.D., seven years rector of Armagh, died in 1872, aged forty-eight. Mural tablets in various parts of the church commemorate Rev. Robert Miller, A.M , died 1840 ; Wm. Lodge Kidd, M.D., 1851 ; Chas. Smyth Cardwell, 1859 ; Robert Riddall, J.P., 1873 ; Rev. Rt. Hay, A.M., 1847; Arthur Irwin Kelly, sovereign of Armagh, 1841 ; Mary Helen Chomley, daughter of Rev. C. R. Elrington, 1884 ; John Stanley, 1846 ; Rev. Wm. Ball, LL.B., 1821 ; Meredith Armstrong, 1868.

THOMAS MOORE & Co.,

WHOLESALE

𝕸𝖎𝖓𝖊 & 𝕾𝖕𝖎𝖗𝖎𝖙 𝕸𝖊𝖗𝖈𝖍𝖆𝖓𝖙𝖘,

𝕺𝖋𝖋𝖎𝖈𝖊:

MARKET SQUARE.

𝕭𝖔𝖓𝖉𝖊𝖉 𝖂𝖆𝖗𝖊𝖍𝖔𝖚𝖘𝖊:

DOBBIN STREET,
ARMAGH.

The Very Rev. George A. Chadwick, D.D., Dean, is rector of St. Mark's

There are three Presbyterian churches in Armagh. Two are on the Mall and one in Abbey Street. The finest of the number, architecturally, fills a large space at the corner of Russell Street and the Mall; and although it is in the "low ground," its graceful spire of chiseled limestone rises to such a height as to impress itself in views of the city from many points. The walls are constructed of limestone "shoddies" from the neighboring quarries, faced with Dungannon freestone. Richly-sculptured doorways, a pinnacled roof, a broad flight of stone steps, and an ornate delicately-hammered iron railing, are among the attractive external features. The interior is fitted throughout in pitch pine: seatings, three galleries, roof, and reading-desk. Messrs. Young & Mackenzie, Belfast, were the architects. The church was finished in April, 1879, and cost between £10,000 and £11,000. Rev. Jackson Smyth, D.D., is the minister.

"Second Armagh" is situated in Abbey Street. It bears date 1722, and was built with material from the ruins of the Abbey of St. Peter and St. Paul. The front is partly castellated, and faces the backs of the houses on the left side of the street. Interest in the church is enhanced by the seclusion. It was remodeled in 1880. The seatings, wainscotings, and pulpit are in pitch pine, and the ceiling groined. The Rev. Silas E. Wilson is minister.

The third Presbyterian church is situated on the Mall, between College Street and Russell Street. It has a handsome gable front, strengthened by engaged columns, with Ionic capitals. The interior is chaste, the seatings being in pitch pine, partly in Cathedral style. One gallery suffices for the requirements of the congregation. It is supported on decorated iron pillars. All the fittings are in strict keeping. The pulpit is surrounded by mahogany uprights bearing a single mahogany rail. A narrow gallery for the choir, raised above the level of the pulpit, has a perforated pitch pine front. The date of the church is 1837. A tablet in the vestibule was erected to the memory of the Rev. John Richard M'Alister, D.D., who died in 1871, aged 55 years. The present minister of the church is the Rev. John Elliott.

Wesleyan Methodism received an impetus in Armagh through the personal influence of John Wesley. It is recorded that he frequently preached in Abbey Street in 1767. The first church was built in 1786. The present church in Abbey Street was remodelled this year, 1888. A new gable, in the Grecian style of architecture, was substituted for one which bore date 1835. An

increase of twelve feet was made in the main structure, and the interior fitted in pitch pine. A new pulpit also of pitch pine, and a handsome railing, hammered iron, fronting the gallery, are among the improvements. Mr. J. J. Phillips, Belfast, was the Architect, and the contract for the work, amounting to over £800, was carried out by Messrs. Thomas Collen & Son, Armagh. The only mural tablet commemorates John Noble, of the City of Armagh, who for half a century performed the duties of a local preacher " with unswerving fidelity."

The Congregational body, after a period of over 90 years, consists of only about 26 members. The church in College Street, is in a good state of repair, and free from debt. It has a gallery on three sides, and a total seating capacity of over 300. Until May, 1887, the Society in London helped to sustain the expenses. Not feeling disposed to continue the stipend any longer, the last minister, Rev. R. H. Smith, was obliged to leave. There is no immediate prospect of a successor being appointed.

A denomination known as Christians, has a meeting-place in Russell Street, next door to the Post Office. It has had an organization in Armagh for about 20 years. At present there are over 50 members. The following paragraph, kindly given by one of the number, is suggestive :—

"Christians meet in the name of the Lord, on Lord's Day at 11.45, for breaking bread, reading of the Scriptures at 3.30, Sunday School at 5.30, and occasionally for preaching the Gospel at 8 o'clock."

ROMAN CATHOLIC CATHEDRAL, OLD CHAPEL, CONVENT, ST. PATRICK'S COLLEGE, CHRISTIAN BROTHERS.

ACCORDING to a paragraph in the *Book of Armagh*, the Roman Catholic Cathedral of St. Patrick occupies the hill to the north of the ancient Cathedral, which was visited by St. Patrick in circumstances of considerable interest. When Daire, chieftain of the district, called on the saint to inform him that he had decided to grant the " Hill of Sallows," in accordance with the original request, they went forth together from *Na-Fertae*, the Abbey in the low ground. On ascending the hill "to view the admirable and well-pleasing gift," they found a roe and fawn ; Daire attempted to catch and kill the fawn, but St. Patrick interposed and took it upon his own shoulders to the other hill, the roe following " like a pet sheep." This story is told in the translation by Dr. Reeves. The foundation stone of the Cathedral was laid in 1840, and the ceremony of dedication took place on the 24th of August, 1873. The site, then called Sandy Hill, was procured by

G

Primate Crolly from Lord Cremorne, and Counsellor Robinson, an outcome of the friendly relations he endeavoured to establish with Protestants, from the date of his appointment, 1835. The building of the Cathedral was continued until the death of Primate Crolly in 1849. He was succeeded in the year following by Dr. Paul Cullen, afterward Cardinal; transferred to Dublin in 1852. Dr. Cullen seemed to think the structure altogether too large for the requirements of Armagh, and as it was not then roofed, suggested that a portion of the walls might be covered. Dr. Joseph Dixon was appointed to the Primacy in 1852. He soon took measures for the completion of the Cathedral. Mr. Duff, the Architect, had died a few years previously, and in the employment of a new Architect, Mr. J. J. M'Carthy, Dublin, a change of plan was also effected. The resumption of the work was celebrated on Easter Monday, 1854, in the midst of a storm which is realistically described by the Rev. John Gallogly, C.C., as follows:—"Father O'Rourke, S.J., occupied the pulpit, but neither he nor the choir, nor any human voice could be heard, for the pitiless storm that raged at the time hushed every voice in order to proclaim its own uncontrollable power. * * * Large beams of timber were placed at intervals across the nave and aisles, and an abundant supply of tarpaulins was procured to cover the space underneath. * * * When 12 o'clock arrived, the appointed hour, the storm assumed the violence of a hurricane, and showers of hail, driven furiously by a south-east wind along the whole length of the Cathedral, plattered on the awning above, which swelled and roared as the billows of an angry sea when lashed into fury by the tempest. * * * Just after the consecration, when the tempest had reached its height, a gust of wind swept the whole Cathedral, extinguished the candles, and would have upset the altar had not the deacon, to the great relief of His Grace, placed the patena on the Host, and secured the Chalice with one of his hands till after the Communion." The Irish people in the United States and Canada contributed largely toward the building fund, one collector, Rev. John McMahon, sending from New York alone £5,000, and £300 for the Virgin's altar. A bazaar netted £7,000. In 1866 Primate Dixon died, leaving the Cathedral unfinished. Dr. Michael Kieran was elevated to the Primacy in 1867, but owing to the delicate state of his health did nothing toward the completion of the work of his predecessor. He died in 1870. Dr. Daniel McGettigan succeeded, and he at once determined that the finishing touches should be made in his own time. Accordingly, on the 24th of August, 1873, two years after his appointment, the Cathedral was dedicated. It is estimated that from 50,000 to 100,000 persons visited Armagh to

participate in the ceremonies of the occasion. Rev. Thomas Burke, O.P., the eloquent Dominican, preached the dedication sermon, and at the close £8,200 was collected. The total sum expended upon the cathedral was about £70,000. Decorated gothic was the style of architecture followed by Mr. McCarthy. Mr. Duff in his part of the work had adhered to the perpendicular. The building is cruciform, with nave, aisles, transepts and chancel. The 16 splendid columns supporting the nave are of Dungannon freestone, but the greater part of the material in the construction of the edifice is limestone, from the celebrated Navan quarries. Two towers and spires rise from the western side to a height of 210 feet. The exact measurements in the interior are as follows :—Nave and aisles, 72 feet wide ; across transepts, 112 feet ; height from floor to ridge, 110 feet ; total, length, 210 feet. There are some fine stained windows, notably one over the high altar, erected in 1879, to the memory of Primate Crolly and Primate Dixon, at a cost of £920. The remains of Primate Crolly were removed to the Cathedral from Drogheda, where he died, and are deposited under the high altar. The remains of Primate Dixon repose in the cemetery attached to the convent of the Sacred Heart. The high altar, in Caen stone and native marbles, is a creditable work of art. The pulpit, also of Caen stone, is supported on eight pillars of Cork marble. There is a very good organ. Statues in Caen stone, with gilt background, typify the several Stations to the Cross. Not the least of the attractions of the Cathedral are the handsome grounds which surround it, and the terraced approach from Mill street, where a highly ornamental railing runs for a short distance at both sides of the gate, fronting a handsome cutstone lodge, built in 1884 for the Sexton. The palace of the Primate—modest, but in good taste—occupies a partly-secluded spot at the back of the Cathedral. Primate McGettigan died in 1887. His remains are interred in the cemetery on the hillside below the Cathedral, in accordance with a desire expressed by himself. The present Primate is the most Rev. Michael Logue, D.D.

The Old Chapel, in Chapel Lane, is still used for early morning Mass. It occupies part of the site of Temple Bridget.

The Covent of the Sacred Heart also stands on a hill, Mount St. Catherine, in view of the Cathedral. It has a school for the education of ladies, and a National School. Mrs. Harbison is the Superioress.

St. Patick's College is situated in extensive grounds, to the right of the Roman Catholic Cathedral. It was founded in 1836 by the Congregation of the Mission of Vincentians, and is devoted chiefly to the preliminary instruction of young men

ROBERT TURNER & CO.,

Merchants,

ENGLISH STREET,

ARMAGH.

Departments.

House, Steam and Smiths' Coal
Timber of every description
Steam Saw Mills
Bar, Rod, Sheet and Hoop Iron
Slates, Tiles, Bricks
Drain Pipes
Cement and Alabaster
Fence Wire, plain and barbed
Farm Boilers
Eave Gutters and Down Pipes
Ranges and Grates
House Furnishing and Builders' Hardware
Artificial Manures
Garden Tools.

intended for the Priesthood. Rev. M. Carrigy, C.M., is President, and the Professors are—Rev. John Boyle, C.M. ; Rev. R. T. Jones, C.M., and Mr. Felix Beggan.

At Green Park, in the outskirts of the city, the Christian Brothers have schools. The connection of the Brotherhood with Armagh began in 1852. About 200 boys take advantage of the methods of education which they employ, intermediate and primary, and have the benefit of good air and extensive recreation grounds. Rev. Bro. R. B. Dunne is the present Director.

THE ARMAGH CLUB, NATURAL HISTORY AND PHILOSOPHICAL SOCIETY, PHILHARMONIC SOCIETY, CRICKET AND FOOT-BALL CLUBS, ORNITHOLOGICAL SOCIETY, PROTESTANT ORPHAN SOCIETY, YOUNG WOMEN'S CHRISTIAN ASSOCIATION, UNITED PROTESTANT MUTUAL IMPROVEMENT SOCIETY, CATHOLIC READING ROOM.

 CLUB for the County and City of Armagh has been in existence since 1869. It is called The Armagh Club, and has first-rate quarters in English Street. Mr. John G. Winder, J.P., took the initiative in effecting an organization, and succeeded in securing a membership of 126. At present there are 108 members, who pay an annual subscription of £3. The entrance fee is £5. Sir John Calvert Stronge, Bart., and St. John Blacker Douglas, are the trustees ; Mr. W. C. Hobson, J.P., is treasurer ; and the secretaries are Mr. John G. Winder, J.P., and Mr. A. W. M'Creight.

The Armagh Natural History and Philosophical Society occupies a building on The Mall, in the Grecian style of Architecture. It has about 275 members, paying an annual subscription of 5s. each. The object of the society is to maintain a museum, library, and reading-room, procure qualified persons to deliver lectures, and to hold meetings for mutual improvement, at which occasional debates may be held. To economise space, the reading-room, by the withdrawal of a partition formed of shutters, becomes the stage of the theatre, and the theatre and museum are one. A good collection of specimens has been secured for the illustration of lectures on natural history. The library is well stocked with books in the following departments :—Antiquities, Astronomy, Arts, Biography, Chemistry, Economics, Geography, Geology, and Mineralogy, History, Mechanics, Metaphysics, Microscopy, Natural History, Natural Philosophy, Poetry, and general literature. Nearly all the leading magazines, and reviews, and

a fair representation of the useful weekly and daily newspapers, are supplied to the reading-room. Members may take out books for family use by paying 2s. 6d. a year extra. Every year the Society makes an excursion, to stimulate the taste of the members for natural history and antiquities. The officers for 1888 are Rev. Geo. Robinson, A.M., President ; Mr. E. R. Johnson, Secretary ; Mr. F. L. Martin, Treasurer, and Mr. James Roberts, Librarian. Miss Susan Reid is the Curator. The reading room is open from 10 a.m. to 10 p.m. daily.

In 1887 the Armagh Philharmonic Society was established. In spite of the fact that there are so many societies in the city, it immediately became an assured success. Opportunities are afforded to the members, who now number about eighty, for instruction in instrumental as well as vocal music. The concerts given under the auspices of the society, thus far, have been well attended, and the efforts of the management fully appreciated. Outside help has been freely provided. Meetings are held in the Mall Female School and in the Music Hall, Vicars' Hill, for instrumental practice. The subscription is 7s. 6d. for performing members, and from 5s. to 21s. per annum for honorary members. Mr. George De La Poer Beresford, D.L., is president, Rev. W. F. Johnson and Mr. Arthur Nelson, secretaries, Mr. W. J. Gibson, treasurer, and Mr. Thomas Osborne Marks, Mus. Doc., conductor.

The Archery and Lawn-tennis Club is described at page 51.

Armagh has had a first-rate Cricket Club since 1859. At present there are 120 members, paying an annual subscription of 10s. each. A portion of The Mall green is rented at £25 a year, and maintained in excellent order. There is a good pavilion and seats for guests. The club is really an " institution " of Armagh. It has some good men, and its matches, being open to the public, are usually witnessed by a large number of people. This year, out of 28 matches, 17 were played at The Mall. Mr. Geo. D. Beresford, D.L., is president, Mr. Thomas Gordon, treasurer, Mr. W. J. Girvin, secretary. The committee, 1888, includes Messrs. J. A. Allen, G. W. Bowen, W. J. Griffiths, H. J. Harris, E. R. Johnson, Rev. W. M. Morgan, C. H. M'Callum, W. H. M'Combe, W. M'Crum, E. S. Obré, J. G. Sharkey, James Wilson.

Several football clubs maintain an active existence in Armagh and vicinity. The Armagh Rugby Football Club has been established for many years. It has 33 members at present. The subscription this season, 1888, is 7s. 6d. Nearly all the members belong to the Cricket Club, and share its hospitality in the use of The Mall ground. The students of the Royal School have a Rugby club, and good ground at the back of the

college. Frequently on Saturdays, matches are played at The Mall. Members of the Catholic Reading Room have had a club for two seasons—Association—and there is a flourishing club at Milford, also Association.

A desire to improve the breed of poultry and to cultivate a taste for the keeping of song-birds suggested the establishment of the Armagh Ornithological Society. It began its career in 1883, and had the first show in 1884. Mr. Alexander Wallace, 15 Scotch Street, is president, and Mr. James Wilson, secretary and treasurer. There are 50 members. The subscriptions are from 5s. to 21s. The show is held in the Tontine Rooms. Mr. W. H. Gillespie won the principal prizes at the last show.

This year the County Armagh Protestant Orphan Society met at Armagh to consider its twentieth annual report. In 1888 the number of orphans was 134, including four apprentices. The total income for 1887 was £1,060 12s. 1d., leaving a balance to credit of £72 5s. 6d., after paying off a debt of £80, incurred in 1886. A bazaar held at Lurgan proved to be the chief source of income. It netted £464 15s. Rev. W. G. Murphy is hon. sec.

Ten years ago the Young Women's Christian Association, was established. There are 60 members, paying each a subscription of one shilling a year. Honorary members pay 2s. 6d. Miss Mary A. Kidd is secretary, and Mrs. John S. Riggs, treasurer. A Bible Class is held once a week. Once a month there is a Recreation Class, the programme of which consists of vocal and instrumental music, and fancy work for charity bazaars. The special object of the Society is to look after and help girls. Members visit other towns with this view. A social tea meeting is held annually. In this friends participate.

Since 1864 the Armagh United Protestant Young Men's Mutual Improvement Society has been in existence. It assembles in the Protestant Hall, Abbey Street, during the session, October to April. There are stated meetings for essays and debates. In February the annual meeting is held. Over 200 members are in good standing. Mr. Maxwell C. Close, A.M.D.L., is President, Mr. Thomas Newton, Treasurer, and Messrs. Thomas Wright and Richard Patterson, secretaries.

The Catholic Reading Room was established by Dean Byrne, of Dungannon, while Administrator of the parish of Armagh, in 1875. Its headquarters were then in Castle Street. Now they are in Ogle Street. The late Primate McGettigan took a warm interest in the undertaking, and gave it substantial monetary help. The Reading Room is well supplied with newspapers and magazines, and about 400 standard books form the nucleus of a library. There are 100 members paying 1s. per quarter. Honorary members pay 2s. 6d. per quarter. A

billiard room, with two tables, is among the attractions. The house belongs to the members. It was bought in October 1887, for £300. Rev. Hugh McOscar, Adm., is spiritual director, Mr. Joseph McParland, treasurer, Mr. John Toole, secretary, Mr. P. Corr, assistant secretary, and Mr. John Campbell, librarian.

BUILDING IMPROVEMENTS, CHIEF PROPERTY OWNERS, MASONIC HALL, SHIEL'S INSTITUTION, DRELINCOURT CHARITY, BLIND ASYLUM, COUNTY INFIRMARY, LUNATIC ASYLUM, GAS WORKS, BANKS, UNION WORKHOUSE, TONTINE BUILDINGS, COURT HOUSE, GAOL, THE CAMPBELL-BOYD DUEL.

DURING the past twenty years building improvements of a most substantial nature have been made in various parts of the city. Hartford Place, Mall, received several handsome additions, notably the houses of Mr. James Best, and Mr. William J. Best, J.P., and those occupied by Mr. John S. Riggs and Mr. W. W. B. Faussett. The two latter belong to Mr. Joseph Anderson, J.P. He built Winder Terrace, Victoria Road, 5 houses, in 1877, and The Mall houses in 1879 ; in 1880 Richmond Terrace, Victoria Road, 6 houses, and in 1887-8 Grantham Villas, Victoria Road, 6 houses. Mr. Thomas George Peel, coroner, built Mel Villas, just outside the city boundary, above Deansbridge, and Oulart Villa, further away in the same direction. There are two handsome brick villas at Deansbridge, erected within the time mentioned. They belong to Mrs. Boyd. Mr. George A. Edwards, J.P., in 1886, built Edwards' Terrace, Railway Street, 5 houses, and in 1887-8 Edwards' Street, 20 houses. The Masonic Hall, First Presbyterian Church, Post Office, and Parochial House are new buildings. The Masonic Hall was erected in 1884, at a cost of £1,400, from a design by Mr. J. H. Fullerton, F.R.I.A.I. It is in the early Gothic style. The principal gable faces The Mall, next to the First Presbyterian Church, and is flanked on one side by a tower and spire, and on the other by a circular-ended staircase with steep conical roof. The largest lodge room is 40 feet by 20. Full accommodation is provided for the four lodges (39, 299, 400 and 623) which indicate the flourishing condition of Masonry in Armagh. The chief owners of property in Armagh are Colonel George Dobbin, Colonel Rbt. Simpson, Cuppy House, Enniskillen ; Colonel H. Robinson, Lord Dartrey, the Lyle Family, Mr. John Y. Burgess, Tyrone ; The Misses

Waller, Clarinda Park, Kingstown ; Mr. Joseph Anderson, Messrs. James Best & Sons, Mr. William Couser, Mr. Geo. A. Edwards, Vicars Choral, Madame Ferris, Paris ; Mr. Samuel Davidson, Miss Sarah Bella Thompson, Belfast ; Representatives of Geo. Dunbar, Representatives of H. L. Prentice, and Miss Mary Ann Quinn.

Sheil's Institution comes under the head of recent improvements. It occupies a part of Tower Hill, an eminence within the city limits, embracing five statute acres. The buildings include 25 houses, one of which is occupied by Mr. Simeon Hicks, the Superintendent, and date from 1868. Each adult inmate receives £10 a-year, children between 10 and 15 years old, £5, and under that age £2 10. The design of the founder was to help persons of small income, who have seen better days. He was a native of Killough, County Down, who made a substantial fortune in Liverpool.

In 1738 the widow of Dean Drelincourt endowed a school or "hospital" for the maintenance and education of 20 boys and 20 girls. The Corporation of Armagh granted waste lands for the buildings, &c. From time to time circumstances required modifications in carrying out the trust, until at length, in 1878, the school came partly under the jurisdiction of the National Board of Education. The charitable intention is fulfilled as far as possible. This year 27 boys and 27 girls received a full suit of clothing each, as a reward for good conduct ; and last winter 100 children were provided with boots. A limited number of the best boys are given an apprentice fee of £6 each. Mr. Geo. Strong, is Principal of the Male Department, and Miss Susanna Strong, of the Female Department. The Schoolhouse is in Charter School Lane.

Arthur Jacob Macan, who died in India in 1819, made a bequest to the Sovereign and Burgesses of Armagh, under which an Asylum for the Blind was opened in 1854. Until the death of Mr. Richard Macan, last surviving nephew, the full amount of the bequest was not available. The Fever Hospital, built in 1825 by Lord John George Beresford, and fitted at an expense of £3,500, was purchased by the Trustees for £1,200. Applications for admission are received from Louth, Down, and Tyrone, but natives of Armagh receive the preference. The inmates this year, 1888, number 17. Basket-making is the chief occupation. Armagh merchants are the best customers for the work turned out. The officers are Mr. Thomas Smith, Secretary, Dr. Henry Frazer, Physician, and Miss Margaret Wilkin, Matron.

The County Infirmary is situated near the Public Library, in the vicinity of the ancient Cathedral of St. Patrick. It dates

from 1774, and originally cost £2,150. There are 72 beds, 36 for Male and 36 for Female free patients, and 2 beds for paying patients in a separate ward. The chief contribution to the maintenance comes from presentments by the Grand Jury. About £400 a-year is derived from Dr. Lill's Charity, used exclusively for the treatment of scrofulous diseases. Dr. J. M. Palmer is Resident Surgeon, Dr. Henry Frazer, Apothecary, Registrar and Medical Assistant, Mr. James Gardner, Treasurer, and Mr. Samuel Gardner, Secretary.

In 1825 the Armagh Lunatic Asylum, first of the kind in Ireland, was opened for the reception of patients. A total sum of £20,900 was spent in the purchase of the site, erection of buildings, &c. It originally received patients from Monaghan, Cavan, and Fermanagh, but now the admissions are confined to natives of the County and City of Armagh. In 1825 the accommodation was for 122 patients. Now there are facilities for the treatment of 304. The asylum stands in handsomely-planted grounds. Of the total area—32 acres, 2 roods and 8 perches—7 acres are under buildings. A pretty gothic chapel is used for worship by Episcopalians, Presbyterians, and Roman Catholics. On the 5th May, 1888, the patients numbered 280, of whom 141 were males and 139 females. Dr. Wm. Graham has been resident Medical Superintendent since December, 1886.

Armagh was first lighted by gas in 1833. The works are in Callan Street Lane, and are in excellent condition. Although a liberal expenditure appears to be made for maintenance, and the general consumers are charged only 4/2 per 1,000 feet, the Company, a limited liability one, has managed to pay its shareholders 10 per cent. for some years past. Mr. John S. Riggs is Chairman, and Mr. James Whimster, Engineer and Manager.

There is probably no place in Ireland of the size that has so many banking establishments. It has branches of the Bank of Ireland, Provincial, Ulster, Belfast, Northern, and Hibernian banks, and one of the old-style institutions for savings (the Armagh Savings' Bank), managed by Mr. Thomas Smith. This was founded in 1818, chiefly to encourage small depositors, but large ones also use it. The limit is £200 for one depositor. There were 4,031 depositors in November, 1887, and the amount of their deposits was £190,435 4s. 11d

The Union Workhouse occupies one of the prettiest sites in the city. It has a farm of 11 acres, the greatert part of which is cultivated by the inmates. Mr. Robert Turner is clerk and returning officer, and Mr. David Gillespie master. The names of the officers and guardians appear in the directory.

The Tontine Building, in English Street, was erected by a company to provide the city with a music-hall, theatre, &c. As

H

an enterprise it was not successful. The company gave it to trustees, by whom it is now managed. It has a hall capable of seating between 400 and 500 people, and rooms let for various purposes. The Town Commissioners have a part of the grounds floor for Office and Board Room. Accommodation is also provided for Grand Jury dinners, &c.. A wine cellar is maintained. Each High Sheriff entertains the Grand Jury here.

Armagh has a very fine Court House with a handsome portico, in College Street, facing The Mall. It was built in 1809.

At the south end of The Mall the front of the County Gaol occupies one side of the square to which it gives name. It is a substantial, sightly structure, with large windows, and, in fact, is very much more like a benevolent than a penal institution. This is the "old part," three stories high. The Governor, Captain J. A. Chippindall, occupies a portion of it, and the rest is used for offices, officers quarters, hospital ward, and cells, 9 in number, for the reception of prisoners awaiting examination by the doctor, preparatory to classification. The new portion of the prison dates from 1846. Here there is the usual Central Hall, with which the male and female wards are in communication. The cells in both wards are maintained in perfect condition, the most sensitive nose failing to perceive the faintest trace of that odor expected to be found associated with bolts and bars. There are two tiers of cells, one at each side of the ward. An iron gallery surrounds the upper tier, and a substantial rope netting covers the open space, as a precaution against suicide. There are good bathing facilities, and the sanitary arrangements throughout are excellent. A well filled bookcase in the central hall supplies material for improving the mind. During the first month of confinement the prisoner has an opportunity to become acquainted with the " plank bed "—a bare board. If he takes to it philosophically, he can earn two good conduct marks a day, and rise triumphant from the " plank " to a mattress in thirty days. The cells are each twelve feet by seven, and nine feet high, and are heated by hot-air flues. The buildings and premises include three and a-half acres. Prisoners are received from the whole of Armagh, Cavan, and Monaghan, and from a portion of Down and a portion of Fermanagh.

The last execution for murder was in 1876. In 1808 Major Alex. Campbell was hanged for killing a brother officer, Capt. Alexander Boyd. in a duel. Major Campbell was descended from an ancient Highland family, and had distinguished himself in Egypt, under Sir Ralf Abercrombie. He was transferred to the 21st Regiment from a Highland corps, and it is said that his promotion to a brevet majority gave offence to the senior

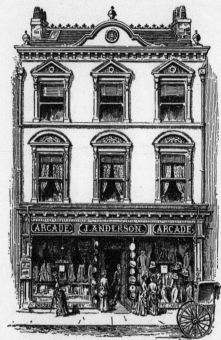

captain. The 21st Regiment was quartered at Newry. Major Campbell commanded at the half-yearly inspection. After dinner Captain Boyd, in the course of conversation, sneeringly remarked that Campbell had given an incorrect order on parade. Later in the evening, while the other officers were at the theatre, Campbell and Boyd continued to converse in bitter terms. At last, heated with wine and stung by the remarks of Boyd, Campbell went to his room and returned with loaded pistols. He sent for Capt. Boyd and, with closed doors, insisted on immediate "satisfaction." At the first fire Boyd was mortally wounded. He was removed to his own quarters. Campbell immediately followed, and found him supported in the arms of his grief-stricken wife and surrounded by his young family. Campbell begged him to acknowledge that all had been fair. "Yes," said Captain Boyd, "it was fair; but you are a bad man. You hurried me." Having gasped out the completion of the sentence, he expired. Major Campbell, after some time, gave himself up. He was tried, found guilty of murder, and sentenced to death by Judge Mayne. A great deal of sympathy was excited for him; but, although respited, his friends were unable to save his life. At the execution, a company of his old regiment formed the gaol guard.

EMANIA ("THE NAVAN"), RESIDENCE OF THE KINGS OF ULSTER FOR SEVEN HUNDRED YEARS.

THE remains of the earthworks belonging to the famous royal residence of Emania are still extensive. At one time they encircled twelve acres, and within this space the Kings of the line of Ir had their palaces during a period of 700 years. Ir was one of the sons of Milesians, of Spain, also called Gael from a remote ancestor, and Scoti, from Scota, mother of Milesius. The Milesians conquered the *Tuatha da Danans*, and two of the sons of Milesius, Heber and Heremhon, divided the country between them. Jealousy speedily resulted from their use of the kingly power. A battle followed, and Heber was slain. Heremhon then became King of Ireland.

By a slight addition to the original Irish word from which Emania has been evolved, the pronunciation easily suggests

Navan. The inhabitants of the district, and also those of the City of Armagh, two miles to the east, know it as The Navan. A green fort, surrounded by a hawthorn hedge, stands near the part of the entrenchment that continues intact. It bears evidence of having been frequently explored by antiquaries. There was a second mound at a lower elevation. The view from the summit of the one remaining takes in the principal features of a wide range. It was, of course, much higher when first constructed, and was a splendid point from which to estimate the strength of an approaching enemy.

It is believed that the first palace was erected at Emania either by Cimbaoth, King of Ireland, in the year of the world 3603, or by his consort, Queen Macha. Cimbaoth and his two cousins, Aed Ruadh and Dihorba, were the sons of three princes, brothers. One of the number was entitled to become king, but owing to the vigor of the fight made by all for the possession of the crown, an understanding was ultimately arrived at, according to which each was to rule during a term of seven years. After having completed two terms, and almost a third, Aed Ruadh was drowned. His only child was a daughter, Macha. She appears to have inherited her father's courage and warlike disposition, and boldly asserted her right to share in the government of the kingdom as he had done. Her cousins having declined to seriously consider her claim, she decided to enforce it in battle. She was beautiful as well as valiant, and the novelty of the contention, no doubt, attracted to her standard the most chivalrous of the subjects. The result was the defeat of Cimbaoth and Dihorba. Dihorba lost his life in the encounter, and a truce having been proclaimed, Cimbaoth gallantly offered his hand and heart to Macha. As queen she probably shared in the rule of Cimbaoth, and after his death became supreme.

The famous Red Branch Knights were quartered in an enclosure near Emania, and went forth from there to uphold the dignity of the King of Ulster, and spread terror among his foes. Within the camp which they occupied there was a house called " The Soldier's Sorrow " for the treatment of the wounded.

In 332, A.D., the palaces of Emania were destroyed by the

ROBERT SMYTH,

Linen Manufacturer,

TULLYELMER,

ARMAGH.

Collas, who had, during the same year, defeated and slain
Fergus Fodha, last of the Irian Kings. One of the Collas
had been King of Ireland through usurpation. In 315 he slew
his uncle Friachadh in battle, and was proclaimed in his stead.
Four years later Muireadhach, son of Friachadh, at the head
of a formidable army, attacked Colla, and drove him into exile,
with his two brothers. A few years' residence at the Court of
the King of Scotland made him so weary that the prospect of
immediate death in his own land seemed more agreeable than
a continued life of inactivity. Moreover, it had been prophesied
that if he or his brothers should be put to death by the King of
Ireland, their descendants would come to the throne. They
returned, and surrendered to Muireadhach, making pretence of
being no longer able to bear the remorse occasioned by thoughts
of the wickedness which had stimulated them to murder his
father. Muireadhach was aware of the prophecy concerning
the change of dynasty, and was not sufficiently revengeful to
take the chances for its fulfilment. He received the three
princes in a kindly spirit, and won their respect by assigning
them posts of importance in the Federal Army, with revenues
in proportion. Having taken a little time for reflection it struck
the King that the constant presence of the brothers might eventually work his own ruin. In this belief he promptly decided to
set them upon Fergus, King of Ulster, who had burned the
beard of one of Muireadhach's kinsmen. With the outrage as
a pretext, the Collas marched from Tara against Fergus, receiving on the way contingents of his disaffected subjects, until
their forces were swelled to the importance of a. *corps
d'armée*. They encountered Fergus in a part of the present
County Monaghan, and overthrew him after a battle continued
for seven days successively. One of the Collas also lost his life
in the struggle The other two seized and destroyed Emania,
and ruled conjointly in the conquered territory. The ruined
palace never was rebuilt.

A " ground plan and sections of Navan Fort," drawn by Mr.
J. C. McBride, C.E., Armagh, was published in the " Journal
of the Royal Historical and Archaeological Association of Ireland for July, 1884. in connection with an exceedingly interesting paper, descriptive of Emania, by the Rev. John Elliott,
Armagh.

MILFORD FACTORY, ARMAGH.

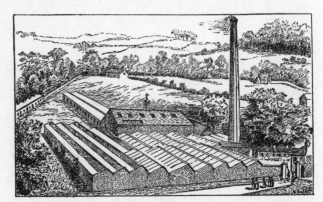

GILLIS FACTORY, ARMAGH.

Belfast Warehouse:

5 LINEN HALL STREET.

THE MILFORD AND GILLIS FACTORIES.

ILFORD, on the river Callan, is distant from Armagh two miles. The inhabitants, with few exceptions, work in the weaving factory of Messrs. Robert M'Crum & Co. Mr. William M'Crum, some years deceased, built a mill here in 1808, and it is claimed to have been the first in Ulster used for spinning flax by the dry process. All the machinery for it was brought from Leeds. In 1850 Mr. Robert G. M'Crum, J.P., changed the spinning mill into a factory for the weaving of damasks. At present there are 270 looms in full operation, driven by a 200 horse-power steam engine, and a turbine of 120 horse. About 450 people are constantly employed. Diapers and towellings are also woven at Milford, and yarn bleaching is done for the use of the concern only. Since 1850 Mr. Robert G. M'Crum has made substantial structural additions to the factory, and has almost entirely built the village, of which it may be truly said, that it is a model of cleanliness and good order, the humblest dwelling bearing evidence internally and externally of a beneficent proprietary control. Mr. M'Crum's handsome private residence, Milford House, stands in a richly-planted and highly ornamented park at the verge of the village, and commands a beautiful view of the surrounding country.

The Gillis factory adjoins the Railway Station at Armagh. It contains 220 power looms, and gives employment to over 250 people. The manufactures are linens, towellings and damasks, and the buildings are of brick, stone and slate. The Gillis factory was built by the late Mr. John Gass about the year 1863, and was purchased by Messrs. Robert M'Crum & Co. in 1872. The premises consist of nine acres. A steam engine, 120 horse, provides the motive power. The warehouse for Milford and Gillis is at 5 Linen Hall Street, Belfast, where the business is conducted under the style of M'Crum, Watson and Mercer— Mr. Robert G. M'Crum and Mr. Wesley Watson. Mr. Mercer has been dead for some time.

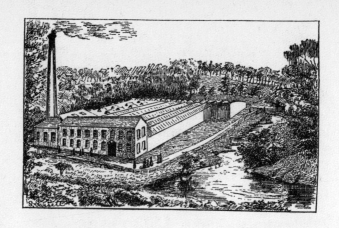

JOHN COMPTON,

Linen, Drill and Damask

MANUFACTURER,

UMGOLA POWER-LOOM FACTORY,

ARMAGH.

Telegraphic Address—"COMPTON, ARMAGH."

THE UMGOLA WEAVING FACTORY.

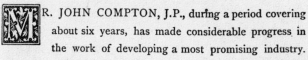R. JOHN COMPTON, J.P., during a period covering about six years, has made considerable progress in the work of developing a most promising industry. His factory at Umgola is devoted to the weaving of linen drills and damasks. Twenty years ago Mr. Thomas Wynne founded the enterprise. Mr. Compton, immediately after purchasing, began to remodel, enlarge and improve, until he secured more than double the original capacity. The buildings, which are of brick and stone, are more extensive than the illustration indicates. They now contain 200 perfected power looms, and the other necessary machinery and equipments, including a steam engine capable of driving up to 120 horse.

Yarns are procured from the principal Irish mills, from Dundee, Scotland, and some from Lille, France. The manufactured goods are sold in Belfast, Manchester, London and Northampton.

In addition to the other substantial improvements effected since Mr. Compton's accession, it may be mentioned that he has had twenty houses erected for workers. About 200 people are employed. Of this number the greater part live in Armagh, and some with their parents who are small farmers of the neighborhood. The Market Square of Armagh is less than an English mile distant from the factory, and the railway station is within a mile and a quarter.

Umgola takes a front rank with the many charming places in the immediate vicinity of Armagh. Mr. Compton's factory and premises occupy between nine and ten acres of the Callan valley, close to the Caledon Road. They are almost surrounded by hills. Half a mile further west the site of the palaces of the Kings of Ulster comes prominently into view.

WM. H. ADDEY & CO.,

P. L. LINEN MANUFACTURERS AND FINISHERS,

ALLISTRAGH MILLS,

ARMAGH.

MESSRS. WM. H. ADDEY & CO.

ESSRS. WM. H. ADDEY & CO.'s Weaving Factory and Beetling Works, at Allistragh, are situated at a distance of two miles from the Armagh Railway Station. They communicate with the direct road to Moy, a border town in Tyrone, celebrated for horse fairs, and are within two miles of the Ulster Canal, at Blackwatertown.

Messrs. Wm. H. Addey & Co. are manufacturers and finishers of coarse linens, known to the trade as "beetlers," and sell all their output in Manchester, where they are represented by Messrs. Jacob Addey & Co., Marsden Square.

About 36 years ago the father of Mr. Wm. H. Addey was attracted by Allistragh, and looked upon it as a most favorable site for founding an important industry. The river seen in the illustration is the Callan. Upon its banks many enterprises have been initiated, and are now deeply rooted. This fact, coupled with others equally encouraging, induced Mr. Addey to acquire premises, consisting of sixty acres, as a basis for operations. Some of the houses now used for beetling purposes, forty years ago, were owned by Mr. W. C. M'Bride, a corn merchant. More than sixty years previous to that time Mr. M'Bride's father had a bleach green here.

Mr. Addey remodeled the corn mill, and put in beetling engines. The weaving factory, which also occupies the site of a corn mill, was built by Messrs. Wm. H. Addey & Co. in 1882. It contains power looms, having the latest improvements, driven by water and steam. Two turbines, with a 40-horse engine as an auxiliary, supply the necessary driving force. A portion of the work-people live in cottages belonging to the property, and the remainder have houses of their own, and small farms in the neighborhood.

Mr. Wm. H. Addey's private residence, approached through a beautifully planted avenue, stands on the side of a gentle acclivity, commanding a charming prospect.

THE RETREAT, ARMAGH.

A HOUSE OF RECOVERY FOR MENTALLY AFFLICTED AND NERVOUS INVALIDS OF BOTH SEXES.

THIS Institution has enjoyed the confidence of the Medical Profession and the Public for nearly sixty years. The greatest care is taken to render it a Domestic Home and House of Recovery rather than an Asylum, in the general acceptation of the term.

The inmates receive the mildest and most careful treatment, and enjoy the greatest liberty compatible with their condition.

Terms from £15 to £20 per Quarter for Ordinary Patients, and from £25 to £35 for those requiring a separate Attendant, paid quarterly in advance.

ALEXANDER D. ALLEN,
PROPRIETOR.

Visiting Physicians—
W. W. LEEPER, M.D.; J. G. ALLEN, L.K.Q.C.P.I., &c.
Telegraphic Address—LOUGHGALL.

THE RETREAT.

R. ALEXANDER D. ALLEN'S institution for the treatment of mental diseases, is three miles from Armagh, and one mile and a half from Richhill railway station. Its situation, in the midst of hills, gives to the name Retreat a most agreeable significance.

There is nothing to be seen in the immediate surroundings to indicate restraint. The buildings stand in tastefully kept grounds, the view of which, from the public road, is unobstructed. Walks for exercise lead for a mile through lands, the property of Mr. Allen, passing for some distance along the banks of a shallow stream, shaded by trees, and at every point suggestive of repose. The late Mr. John Allen, a member of the Society of Friends, and father of the present proprietor, founded the Retreat, in 1824. He had had many years experience at the asylums of York, and Bloomfield, Donnybrook, and approached the work on his own account under the conviction that the strict application of the humane principle would enable him to effect a large percentage of permanent cures. The blessings of the system which he practised soon became known, and the Retreat, from a very small beginning, grew to the present extensive proportions. Mr. Alexander Dawson Allen was associated in the management with his father, and practically succeeded him in 1854. The capacity of the Retreat is for thirty-five patients, a fact which occasions surprise to the visitor, considering the extent of the buildings. The explanation is that the patients have the freedom and comforts of a comfortable home, roomy apartments for social intercourse, lofty halls, and single bed-chambers. The proprietor and members of his family live in the Retreat, and patients who are progressing toward recovery have their meals at the same table. Servants' quarters also take a considerable space. The facilities for service are so ample that any patient willing to pay for it may have a special attendant. Invalids of both sexes are admitted. The ladies are cared for under the supervision of the Misses Allen, and the gentlemen under the supervision of Mr. Joseph Allen. Lawn tennis, cricket, quoits and bowls form the principal out-door amusements. Various simple games, and dancing are provided for pastimes in-doors. Shower, reclining and sitz baths are given freely. Restraint is never used unless it can't be avoided, and it is very rarely required. Religious services are held by clergymen of the Church of Ireland and Presbyterian Church once a fortnight, alternately. The farm attached to the Retreat, consisting of twenty-nine acres, supplies it with plenty of fruit, vegetables and milk.

I

ARMAGH CITY DIRECTORY.

——:o:——

BUSINESS BRANCHES, PROFESSIONS, PUBLIC BODIES, &c., &c.

——:o:——

[Arranged Alphabetically. Names of individuals not found here should be sought in the Armagh City Alphabetical Directory. For institutions not mentioned see County Directory, page 53.]

——:o:——

ARCHITECT.
Fullerton, J. H., College st

ARMY.
(See Co. Directory.)

AUCTIONEERS.
Bell, Matthew A., English st
Hewton, Thos. W., Thomas st
M'Cullough, Jno., Thomas st
M'Garity, P. J., Thomas st
M'Ginity, Jno., Thomas st
Reilly, Henry, Scotch st
Williamson, Saml., Scotch st.

BAKERS.
Brooks, Thos., Scotch st
Collins, J. & A., Scotch st
Fox, Daniel, Lr. English st
Hamill, Patrick, Thomas st
Hughes, Thos., Thomas st
rwin, James, Scotch st
M'Kenny, Andw., Charter Schl le
M'Parland, Owen, English st
Rolston, Andrew, English st
Wilson, Thomas, English st

BANKS.
Bank of Ireland, Scotch st. : Wm. C. Hobson, agent. Chas. H. A. Davis, sub-agent. J. H. Johnston, cashier

Belfast Bank, English st.: E. Moorehead, mgr. Jas. C. Murphy, sub-mgr. J. W. West, Cashier

Hibernian Bank, Russell st.: W. O'Shaughnessy, mgr. Jno. H. Mostyn, cashier

Northern Bank, Scotch st.: Thos. M'Dowell, mgr. Geo. W. Bowen, sub-mgr. Geo. W. Waddell, cashier

Provincial Bank, Abbey st.:

Chas. Griffith, mgr. Wm. Gibson, sub-mgr. and cashier

Savings Bank, Victoria st. and Gaol sq. : Thos. Smith, actuary. Benjamin P Davidson, auditor. Clerks : Edward Parkinson, Thos. W. Cowan

Ulster Bank, English st.; Fras. L. Martin, mgr. Jas. Moore, cashr.

BIRTHS, DEATHS AND MARRIAGES.
Supt. Registrar — William M'Cartney, English st.

Registrar—Dr. Robert Gray, Dispensary, The Mall.

BLACKSMITHS.
Horse shoers [*]
Carson, Jno., Lr. Irish st
Cullen, Bd., Lr. English st
* Hill, Rt., Lr. English st
* M'Kenna, Jas., Dobbin st
* M'Quaid, Jas., Lr. English st
* Newbank, Bros., Abbey lane
* Newbank, Jas., Scotch st
Rafferty, Owen, Up. Irish st

BLIND ASYLUM, MACAN.
Trustees and Governors—Most Rev. Rt. B. Knox, D.D., primate ; Philip Lavery, J.P. ; Very Rev. G. A. Chadwick, D.D. ; Arthur Macan, J.P. ; Most Rev. Ml. Logue, D.D., primate; Major Chas. E. M'Clintock ; Rev. Jackson Smyth, D.D. ; Jas. Gardiner, Rt. G. M'Crum, J.P. ; Jno M'Parland, J.P. ; Rev. John Elliott

Medical Officer—Hy. Frazer, M.D.
Secretary—Thos. Smith
Matron—Miss M. Wilkin

ALEXANDER WALLACE,

IMPORTER OF HAVANA CIGARS

——AND——

FANCY TOBACCOS,

15 SCOTCH STREET,

ARMAGH.

THOMAS W. HEWTON,

Auctioneer and Valuator,

THOMAS STREET,

ARMAGH,

General Drapery and Clothing Establishment

——AND——

MUSICAL INSTRUMENT WAREHOUSE.

Valuations made for Probate and Land Courts. Sales Undertaken in any part of Ulster. Prompt Cash Settlements. Bills Discounted if required.

BOOTMAKERS
Who have shops.
Marked thus [*] sell leather

Carson, Saml. E., English st
Clarke, Chas., Scotch st
* Farley, Paton, Thomas st.
Geough & Son, Thomas st
Harrison, John, Thomas st
Hodgens, Thos., Thomas st
Hoy, Matthew, Thomas st
Hughes; Patk., Thomas st
Kearney, Patk., Thomas st
Kerr, John, English st
Nixon, John, Thomas st
* Wilson, James, Scotch st

BUILDERS.
Collen, Thomas & Son, Railway st
MacMurray, Thomas, Scotch st

BUTTER AND EGG EX-
PORTERS.
* Eggs only.

Adams, Frank, English st
Benson, Thomas, Dobbin st
Gorman, Ml., Tassagh
Lonsdale, J. & J., The Pavilion
*M'Mahon, James, Railway st
The Co-operative Wholesale So-
ciety, Limited, Dobbin st

CABINET MAKERS.
See Draper's announcements.

Allen, Robert, Barrack st
Clancy, Henry, Barrack st
Frizell's Works, 7 Houses

CARPENTERS.
Bloomer, Lower English st
Carson, James, Lower Irish st
Connolly Brothers, Abbey st
Corr, Neece, Banbrook
Donohue, James, Dobbin st
Farr, Brothers, Mall
M'Cashel, Daniel, Thomas st
M'Manus, Charles, Up. Irish st
O'Hagan, Charles, Castle st

CARRIERS (FURNITURE &c).
Bell, M. A., English st
Reilly, Henry, Scotch st

CIVIL ENGINEERS.
Davison, T. W. J., Abbey st
Davison, Henry, Russell st
M'Bride, James C., English st

CLOG MAKER.
Harrison, John, Thomas st

CLOTHIERS.
New and Second Hand.

Gribbon, J., Castle st
M'Creesh, John, Market square
M'Keown, M., Castle st
Slevin, James, Thomas st

CLUBS.
See Index.

COACH BUILDERS.
Hughes, William, Scotch st
Johnston, James, Thomas st
Taylor Brothers, The Mall

COAL MERCHANTS.
Boyd & Co., Dobbin st
Edwards, Geo. A., Ry. Station
Hillock, Henry, Thomas st
Turner, Robert & Co., English st

COFFEE HOUSES.
Black, W. J., Scotch st
Coffee House Company, Limited,
Scotch st
M'Kee & Co., Scotch st

COLLEGES.
See Education

CONFECTIONERS.
Bright, William, English st
Hazelton, Hamersley, English st
Irwin, Jas., Scotch st
M'Kee, John, Thomas st
Rolston, A., English st

COOPERS.
Cosgrove, James, Abbey lane
Hamill, William, Castle st
Hill, George, Abbey lane

CORK CUTTERS.
Kelly, Charles, Callan st
Kelly, J., Lower English st
M'Carter, Thomas, Lr. English st

CHURCHES.
Church of Ireland—Cathedral of
St. Patrick—Most Rev. Robert B.
Knox, D.D., Archbishop and Pri-
mate of all Ireland; Very Rev.
George A. Chadwick, D.D., Dean;
Ven. Wm. E. Meade, D.D., Arch-
deacon; Rev. Augustine Fitzger-
ald, D.D., Precentor; Rev. Ben-
jamin Wade, M.A., Chancellor;

Rev. Charles K. Irwin, D.D., Treasurer; Rev. W. F. Johnson, M.A., Rev. Charles Faris, M.A., Rev. Wm. M. Morgan, LL.D. (Honorary), Vicars Choral; T. O. Marks, Mus. Doc., Organist; Robert Farr, Assistant

Church of Ireland—St. Mark's— Very Rev. George A. Chadwick, D.D., Dean, Rector; Rev. R.R. Thacker, M.A., Rev. Perceval Waugh, Curates; T. O. Marks, Mus. Doc., Organist; Robt. Farr, Assistant

Methodist Church, Abbey street —Rev. William M'Mullen, Rev. W. S. M'Kee

Presbyterian Church—1st, Russell street, Rev. Jackson Smyth, D.D.; 2nd, Abbey street, Rev. Silas E. Wilson; 3rd, Mall, Rev. John Elliott

Roman Catholic—St Patrick's Cathedral—Old Chapel, Most Rev. Michl. Logue, D.D., Archbishop and Primate of all Ireland; Rev. Hugh M'Oscar, Administrator; Rev. Henry M'Neece, C.C., Rev. Francis M'Elvogue, C.C., Rev. John Quinn, C.C.; James Lalor, Organist

DENTIST.

Chapman, W. M., Melbourne ter

DISPENSARY.

The Mall—Dr. Robert Gray, M.O. Attendance — Monday, Tuesday, Thursday, and Saturday, 9 a.m. to 11 a.m.

Meetings, 1st Saturday every month, 11 a.m.

Committee:—John G. Winder, J.P., Armagh; Hugh Boyle, J.P., Armagh; Capt. Beresford, J.P., Castledillon, Armagh; St. J. T. Blacker-Douglas, J.P., Elm Park, Killylea; Colonel Simpson, J.P., Ballyards, Armagh; John Douglas, J.P., Mountain Lodge, Keady; J. W. M. Bond, J.P., Drumsill House, Armagh; Colonel Dobbin,

J.P., The Mall, Armagh; John Compton, J.P., Armagh; Henry B. Armstrong, J.P., Killylea; John Barcroft, J.P., Ennislare House, Tassagh, Armagh; Robert Gillespie, J.P., Armagh; James Lonsdale, J.P., Armagh; Dr. Philip Lavery, J.P., Armagh; John S. Riggs, Armagh; William R. Ferris, Armagh; William Simpson, Killeen, Armagh; Jacob Jenkinson, Armagh; John Trotter, Mullyleggan, Blackwatertown, Moy; Andrew M'Creight, Armagh; Jas. Best, Armagh; Thomas Wynne, sen., Lislea, Armagh; John Knipe, Derrydarragh, Armagh; George Rice, Armagh; John Davidson, Linen Hill, Armagh; Thompson Brown, Killynure, Armagh; John M'Parland, J.P., Armagh; R. P. M'Watters, Armagh; Joseph Anderson, J.P., Armagh

Wardens—Robert Corrigan, Annamoy; Thomas Knipe, Bellaghy; John Kilpatrick, Ballyards; Thomas Montgomery, Milford; John Gray, Rokeby Green

DRAPERS.

Acheson, David, Scotch st
Adams & Co., English st
Anderson, Joseph, Market sq
Bowes, James, Thomas st
Bronté & Co., Market sq
Collins, James, Scotch st
Davison, Wm. & Son, Scotch st
Fullerton, David, Market sq
Hewton, Thos. W., Thomas st
Leeman, H. G. & Co., Market sq, Scotch st., and Thomas st
Lennox, William J., Market sq
M'Garity, P. J., Thomas st
M'Lorinan, P., Scotch st
Newton, Thomas J., Market sq
Reilly, William Jas., Scotch st
Taylor Mrs., Thomas st
Walker, Miss Louisa, English st
Warnock, John, English st
Williamson, S., Scotch st

DRUGGISTS.
*Dispensing Chemists
*Brice's Medical Hall, English st (Dr. Herron)
*City Medical Hall, English st (Dr. Frazer)
Gray, John, English st
Hillock, James, English st
*Peel, Josiah, Thomas st

EDUCATION.
COLLEGE : ROYAL SCHOOL
Head Master — Rev. William Moore Morgan, I.L.D.
Senior Master—Thomas Gordon, M.A.
Assistant Masters—Rev. Herbert B. Sandford, B.A., Edward R. Johnston, B.A., S. Deschamps, B.A., T. O. Marks, Mus. Doc. ; R. Smeeth.
COLLEGE (ST. PATRICK'S).
President—Very Rev. M. Carrigy, C.M.
Professors — Rev. John Boyle, C.M. ; Rev. Robert Jones, C.M. ; Felix Beggan
CHRISTIAN BROTHERS Schools, Green Park.
Director—Rev. Bro. R. B. Dunne
INTERMEDIATE ACADEMY, &c.
Masters—Alex. Gibson, and A. J. Boyd.
Classical School—Alex. Gibson.
LADIES' BOARDING AND DAY SCHOOLS.
Abbey st.—Mrs. Davidson
Abbey School — The Misses L'Estrange
Abbey st.—Mrs. Allandar
Beresford Row — Misses St. George
Convent (Sacred Heart) — Madame Anastatias
Palace Row—Miss Bell
Railway st.—Mrs Hardy
Russell st.—Miss Bell
St. Marks place—Miss M. W. Calvert
Vicars' hill—Miss Wilkin

NATIONAL SCHOOLS
District Inspector—John W. Rodgers, Deansbridge house
Ballinahone—Miss S. G. Strong
Banbrook — Arthur McGurk, Miss M'Kenna, Mrs. McDonald
Callan st.—Miss M. Roberts
Chapel lane — Hugh Scanlan, Miss M. M. O'Reilly
Churchwalk—Miss Tyrrell, Miss Shegog
College st. — Samuel M'Kimm, Miss H. J. M'Cleery
Convent—Mount St. Catherine
Drelincourt, Charter school lane—George Strong, Miss Susana Strong
Drumcairne — Miss Sarah A. Robinson
Gosford, Mall—James Shields
Mall — Duprez A. Simmons, Miss L. Cowan
Methodist—John Abraham, Miss Jane M'Cauley

EMIGRATION AGENTS.
O'Hare, Chas., Barrack st
Thompson, Wm. C. B., English st
Young, John, Scotch st

FANCY WAREHOUSES.
(See also Stationers.)
Morrison, Miss M. J., Scotch st
Wallace, Miss M., Scotch st

FIRE BRIGADE.
Station, Lower English st.
C. H. M'Callum, Beresford Arms Hotel, Captain ; J. J. Ovens, Abbey st. ; J. H. Fullerton, College st. ; A. G. Bright, English st. ; R. Nesbitt, Linenhall st. ; M. Walker, Barrack st. ; A. Nesbitt, Linenhall st. ; J. Black, Scotch st.; P. Gorman, Linenhall st, ; T. H. Murphy, Winder terrace ; J. M'Quade, Beresford Arms Hotel. D. Gillespie, English st.

FLAX AND TOW SPINNERS.
Armagh Spinning Co. (A. Wilson), Loughgall road

FLORISTS.
Lockhart, Wm., Deansbridge
Somers, James, English st

FOWL DEALERS.

Corrigan, Francis, Irish st
Corrigan, Michael, Ogle st
Donaghy, James, Ogle st
Gregory, Thos., Lower Irish st
M'Ardle, Pat., Charterschool lane
Morrow, Thomas, Linenhall street
Stuart, James, Barrackhill
Stuart, Richard, Barrackhill
Stuart, Richard, jun., Linenhall st

GAS COMPANY, LIMITED.

Works, Callan street lane
John S. Riggs, chairman of
directors; J. Whimster, manager
and engineer; J. G. Deacon,
secretary; Norton Riggs collector

GLASS, CHINA. DELF, &c.

Hart, John, Lower English st
M'Loughlin. James Ogle st
Ross, L. & C., English st
Willis, James, Scotch st

GRAIN MERCHANTS.

Best, James, & Sons, Lower
English st
Ferris, Wm. R., Market square
Loughran, Geo., Ballyrath
M'Connell, Javanna, Scotch st
Murray, James, Thomas st

GREEN GROCERS.

Kelly, Francis, Shambles
Kelly, James, Market square
Kelly, Mrs., Market square

GROCERS.

Marked thus [*] sell spirits. Thus
[†] are seed merchants.
*Aiken, James & Co., Barrack st
Armagh Spinning Company, Lough
gall road
Baxter, Thomas, Charter School lne
Byrne, Patrick, Lower English st
*Campbell, Henry, Lr. English st
Carson, R., English st
*Carter, William, English st
Cleeland, James, Railway st
*Couser, William, English st
Donnelly, Michael, English st
*Downey, John, Lower English st
Downey, Miss Mary, Castle st
*Elliott, Wm., 17 & 18 Thomas st
*Ferris, William R., off Market sq

*Gamble, James, Barrack hill
Geough & Son, Thomas st
*Gillen, John, Lower Irish st
*Gillespie, David, English st
†Gillespie, J. & R., English st
Gray, William & Co., Thomas st.
and Ogle st
Hanlon, John, Charter School lane
*Hanna, W. M'Clure, Market sq
*Hawthorn, Thomas, Scotch st
Hillock, James, English st
Irwin, James, Scotch st
Loughran, Mrs. S. A., Irish st
*M'Alevey, Robert, Thomas st
*M'Cann, Nicholas V., Ogle st
*†M'Clelland, John, English st
*M'Connell, Javanna, Scotch st
and Mill st
M'Guirk, Mrs., Castle st
*M'Kee, Miss Eliza, Ogle st
M'Kenna, John, Thomas st
*M'Loughlin, Robert J., Lower
English st
*Magowan, W. C., English st
Mason, James, Scotch st
†Massey, Francis A., Scotch st
*Mullen, James, Thomas st
Mullen, Mrs., Castle st
*†Murray, James, Thomas st
*O'Hare, Mrs. Catherine, Barrack
st
*Riggs, John S., English st
Smith, Robert, Edwards st
†Somers, James, English st
Stephenson, Miss, Barrack st
Vogan, Robert, Scotch st
Wallace, Alexander, 15 Scotch st
*Wallace, Robert & Co., Scotch st
and Thomas st
†Watson, J. & Co., Thomas st
*Wilkin, Miss Anne E., Scotch st
Wilson, Thomas, English st
Wright, Samuel, Lower English st

HARDWARE.

Boyd & Co., Dobbinst
Hillock, Henry, Thomas st
Turner, Robert & Co., English st
Wallace, Alexander. Scotch st
Watson, J. & Co., Thomas st
Whitsitt Brothers, Market square

H. M. PRISON.

Governor—Capt. J. A. Chippindall

Chief Warder—J. Murphy
Matron—Miss Jane Simons
Clerk—Thomas Furlong
Storekeeper—Alexander Spence
School Teachers—Ralf Foster, Miss M. J. Boyle
Medical Officer—Dr. J. M. Palmer
Chaplains—Rev. R. Thacker, C.I. ; Rev. Jackson Smyth, Presbyterian ; Rev. Hugh M'Oscar, R.C.

HIDES AND SKINS.

Carbery, Patrick, Lr. English st

HOTELS.

All but one have spirit licenses.

BERESFORD Arms (W. Campbell), English st
CHARLEMONT Arms (J. H. Mann), English st
Linen Hall (Mrs C. Lynch), Dobbin st
Plough (Mrs. E. Byrne), English st
Railway (James M'Mahon), Railway st
Temperance (Mrs. Lowden), English st
Wellington (Thomas English), Lr. English st

HOUSE AGENTS.

See Rent Agents

INLAND REVENUE.

Office Scotch street
Supervisor—Mark J. Blake, 3 Victoria st
Officer—John Torhy. 1 Dobbin st

INFIRMARY, ARMAGH CO.

Surgeon J. M. Palmer, F.R.C.S.I. ; Apothecary, Registrar and Medical Assistant, Henry Frazer, M.D. ; Treasurer, James Gardner ; Secretary, Samuel Gardner ; Matron, Mrs. Eno

LAND AGENTS.

See Rent Agents.

LEATHER MERCHANT.

See also Boot Makers.
Watson, James Alex., Thomas st

LIBRARY, PUBLIC.

Rev. Benjamin Wade, Librarian.
Edward Rogers, Deputy Librarian

LINEN MANUFACTURERS.

Addey, W. H. & Co., Allistragh
Compton, John, Umgola
M'Crum, Robert & Co., Milford
Smyth, Robert, Tullyelmer
The Gillis Linen Co., Armagh
Wynne, Thomas & Co., Lislea

LUNATIC ASYLUM, ARMAGH DISTRICT.

GOVERNORS :

Hugh Boyle, J.P. ; M. C. Close, D.L., J.P. ; J. Hughes ; St. J. Blacker-Douglas, D.L., J.P. ; The Earl of Charlemont, K.P. ; Rev. John Elliott ; G. D. Beresford, D.L., J.P. ; J. G. Winder, J.P. ; Rev. Jackson Smyth, D.D. ; J. G. Richardson ; C. Reynolds ; R. Gillespie, J.P. ; T. Shillington, J.P ; Lord Lurgan ; William Simpson ; H. B. Armstrong, D.L., J.P. ; W. J. Best, J.P. ; Very Rev. George A. Chadwick, D.D. ; Colonel G. M. Dobbin, J.P. ; P. Lavery, J.P. ; J. Lonsdale, J.P. ; J. Murphy, J.P. ; The Right Rev. W. Reeves, D.D., Bishop of Down and Connor and Dromore ; Most Rev. R. B. Knox, D.D., Archbishop of Armagh ; J. H. Stronge, J.P. ; Henry Hillock. Wm. Graham, M.D., Resident Medical Superintendent ; J. M. Palmer, F.R.C.S.I., Visiting Physician ; J. A. Allen, Clerk and Storekeeper ; Mrs. E. Bright, Matron ; Chaplains : Rev. C. Faris, C.I., Rev. H. McNeece, R.C., Rev. S. E. Wilson, Presbyterian

LUNATIC ASYLUM (Private).

The Retreat, Alex. D. Allen

MANUFACTURERS.

(See Linen Manufrs. & Spinners).

MARINE STORES.

M'Loughlin, J., Ogle st
O'Neill, Chas., Scotch st
Quinn, Peter, Ogle st

MARKETS.

Every Tuesday—hay, straw, butter, eggs, pork, fowl, potatoes, flax, &c ; every Wednesday and Saturday, grain and grass seed

Toll Trustees — J. G. Winder, T. A. Prentice, John S. Riggs, Wm. Couser, James Gardner, Hon. Treasurer

Committee—J. S. Riggs, Chairman ; Jas. Gardner, Secretary ; T A. Prentice, Robert Gillespie, W. R. Ferris, John McClelland, Wm. J. Best, Jacob Jenkinson, Andrew Rolston

MARRIAGES (Registrar).

See Co. Directory.

MERCHANT TAILORS.

See also Drapers.

Gray, Bros., English st

MILITIA.

See Co. Directory.

MILLERS, &c.

Best, Jas. & Sons, Lr. English st

MILLINERY, DRESS, &c.

See also Drapers.

Boyd, Mrs. Wm. C., English st
Shiels, Mrs. E. A., English st

MONUMENT WORKS.

Corr, P. & Co., Dobbin st
Donnelly, P., Ogle st
Johnston, Samuel, Dobbin st
McCullough, John, Thomas st

NATURAL HISTORY AND PHILOSOPHICAL SOCIETY.

See Index.

NEWS AGENTS.

See Stationers.

NEWSPAPERS.

Guardian, Friday, 2d., English st, Wm. C. B. Thompson
Standard, Friday, 1d., Scotch st, John Young
Ulster Gazette, Saturday, 1½d., Scotch st, McClelland & Peel

NURSERY.

Lockhart, Wm., Deansbridge

OBSERVATORY, ARMAGH.

See Index.

ORNITHOLOGICAL SOCIETY.

See Index.

PAINTERS & DECORATORS

Fawkner, J., Abbey st
Grimes, Patrick, Irish st
Kimmitt, Joseph, Dobbin st
McGahan, Patrick, Chapel le
Maxwell, James, The Mall
Murphy, Michl., Ballyharden

PAWNBROKERS.

Gibson, Mrs., Market sq
McAllen, Mrs., Market sq
Reilly, John, Abbey st

PETTY SESSIONS.

Held every Thursday at 10 a.m.

Clerk, S. M. Steel, Abbey st

PHOTOGRAPHERS.

Hunter, Mrs., Scotch st
Loudan, B. M., & Co., English st

PHILHARMONIC SOCIETY.

See Index.

PHYSICIANS, &c.

Frazer, Henry, Seven Houses
Graham, Wm., Lunatic Asylum
Gray, Robt., Melbourne ter
Herron, Robt. T., English st
Hunter, Chas. R., Scotch st
Lavery, Philip, J.P., English st
Lynn, J. M., Melbourne ter
Palmer, J. M., Infirmary

PIANOFORTE WAREROOMS.

Lee, Jas. & Sons, Market sq

PICTURE FRAME MAKERS.

Gray, J., English st
Hillock, James, English st
Hunter, Mrs., Scotch st
McWatters, Robt. P., English st

PLUMBERS.

Cochran, J., Scotch st
Donnelly & Somerville, Barrack st
Hillock, Henry, Thomas st
Morrison, John, Dobbin st
Whitsitt Brothers, Market sq

POSTING CAR OWNERS.

Beresford Arms Hotel, English st.
Campbell, James, Mill street
Charlemont Arms Hotel English st
Cooke, Wm., Edwards street
Corr, James, Banbrook hill

Corr, Mrs. Sara, Russell street
Hamill, D., Lr. Irish street
Hawthorn, Thomas, Scotch street
Hillock, James, College street
Hughes, John, Cathedral place
Kennedy, Patrick, Scotch street
Loudan, R. R., English street
McArdle, Mrs. Ann, Mill street
McKee, Peter, Boyd's row
McGeough, Frank, Thomas street
McNeese, Patrick, Lr. English st
McWhirter, Hugh, Lr. English st
Molloy, Mrs. M., Thomas street

POST OFFICE.
Russell street.

post mr.
Clerks—Thomas J. Uprichard
(chief); John Pillow, William H.
Uprichard, W. B. Brownlee, David
Semple, Huston Doak, William G.
Reid, Charles Mulholland, Edwin
Uprichard

PRINTING WORKS (Job).
Guardian Office, English street,
McWatters, Robert P., English st
Standard Office, Scotch street
Ulster Gazette Office, Scotch st

PROBATE COURT.
(See County Directory.)

PROCESS SERVERS.
Robert Woods and Richard Nesbit

RAILWAY (G.N.R.)
John Foster, Station Master

RENT AGENTS.
Babington, H., B'nahone ho
Boyle, Hugh, Charlemont place
Davison, Benjamin, Abbey street
Fullerton, Ephraim, Tontine Bldgs.
Jenkinson, Jacob, Barrack st
Martin, D. P. & Co., English st.
Smith, Thomas, Savings Bank
Winder, John G., Tontine Bldgs.

ROPE AND TWINE
MANUFACTURER.
Griffin, Jackson, Scotch street

R.I. CONSTABULARY.
(See also Co. Directory.)
Barracks, Russell street and Upper
Irish street.
District Inspector—

Head Constable—David Magee

SADDLERS.
Cassidy, Joseph, Ogle street
Greer, Arthur, Thomas street
Hughes, Charles, Thomas street
Loughrane, Francis, English street
McKenna, O., Scotch street
Nesbit, Richard, Linen Hall street

SAUSAGE SKIN
MANUFACTURER.
Baxter, Thos., Charter School lane

SAW MILLS.
Edwards, Geo. A., Railway Station
Hillock, Henry, Thomas street
Turner, Robert & Co., English st

SCHOOLS.
(See Education.)

SEED MERCHANTS.
(See also Grocers.)
Bell, Matthew, English street
Peel, Josiah, Thomas street

SEWING MACHINE CO.
Singer and Co., Ogle street

SHEIL'S INSTITUTION.
Local Governors—Very Rev. Geo.
A. Chadwick, D.D.; Rev. Jackson
Smyth, D.D.; Rev. Hugh McOscar,
Adm.; Rev. John Elliott; Colonel
Thomas Simpson, J.P.; Colonel
G. M. Dobbin, J.P.; John G.
Winder, J.P.; William C. Hobson,
J.P.; James Gardner; Robert G.
McCrum, J.P.; Robert Gillespie,
J.P.; Philip Lavery, J.P.; James
C. Bell; James H. Stronge, J.P.;
Hume Babbington, J.P.; Joseph
Anderson, J.P.
Superintendent—Simeon Hicks
Medical Officer—H. Frazer, M.D.

SOLICITORS.
Bell, James C., Beresford row
Best, Edwin, Beresford row
Gallagher, Wm., Seven houses
Girvin, Wm., St. Mark's place
Harris, Henry J., Beresford row
Kilpatrick, T. W., English street
Lavery, Patrick, College street
McCombe, Alexander, English st
Monroe, Samuel H., Russell street
Peel, Joshua E., English street

Sharkey, J. G., Russell street
Simpson, Wm. A., Russell street
Williamson, James, College street

SPINNERS.

(See Flax and Tow Spinners.)

SPIRIT MERCHANTS.

(Wholesale licenses.)

Aiken, James & Co., Barrack st.
Couser, William, English street
Ferris, Wm. R., off Market square
Hanna, Wm. McClure, Market sq
McClelland, John, English street
Moore, Thomas & Co., Market sq
Wallace, Robt. & Co., Scotch and Thomas streets

SPIRIT RETAILERS.

See also Hotels and Grocers marked thus [*]

Baldock, John, Barrack st
Boyle, Mrs. C., Lr. English st
Cooper, Thos., Scotch st
Corr, Mrs. A. Lr. Irish st
Cowan, Ter., Barrack st
Gorman, J., Linen Hall st
Hamill, Danl., Lower Irish st
Hughes, Chas., Thomas st
Hughes, Patk., Scotch st
Irwin, Hugh, Thomas st
Keating, Danl., Lr. Irish st
Kindness, John, Scotch st
Lavery, Philip, Dobbin st
McAleavy, Mrs. M., Ogle st
McAlinden, Hugh, Castle st
McGahan, Bernard, Market sq
McKenna, Patk., Scotch st
McKinney, Andrew, Thomas st
Magowan, John T., Barrack st
Magowan, Mrs. Ellen, Scotch st
Mann, Jas., Railway st
Mann, Robt., Lr. English st
Molloy, Mrs. Martha, Thomas st
Monaghan, Wm., Up. Irish st
O'Hanlon, John F., English st
Pillow, Saml., English st

STATIONERY WARE-HOUSES.

(Nearly all are News Agencies.)

Bourke, Mrs. M., English st
Guardian office, English st
Johnston, Jos. B., Ogle st
M'Loughlin, Jas., Ogle st

M'Mahon's, Thomas st
M'Watters, Rt. P., English st
Standard office, Scotch st
Ulster Gazette office, Scotch st
White, S., English st

TIMBER MERCHANTS.

Boyd & Co., Dobbin st
Edwards, Geo A., Railway station
Hillock, Henry, Thomas st
Turner, Rt., & Co., English st

TINSMITHS.

Baxter, Rt., Castle st
Cochran, Mrs., Market sq

TONTINE ROOMS,
English st

Trustees—Col. Geo. Dobbin, J.P.; Henry Davison, Thos. A. Prentice, St. John T. Blacker-Douglas, John G. Winder, secretary; Ephraim Fullerton, ast. secretary; Kingsbury Smith, keeper.

TOWN COMMISSIONERS.

Meet 1st Monday of every month at Tontine Rooms, Patrick M'Lorinan, Chairman; David Acheson, Joseph Anderson, J.P.; Saml. Davison, Geo. A. Edwards, J.P.; Wm. R. Ferris, Wm. Gray, John Harrison, Henry Hillock, James Irwin, Jacob Jenkinson, John M'Clelland, Wm. C. Magowan, James Mann, James Maxwell, jun.; T. J. Newton, Josiah Peel, Andrew Rolston, Saml. C. Sloane, Jas. Alex. Watson, James Whitsitt

Clerk & Executive Sanitary Officer—Thos. G. Peel

Sanitary Inspector—Dr. Robert Gray

Town Sergeant—James Nelson

UNDERTAKERS.

Boyd & Co., Dobbin st
Frizell, Alex., Seven houses
Hillock, James, English st
Loudan, R. R., English st

UNION WORKHOUSE.

Guardians meet every Tuesday at noon.

Chairman—Sir John Calvert Stronge, Bart.

Vice-Chairman—A. Small, J. P.
D. V.-Chairman—John S. Riggs
Magistrates who are ex-officio members of the Board : (For post office addresses see magistrates in County Directory.)

Joseph Atkinson, Joseph Atkinson, jun.; Henry B. Armstrong, John Barcroft, George De La'Poer Beresford, St. John T. Blacker-Douglas, Joshua W. M. Bond, Samuel Byers, Hugh Boyle, Matthew Burke, Earl of Charlemont, Robert Clarke, John Compton, John A. M. Cope, Col. G. M. Dobbin, John Douglas, Charles Ensor, Robert Gillespie, The Earl of Gosford, George Gray, Thomas Hall, Captain Irwin, Philip Lavery, James Lonsdale, Robert J. M'Geough, R. G. M'Crum, James Orr, Jacob Orr, Colonel Simpson, Thomas Small, Major T. Stronge, Major Tenison, Ormsby Vandeleur, Annaghroe, Caledon ; John G. Winder, James C. Wann, John Wilkin, Tannaghlane, Caledon

Elected Guardians, and electoral Divisions—John S. Riggs, William R. Ferris, Jacob Jenkinson, Andrew M'Creight, Armagh; Isaiah Fulton, Armaghbreague; Jacob Orr, J.P., Annaghmore ; Thompson Brown, Ballyards ; John Knipe, Ballymartin ; John Gamble, Brootally ; William Naye, Joseph Wright, Caledon ; Thomas Gilpin, John Trotter, Charlemont; Robt. Dodds, Clady; Joseph Gibson, Crossmore; Patrick Moan, Peter Campbell, Derrynoose; Moses Gillespie, Glenaul; George Rice, Grange ; Thomas Wynne, jun., Hamiltonsbawn ; Edward Reilly, Hockley ; Francis Carville. John Gormill, Keady ; William Simpson, Killeen; James Hobson, Kilmore ; Timothy Fox, Killyman ; William Cuming, Lisnadill; Moses Robinson, Henry Lamb, Loughgall ; William Byers,

Robert Black, Markethill ; John M'Namee, James Deighan, Middletown ; James Best, John Jackson, Richhill ; Joseph Marshall, John Gillespie, Tynan ; Thomas W. Sinclair, Tullyroan

Local Gov. Bd. Officers—R. T. Hamilton, Inspector ; Col. R. M. Studdert, auditor

Clerk and Returning Officer, Executive Sanitary Officer, &c.—Robert Turner ; Assistant Clerk, Wm. Calvert

Chaplains—Rev. Richard R. Graham, C. I.; Rev. John Elliott, Presbn. ; Rev. P. M'Geaney, R. C.

Medical Officer—H. Frazer, M.D.

Veterinary Inspector — John Moir, V.S.

Master and Matron — David Gillespie, Miss Margt. M'Master

Relieving Officer—Thomas Bennett, Barrack hill

VETERINARY SURGEONS.

Huston, Rt. T., Dobbin st
Moir, John, Marine lodge
Murphy, James, Scotch st
Quinn, Ml., Scotch st

VICTUALLERS.

Ballantine, Rt., Scotch st
Edgar, Geo., Scotch st
M'Kee, James, Thomas st
M'Kenna, John, English st
Nugent, Wm., Ogle st
Parr, John, English st
Sherry, John Geo., English st
Sherry, John, Lr. English st
O'Neill, Jas., Lr. English st
Ward, Constantine, Ogle st
Warmoll Bros., Thomas st
Warmoll, Charles, Market sq
Warmoll, Edward, English st

WATCHMAKERS, &c.

Biggart, Wm., Market sq and English st
Clarke, Gabriel, Scotch st
Hazelton, H., English st
Humphreys, Meredith, Scotch st
Sloane, Samuel C., English st
Wilkin, James, Scotch st

ARMAGH.

Alphabetical Directory,

FARMERS AND RESIDENTS.

*For names not found here, see Armagh Business Branches, Professions,
&c., and Armagh Sub-Post Offices.*

Abbreviations—Sub-Post Offices—Al-Allistragh ; M-Milford.

Adams, G. W,, Drummondmore
Adams, John C., English street
Adams, W., Drumbeebeg
Addey, Wm. Hardy, Allistragh
Alexander, Robert, Mullinure
Alexander, William, Mullynure
Allen, Alexander D., The Retreat
Allen, Benjamin, Ballyknick
Allen, George, Magheryarville, M
Allen, James A., Abbey street
Allen, Joseph, The Retreat
Allen, Thomas, Drumbee
Allen, William, Drumbee
Anderson, F., Ballymartrim otra
Anderson, James, Tullygarran, Al
Anderson, John, Ednavase
Anderson, Jno. W., Richmond ter
Anderson, Jos. (J.P.), Winder ter
Anderson, Mrs. A. J. T'garron, Al
Anderson, Thomas, Corporation
Anderson, Wm., Ballyscandle
Armstrong, H. B. (D.L.), The
    Deanery
Babington, H. (J.P.), Ballinahone
    House
Barcroft, J. (J.P.), Ennislare house
Barrett, James, Altaturk
Beggs, Joseph, Annacramp
Bell, J. W. C., English street
Beresford, George De La Poer,
    (D.L.), Castle Dillon
Best, James, Hartford pl
Best, Richard, Hartford pl
Best, Wm. J. (J.P.), Hartford pl
Best, William, Barrack hill
Best, Wm. (J.P.), Melbourne ter
Blake, Mark J., Victoria st
Blane, Alex. (M.P.), Scotch st

Bond, J. W. M,, (J.P.), Drumsill ho
Bond, W. A. M'G., Drumsill ho
Bond, Walter M'G., Drumsill ho
Bothwell, John, Enagh, M
Bowen, Geo. W., St. Mark's pl
Bowman, Misses, Victoria st
Boyd, Andrew, Deansbridge
Boyd, John, Deansbridge
Boyd, Mrs., Deansbridge
Boyd, Wm. C., English street
Boylan Patrick, Lenalea
Boyle, Hugh (J.P.), Charlemont pl
Brady, John, Red Barns
Brannigan, Arthur, Tullygarron
Brannigan, James, Lisadian
Brannigan, Patrick, Grangemore
Brawley, Francis, Drumcairn
Brawley, Wm., jun., Terreskane
Broderick, Jos. J., English st
Brolly, William, Terreskane
Brooks, David, Dobbin st
Brown, Alex., Drumbeebeg
Browne, Rev. W. J., Red Rock
Brown, Rt., Lisdrumbroughas
Brown, T., Killynure, M
Brown, W. H., Drumbeebeg
Burrows, James, Lisdonwilly, Al
Calvert, James E., Boyd's ter
Campbell, Henry, Ballyharridan
Campbell, Hugh, Aughanore
Campbell, Rd., Ballybrockey
Carmichael, John, Ballybrockey
Cardwell, W. F., Tullyelmer
Carrick, William, Lisbane
Carson, Henry, Bellaghy
Carson, James Tullysarron
Carson, William, Lisdown
Cartmill, James, Tullysarron

Clements, J. W., Vicar's hill
Compton, J. (J.P.), Richmond ter
Connolly, Stephen, Edward st
Conway, John, Drummondmore
Conroy, Daniel, Cloughfin
Coote, Capt. A. E., Bow house
Corr, M., jun., Maheryarville, M
Corvan, W., Ballinahonemore
Cotter, George, Barrack hill
Couser, David, Aghavilly
Couser, Samuel, Aghavilly
Couser, W., jun., Killynure
Cowan, T. W., Abbey street
Craig, Mrs., The Hall
Crozier, Richard, Cavanacaw
Crummy, Patrick, Drumcairn
Cullen, F. N., Charlemont pl
Cullen, Owen, Tullygarron, Al
Cumming, Robert, Ballaghy
Cunningham, J., Farmacaffly
Cunningham, T. M., Lisbanoe, M
Cunningham, William, Baltarran
Davidson, B. P., Abbey st
Daly, Owen, Lisbane
Davidson, Henry, Russell st
Davidson, J. W., Linen hill
Davidson, J., Ballinahonemore
Dawley, Connor, Bracknagh
Delany, C. J., Lurgyvallen
Delany, James, Liberty Hall
Delany, P., Lisbanoe, M
Deschamps, S., Killoney
Diamond, James, Edward st
Dickenson, R., Lisbanoe, M
Diffin, Henry, Garvaghy
Diffin, W., Ballybrockey
Dignam, John, Legarhill
Dixon, John, Lenalea
Dobbin, F. W., Lenalea
Dobbin, John, Enagh, M
Dobbin, Mrs., Tullymore house
Dodd, John, Aghavilly
Dolan, Thomas, Thomas st
Donnelly, Alex., Navan
Donnelly, Daniel, Terreskane
Donnolly, John, Tullyloist
Donnelly, Owen, Ballinahonemore
Donnelly, Patrick, Terreskane
Donnelly, Thomas, Bracknagh
Donnelly, William, Ballyrea

Doughan, John, Ballyharridan
Douglas, John, Scotch street
Downey, Bernard, Drumcairn
Dreyer, J. L. E. Observatory
Duncan, Samuel, Ennislare
Edgar, James, Mount Pleasant
Edgar, John, Ballinhonemore
Edwards, G. A. (J.P.), Prospect ho
Emerson, William, Edenavase
Erskine, H. W., Ballyards
Faris, Rev. Chas., Cathedral close
Faussett, W. W. B., Hartford pl
Fegan, Alex., Lisdrumbroughas
Fegan, Patrick, Lisdrumbroughas
Fegan, Peter, Magherkilcranny, M
Feehan, Joseph, Baltarran
Ferguson, John, Lenalea
Finlay, Alexander, Cavanacaw
Flannagan, Patrick, Lurgyvallen
Fluke, John, Ballydoo
Foster, Samuel, Lisdrumbroughas
Foster, Thos. (Boyd & Co.) Dobbin st
Foster, Thos, Maherykilcranny, M
Foster, Wm., Maherkilcranny, M
Fox, Samuel, Killylyn, Al
Fox, Terence, Tirgarve
Gamble, Mrs., Edward street
Gardiner, Thomas, Abbey street
Gardner, James, Richmond terrace
Gardner, Saml., Richmond terrace
Garland, Geo., Edward street
Garland John, Aughrafin
Garvey, John, Ballytrodden
George, James, Cabragh
George, John, Tirearly
George, Thomas, Cabragh
George, William, Cloughfin
Gibb, Joseph, Dobbin street
Gibson, Alex., Market street
Gibson, John, Ballyknick
Gibson, Nathaniel, Annacramp
Gillen, George, Tullynicholl
Gillespie, James, Callan street
Gillespie, Thomas, Cavanacaw
Gillespie, W. H., Edwards street
Gillin, George, Ballyscandle
Gillow, Mrs. E., Ballyhoy, M
Glass, Thomas, Allistragh,
Godfrey, Patrick, Aghanore
Gordon, Thomas, Charlemont pl

Gray, John, Rokeby green
Gray, Samuel, Russsell street
Gray, William, English street
Greer, H. F., Grantham villas
Greer, Wm. H., Grantham villas
Greer, W. J., Abbey street
Greer, William, Drumsill
Gribben, Patrick, Granemore
Griffin, Daniel, Lenalea
Griffin, Jackson, Scotch street
Grimley, Patk., Lisdrumbroughas
Grimshaw, N. W., Winder terrace
Gubbin, F., Lisdrumbroughis
Haffey, Bernard, Tray
Haffey, Joseph, Magheryarville, M
Hagan, Charles, Castle street
Hagan, J., sen., M'kilcranny, M
Hagan, J., jun., M'kilcranny, M
Hagan, James, Ballyhoy
Hailigan, William, Drumart
Hamill, Edward, Iiish street
Hamill, Patrick, Thomas street
Hamilton, John, Milford
Hamilton, J. G. Milford
Hamilton, Robert, Lisadian
Hamilton, R. J., Killeen
Hanson, David, Cloughfin
Hanson, Joseph, Tullygarron
Hanson, Thomas, Cloughfin
Harding, Dr. W. T., Hartford pl.
Hardy, Mrs. E., Charlemont place
Hardy, Mrs., Winder terrace
Harson, Fr., Aughrafin
Hart, John, Lower English street
Hart, Patrick, Killeen
Hegarty, Edward, Lisadian
Henry, John, Barrack hill
Herron, A., Railway view
Hewitt, James, Killeen
Hillock, R., Lisdrumbroughas
Hillock, Thomas, Edwards street
Hobson, Wm. C. (J.P.), Scotch st
Hogg, John, Drumgaw
Holland, John, Dobbin street
Hooks, William, Drumadd
Hopton, Col. Edw., Mel Villas
Houston, William, Bracknagh
Hutchinson, William, Aghavilly
Hughes, Edward, Ballytrodden
Hughes, Francis, New street

Hughes, Francis, Baltarran
Hughes, Henry, Ogle street
Hughes, James, Tullysarron
Hughes, John, Ballytroden
Hughes, John, Baltarron M
Hughes, Peter, Baltarron M
Hughes, Thomas, English street
Hughes, William, Scotch street
Hutton, Wolsey H., Cullentragh
Irwin, Hugh, Thomas street
Jenkinson, Benjamin, Tamlaght
Jenkinson, Jno., Tamlaght
Johnston, Rev. W. F., Winder ter
Johnston, Wm., Ballyknick
Jones, R., Ballinahonemore
Johnston, Sl., Ennislare
Kearney, J., jun. Linen hall st
Kearney, Mrs. E., Edwards st
Kearney, Rd., Tamlaght
Keating, Dl., Irish st
Keating, F., Magherykilcranny M
Keating, J., Magherykilcranny M
Keating, Ml., Lisdrumbroughis
Kennedy, Geo., Kennedies, M
Kennedy, R. J., Kennedies, M
Kennedy, Thos., Edenavase
Kernaghan, Jas., Grangemore
Kerr, Wm., Edwards st
Keyes, Alex., Aghavilly
Keyes, D., Magheryarville, M
Keyes, Andrew, Lisbanoe, M
Keyes, J., Magheryarville, M
Keyes, Robt., Aghavilly, M
Kilpatrick, James, Tullysarron
Kilpatrick, John, Ballaghey
Kirkwood, Sl., Lisbanoe, M
Knipe, John, Tonnagh
Knipe, Thomas, Ballaghy
Lang, James, Broughan
Lappan, Alexr., Grangemore
Lappan, George, Grangemore
Lappan, James, Cabragh
Lappan, William, Drumbee
Largey, J., Ballinahonemore
Largy, Patrick, Drumbeebeg
Lavery, Dr. P. (J.P.), English st
Lawson, Samuel, Augherafin
Leeman, Hans. G., Cathedral close
Leemon, John, Navan
Leeman, William, Navan

K

Leeman, William, Lisdrumard
Leemon, John, Rosebrook
Leemon, Thomas, Culentragh
Leeper, W. R., Victoria st
Lennon, John, Tullygarron
Linton, Sl., Augherafin
Lonsdale, James (J.P.), Pavilion
Lonsdale, Thos., Pavilion
Loughran, George, Ballycrumney
Loughran, John, Lurgyvallen
Lowry, Sl., Augherafin
Lynas, Bernard, Drumart
Lyons, John Lisdrumbroughis
Lyons, John, Tyrearly
Lyons, Wm., Ballyrea
Lyster, Wm., Lisdown
M'Adam, Robt., Drumcairn
M'Alevy, F., Ballyards
M'Alindon, Hugh, Castle st
M'Ardle, P., Charter school lane
M'Auley, John, Irish st
M'Caffry, Patrick, Drumarg
M'Callum, C. H., English st
M'Cann, John, Killooney
M'Carragher, James, Bracknagh
M'Carragher, Joseph, Ballybrockey
M'Carragher, J., Baltarran, M
Macartney, David, Ballybrockey
M'Cartney, Thos., Scotch st
Macartney, William, Killuney
M'Clelland, Samuel, Lenalea
M'Connell, Wm., Gillis
M'Creedy, Thomas, Tergarve
M'Creight, A., Barrack Hill
M'Crum, R. G. (J.P.), Milford ho
M'Cullagh, James, Ballytrodden
M'Cluskey, B., Ballyhonebeg, Al
M'Culla, Robt., Edwards ter
M'Cully, Wm., Baltarran, M
M'Cuskey, Arthur, B'kilmurray
M'Cuskey, H., B'lemurray Al
M'Cuskey, Ml., B'kilmurray, Al
M'Dermott, T., sen., L'willy Al
M'Farlane, S., The Cottage
M'Gahan, F., Ballinahonemore
M'Gleenan, M., Ballytrodden
M'Glone, John, Lurgyvallen
M'Gow, Thos., Edwards st
M'Grane, Ml., Ballytrodden
M'Gurgan, P., Enagh, M

M'Hugh, Edw., Edwards st
M'Kee, Dl., Edwards st
M'Kee, John, Thomas st
M'Kee, William, Thomas st
M'Kendal, Thos., Killylyn, Al
M'Kendle, John, Allistragh
M'Kenna, C., Tamlaght, M
M'Kenna, George, Ballydoo
M'Kenna, James, Ballycoffey
M'Kenna, Jere., Drumgaw
M'Kenna, John, Terreskane
M'Kenna, John, Thomas st
M'Kenna, J., jun., Lr. English st
M'Kenna, Peter, Ballyherridan
M'Kenna, T., sen., Teeraw
M'Kenna, T., Ballynahonebeg, M
M'Kenzie, James, Creaghan
M'Keown, J., Lisdrumbroughas
M'Kinley, Alex., Dobbin st
M'Kinley, Thomas, Dobbin st
M'Kinney, Andrew, Thomas st
M'Laughlin. Geo., Edwards st
M'Loughlin. John. Edwards ter
M'Laughlin, Mrs. M., Ballyboy, M
M'Mahon, Jno., Aghavilly, M
M'Murray, Jos., Killooney
M'Murray, Thos., Lisdown
M'Parland, John (J.P.), English st
M'Parland, Jos., English st
M'Parland, Pk., English st
M'Veigh, Robt., Edwards st
M'Watters, Jno., Hartford pl
M'Whirter, T. G., Creeverow, Al
M'William, G., Ballyhonebeg, M
Magill, Henry, Ballymartrim
Magill, James, Mullinure
Mahaffy, W., Castle st
Maguire, Mrs. S. J. (P.M.), Allistragh
Major, Jno., Edwards st
Mallon, James, Drumart
Mallon, John, Creaghan
Mallon, Michael, Ballycoffey
Mallon, Ptk., Tullygarron, Al
Mallon, T., Tullygarron, Al
Mallon, Wm., Edwards st
Mann, Wm., Drumbeemore
Marks, T. O., Cathedral hill
Marshall, Mrs., Drumadd cottage
Martin, David P., Martinville
Martin, D. P. Walker, Martinville

Martin, Hugh, Edwards st
Marton, James, Lisdown
Maxwell, Jas., jun., College st
Menary, W., Aghavilly, M
Mills, John, Ballyscandle
Minnis, Hugh, Lisadian
Mitchell, W., Ballinahonebeg
Moan, James, Farmacaffly
Molloy, Bernard, Edwards ter
Molloy, J., Charter school lane
Monaghan, Wm., Irish st
Monteith, Thos. J., Dobbin st
Montgomery, N., Market st
Montgomery, R., Killynure, M
Montgomery, Thos. A., Milford
Moore, George, Tyrearly
Moore, Mrs., The Nursery
Morgan, Wm., Drumgaw
Morgan, Dr. W. M., The College
Morrison, Jas., Scotch st
Morton, James, Tray
Morrow, Alex., Aughrafin
Morrow, John, Drumarg
Morrow, Rd., Aghanore
Mullen, Fr., Ballytrodden
Mulligan, Nl., Lisdrumbroughis
Murphy, Isaac J., Winder ter
Murray, David, Aughrafin
Murphy, Rev. W. G., Cabragh
Neill, Robert, Killeen
Nelson, Arthur, Ardmore
Nelson, George, Tyrearly
Nelson, Thomas, Tullylost
Nelson, William, Ballydoo
Newton, R. Alex., Killooney
North, Mrs., Richmond ter
Nugent, Wm., Ogle st
O'Hanlon, J., Charter school lane
O'Neill, Bernard, Irish st
O'Neill, Charles, Lower English st
O'Neill, Felix, Killynure
O'Neill, Joseph, Ballymartrim
O'Neill, Patrick, Ogle st
Oliver, Bradford, Ballyscandle
Oliver, John, Ballycrummy
Orr, James, Ballyknick
Orr, Tobias, Ballyknick
Ovens, John J., Abbey st
Parkinson, Edward, Abbey st
Patterson, R. J., Milford
Payne, Hy., Edward st

Peel, Thos. Geo., Oulart villa
Pillow, Hamilton, Altaturk
Pillow, Robert, English st
Pillow, Thos., Drumsavage
Pooler, Misses, College st
Porter, Alex., Altaturk
Porter, Hugh, Abbey st
Prentice, John, Ballybrockey
Prentice, T. A., Seven houses
Prentice, William, Drumbee
Preston, Capt. (R.M.), Charlemont pl
Preston, Geo., Cullentragh
Price, Jas. D., Vicars' hill
Quigley, William, Ballyrea
Quinn, Patrick, Ballytrodden
Quinn, Thos., Teeraw
Rafferty, Dl., Aghamore
Reade, Mrs. M., Hartford pl
Reilly, E., Drummondmore
Reilly, John, Abbey st
Reilly, Wm., Drummondmore
Rice, Geo., Armagh
Rice, Wm., Primrose st
Richardson, Adam, Annacramp
Riggs, John S., Hartford place
Riggs, Mrs., Richmond ter
Riggs, Norton, Hartford pl
Roberts, Jas., Vicars' hill
Robinson, Capt. W., Cathedral ter
Robinson, Geo., Market sq
Robinson, H. J., Lisdrumbroughis
Robinson, Rev. Geo., Beechhill
Robinson, Thos., Greenan
Robinson, Wm. G., Beechhill
Robinson, Wm., Greenan
Roberts, Major A. J., Rookford M
Rocks, Bd., Drumcoote
Rocks, Edward, Creeveroe, Al
Rocks, John, Ballyrea
Rocks, Mrs. M., Ballyboy, M
Rocks, Ptk., Drumcairn, Al
Rocks, Ptk., Drumcoote
Rocks, Simon, Ballycoffey
Rogers, Edward, Abbey st
Rolston, Richard, Drumsill
Rolston, Walter, Drumcairn
Rountree, John, Ballaghey
Sally, James, Tullynichol
Saunderson, A., Greenan, Al
Saunderson, Jas., Annacramp
Saunderson, Wm., Greenan, Al

Scott, Henry, Annaclare
Scott, James, Annacramp
Scott, James, Killeen
Scott, Oliver, Drumaugher
Shaw, John, George st
Sheridan, P., Maheryarville, M
Sherry, Hugh, Tullyworgle
Sherry, John, Tullyard
Silvey, Nl., Aghavilly, M
Simpson, Col. T. (J.P.), Ballyards ho
Simpson, Robt., Cavanacaw
Simpson, Wm., Killeen
Simpson, Wm. A., Russell st
Skeith, H., Ballynahonemore
Slavin, James, Thomas st
Sleator, Geo., B'murry, Al
Sleator, James, Thomas st
Sling, Henry, English street
Sloan, William, Grangemore
Sloan, William, Killylyn, Al
Smith, George H. (B.L.), Killuney
Smyth, Robert, Tullyelmer
Somerville, Rt., Ballinahonemore
Sparks, James, Cullentragh
Spark, Robert, Lisdown
Sparks, George, Lisdown
Speer, Thomas, Cullentragh
Stanley, Colonel E. S., Summerhill
Steele, Samuel M., Abbey st
Stokes, Rev. W. F., Cloghery
Stoops, Benjamin, Killooney
Stoops, John, Killooney
Stoops, J., Drummondmore
Stoops, Robert, Drummondmore
Stoops, Thos., Killooney
Stoops, T., jun., Drummondmore
Strain, John, Killeen
Stronge, J. H. (J.P.), Hockley lodge
Symington, W., Teeraw
Taggart, David, Edenknappa
Taggart, James, Lisdonwilly
Tarleton, T. R., Vicars' hill
Taylor, E. B., The Mall
Taylor, Henry, The Mall
Taylor, Robert, Greenan
Taylor, Samuel, Ballyknick
Taylor, Samuel, Greenan, Al
Templeton, John, Terreskane
Thackeray, Duncan, Vicars' hill
Thompson, Adam, Cloghfin
Thompson, David, Cloghfin
Thompson, George, Lisadian

Thompson, Hugh B., English st
Thompson, James, Cloghfin
Thompson, Jas., Loughgall road
Thompson, Wm., Ballytrodden
Thompson, Wm., Cloghfin
Thompson, Wm., Terreskane
Thompson, W. C. B., English st
Toner, F., Lower English st
Toner, Fr., Lisdonwilly, Al
Turner, W., Ballynahonemore
Turpin, Mrs., Grantham villas
Vallely, M., B'macklemurry, Al
Vallely, Patrick, Aughanore
Villiers, James, Drumsavage
Waddell, Mrs., The Mall
Walker, Jno., English st
Wallace, Alex., Ballyards
Walsh, Robt., City Mills
Ward, John, Edwards st
Warden, John, Lisdrumard
Warden, William, Ballydoo
Warmoll, James, Barrack st
Warnock, J., Drummondmore
Watson, Jas. Alex., Avon lodge
Watson, Wesley, Kennedies M
Webb, John, Castle st
Webster, John, Cavanacaw
Webster, Wm., Cavanacaw
Wier, John, Lisdonwilly
Weir, Mrs. H., Victoria st
West, Mrs., Meredith pl
White, William, Ballydoo
Wilkin, Rd., Scotch street
Wilkin, W. B., Drumbeemore
Willis, J., Ballymucklemurry, Al
Williamson, B., Lisbane
Williamson, C., Garvaghy
Wilson, Alexander, Lisbane
Wilson, James, Cathedral Hill
Wilson, Jas., Cathedral ter
Wilson, Joseph, Aghanore
Wilson, Rev. S.E., Greenfield Manse
Wilson, Thos., Tonnagh
Wilson, Thos., English st
Wilson, Wm., Bracknagh
Winder, John G., Seven houses
Woods, Charles, Vicars' hill
Woods, Wm. L., Market sq
Wood, William, Lr. English st
Wright, Alex., Lisbane
Young, Mrs. T., Gosford pl

SUB-POST OFFICES

IN THE ARMAGH DISTRICT.

ETTERS addressed to residents of sub-postal districts should bear the name of the head office, thus : Collone, Armagh.

CLADYMILLTOWN.

LADYMILLTOWN is a rural post-office 7 miles south east from Armagh. Markethill, 2 miles, is the nearest railway station. The land of the district is fair for oats, potatoes and flax. Although there is no village here the houses for a considerable distance all around are near each other. Dairying is done on a modest scale, most of the butter being sent to market in "bricks."

Grocers (*) retails spirits—Jas. Carr, P. Carr, H. Coulter, Thos. Corr, Jno. Donnelly, Ptk. Lennon*, Ml. Loughran, Mrs. Mt. Loye, J. M'Cartney, Wm. D. M'Cullagh, Miss E. Martin, Edw. Rocks, Bernard Vallely

Post M. : Wm. D. M'Cullagh
Presbyterian Church : Rev. Rt. Shannon
R.C. : Rev. F. Corr, P.P.
Scutch Mills : Sl. Black, Hh Gass (corn also), Mrs. G. Gray, Sl. Martin

Farmers & Residents

Agnew, Francis, Lisnaget
Black, James, Enagh
Black, Robert, Enagh
Black, Samuel, Ballylane
Blair, Hugh, Lisnaget
Corr, Thomas, Lisnaget
Cosgrove, John, jun., Cladybeg
Coulter, Hugh, Cladymore
Dalzell, Henry, Lisnagat
Dougan, George, Killymachugh
Dougan, Robert, Damoily
Gass, Mrs. E., Killymachugh
Gollogly, Henry, Cladybeg
Gollogly, Terence, Cladybeg
Gray, James, Enagh
Gray, John, Ballylane
Gray, John, Ballylane
Gray, Mrs. Gordon, Killymachugh
Gordon, Robert, Enagh
Holmes, Thomas, Lisnaget
Gray, Wm., Enagh
Lee, Alex., Lisnaget
Lennon, John, Cladymore
Loughran, Peter, Cladymore
Kilpatrick, Thos., Cladybeg
M'Ardle, John, Cladymore
M'Cairn, Hugh, Cladybeg
M'Cammon, Jas., Damoily
M'Clenaghan, James, Cladybeg
M'Clenaghan, Wm., Cladybeg
M'Clure, James, Cladymore
M'Clure, James, Greyhillan
M'Clure, Samuel, Cladymore
M'Clure, Samuel, Damoily
M'Clure, Samuel, Enagh
M'Cullagh, Alex., Cladymore.
M'Cullagh, John, Cladymore

M'Gaughey, James, Damoily
M'Gaughey, Robert, Enagh
M'Kean, Archd., Cladymore
M'Mullin, David, Cladybeg
M'Mullin, John, Cladybeg
M'Mullin, John C., Damoily
Mackey, Jos. N., Killyhugh
Mann, Jacob, Cladybeg
Mann, Thomas, Cladybeg
Marshall, Mrs. E. E., Lisnegat
Martin, Jno., Ballylane
Marshall, William, Cladybeg
Murphy, Michael, Cladybeg
Nugent, Patrick, Cladybeg
Porter, Alex., Cladybeg
Porter, Alex., jun., Cladybeg
Porter, Hugh, Cladybeg
Rafferty, Dl., Cladymore
Rafferty, Jas., Cladymore
Rafferty, Patk., Cladymore
Rafferty, Patk., Cladymore
Rocks, Edwd., Cladymore
Rocks, Hy., Cladymore
Shannon, Rev. Robert, Cladymore
Sleith, Alex., Enagh
Taylor, George, Cladymore
Taylor, Mrs. Mt., Cladymore
Taylor, Thomas, Cladymore
Traynor, Thomas, Enagh
Vallely, Arthur, Cladymore
Vallely, Daniel, Cladybeg
Vallely, Edward, Cladybeg
Valelly, John, Cladymore
Valelly, Mrs. C., Cladymore
Vallely, Mrs. M., Cladymore
Vallely, Terence, Cladybeg
Vallely, Hugh, Cladybeg
Wallace, James, Cladymore

COLLONE.

COLLONE is a rural post-office 2½ miles east by south from Armagh, on the road to Markethill. Potatoes, oats and flax are the crops of the district. The land is of medium quality. Nearly all the farmers grow a little flax, and make some butter, which they send to market chiefly in "bricks."

National School : Mrs. R. Gray
Post Master : Wm. Gray

Presbyterian Church : Rev. W. J. Browne, Red Rock, Armagh

Farmers & Residents

Alexander, J. H., Carnavanaghan
Armstrong, Fras., Edenknappa
Armstrong, Hugh, Edenknappa
Black, John, Collone
Black, Joseph, Collone
Broomfield, Sl., Carnavanaghan
Conlan, D., jun., Carnavanaghan
Conlan, Rt., Carnavanaghan
Crozier, David, Seagahan
Crozier, James, Edenknappa
Crozier, James, Seagahan
Crozier, Jno., Carnavanaghan
Crozier, Thomas, Seagahan
Dodds, Robert, Seagahan
Donaldson, James, Cavanagrove
Donnelly, Henry, Drumbeemore
Dougan, Alexander, Cavanagrove
Dougan, George, Ballymacaully
Dougan, John, Collone
Dougan, J. jun., Carnavanaghan
Dougan, Mrs. E., Ballymacaully
Dougan, Simpson, Cavanagrove
Dougan, Wm., Seagahan
Farley, Sl., Carnavanaghan
Ferguson, Robert, Kilcopple
Finn, John, Edenknappagh
Frazer, Mrs. L., Collone
Gilmore, Rt., Edenknappagh
Gray, Thos. H., Seagahan
Gray, William, Killycopple
Hamilton, W., Killycopple
Hart, Bernard, Edenknappagh
Henning, George, Killeen
Hutchinson, Mrs. J., Collone
Jamison, Robert, Killeen
Kennedy, James, Cavanagrove
Kennedy, Mrs. R., Cairn
Kennedy, W., Carnavanaghan
Kilpatrick, James, Collone
King, Samuel, Killycopple
Largey, Hugh, Collone
Lyons, James, Cavanagrove
M'Call, George, Carnavanaghan
M'Call, Jas., Carnavanaghan
M'Call, Jno., Carnavanaghan
M'Call, R. S., Carnavanaghan
M'Call, Samuel, Seagahan
M'Cartney, W., Carnavanaghan
M'Cune, James, Carnavanaghan
M'Mahon, George, Collone
Magill, John, Killycopple
Megarity, George, Killeen
Mitchell, George, Killycopple
Mitchell, Robert, Killycopple
Montgomery, Wm., Cavanagrove
Phœnix, William, Edenknappa
Porter, James, Edenknappa
Semple, Robert, Killycopple
Shillington, Edward, Killycopple
Simpson, George, Collone
Simpson, James, Collone
Simpson, John, Cavanagrove
Simpson, William, Killeen
Tate, James, Killycopple
Tate, John, Collone
Tate, Misses, Collone
Tate, Thomas, Killycopple
Whiteside, James, Killycopple
Wilson, Thomas, Cavanagrove
Wilson, William, Cavanagrove

CALEDON, CO. TYRONE.

THIS village is on the border of County Armagh, less than a mile from the Tynan Railway Station, with which it is connected by the Clogher Valley Steam Tramway. The following residents of County Armagh receive letters from the Caledon Post Office :—

Curry, Ptk., Clontycarty
Lee, Wm , Drumgolliff
M'Elroy, James, Clontycarty
Marshall, Thos., jun., Drumgolliff

SHERRARD SMITH & CO.,

WOOLLEN

MANUFACTURERS,

CALEDON,

CO. TYRONE.

THE CALEDON WOOLLEN MILLS.

DURING the past few years the goods manufactured at the Caledon Woollen Mills have been dividing attention with those of the best known manufacturers in the country. The history of the woollen industry here dates from 1882. In that year Mr. John Charles Smith became lessee of the great flour mills, built by the Earl of Caledon thirty years previously, at a cost of £47,000. While the palmy days of flour milling continued, it was said that they produced a profit of £20,000 a year. The buildings, of stone and slate, as seen in the illustration, partly cover premises about five acres in extent. Mr. Smith formed the firm of Sherrard, Smith & Co., consisting of Mr. William O. Sherrard, himself, and Mr. Geo. H. Thompson, and, having had an experience of twenty years in the woollen and worsted manufacturing business at the Shannon and Burnbrook Woollen Mills, Athlone, he began at once to lay the foundation of an industry which promises in the near future to rank among the most important in Ireland. The flour mills had to be entirely remodeled internally to suit the demands of woollen manufacture. Forty looms of the best description, sets of carding engines, with selfacting mules to match, and all the requisite machinery for preparing, dyeing, and finishing were put into position, and the work begun under the most encouraging auspices. Power is provided by a 200 horse engine, a breast wheel 30 feet in diameter, and an undershot wheel 20 feet in diameter, driven by the Blackwater. The water supply continues fair all the year round. Steam is used as an auxiliary. The manufactures consist of tweeds, friezes, serges, blankets, flannels, coatings, costume cloths (ladies' dress goods), and knitting yarns. Messrs. Sherrard, Smith, & Co. do business only with the wholesale trade of the United Kingdom, the European Continent, the United States, and the Colonies. They were exhibitors at the Cork International Exhibition in 1883. Their exhibit at the Artisans' Exhibition, Dublin, 1885, won a diploma of merit. They were represented at the Manchester Exhibition, and received the appointment of Woollen Manufacturers to Her Majesty the Queen in 1886. The Caledon Woollen Mills are actually in Tyrone, separated from Armagh by the Blackwater. Identification with the latter-named county arises mainly by reason of the fact that the shipping place of the firm is at Tynan.

DARKLEY.

DARKLEY, on the Callan, is 8 miles south by west from Armagh, and 2 miles south-east of Keady. It had a population of 810 in 1881. The village is situated on an eminence, which commands a splendid view of the surrounding country. An industry, which gives employment to nearly the entire population, will be found described and illustrated in association with the "Kirk enterprises," under the head of Keady. Tullynawood Lake, about 80 acres in area, is a mile above Darkley. It is well stocked with pike and perch, and occasionally affords good snipe shooting. A reading room and library for the working people are maintained by a subscription of one penny per week from each member. A cricket club, with about 50 members, has been in full swing for a few years. The land in the district is rather poor, and boggy in some parts. Oats and potatoes are the principal crops.

Blacksmith : Thomas Ruddox

Drapery : Co-operative stores

Flax Spinners and manufacturers of Linen Diapers, &c.: William M. Kirk & Co

Grocers : Co-operative stores, Jno. Duffy, Owen Traynor

Post M : Miss M. J. Mahaffy

School,National : Robert Johnston, Miss English

Spirit Retailers : None.

Farmers & Residents

Best, John, Tullyglush
Blackstock, James, Aughnagurgan
Blackstock, Joseph, Aughnagurgan
Breen, Bernard, Clay
Breen, Matthew, Clay
Bryson, Samuel, Darkley
Campbell, John, Tullyglush
Carter, William, Darkley house
Cowan, James, Darkley
Cartmill, Thomas, Darkley
Dailey, Hugh, Crossdened
Daley, James, Clay
Daly, Owen, Crossdened
Douglas, Hugh, Aughnagurgan
Douglas, W., Aughnagurgan
Doyle, James, Tullyglush
Finnegan, John, Aughnagurgan
Flannigan, Francis, Cargaclogher
Gorman, James, Tullyglush

Gorman, Bernard, Rathcarberry
Gordon, David, Tullyglush
Gordon, James, Tullyglush
Graham, John, Aughnagurgan
Hannaway, Patrick, Aughnagurgan
Hillis, John, Tullyglush
Hughes, George, Crossdened
Hughes, Henry, Aughnagurgan
Hughes, Robert, Aughnagurgan
Kavanagh, John, Aughnagurgan
Kennedy, John, Aughnagurgan
Lee, Joseph, Clay
M'Coey, Hugh, Rathcarberry
M'Coey, John, jun., Rathcarberry
M'Gurk, Michael, Darkley
M'Kee, Alex., Aughnagurgan
M'Kee, Aaron, Corkley
M'Kee, David, Corkley
M'Kee, Hugh, Darkley
M'Kee, Joseph, Corkley
M'Kee, Robert, Darkley
Magill, Joseph, Aughnagurgan
Moan, James, Crossdened
Moan, Patrick, Crossdened
Mulligan, William G., Darkley
Nugent, Edward, Aughnagurgan
Nugent, Edward, Tullyglush
Nugent, Hugh, Aughnagurgan
Nugent, James, Aughnagurgan
Nugent, Lawrence, Aughnagurgan
Nugent, Neill, Aughnagurgan

Nugent, Patk., Aughnagurgan
Nicholl, Robt., Aughnagurgan
Pattison, Thomas, Darkley
Reilly, Alex., sen., Tievenacree
Renaghan, Patrick, Crossdened
Robb, James, Clay
Shanks, John, Aughnagurgan
Shanks, Samuel, Corkley
Shillady, Samuel, Tullyglush
Shillady, Thomas, Darkley
Short, Cornelius, Clay
Simington, James, Corkley

Silvey, James, Clay
Stuart, John, Corkley
Tatton, David, Darkley
Thompson, Hugh, Aughnagurgan
Thompson, John, Aughnagurgan
Toner, Bernard, Aughnagurgan
Twynam, Thomas, Tullyglush
Warnock, Joseph, Corkley
Warnock, Joseph, jun., Corkley
Warnock, Thomas, Corkley
Warnock, William, Corkley
Wilson, Samuel, Aughnagurgan

DERRYNOOSE.

 ERRYNOOSE is a rural post-office within 2½ miles of Keady. The land of the district is rocky. Crops : oats, poatoes, and some flax. The farmers nearly all do a little at butter-making.

Postmistress—Mrs. Susan Murtagh

Farmers & Residents

Baird, George, Curryhugh
Baird, John, Cargalisgarron
Baird Samuel, Cargalisgarron
Baird, William A., Cargalisgarron
Barker, James, Fergort
Callaghan, Michael, Carrickabone
Callaghan, Michael, Mullyard
Callaghan, Peter, Rowan
Callaghan, Thomas, Carrickabolie
Campbell, Alex., Tievenacree
Campbell, Andrew, Ratchcumber
Campbell, Andrew, Tievenacree
Campbell, Thos., Cargalisgarron
Carberry, Michael, Sheetrim
Cassely, James, Crossnamoyle
Clarke, John, Crossbane
Connolly, Patrick, Crossnamoyle
Corrigan, Patrick, Crossbane
Corrigan, Thomas, Mullyard
Couser, William, Curryhugh
Curry, Hugh, Rathcumber
Dalzell, William, Rowan
Fox, Edward, Carrickabolie
Gaffney, John, Rawes
Gaffney, Patrick, Tievenacree
Haffey, Patrick, Tievenacree
Hops, Robert, Cavanagarvin
Hughes, Daniel, Doohat

Hughes, Owen, Tullyherm
Keenan, James, Fergort
Kelly, Miles, Listrakelt
Kelly, Patrick, Curryhugh
Kerr, James, Carrickabolie
Kerr, James, Tullyherm
Kinnear, Thomas, Listrakelt
Kinner, Alex., Rowan
Lennon, John, Tullyherim
Lennon, Matthew, Fergort
M'Aleavey, Arthur, Carrickabolie
M'Alevey, Charles, Rawes
M'Aleavey, James, Drumnahavill
M'Aleavey, Patk., Drumnahavill
M'Anally, Edward, Fergort
M'Crea, James, Tievenacree
M'Grane, Patrick, Drumeland
M'Kearney, Patrick, Mullyard
M'Kee, John, Cavanagarvin
M'Keown, James, Mullyard
M'Keown, John, Fergort
M'Noghton, John, Mullyard
Macklan, John, Curryhughes
Moan, Patrick, Crossnamoyle
Moan, Thomas, Mullyard
Morgan, Francis, Fergort
Morgan, John, Listerkelt
Montgomery, T., Cargalisgerron
Murphy, David, Lislea
Murphy, Patrick, Listerkelt

Murphy, Thomas, Listerkelt
Murray, Daniel, Crossbane
Murray, Hugh, Doohat
Murray, James, Doohat
Murray, James, Rawes
Murray, Terence, Crossbane
Murray, Terence, Mullyard
Murray, Thomas, Doohat
Murray, Thomas, Mullyard
Murray, Arthur, Crossbane
O'Neill, John, Fergort
Patterson, James, Drumnahavill
Quinn, Bernard, Sheetrim
Reid, Alexander, Cargalisgerron
Reid, Joseph, Drumeland
Reilly Patrick, Rowan
Renaghan, Bernard, Drumnahavill
Renaghan, Michael, Drumnahavill
Renaghan, Nicholas, Listrakelt
Renaghan, Patrick, Crossbane
Renaghan, Peter, Crossbane
Rule, Robert, Curryhugh
Scott, William, Rowan
Singleton, John, Tullyherim

Singleton, William, Listerkelt
Slevin, Owen, Crossnamoyle
Stewart James, Curryhugh
Tait, Thomas, Crossnamoyle
Treanor, Patrick, Rowan
Vallely, Henry, Tullyherim
Vallely, John, Tullyherim
Vallely, Patrick, Tullyherim
Vallely, Peter, Tullyherim
Vallely, Thomas, Tievenacree
Vallely, Thomas, Tullyherim
Walker, William, Curryhugh
White, Arthur, Crossnamoyle
White, John, Drummeland
White, Nicholas, Crossnamoyle
Wilson, Francis, Rawes
Wilson, Dichard, Rawes
Wilson, Thomas, Rawes
Wilson, William, Rawes
Woods, James, Drumnahavill
Woods, James, Mullyard
Woods, Patrick, Mullyard
Woods, Peter, Mullyard

DRUMACHEE.

DRUMACHEE is a rural post office 4 miles to the south-east of Armagh, and 2½ miles west by north from Markethill, its nearest railway station. The land of the district is fair for oats, flax and potatoes. Dairying is carried on to some extent, the butter being sent to market chiefly in "bricks." A lake of 15 acres, formed from a small stream to drive Mr. Jackson Pillow's mill, has a supply of eels and pike. The country-people purchased a boat by subscription, and in summer have a good time on the lake. Mr. John Jenkinson, a tenant-farmer residing in this townland, on the property of Lord Charlemont, has reached the splendid age of 105 years. He is able to walk about with slight aid from sticks, and makes many social calls on his neighbors, He was in the Yeomanry in 1798. His wife died about 20 years ago at the age of 76. Forty years have passed since he gave up tobacco. A daughter, unmarried, keeps house for him. Simple habits and regularity have done much to make his life comfortable. With the exception of an occasional "touch" of rheumatism, he enjoys good health. At eight o'clock in the evening he goes to bed, and rises at ten in the morning. For breakfast he takes a slice of toast and a cup of tea; for dinner—one o'clock—one potato, and a slice of ham ; one slice of bread and butter, and a cup of tea, at six o'clock in the evening, ends the food programme for the day.

Corn and Scutch Mills, Jackson Pillow

Postmistress : Mrs. J. Moffett

Farmers & Residents.

Allen, John, Drumbeecross
Atcheson, William, Lurgaboy
Bell, Mrs. A., Drumachee
Black, John A., Drumachee
Coburn, Wallace, Drumachee
Cordner, James, Cavanagrove
Cosgrove, John, Ballymacawley
Dixon, Joseph, Drumachee
Dixon, Thomas, Drumachee
Dougan, Robert, Cavanagrove
Fullerton, William, Cavanagrove
Gray, Samuel, Ballymacawley
Hamilton, George, Drumachee
Hamilton, Robert, Drumachee
Hanna, David, Drumachee
Harvey, Joseph, Cavanagrove
Hooks, J. & T., Drumbeecross ho
Hutton, Jas., Drumachee

Jenkinson, John, Drumachee
Kidd, John, Ballymacawley
Kidd, William, Ballymacawley
Lenehan, Robert, Drumachee
Lyster, William, Cavanagrove
M'Call, James, Drumbeecross
M'Carron, John, Drumatee
M'Clelland, John, Drumachee
M'Cullagh, James, Cavanagrove
M'Mullen, John, Lurgaboy
M'Parland, Bernard, Drumachee
M'Parland, Eneas, Drumachee
Moffitt, William, Lurgaboy
Pillow, Jackson, Drumachee
Speers, Alexander, Cavanagrove
Taggart, Mrs. E., Drumachee
Tweedie, Wm. John, Drumachee
Waugh, Mrs. R., Drumachee
Wilson, James, Drumbeecross
Wilson, Robert, Ballymacawley
Wilson, Wm., Ballymacawley

GLENANNE.

GLENANNE is one of the handsomest villages in the county. It is situated on the side of a hill overlooking the glen, and forms part of the property owned by Messrs. George Gray & Sons. The workers in the mills of Messrs. Gray live in various parts of the immediate district, as well as at Glenanne. In the village a library and readingroom, established by Miss Gray, are popular with the workers, who contribute 2d. per month each toward maintenance. The land of the neighborhood is fair for oats, potatoes and flax. Many of the farmers have dairies. The butter is, for the greater part, sent to market in "bricks." An ancient earthen fort, near the village, occupied by Mr. John Patterson, has been turned into an apple-orchard. Glenanne is 2½ miles west by south from the Loughgilly railway station, which is 12 miles by rail from Armagh.

GEORGE GRAY & SONS

Linen Manufacturers,

Bleachers & Finishers,

GLENANNE.

Railway Station, Loughgilly.— Telegraphic Address, "Grays, Glenanne."

MESSRS. GEORGE GRAY & SONS.

GLENANNE is one of the places in the County Armagh possessing features of interest apart from those connected with it as a centre of industrial activity. The Glen, for a mile and a half, is charmingly diversified by trees, rocks, green banks, and rugged acclivities. The buildings seen in the illustration extend from a point within about a mile of the Railway station at Loughgilly, to the head of the Glen, helping to accentuate the picturesque effects. At the lower end the water-wheels, and in the upper region, the tall chimney-shafts, sending their clouds of smoke above the tree-tops and beyond the cliffs, are striking accessories.

Shaw's Lake, a body of water forty acres in extent, with a depth of about thirty feet, is the reservoir for power purposes. It impounds the Tate river and other smaller streams, and lets out from day to day sufficient of its store to drive six breast wheels and one Macadam turbine, aggregating 200 horse. Three steam engines, aggregating 180 horse, are used as an auxiliary. With these appliances 316 looms are kept at work weaving, and 34 engines beetle-finishing linen of all grades from coarse to fine. Messrs. George Gray & Sons bleach as well as finish the products of their looms, having plenty of spread ground available in the limits of a property embracing 250 acres. From 400 to 500 people are employed in the various departments. Most of these live in the village of Glenanne, which contains about 60 houses belonging to Messrs. Gray. The firm consists of Mr. George Gray, J.P., Mr. Joseph H. Gray, J.P., and Mr. Wm. B. Gray. Bleach greens were established in the Glen at an early period, and about the year 1818, the late Mr. William Atkinson settled at Glenanne and erected extensive cotton spinning and weaving mills. In 1841 Mr. George Gray acquired possession of the mills and premises, and continued the cotton manufacture for fifteen years. He then remodeled the buildings to suit the manufacture of linen, and the mills have since been much enlarged.

Churches: Presbyterian, Rev. J.D. Martin, Rev. John Entrican

Corn and Scutch Mill: Mrs. E. M'Cullagh, P. Toner

Drapers: Co-operative Stores, Rt. Corkey

Grocers: Co-operative Stores, Rt. Corkey, Mrs. J. Halliday, Jas. Moffett, Jas. Patterson, Jno. Waddell

Linen Manufacturers, &c.: Geo. Gray & Sons

Postmaster: John Patterson

Schools, Natl., Glenanne: Miss S. E. McPherson; Lisdrumchor, Isaac Thompson; Ballylane, P. Bartley

Farmers & Residents.

Boyle, Patk., Maytone
Corkey, Alex., Ballylane
Corkey, Robt., Ballylane
Corkey, Sl., sen., Ballylane
Corkey, Samuel, jun., Ballylane
Cully, Rd., Lisdrumchor up
Douglas, John, Ballylane
Feenan, Hugh, Maytone
Finnigan, James, Ballylane
Gray, Geo. (J.P.), Glenanne ho
Gray, Geo., junr., Maytone
Gray, Jos. Hy. (J.P.), Maytone ho.
Gray, Wm. B., Glenanne house
Haddon, John, Ballylane

Haddon, Robert, Ballylane
Hawthorne, John, Maytone
Henderson, Daniel, Lisdrumchor L
Hook, Thos. R., Lisdrumchor U
Ingram, Thomas, Tullyallen
Irwin, David, Maytone
Irwin, William, Maytone
Johnston, Joseph, Lisdrumchor U
Kilpatrick, Arthur, Ballylane
Kilpatrick, David, Ballylane
Kilpatrick, John, Ballylane
Kilpatrick, John, Lurgyross
M'Call, Thomas, Tullyallen
M'Comb, W. J., Lisdrumchor U
M'Dowell, James, Lisdrumchor U
M'Dowell, John, Lurgyross
M'Elroy, J. A., Lisdrumchor U
M'Giffin, Charles, Lurgyross
M'Kenna, Thomas, Ballylane
M'Kinney, Robert, Lurgyross
M'Partland, John, Lisdrumchor U
M'Sherry, Arthur, Lisdrumchor U
M'Sherry, Patrick, Lisdrumchor U
M'Whirter, Robert, Tullyallen
Shaw, Alexander, Lisdrumchor U
Smyth, E., Glenanne
Stewart, John, Lisdrumchor U
Stewart, Wm., Lisdrumchor U
Toner, Hugh, Ballylane
Toner, John, Maytone
Toner, Patrick, Maytone
Trimble, David, Lurgyross

DRUMANNON.

RUMANNON is a rural post office 9 miles north-east of Armagh, and 4 miles north-east from Loughgall. The nearest railway station is Annaghmore, one mile and a quarter.

Postmaster: Sl. Reid

Farmers & Residents

Atkinson, Joseph, J.P., Crowhill
Benson, Mrs. J., Tague
Benson, Mrs. Mt., Tague
Caddell, Hugh, Tague
Cochrane, Mrs. I., Drumannon
Crilly, Thomas Teagy
Devlin, Joseph, Clonacle

Duke, Robert, Drumannon
Dunlop, Charles, Drumannon
Dunlop, James, Broughas
Dunlop, Misses A. & M., Clonacle
Dunlop, Mrs. M. A., Clonacle
Dunlop, Robert, Clonacle
Ferguson, James, Drumannon
Frazer, Misses S. & R., Clonacle
Gardner, John, Drumanphy

Greer, John, Magarity
Henderson, Sl., Drumanphy
Hunter, John, Teagy
Hyde, Robert, sen., Cranagill
Livingstone, John, Teagy
Melwin, Mrs. E., Tague
Nicholson, C. J., Crannigael house
Nicholson, William, Drumannon
Potts, William, Teagy
Price, David, Clonacle

Redmond, Edward, Drumannon
Robinson, Archibald, Eglish
Robinson, David, Eglish
Robinson, John, Eglish
Robinson, Mrs., Eglish
Robinson, Mrs. N., Magarity
Robinson, Mrs. R., Eglish
Smith, Mrs. M., Dromanphy
Watt, James, Drumannon
Woods, Robert, Teagy

HAMILTONSBAWN.

HAMILTONSBAWN is 4 miles east of Armagh by road, and 5 miles by rail. The railway station is an eighth of a mile from the village. A pretty good farming country surrounds Hamiltonsbawn, and to this fact is due the maintenance of old-established fairs twice a year, and hiring fairs, when nearly all the other villages of the county, situated near large towns, have lost these much-prized helps to prosperity. In 1619, during the plantation of Ulster, James I. granted a tract of land in this district to J. Hamilton. He built

L

a strong "bawn" of lime and stone, 60 feet square, with flankers, and settled 26 British families. Protection was afforded by 30 armed men under authority of the King. In the Parliamentary War of 1641 the "bawn" was terribly battered by a portion of Sir Phelim O'Neill's troops, and the inhabitants suffered very much. The property afterward came into possession of the Achesons, one of whom was raised to the peerage as Lord Gosford. At the time Dean Swift was living at Markethill, 1729, his host, Sir Arthur Acheson, evidently had some project under deliberation for utilizing Hamiltonsbawn, and the Dean finding the matter to his taste, wrote a poem upon the subject, from which I extract the following passages :—

THE GRAND QUESTION DEBATED

WHETHER HAMILTON'S BAWN SHOULD BE TURNED INTO A BARRACK OR A MALT-HOUSE.

Thus spoke to my lady the knight full of care :
" Let me have your advice in a weighty affair.
This Hamilton's Bawn whilst it sticks on my hand,
I lose by the house what I get by the land ;
But how to dispose of it to the best bidder,
For a barrack or malt-house, we now must consider.
First let me suppose I make it a malt-house ;
Here I have computed the profit will t'us ;
There's nine hundred pounds for labour and grain ;
I increase it to twelve, so three hundred remain,
A handsome addition for wine and good cheer,
Three dishes a day and three hogsheads a year ;
With a dozen large vessels my vault shall be stored.
No little scrub joint shall come on my board ;
And you and the Dean no more shall combine
To stint me at night to one bottle of wine.

   *   *   *   *

If I make it a barrack, the Crown is my tenant,
My dear, I have pondered again and again on't ;
In poundage and drawbacks I lose half my rent ;
Whatever they give me, I must be content."

   *   *   *   *   *

Thus ended the knight ; thus began his meek wife :
" It must and it shall be a barrack, my life !
I'm grown a mere *mopus* ; no company comes
But a rabble of tenants and rusty dull Rums ; [parsons]
With parsons what lady can keep herself clean ?
I'm all over daub'd when I sit by the Dean ;

But if you will give us a barrack, my dear,
The captain, I'm sure, will always come here;
I then shall not value his deanship a straw,
For the captain, I warrant, will keep him in awe."

*　　　*　　　*　　　*　　　*　　　*

Hamiltonsbawn at the present day consists mainly of one long street. A portion of the famous barrack still exists. Mr. M'Roberts, by permission of Lord Gosford, removed the fortification for improvement purposes. In the village, on the holding of Mr. P. M'Geary, there are five fine cedars of Lebanon, each from 35 to 40 feet high. At a distance of a quarter of a mile, the celebrated Shelah well is on the farm of Mr. Robert Palmer. About 100 hand-loom weavers live in Hamiltonsbawn and neighborhood.

Blacksmith: Robert McCortney
Churches, C.I., Mullabrack, Rev. Dr. Maclaurnin; Methodist, George Connor; Presbyterian, Rev. William Jordan; R.C., Rev. P. McWilliams
Draper: W. F. Sinton
Education: Nat. School, Mrs. Clements, Jos. Anderson; Private, Mrs. Little
Grocers: [*]retail spirits; [†]sell hardware; [‡] seeds. William Alexander, James Fergus, Benjn. McConnell,* James McRoberts* ; W. F. Sinton,†‡
Post M.: William F. Sinton
Railway Station: Patk. Gorman, Toll Collector
Spirit retailer (see also grocers) Sarah Beck

Farmers & Residents
Albin, Hugh, Hamiltonsbawn
Albin, Samuel, Hamiltonsbawn
Anderson, J. W., Drumman
Bain, Jacob, Drumman
Barrett, Robert, Killyrudden
Beatty, Hugh, Hamiltonsbawn
Beatty, J. H., Hamiltonsbawn
Beatty, Mrs., Mullabane
Beck, James, Drumeniss
Bell, Benjamin, Derryraine
Bell, Isaac, Derryraine
Bell, John T., Drumorgan
Bell, Thomas, Derryraine

Black, Brabazon, Retarnet
Bradford, James, Drumeniss
Bradshaw, Wm., Drumman
Brown, James, Derrynaught
Brown, William J., Rocks
Caldwell, Thomas, Corry
Callaghan, Hans, Johnstown
Carson, Henry, Ballygroobany
Carson, Thomas, Ballygroobany
Dorey, John, Derryane
Duggan, John, Mullaghbane
Ferris, Mrs. E., Drumorgan
Fullerton, Thomas, Killyrudden
Fullerton, William, Derrynaught
Gillyland, Robert, Drumman
Graham, John, Johnston
Grant, James, Carrowmoney
Gray, Mrs. S., Drumman
Greer, Alex., Hamiltonsbawn
Greer, Robert J., Mullaghbane
Hamilton, Alex., Derrynaught
Hamilton, Alex., Drumsavage
Hamilton, James, Derrynaught
Hamilton, John, Derrynaught
Hazley, James, Macantrim
Heatley, James, Ballynewry
Heatley, Thomas, Ballygroobany
Heatley, Thomas, Drumman
Heatley, William, Drumman
Hill, David, Drumman
Hooks, William, Derrynaught
Hutchinson, John, Drumman
Jackson, Joseph, Corry
Jackson, Joseph, Killyrudden

WATTERS & SMYTH,

Merchant Tailors, General Drapers, Shirt Manufacturers, Watchmakers,
Jewellers and Fancy Warehousemen, KEADY.

☞ Orders by post a speciality. Full particulars on application.

Jackson, William, Corry
Johnston, Baptist, Drumorgan
Johnston, William, Drumman,
Kenny, Patrick, Druminnis
Kilpatrick, Robert, Derrynaught
Kilpatrick, Samuel, Derrynaught
Kilpatrick, Wm., Ballygroobany
King, John, Hamiltonsbawn
M'Cartney, David, Drumsavage
MacCartney, Robt., Mullaghbane
M'Cartney, Samuel, Derrynought
Macartney, William, Derryraine
M'Hugh, William, Retarnet
M'Clure, William, Retarnet
M'Connell, James, Killyrudden
M'Connell, Patk., Hamiltonsbawn
M'Cullough, Mrs. M., Brackley
M'Garity, Robert, Drumsavage
M'Kew, Samuel, Hamiltonsbawn
M'Loughlin, J. G., Killyrudden
M'Loughlin, Mrs. A. J., C'money
M'Loughlin, Richd., Derrynaught
M'Parland, Francis, Drumsavage
M'Whirter, Wm., Drumsavage

Meegary, Patrick, Hamiltonsbawn
Mulligan, John, Retarnet
O'Hanlon, Edward, Garvagh
O'Hanlon, John, Garvagh
Parkes, Jas., Ballygroobany
Parkes, M. W., Ballygroobany
Parks, J. R., Ballygroobany
Patterson, William, Killyrudden
Quinn, John, Drumeniss
Quinn, John, Rathdrumgan
Quinn, Thomas, Drumeniss
Rice, Edward, Garvagh
Rolston, Jas., Drumeniss
Rountree, Wm., Drumsavage
Rutherford, James, Drumenisss
Scott, Adam, Derryraine
Shepherd, Andrew, Derrynaught
Sinton, William, Drumorgan
Snodden, Mrs., Macantrim
Todd, James. Drumorgan
Williamson, Wm., Drumman
Wilson, John, Killyrudden
Wilson, Thomas, Macantrim

KEADY.

Population 1,598 in 1881.

EADY lies to the south south-west of Armagh, at a distance of 6 miles, Irish. It is in the parish of the same name, and in the barony of Armagh. The principal streets occupy the side of a hill which rises high enough at different points to afford commanding sites for churches and other buildings. In the valley, at the foot of the town, the river Callan winds along through meadows, plantations and bleach greens, forming a picture of rural beauty rarely excelled.

Toward the north and north-west the land is fair. To the south, south-east, and south-west it is not good. Oats, potatoes, and flax are the chief crops of the district. Dairying is carried on to some extent by nearly all the farmers. The markets of Keady are held three times a week. Monday and Thursday for grain, and Friday for butter, eggs, and pork. Most of the butter is made up in rolls. A handsome Market House stands at the junction of the main thoroughfares. It is constructed of red brick on a freestone base, and has a clock tower and spire; cost £1,370, and dates from 1870. The Town Commissioners rent the Market House and tolls from the representatives of the late

Mr. John Kirk, and sublet to Mr. Laurence McShane, who acts as Crane Master and Collector. Trinity College, Dublin, receives a head rent from the Kirk representatives for the town and district. A fair is held on the second Friday of every month for cattle, sheep, pigs and horses. It is usually well attended.

Keady came under the provisions of the Towns Improvement Act in 1862. The first commissioners elected were Henry Kirke, Thomas Small, Dr. John Dobbin, Joseph Graham, James Jelly, Henry Kelly, Thomas Raverty, John McGrath, and W. Hoste McKean. Each commissioner holds office for three years. Three commissioners go out of office every year, the electors having, in this way, an opportunity to infuse new blood if considered desirable. In 1862 the valuation of the town was £1,810. Three years later it was £2,096 10s. In 1875 it was £2,408 15s., and in 1888 it was £2,412 15s. The rate for general purposes is 4d. in the £. Expenses for lighting, cleansing, and repairing foot-paths are covered by this. The Guardians of Armagh Union provide for sanitary improvements. Thus far no debt has been incurred on behalf of the ratepayers. Keady was first lighted by gas in 1851. At present 40 lamps are maintained in the public streets and places, at a total cost of £47 per year. For the year ending 1887 the cleansing of the town cost £19 10s.

Manufacturing is carried on extensively within the parish, notably at Annvale and Darkley. The works are fully described and illustrated in the next chapter. Evidence of the popularity of the founder of these industries, the late Mr. William Kirk, and of the gratitude of the people who benefited by his enterprise, was manifested by the erection of a beautiful monument to his memory. It stands opposite the Market House, and bears this inscription :—" Erected by many friends in remembrance of William Kirk. For forty years he was the mainspring of the industrial activity and social progress of this town and district." Mr. Kirk died in 1871.

Keady has earned a reputation for superiority in tailor-made clothing and shirt manufacture, which extends all over Ireland. In the development of these special features large employment is given.

The churches include the Protestant Episcopal (C.I.,) Roman Catholic, and Presbyterian. The Presbyterian Church, in Meeting street, is an unpretending gabled structure of the old style, with an extensive and interesting burial ground. The Protestant Church occupies a hill at the head of the town. It is in the early English style of architecture, and was built by Primate Robinson in 1776. A battlemented pinnacled tower was added in 1822, during the rectorship of the Rev. Henry Stewart. The interior is plain. A handsome stained chancel window com-

WILLIAM M. KIRK & PARTNERS,

FLAX SPINNERS,

LINEN MANUFACTURERS, BLEACHERS, DYERS & FINISHERS.

Factories & Works. { ANNVALE and DARKLEY, } KEADY. BALLYARDS, ARMAGH.

Warehouse, 11 DONEGALL SQUARE WEST, BELFAST.

Telegraphic Address—"DARKLEY," BELFAST.

memorates William Gardiner, of Annvale, who died in 1883. Among the monuments in the churchyard, the most striking is a granite obelisk, inscribed to the memory of members of the McKean family—James McKean, R.N., 1841 ; Henry McKean, 1847. The Roman Catholic Church also stands on a hill. It is a large edifice, has a fine pinnacled tower, and cost about £4,000. The work was completed in 1861. Keady is united to the parish of Derrynoose.

St. Clare's Abbey occupies a commanding height inside the town boundary. It was completed in 1879, at a cost of £6,000. Five sisters, "Poor Clares," came here from the Convent of the Order at Newry in 1871—Mrs. McHugh, in religion, Mary Josepha, is the superioress.

Keady is well supplied with schools, national and intermediate.

The Keady river rises in Clay Lake, about a mile to the south-west, and at a short distance to the east joins the Callan. Perch, pike and eels are found in the lake, and in the season it has plenty of duck, widgeon and snipe.

A lead mine was opened in the district by the Mining Company of Ireland more than 50 years ago, but it did not prove a profitable speculation.

In 1798 many of the inhabitants were enrolled among the United Irishmen. The King's troops spent a short time in the town. One house, supposed to be the property of a leader, was burned.

THE KIRK ENTERPRISES AT ANNVALE AND DARKLEY.

THE enterprises growing out of the life-work of the late Mr. William Kirk, a native of the County Antrim, flourish at various points along the banks of the Callan. Mr. Kirk began his career at Annvale, near Keady, in 1840, using one small building, now devoted to beetle finishing, in connection with his efforts as a bleacher. Annvale afterward became one of the finest bleach greens in Ireland, including in spread grounds, works and factories, about 250 acres. The work done during his time, and still continued, included linen weaving, bleaching, dyeing and finishing. There are 200 power looms, and beetling works at different points on the Callan, extending for six miles—Ballyards, Moneyquin, Tassagh, Greenmount, Annvale, Millmount, upper and lower, the Glen, Corclea and Darkley. Some 600 people are employed at Annvale and its beetling connections.

The extensive buildings at Darkley, a mile and a half higher up the river, were erected by Mr. William Kirk, in conjunction with his son, Mr. William M. Kirk, and are devoted to flax spinning and linen weaving. The mill contains 8,000 spindles, and the factory 200 power looms. There are 137 acres in the premises and farm belonging to this enterprise. About 700 work-people are employed. Mr. William Kirk died in 1871, leaving the business and estate to Mr. John Kirk, his eldest son. He died in 1873, and his brother, Mr. William M. Kirk, as trustee, then formed a partnership under the style of William Kirk and Son. Four years later he founded a second partnership under the style of William M. Kirk and partners. Two years afterward this firm, with the sanction of the Court, acquired title to the business of William Kirk and Son. The partners were Mr. William M. Kirk, Mr. William Gardiner, Mr. Samuel C. Magee and Mr. Alex. Wallace. Mr. Gardiner died in 1883, Mr. William M. Kirk in 1884, and Mr. Magee in 1886. The present partners are Mr. Alex. Wallace, Mrs. Mary Gardiner and Mr. Robert George Wallace.

The business at Darkley is conducted under the style of Wm. M. Kirk and Co. Nearly all the linen woven there is taken over by Messrs. Wm. M. Kirk and partners. The two firms work in unison, but the interest in Darkley is owned by the trustees of William M. Kirk. One of the handsomest warehouses in Belfast belongs to Messrs. Wm. M. Kirk and partners. It stands at the corner of Donegall Square, West. There are agencies of the firm at 44 White Street, New York; Red Lion, Court, Cannon Street and Bread Street, London; Portland Street, Manchester, and Rue D'Aboukir, and 24 Rue St. Marc, Paris.

KEADY DIRECTORY.

Auctioneers: John Nugent & Co., Robert Thompson.

Bakers: Edward & John Connolly Anthony Daly, Patk. Hughes, Jos. M'Bride & Son, Chas. Mallon, Thos. Mone, F. & J. Nicholson.

Bank Northern: Samuel Johnston, manager; Alex. Whitford, cashier.

Blacksmiths: John Cunningham, Pat. Donnelly, John M'Ateer.

Bootmakers & Leather Dealers: Joseph M'Bride & Son, Wm. M'Knight, John Thompson.

Churches and Meetinghouses; C. I., Rev. M. B. Hogg; Christians; Presbyterian, 1st, Rev. ——; 2nd, Rev. George Steen; R.C., Very Rev. Patrick Kelly, P.P.; Rev. Peter Quinn, C.C.; Rev. Peter J. M'Ardle, C.C.; Rev. Patrick Vallely, C.C

Coal Merchants: A. & W. F. M'Cormick, W. J. Reilly.

Convent (Poor Clares): Mrs. M'Hugh (Mary Josepha), Superioress.

Coach Builders: O'Neill, Bro's.

Cooper: David M'Clung.

Dispensary: Dr. John Gower Allen, Medical Officer; attendance, Monday, Wednesday and Friday 9 to 11 a.m.

Committee :—Sir John Calvert Stronge, Bart., J.P., Tynan Abbey Tynan; John Douglas J.P.,, Mountain Lodge, Keady; Captain Irwin, J.P., Carnagh House, Carnagh; John Barcroft, J.P., Ennisclare House, Tassagh, Armagh; William M'Kean, J.P., Millmount, Keady; Robert John M'Geough, J.P., The Argory, Moy; Francis Carville, Keady; Peter

Campbell, Keady ; William Simpson, Killeen, Armagh ; John Gormill, Drumgreenagh, Keady ; Isaiah Fulton, Corran, Lisnadill ; Robert Dodds, Segahan, Lisnadill, Thomas Small, J.P., Hermitage, Keady ; James Gibson, Dunlargue House, Keady ; Patrick Mone, Keady ; John S. Riggs, Armagh ; William Cuming, Markethill ; John Hughes, J.P., Keady.

Meeting of Committee second Thursday every month at noon.

Wardens : James Anderson, Drumnacanver, Madden; William Boyd, Blackley ; James Callaghan, Brackley ; James R. Girvan, Roan; David Murphy, Lislea ; Hugh M'Kernan, Cashel ; Rev. S. Ratcliffe, Lisnadill ; William J. Reilly, Keady ; Joseph Turner, Carrickduff ; W. Carter, Darkley.

Drapers : Peter Campbell, Jas. English, E. Fegan, Jos. Graham, Hughes & Co., Nicholson & Co., W. J. Reilly, Miss A. Rolston, A. & S. Small, Watters & Smyth.

Education, Intermediate School; Henry Gray ; Music, Miss Johnston ; National School : Teachers, Edward Quinn, Ellen Quinn, E. Irons, J. M'Kenna.

Emigration Agents : Thomas Mone, R. H. Roleston, A. & S. Small.

Gas : Keady Gas Co., Ld., Geo. M'Bride, Peter Campbell, managing directors ; Edward Quinn, secretary ; Patrick M'Givern, manager, 7s. 6d. per 1,000 feet.

Glass, China & Delf : James Arthurs, Wm. Peatt.

Grain Merchant : Laurence M'Shane.

Grocers, marked thus [*] sell spirits ; thus [†] hardware ; thus [‡] seeds—John Bailie*†‡, Miss Bt. Callaghan, Jno. Carbery, Edw. & Jno. Connolly, Jno. Conory*†‡, Hugh Eccles*, Robert I. Eccles &

Co.†‡, Felix Fegan, Patk. Hughes, Chas. Kavanagh, Jno. Kerr, Jos. M'Bride & Son‡, A. & W. F. M'Cormick‡, Wm. M'Cormick, James M'Kenney*‡, Laurence M'Shane, Patk. Mone*‡, Thos. Mone, F. & J. Nicholson†‡, Jno. Nugent & Co†‡., William J. Reilly†‡, William Richardson*, Robert H. Roleston, Jno. Thompson, Robert Waddell (spirit grocer)‡ Jos. Walker, B. & T. Woods*‡.

Hospital : Keady Cottage Hospital, J. Gower Allen, Surgeon.

Hotel keepers: Peter Campbell, James English

Linen Manufacturers, &c.: Wm. M. Kirk and partners

Markets : Monday and Thursday, grain; Friday, general (pork, October till May). Laurence M'Shane, Cranemaster, &c.

Merchant Tailors: E. Fegan, A. and S. Small, Watters and Smyth

Newsagents: John Baillie, Peter Campbell, Miss Hughes, Joseph McBride and Son, Miss Rolston, Robt. Waddell

Physician : J. G. Allen

Painters: Sl. McCabe, M'Gurk

Petty Sessions : second and last Thursdays of every month. Robt. Thompson, P.S.C.

Posting Car Owners: John Campbell, Peter Campbell, Frank Carvill, Jas. English, Mrs. E. Dumigan, Chas. Kavanagh, Jno. Kerr, Jas. Woods, Owen Woods

Post Master and Stamp Distributer : Alex. Small

Process Server: John Nugent

R. I. Constabulary: Jas. Reid, Sergeant

Saddlers : J. Cassidy, J. T. Gallagher.

Schools— See Education.

Sewing Agent: Miss Mt. McAfee

Spirit Retailers (See also grocers and hotels) : John W. Campbell, Mrs. Ann Campbell, Frank Carvill,

(*Directory continued on page* 173.)

E. FEGAN,

Merchant Tailor, Shirt Manufacturer, Watchmaker & Jeweller,
KEADY.

☞ Patterns, samples, forms for self-measurement, and price list sent to any part of Ireland.

THE PEOPLE'S TEA HOUSE.

B. & T. WOODS,
General Merchants.
THE CORNER HOUSE,
KEADY.

DEPARTMENTS:

Groceries (wholesale and retail).
Home and Foreign Provisions.
Bacon curing.
Flour.
Meal.
Feeding Stuffs.

Seeds.
Artificial Manures.
Wines and Spirits.
Bottlers of Guinness' Porter and
Bass's Ales.

UNDERTAKERS.
☞ *Funeral furnishings on the most moderate terms.*

Mrs. Eliza Clarke, Mrs. Ellen Dumigan, Patk. Reynolds, Henry Short, James Woods, Owen Woods

Tailors' Amalgamated Society: Thomas Devlin, Patk. Brennan, Peter Lynch, Secretary

Tinsmiths : B. Carolan, P. Carolan

Town Commissioners: Dr. John Gower Allen, Chairman ; John Hughes, J.P. ; Patrick Mone, Peter Campbell, Charles Kavanagh, James English, Bernard Woods, Patrick Hughes, Thomas Mone. Edward Quinn, Clerk; Patrick Houston, Inspector

Undertakers: Rt. I. Eccles and Co., F. and J. Nicholson, B. and T. Woods

Victuallers : Thos. Boyd, Jno. Heenan, Mrs. Mary A. McGinn, Thos. McKee

Watchmakers: E. Fegan, E. Finlay, Watters and Smyth

Farmers & Residents

Adam, James, Dunlarge
Adams, Robert, Tullynamallogue
Armstrong, John, Camagh
Armstrong, John, jun., Camagh
Armstrong, Sl., Drumderg
Armstrong, Wm., Curryhugh
Bailie, John, Crossmore
Bailey, Thomas, Curryhugh
Bain, Thomas, Corkley
Blackstock, John, Corkley
Blackstock, Thos., Corkley
Boyd, Andrew, Brackley
Boyd, James, Tullynamallogue
Boyd, Samuel, Clay
Bradley, James, Mowillan
Bratty, Wm., Iskeymeadow
Brown, James, Kilreavy
Burke, Francis, Rathcarbery
Callaghan, James, Brackly
Campbell, Fr. A'brague
Campbell, George, Lagan
Campbell, John W., Crossmore
Campbell, Nathl., Dunlarge
Campbell, Peter, Crossdened
Campbell, Saml., Kilreavy

Campbell, Wm. Brackly
Carberry, John, Rathcarberry
Carson, Rev. H.W., Tullynamaloge
Clarke, Alex., Corkley
Clarke, John, Armaghbrague
Clarke, Samuel, Corkley
Clarke, William, Corkley
Coleman, Arch., A'brague
Conn, Andrew, Corkley
Coulter, John, Cargaclogher
Craig, James, Knockraven
Cummins, Wm., Keady
Curry, James R., Iskeymeadow
Curry, Robert, Iskeymeadow
Davidson, Robert, Corkley
Devlin, John, Tullyglush
Donnelly, Francis, Cargaclogher
Douglas, Hh., Mountain Lodge
Douglas, J. (J.P.), Mountain Lodge
Doyle, Charles, Armaghbrague
Doyle, Edward, Corkley
Doyle, James, Armaghbrague
Dunwoody, Geo., Iskymeadow
English, Saml., Knockrevan
English, Wm., Kilreavy
Ewart, James A., Drumderg
Ewart, John, Drumderg
Falloon, James, Drumderg
Flemming, John. Corkley
Foster, John, Mowillan
Gardiner, George, Annvale house
Gardiner, Mrs. M., Annvale house
Gibson, Jos., Dunlargue house
Gibson, Sml., Tullynamallogue
Griffin, Samuel, Clay
Gillespie, I., Tullynamallogue
Gollogly, Francis, Knockraven
Gorman, Peter, Drumlarge
Hall, James, Farnaloy
Hall, W. J., Mowillan
Harvey, Hh., Armaghbrague
Haughey, Hh., Armaghbrague
Haughey, John, Armaghbrague
Haughey, John, Dunlarge
Haughey, Ml., Armaghbrague
Hazlett, James, Corkley
Herron, Wm., Armaghbrague
Hill, John, Dunlarge
Hughes, James, Armaghbrague
Hughes, John, Knockraven

Hughes, John, Lagan
Hughes, Jno. (J.P.), Glenview ter
Jenkins, Andw., Armaghbrague
Jenkins, Jas., Armaghbrague
Kavanagh, Charles, Crossdened
Kelly, Adam, Armaghbrague
Kelly, Adam, Corkley
Keoghan, Wm. James, Lagan
Kernaghan, Thos., Armaghbrague
Kirker, John, Kilreavy
Lawson, William, Lagan
Lena, Jno., Kilcreevy otra
Lutton, John, Iskymeadow
Lynas, Patk., Rathcarberry
M'Ardle, Hugh, Mowillan
M'Ateer, Farrell, Kilreavy
M'Bride, George, Keady
M'Bride, Robert, Crossdened
M'Bride, W. J., Tullyglush
M'Cabe, John, Keady
M'Cann, Patrick, Drumderg
M'Carten, Wm., Mowillan
M'Coey, Michael, Rathcarberry
M'Coey, Ml., Tullyglush
M'Coey, Ptk., Rathcarberry
M'Coy, Geo., Armaghbrague
M'Elhern, Peter, Drumderg
M'Ilrath, James, Kilreavy
M'Kean, Wm. (J.P.), Millmount
M'Kee, David, Tullyglush
M'Kenna, John, Crossmore
M'Kenna, Wm., Iskymeadow
M'Keown, James, Clay
M'Mullen, David, Aughnagurgan
M'Williams, Ellen, T'namallogue
Magerr, Edw., Tul'namallogue
Mallon, John, Armaghbrague
Mann, Jos., Tul'namallogue
Matchett, Fr., Armaghbrague
Mehaffy, Thomas, Mowman
Menary, Alex., Armaghbrague
Moore, Alex., Tullynamallogue
Moore, James, Iskymeadow
Moore, William, Iskymeadow
Nugent, Neil, Armaghbrague
O'Hara, Ambrose, Lagan
O'Hara, James, Lagan

Porter, Wm., Armaghbrague
Purdy, Jas., Aughnagurgan
Rafferty, Bernard, Clay
Rafferty, John, jun., Lagan
Rafferty, Lawrence, Clay
Rafferty, Patrick, Clay
Raverty, Michael, Clay
Raverty, Patrick, Rathcarberry
Reaney, Geo., Armaghbrague
Reany, John, Rathcarberry
Renehan, John, Cargaclogher
Rice, Mrs., Clay
Robinson, Walter, Iskymeadow
Russell, A., Aughnagurgan
Scarr, David, Aughnagurgan
Shields, Bd., jun., Clay
Short, Terence, Keady
Short, Terence, Rathcarberry
Slavin, Peter, Clay
Small, Alex. (P.M.), Keady
Small, Sl. Sturgeon, Keady
Small, Thos. (J.P.), The Hermitage
Smyth, Ml., Keady
Stewart, Henry, Knockraven
Tughan, Henry, Drumderg
Tughan, John, Knockraven
Tughan, Samuel, Tullyglush
Tughan, Wm. J., Lagan
Waddell, Jas., Tullynamallogue
Waddell, Wm., Drumlarge
Wallace, James, Tullyglush
Walker, John, Mowillan
Warnock, Daniel, Armaghbrague
Warnock, James, Armaghbrague
Watson, Isaiah, Crossmore
Watson, Joseph, Crossmore
Watson, Samuel, Crossmore
Watson, W. J., Crossmore
Watters, Patrick, Keady
Williamson, John, Dunlarge
Wolfenden, Thomas, Rockmount
Wilson, Robert, Clay
Wilson, William, Annvale
Woods, Bernard, Keady
Woods, Bernard, Lagan
Woods, Thomas, Keady

KILLYLEA.

KILLYLEA is handsomely situated on the side of a hill, 5 miles west of Armagh by road, and 4½ by rail. The station is half a mile distant. A good farming country surrounding the village, makes it the centre for a first-rate fair, held on the last Friday of each month. Oats and potatoes are the principal crops. Nearly all the farmers make butter and send it to market in rolls. Killylea is a district parish, formed out of the parishes of Armagh, Tynan and Derrynoose, under a special Act of Parliament in the reign of George IV. The chief attraction of the village, architecturally, is a handsome church, with square pinnacled tower, standing on the summit of the hill. It was erected by subscription in 1832. The present owner of Killylea is Mr. Henry Bruce Armstrong, D.L., Armagh. There are good limestone quarries in the parish.

Baker : John Fitzsimons
Blacksmith : James Glass
Carpenter : David Gordon
Churches, C.I. : Rev. Herbert Sandford ; Presbyterian : Rev. William Waddell

Draper : William Costigan
Grocers and spirit retailers : Wm. Costigan, C. M. Hughes, H. Parr
Nursery : Wm. Bleakley
Painter : James Woods
Post M. : Miss Mt. Esterbrook

Process Server : Jas. Wilson
Railway station : Rt. Marshall,
Toll Collector
   Schools, Natl. : Wm. Anderson,
Miss Margt. Esterbrook

Farmers & Residents

Allen, Greer, Mullintur
Allen, James, Corr
Allen, James, jun., Corr
Allen, John, Corr
Allen, Joseph, Corr
Allen, Robert, Corr
Anderson, Robert, Drum
Archer, John, Cormeen
Bingham, James, Killylea
Blacker, St. J. T. (J.P.), Elm Park
Blacker, Maxwell V., Elm Park
Bole, Mrs. L., Naul
Bloomer, Quinton, Cavanbellaghey
Branigan, Francis, Tullycallidy
Carberry, John, Drum
Clarke, Thomas, Annaghnanny
Clogher, William, Tullycallidy
Conlon, James, Drumsallen up
Conlon, Joseph, Drumsallen lr
Connelly, James, Corr
Coote, Mrs. A., Knappah Manse
Costigan, John, Annaghananny
Cross, Mrs. Fanny, Dartan
Crow, William, Dressogagh
Crozier, William J., Naul
Curry, John, Annaghananny
Davidson, Thomas, Drumgar
Devlin, James, Kilmatroy
Donaldson, Wm., Cormeen
Donaldson, W., sen., Tullycallidy
Donaldson, Wm., jun., Tullycallidy
Donnelly, Arthur, Annaghananny
Donnelly, Cornelius A'hananny
Donnelly, Ptk., Polnagh
Ewart, Clarke, Tullycallidy
Ewart, Jas., Tullycallidy
Ewart, Sl., Tullycallidy
Ferguson, Quinton, Corr
Finnally, Thomas, Killymaddy
Frazer, John, Killymaddy
Frazer, John, Lisnafeedy
Frazer, Joseph, Cabragh
Frazer, Jos., Killymaddy
Frazer, Wm., Lisnafeedy

Gamble, John, Lisagally
Gillespie, Hugh, Killylea
Gillespie, Hugh, Naul
Gillespie, James, Drum
Gillespie, John, Corr
Gillespe, J. W., Cavanbellaghey
Gillespie, Mrs., Annagh
Gillespie, William, Pollnagh
Glass, James, Killylea
Graham, Thomas, Drumrusk
Greer, Benjamin, Drumgar
Greer, John, Mullintur
Greer, William, Drumgar
Greer, Wm., jun., Drumgar
Hagan, Owen, Corr
Hall, George, Cormeen
Henderson, James, Knockenagh
Henderson, William, Dressogagh
Hewton, James, Killymaddy
Hodge, John, Derrydarragh
Hughes, Andrew, Foyar
Hughes, C., Dartan house
Hughes, Edward, Ballymacaulay
Hughes, Edward, Corr
Hughes, Francis, Lisagally
Hughes, Henry, Ballymacaully
Hughes, James, Corr
Hughes, James, Corr
Hughes, John, Cavanbellaghey
Hughes, Joseph, Corr
Hughes, Patrick, Tullycallidy
Hughes, William, jun., Corr
Huston, William, Killylea
Irwin, James S., Cormeen
Johnston, Alex., Cavanapole
Kane, Thomas, Annagh
Knipe, Samuel, Culkeeran house
Lappan, James, Dernasigh
Lawson, Abraham, Drumgar
Lee, David, Eglish
Lester, Geo. Hy., Polnagh house
Lester, Thomas, Dernasigh
Lester, Wm., Kilcarn
Linton, Wm., Tullycallidy
Livingston, John, Drumsallen
Loughead, Timothy, Polnagh
Lowery, Robert, Lisgally
M'Alister, Francis, Dartan
M'Aree, James, Manooney
Macabe, Thomas, Foyar house

M'Carragher, George, Cabragh
M'Carragher, John, Killyquin
M'Carten, Bernard, B'macauley up
Macauley, John, Knockaneagh
M'Clean, James, Killylea
M'Clure, Thos. A., Rose lodge
M'Elroy, Patrick, Annaharap
M'Gee, Arthur, Turry cottage
M'Kenna, Fr., Cormeen
M'Keown, Rt., Annaharap
M'Quade, Bd., Annaharap
M'Williams, John, Lisagally
Magee, John, Eglish
Magee, John, Lisagally
Makeham, Felix, Drumrusk
Marshall, Henry, Killymaddy
Marshall, Michael, Lisnafeedy
Meaghan, John, Corr
Menary, Jno., Knockaneagh
Menary, Wm., Killmatroy
Mooney, Peter, Lisagally
Morton, Alex., Manoony
Murphy, John, Cormeen
Newton, Miss S., Killylea ho
Noble, S., Lisnafeedy ho
Nugent, Alex., Annaghananny
O'Neill, C., Ballymacauley up
Patten, Wm., Killylea
Prentice, Joseph, Killylea

Quinn, Edw., Derrydarragh
Rolston, James, Polnagh
Speer, Robert, Tullycallidy
Speer, Samuel, Tullycallidy
Speers, Robert, Drumgar
Steele, James, Cormeen
Steele, Thomas, Cormeen
Stevenson, Jos., Cavanbellaghey
Stringer, Wm., Cavanbellaghey
Tate, William, Lisnafeedy
Thompson, William, Killyquinn
Toner, Hugh, Drumrusk
Trimble, John, Tullycallidy
Treanor, James, Polnagh
Vogan, Joseph, Ballymacaully up
Ward, John, Manooney
Warden, Joseph, Tannagh
Whitelock, John, Polnagh
Williamson, George, Drumgar
Wilson, Edward, Kilcarn
Wilson, Jas., Drumsallen
Wilson, Jas., Knockaneagh
Wilson, John, Kilcarn
Wilson, John, Lisnafeedy
Wilson, Joseph, Drumrusk
Wilson, Robert, Killylea
Wilson, Thomas, Killymaddy
Wilson, T. A., Drumgoliff

KILMORE.

KILMORE is a village of a few houses, 7 miles north-east of Armagh, 2 miles south-east of Loughgall, and 2 miles north-east of Richhill, the nearest railway station. The land of the district is good. Potatoes, oats, wheat and beans are the principal crops. A great many of the farm-houses are improved in appearance by apple-orchards. Mr. Henry A. Johnston, of St. Adan's, is chief owner of the immediate district. His mansion occupies part of the site of the ancient abbey dedicated to St. Adan (*Aedhain*), by St. Mochtee, founder of Louth. Extensive ruins of Castle Roe are within view. A full description will be found under the head of castles at page 33. Limestone, of excellent quality, is abundant in the parish. Many of the small farmers and cotters receive their letters from the Kilmore post office.

Church of I.: Rev. L. P. T. Ledoux
Grocers & drapers: Misses Gilpin

Postm.: Miss M. J. Greer
Schools, Erasmus Smith's: Miss

M

THOMAS WYNNE & CO.,

Linen Manufacturers,
Dyers and Finishers,

LISLEA,
ARMAGH.

~~~~~~~~

Manchester Agency : **22 CHATHAM BUILDINGS.**

Mary J. Greer; National, Mr. Ruddock
Spirit retailer—Robinson Ruddock

Farmers & Residents.

Atkinson, John, Ballywilly
Atkinson, Richard, Ballytrue
Atkinson, Richard, Money
Derry, John, Kilmacanty
Gardner, Miss Rachel, Annaboe
Greer, James W., Lurgancot
Hall, John, Annaboe
Hampton, Chr., Greenagh
Henderson, John, Ballytrue
Hobson, James, Kilmore
Hutchinson, Rt., Annaboe
Jenkinson, James, Drumard Jones
Johnston, H. A. (B.L.), St. Aidan's
Kane, John, Mullaletra
Kane, Wm., Mullaletra
Kane, W., jun., Drumard Jones

M'Allister, Jonathan, Kilmacanty
M'Cann, Daniel, Lurgancot
M'Coo, Michael, Ballywilly
M'Donnell, J., Lurgancot
M'Geough, John, Ballytrue
Marshall, William, Money
M'Mahon, John, Drumard Jones
Morgan, Felix, Lurgancot
Odgers, Robert, Kilmacanty
Odgers, Thomas, Ballywilly
Palmer, William, Ballywilly
Redmond, Philip, The Cottage
Robinson, Joseph, Annaboe
Troughton, Jones, Annaboe
Troughton, Rt., Lurgancot
Watts, Samuel, Lurgancot
Weir, Henry, Money
Williamson, Wm., Kilmacanty
Winter, Joseph, Ballytrue

LISLEA.

Trout Fishing.

ISLEA is a village 4 miles south-west of Armagh. The houses are scattered. It is in the Callan valley, once, at this point, the site of extensive bleach greens. Now the only industry is operated by Messrs. Thomas Wynne & Co. They are manufacturers by power loom of buckrams, hollands, and packing canvas, and in the factory and beetling mills give employment to about 200 people. The land of the district is good. Oats and potatoes are the principal crops. Higher up the river the Roan Paper Company, Limited, gives employment to about 50 people. Coarse lapping paper is the specialty. Anglers find the Callan fairly good for trout up to the paper mill, but no further. The scenery is charming at Lislea. Armagh is the nearest railway station.

Church of Ireland, Aughavilly: Rev. Hugh Edgar
Linen Manufacturers: Thomas Wynne & Co.
Paper: Roan Paper Manufacturing Co., Ltd.; Jas. R. Girvin, Man. Director; Wm. Girvin, Sec.
Post M.: Jno. McKinney
School, Natl.: Jas. McMenemy

Farmers & Residents

Allen, James, Lislea
Armstrong, John, Kilcreevy-etra
Brooks, Robert, Drumhirk
Broomfield, Mrs. E., Moneyquinn
Broomfield, Robert, Moneyquinn
Brown, Robert, Kilcreevy-otra
Curry, Bernard, Kilcreevy-otra
Dodds, Clarke, Kilcreevy-etra

Dodds, John, Ballynagoland
Dodds, Wm. G., Kilcreevy-etra
Dunwoody, William, Drumhirk
Eccles, John, Drumhirk
English, William, Kilcreevy-otra
Faloon, David, Drumhirk
Faloon, Robert, Drumhirk
Fee, John, Kilcreevy-etra
Feghan, Roger, Kilcreevy-otra
Foster, James, Kilcreevy-etra
Foster, Robert, Kilcreevy-etra
Gibson, Robert, Kilcreevy-etra
Gibson, Samuel, Ballynagolan
Girvin, James R., Roan house
Girvin, Wm., Moneyquin house
Gray, Robert, Roughan
Hall, James, Roughan
Herron, Henry W., Ballynagoland
Heron, John, Ballynagoland
Hughes, Bernard, Kilcreevy-etra
Hughes, Peter, Kilcreevy-otra
Ireland, David, Ballynagalliagh
Ireland, James, Ballynagalliagh
Ireland, James, Moneyquinn
Ireland, William J., Broughan
Irwin, John, Ballynagalliagh
Johnston, Couser, Ballynagalliagh
Johnston, John, Ballynagalliagh
Johnston, Lewis, Moneyquinn
Johnston, Thos., Ballynagalliagh
Johnston, Wm. J., Ballynagalliagh
Kilpatrick, John, Ballyards
Kilpatrick, Robert, Ballyards

Leslie, James, Roan
M'Aleavey, Thos., Balynagalliagh
M'Ardle, James, Ballynagalliagh
M'Ardle, Peter, Kilcreevy-otra
M'Birney, Hugh, Roughan
M'Carten, Bernard, Kilcreevy-otra
M'Caul, Hugh, Kilcreevy-etra
M'Culla, Robert, Kilcreevy-otra
M'Ilrath, Samuel, Drumhirk
M'Quaid, James, Kilcreevy-etra
Mann, James, Ballynagoland
Mann, Wm., sen., Ballynagoland
Mann, Wm., jun., Ballynagoland
Morrison, James, Ballynagoland
O'Hare, John, Moneyquinn
Rafferty, James, Killycreevy-etra
Reid, Robert J., Drumhirk
Robinson, William, Ballynagoland
Rocks, James, Ballynagalliagh
Rooney, Philip, Ballyards
Taggart, Owen, Kilcreevy-etra
Tecey, James, The Cottage
Vallely, Arthur, Lislea
Walker, George, Moneyquinn
Walker, James, Drumhirk
Walker, Jenkinson, Drumhirk
Watson, David, Drumhirk
Wilson, James, Moneyquinn
Wilson, Robert, Moneyquinn
Woods, Arthur, Ballynagalliagh
Wynne, Thomas, Lislea Hill
Wynne, Thomas, Lislea House

LISNADILL.

LISNADILL is a rural post office in the parish of the same name, 3 miles south of Armagh, on the road to Newtownhamilton. A few houses, and the Parish Church of Ireland, occupy an eminence commanding a beautiful view of the surrounding district. An ancient burial ground, in the townland of Drumconnell, is supposed to contain the remains of many distinguished persons who flourished before the Christian period. The townland received its name from the fact that it was the last resting place of Connell, or Conmael, King of Ireland, slain in the year of the world 3,579. An Ogham stone discovered here by Mr. Robert Pillow, Armagh, is described at page 31. In 1833, a gold case containing many beautiful gold ornaments, was dug up at Corran in this parish. A richly carved necklace of jet was included in the "find." There are three large earthen forts in sight of the post office. Lisnadill Church was built by Primate Robinson in 1772. It is still in a good state of preservation, and in front of its fine square tower bears the Rokeby Arms. At the point of two roads, less than a mile further toward Newtownhamilton, there is a curious stone called "The Bulls Track." It has three deep dints like those which might be formed in heavy wet clay by a bull in leaping over a fence. According to the tradition, the beast in this case sprang from the stone to Armagh. The land of the district of Lisnadill is good. Oats, potatoes, and flax are the chief crops. Most of the farmers make roll butter for the Armagh market.

Churches: C.I.: Rev. Stephen Radcliff
R.C.: Rev. Patrick Corr, P.P., Rev. Henry M'Neice, C.C.
Postmaster: William Black
Schools, National: Wm. M'Culla, Miss M. Quinn.

Farmers & Residents

Acheson, Thomas G., Ballyards
Acheson, William, Ballymoran
Agnew, James, Lisdrumbroughas
Agnew, John, Lisdrumbroughas
Agnew, Wm., Lisdrumbroughas
Allen, Graham, Outlack
Allen, Osborne, Outlack
Allen, Robert, Outlack
Armour, Robert, Cavanacaw
Atkinson, Mrs. S., Letmacollum
Beatty, William, Letmacollum
Black, Thomas, Outlack
Blevins, James, Cavanacaw
Boyd, Samuel, Drumgaw
Boyd, William, Cavanacaw
Brooks, David, Drumconnell
Brooks, Robert, Moneypatrick
Conlan, David, Outlack
Cosgrove, Mrs., Letmacollum
Couser, James, Ballymoran
Couser, William, Ballymoran
Coyne, George, Drumgaw
Crummy, Patrick, Letmacollum
Donnelly, Peter, Drumconnell
Erskine, Robert, Ennislare
Farley, John, jun., Cavanacaw
Fehan, Patrick Drumconnell
Gray, George, Outlack
Gray, James, Outlack

Gray, Bernard, Lisnadill
Greer, Joshua, Ennislare
Hanna, Joseph, Outlack
Hughes, William, Ballymoran
Ireland, David, Lisnadill
Ireland, Robert, Drumconnell
Ireland, Samuel, Drumconnell
Jamison, George, Ballymoran
Johnston, Andrew, Ennislare
King, Benjamin, Outlack
M'Alister, Wm., Seagahan
M'Alister, George, Seagahan
M'Kee, Bernard, Seagahan
M'Kee, Henry, Seagahan
M'Kee, Patrick, Ballymoran
M'Kee, Patrick, Seagahan
M'Kee, Peter, Lisnadill
M'Mahon, George, Cavanacaw
Marks, George, Lisnadill
Marks, Mrs. M., Lisnadill
Menary, John, Letmacollum
Moffat, David, Drumgaw
Moffat, Henry, Seagahan
Moffett, Henry, jun., Lisnadill
Moffat, James, Drumgaw
Moffett, James, Lislea
Moore, Thomas, Lisnadill
O'Neill, John, Drumconnell
Nugent, Patrick, Drumconnell
Patterson, James, Lisnadill
Reaney, James, Ballymoran
Redmond, John, Cavanacaw
Robinson, Joseph, Letmacollum
Short, James, Seagahan
Thompson, John, Ennislare
Trodden, Wm., Ballynagalliah
Reaney, Thomas, Drumconnell

LOUGHGILLY.

LOUGHGILLY is a rural post-office and railway station in the parish of the same name, 12 miles south-east of Armagh, and 3¼ miles south-east of Markethill by rail. The lough, from which the parish is named, was drained many years ago, and the land brought into cultivation. It originally extended from Poyntzpass to Mountnorris, and had a strong military fortification at each end. Potatoes, oats, and flax are the principal crops of the district. Flax is grown extensively.

Churches: C. I., Rev. Paul L. Jameson; Presbyterian, Rev. A. F. Hamilton

Postm.: Mrs. S. Gordon
Rail. Station: J. Cochrane, T.C.
Schools, Natl.: Mrs. Mt. Johnston, Loughgilly; Joseph Crawford, Mullaghmore

Farmers & Residents.

Allen John, Cornagrally
Allen, Thomas, Ballyvally
Atcheson, Mrs., Killycarn up
Bradley, John, Lisnalee
Bradshaw, Mrs. Susan, Drumilt
Brown, Jos. S., Lisnisk
Brown, Robert, Killycarn lr
Caherty, Ter., Ballydogherty
Caherty, John, Lesh
Carty, James, Lesh
Clarke, D., Cornagrally
Clarke, John, Lisnisk
Clarke, John T., Cornagrally
Cochrane, John D., Killycarn up
Cochrane, Robert, Killycarn up
Cosgrove, Thos., Ballygorman
Devlin, Hugh, Ballygorman
Dillon, John. Cornagrally
Dillon, John, Mullaghmore
Dillon. Neill, Cornagrally
Douglas, Stephen, Mullaghmore
Donaldson, James, Cornagrally
Douglas, George, Mullaghmore
Douglas, John, Killycarn up
Ferguson, Jas., Mullaghmore
Flack, Hugh, Cornagrally
Gibson, James, Lesh
Girvin, Robert, Kilcon
Girvin, Wm., Kilcon

Gordon, Wm., Lisnisk
Greer, Robert, Mullaghmore
Hale, Thomas, Cornagrally
Hale, Wm. J., Cornagrally
Hamilton, John, Corrinare
Hamilton, Hugh, Lisnisk
Hamilton, J. Ferguson, Corrinare
Hamilton, Wm., Cornagrally
Hanna, Isaac, Ballydogherty
Hanna, Wm., Ballydogherty
Hawthorne, Jas., sen., Kilcon
Hawthorne, James, Kilcon
Henry, James, Creeve
Henry, William, Creeve
Hutcheson, F. G., Killycarn lr
Hutcheson, Thos., Killycarn up
Jennings, James, Mullaghmore
Larkins, John, Mullaghmore
Lennon, James, Drumilt
Lester, Samuel, Killycarn lr
Lowe, Patrick, Cornagrally
M'Cartney, Wm. T., Bolton
M'Clelland, James, Ballygorman,
M'Cune, James, Ballygorman
M'Conville, Andrew, Lesh
M'Conville, Felix, Lesh
M'Kee, Mrs. J., Mullaghmore
M'Kinlay, James, Ballygorman
M'Kinlay, John, Ballygorman
M'Kinlay, Moses, Ballygorman
M'Manus, James, Lesh
M'Parland, Thomas, Drumilt
Madden, Michael, Lesh
Malcomson, Mrs. Mgt., Bolton
Malcomson, Sl. (jun.), Bolton
Marshall, Wm., Killycarn upper
Maxwell, John, Cornagrally
Mitchell, Samuel, Killycarn

Monaghan, Samuel, Ballygorman
Neill, William, Mullaghmore
Nicholl, Mrs., Corrinare
O'Hagan, John, Ballygorman
Paul, James, Ballydogherty
Qua, Benjamin, Bolton
Qua, David, Bolton
Quinn, John, Lesh
Revel, John, Crankey
Ross, Jos., Crankey
Shields, David, Ballydoherty
Shields, John, jun., Ballydoherty

Shields, Mrs. I., Ballydoherty
Shields, Wm., Killycarn lower
Simms, James, Ballygorman
Simms, Joseph, B'gorman
Stewart, Alex. S., Corrinare
Stewart, David, Ballydoherty
Stewart, Gawn, Creeve
Stewart, Hugh, Creeve
Taylor, Mrs. Mary, Ballygorman
Vint, Thomas, Kilcon
Ward, Richard J., Cornagrally
Wilson, James, Cornagrally

LOUGHGALL.

LOUGHGALL is 5 miles north-east of Armagh, and 2¼ miles north by west from Richhill, the nearest railway station. It is situated in a beautiful valley, and surrounded by richly planted demesnes and handsome private residences. The village consists of one street, in which the houses, with few exceptions, are large and well built. A highly ornamented entrance to the Manor House demesne (Mrs. Cope), is almost in the centre. The lough that gives name to the village, is accessible from this point, and is one of the attractive features. Opposite the Manor House gate there is an entrance to the ancient burial ground in which are vaults containing the remains of the Copes, the Verners, and many other well-known county families. The western gable of the church, completely covered with ivy, still continues in a state of preservation. The oldest legible inscription records the death of Richard Taylor, 1706. Not far from it a large slab commemorates Patrick Sheals, who died in 1848, aged 102. Loughgall, as a farming country, is one of the best in Armagh. The lands have a limestone basis, and yield abundantly. Oats, potatoes, flax and wheat are the chief crops. A great many of the farmers are fruit growers, more or less extensively, and in the season of bloom the orchards contribute greatly to heighten the charm of the scenery. Mrs. Cope, it appears, considered that the thirstiest mortal could find enjoyment in such a fair region without the aid of either brewer or distiller. She tested the truth of her opinion by purchasing the "vested rights" of the village publicans, and setting up a coffee tavern as a substitute. To this she has added a library and reading room. The nearest publican hangs out his sign at a distance of one mile from the village. A foot-ball club (Association), established about three years, has 30 members and flourishes upon a subscription of 2s. per member. Mr. Samuel H. Orr is captain.

MILLTOWN WEAVING FACTORY AND FINISHING WORKS.

GRANAGILL MILLS.

JOSEPH ORR & SONS,

Linen Manufacturers, Finishers,

&c.

Office—Cranagill, Loughgall, ARMAGH.

Telegraphic Address: "ORRS, LOUGHGALL."

MESSRS. JOSEPH ORR & SONS.

ESSRS. JOSEPH ORR & SONS are manufacturers by power loom of linens of different kinds. They are also dyers and finishers. The factory of chief importance is situated on the Armagh side of the Blackwater, and is known as Milltown Mills, Benburb, County Tyrone. As may be seen from the illustration, there are few more picturesque places devoted to industrial purposes. The river, the valley, the surrounding heights, and the plantations form a lovely combination.

The factory buildings and beetling mills are constructed of stone, with brick facings. Water and steam are used in conjunction for power purposes. The premises contain 36 acres. At Tullydoey, distant about a mile and a half from Milltown Mills, there is a handsome private residence belonging to this property. It is on the opposite side of the Blackwater, in Tyrone, and has attached to it 157 acres of land.

The warehouse and mills at Cranagill, Loughgall, are eight miles from Milltown Mills. Adjoining them are 86 acres, with a private residence. The late Mr. Joseph Orr founded the industry at Cranagill, fifty years ago. At the time of his death he was head of the firm of Joseph Orr & Sons. It at present consists of Mr. James Orr, J.P., and Mr. Jacob Orr, J.P. The principal market for the manufactures is the United Kingdom. There are agencies at London, Manchester, Leeds, and Belfast. Cranagill is seven miles from the city of Armagh, and Milltown Mills six miles.

LOUGHGALL DIRECTORY.

Bleacher, Finisher, &c.: Anthony Cowdy, jun., Green Hall Mills

Burial Ground : S. Orr, Caretaker

Baker : John McKitterick

Blacksmith : Thomas Wright

Churches : C.I.—Rev. A. M. Dobbs ; Presbyterian, Rev. Wm. Smyth; R.C., Rev. Ml. O'Brien, P.P.

Coffee house : Mrs. T, Jones, mgr

Dispensary : Dr. W. W. Leeper, J.P., Medical Officer. Attendance —Monday, Wednesday and Friday, 10 a.m. to noon.

Committee—Jos. Atkinson, J.P., D.L., Crowhill, Loughgall; John A. M. Cope, J.P., Drummilly house ; Robert J. M'Geough, J.P. ; Charles Ensor, J.P., Ardress east, Loughgall; Joseph Atkinson, jun., J.P., Summer Island, Loughgall ; Thos. Hall, J.P., Eden Cottage, Loughgall ; James Orr, J.P., Cranagill, Loughgall ; Henry Lamb, Castleraw, Loughgall ; Timothy Fox, Derrylee, Verner's Bridge ; Moses Robinson, Grange O'Nieland, Loughgall ; Thomas W. Sinclair, Tullyrone, Moy ; Jacob Orr, J.P., Cranagill, Loughgall; John Nicholson, Tall Bridge, Loughgall ; Alf. R. Goodlatte, Salem lodge, Moy ; George Hayes, Clonytclay, Moy

Committee meeting first Monday every month at noon.

Wardens—Thomas D. Jackson, Derryane ; Robert Taylor, Grange Lower; James Conn, Clonmacash ; W. J. Lawson, Clonmain ; Samuel Orr, Loughgall ; William Smith, Derrycorry north ; Richard Gilpin, Derrycorry

Drapers : Miss M. J. Jackson, Jos. Orr

Education : Eras. Smith's school, James Doherty ; National schools, J. Lindsay, Patrick Bradley

Estate Agent : Hume Babington, Armagh

Groceries, Hardware, Seeds, Boots, Delf, &c. : George Jackson, Joseph Orr.

Library : Mrs. T. Jones

Linen Manufacturers, &c. : Jos. Orr and Sons, Cranagill

Petty Sessions 3rd Wednesday in every month. Rd. Ewing, clerk

Post M.: Samuel H. Orr

Process Server : William Hall

R.I. Constabulary : Sergt. Geo. Tanner.

Schools : see Education

Scutch Mill : James Mallon

Spirit Retailers : None

Farmers & Residents.

Alexander, Henry, Kinnego

Alexander, John, Termacrannon

Allen, Isaac, Caushnagh

Allen, Jacob, Annasamry

Allen, James, Derryloughan

Allen, John, Drumhariff

Allen, Samuel, Dennyloughan

Allen, William, Ballymagerney

Allen, William, Ternagreevagh

Anderson, Henry J., Kinnego

Anderson, James, Aughnacloy

Atkinson, Joseph (D.L.), Crowhill

Atkinson, J., jun. (J.P.), Summer Island

Bates, George, Ardrea

Beggs, John, Ballygasey

Beggs, John, Drumilly

Bates, George, Creenagh

Best, George, Egerlougher

Boland, James, Moneycree

Boland, William, Moneycree

Bothwell, William, Clovenden

Brannigan, Patrick, Knockaconey

Brown, James, Creenagh
Brown, Robert, Creenagh
Burrows, Samuel, Kinnego
Burrows, William, Lisasley
Campbell, Felix, Derrycrew
Campbell, James, Ardress east
Cappagh, Michael, Eagralougher
Carroll, James, Derrycrew
Carroll, Samuel, Mullaghmore
Cartmill, Bernard, B'gassoon
Cartmill, Francis, Grangeblundell
Cartmill, Robert, Grangeblundell
Castles, Robert, Derryloughan
Clancy, Robert, Aughinlig
Clogher, Henry, Ballybrannon
Clogher, John, Drumagher
Connor, John, Ardress
Connor, Thos, Ardress east
Conway, Charles, Clonmain
Cooey, John, Ballygassoon
Cope, J. A. M. (J.P.), Drumilly
Cope, Mrs., The Manor
Corrigan, Wm., Clonmain
Cullen, James, Tullymore
Cunningham, Ml., Mullaghmore
Curry, John, Annahugh
Davison, James, Ardress west
Davison, John, Ardress west
Davison, Sl., Ballymagerney
Davison, Thomas, Caushnagh
Davison, Thomas, Coragh
Davison, Walter, Annasamry
Davison, Wm. H., Ardress west
Devlin, Patrick, Mullaghmore
Donnelly, Peter, Grangeblundell
Dougan, Mrs., Clonmain
Downard, James, Mullagamore
Drainey, Henry, Ballytyrone
Elliott, John, Eagarlougher
Elliott, Joseph, Annasamry
Elliott, Wm., Tullygoonigan
Ensor, Charles (J.P.), Ardress east
Foster, Francis, Drumheriff
Foster, Joseph, Drumharriff
Gilpin, James, Coragh
Gilpin, Johnston, Ardress east
Gibson, Peter, Annacramp
Gibson, Wm., Annacramp
Glass, Saml., Lissheffield
Graham, John, Ballybrannon

Gribben, Francis, Ballybrannon
Gribben, Thomas E., Ballybrannon
Hagan, James, Lislasly
Hagan, John, Aughinlig
Hall, Thos. (J.P.), Eden Cottage
Halligan, Hugh, Ballyhagan
Halligan, Mrs., Castleroe
Halligan, Wm., Drumart
Hamilton, Geo., Ternagreevagh
Hampton, Verner, Ballywilly
Henry, Brown, Annasamry
Higgings, George, Eagralougher
Hobson, Joshua, Drumilly
Hogg, Mrs., Eagralougher
Hughes, John, Termacrannon
Hughes, Bernard, Knockaconey
Hughes, Peter, Ardress west
Hughes, Thomas, Knockaconly
Hunter, William, Lissheffield
Hutchinson, Joseph, Ballytyrone
Hyde, John, Annasamry
Irwin, Archibald, Kinnego
Irwin, John, Cloveneden
Jackson, Joseph, Coragh
Jackson, Walter, Coragh
Johnston, Jervas, Tullymore
Johnston, Jervas, jun., Tullymore
Johnston, Josiah, Ballytyrone
Jones, Mrs. M., Mullaletra
Keane, John, Ardress east
Keegan, Thomas, Annahugh
Keegan, Thomas, Ballyhagan
Kennedy, Robert, Lissheffield
Kimlin, Hh., Ballymagerney
King, George, Creenagh
Lamb, Henry, Castleroe
Lamb, John, Tullymore
Lavery, John, Kinnegoe
Lawson, Wm. J., Clonmain
Lee, Thos. H., Derrycrew
Leeper, Dr. W. W. (J.P.), Loughgall
Livingston, David, Causnagh
Lonsdale, Thomas, Loughgall
Loudan, Wm., Drumhariff
Ludley, John, Salter's Grange
Lynn, Alex,, Clonmain
M'Cann, John, Grangeblundell
M'Cann, Patrick, Mullaghmore
M'Clelland, David, Annahugh
M'Clelland, Robert, Derryloughan

M'Crealy, Joseph, Grangeblundell
M'Cutcheon, Alex., Kinnego
M'Cutcheon, James, G'blundell
M'Donald, Bernard, Lissheffield
M'Donnell, Alex., Annahugh
M'Donnell, Berd., Egralougher
M'Dowell, Wm. H., Ballygassy
M'Guinness, John, Derryloughan
M'Guinness, Michl., Knockaconey
M'Keever, Daniel, Aunahugh
M'Keever, James, Tullymore
M'Keever, John, Annahugh
M'Keever, John, Termacrannon
M'Kenny, Jas., Grangeblundell
M'Kittrick, Joshua, Derrycrew
M'Loughlan, James, Greenagh
M'Mullen, Thomas, Aughnacloy
M'Quaid, Mrs., Ballymagerney
Mackay, William, Kincon
Mackle, James, Aughanlig
Mackle, John, Aughinalig
Marshall, Jacob, Derrycrew
Marshall, Jacob, Ternagreevy
Marshall, James, Derrycrew
Marshall, William, Ternagreevagh
Martin, George, Termacrannon
Montgomery, John, Drumart
Neille, Henry, Cranagill
Neville, Martin, Kinnego
Nicholson, Joshua, Drumnasoo
O'Neill, James, Clonmain
O'Neill, John, Eagerlougher
Orr, James (J.P), Cranagill
Orr, Jacob (J.P.), Cranagill
Orr, Robt. Ballymagerney
Orr, Robert W., Ballymagerney
Orr, Wm., Drumheriff house
Preston, Mrs., Ballymagerney
Preston, A. D., Ballyhagan
Preston, Wm. J., Ballymagerney
Proctor, Richard, Ballytyrone
Proctor, William, Drumilly

Reilly, John, Lissheffield
Robinson, James, Cloveneden
Robinson, John, Derrycrew
Robinson, Moses, Grange up
Rolston, Brown, Aughinlig
Ross, Thomas, Lissheffield
Rountree, Johnston, Causnagh
Sinclair, George, Clonmain
Slevin, Daniel, Ballygasson
Smith, James, Grangeblundell
Spence, Robert, Ballytyrone
Stothers, James, Ternagreevagh
Stothers, Robert, Derryloughan
Stothers, Wm., Derryloughan
Thompson, Wm., Derrycrew
Toal, John, Termacrannon
Todd, Samuel, Salter's grange
Toner, John, Drumhariff
Vallely, Jas., Ardress west
Ward, Wm., Derryloughan
Walker, John, Ballytyrone
Walker, Thomas, Ballytyrone
Walker, John F., Callan Lodge
Wallace, Andrew, Ballytyrone
Weir, David, Kinnego
Weir, James, Kinnego
Weir, Robert, Tullymore
Weir, Thomas, Derryloughan
White, Thomas, Clonmain
White, Thomas, Cloveneden
White, William, Clonmain
Wiley, John, Ardress west
Williamson, Henry, Kilcon
Williamson, Wm., Kilcon
Willis, Joshua, Grangeblundel
Willis, Wm., Grangeblundel
Willis, Robt., jun., Grangeblundel
Willis, Thomas, Grangeblundel
Wilson, Joseph, Castleroe
Wilson, Thomas, Caushnagh
Winter, Daniel, Grange lr

MADDEN.

 MADDEN consists of a church and a few houses in the parish of Derrynoose, 7½ miles south-west of Armagh, and 3 miles north-west of Keady. Several earthen forts exist in the district. The land is good. Oats, potatoes and flax are the principal crops. Most of the farmers make butter in a small way, and send it to market in " bricks." A few have large dairies, and rise to the dignity of firkins.

Churches, &c. : C. I., Rev. Dr. Chas. King Irwin ; Christians ; Presbyn., Rev. Wm. Ingram ; R. C., Very Rev. Canon Kelly, P.P.

Grocers : Jas. Anderson, Denis Gardner, James M'Crea, Natl. Tacey

Miller (corn) : Jas. Anderson

Post M. : Wm. Glasgow

Schools, Natl. : Wm. Glasgow, Madden ; Ptk. Macklin, Madden lr

Scutch Mills : Jas. Anderson, Jos. Keenan, Jas. M'Crum, Roger Marshall, Hugh Smith

Spirit Retailers : James M'Crea, James M'Kenna

Farmers & Residents

Barrett, Edw., Drumgreenagh
Bradshaw, Thomas, Madden
Campbell, Abraham, Camagh
Campbell, John, Camagh
Campbell, John A., Camagh
Campbell, Wilson, Camagh
Clements, Arthur, Drumacanver
Crummy, Mrs. J., Tamlaght
Curry, Francis, Madden
Curry, John, Madden
Delaney, James, Camagh
Dodd, William, Fernaloy
Donnelly, Arthur, Brootally
Donnelly, Jas., jun., Tamlaght
Donnelly, John, Tamlaght
Donnelly, Ptk., Drumacanver
Donnelly, Patrick, Tamlet
English, James, Farnaloy
Fehan, Matthew, Brootally
Finlay, Mrs. S., Drumhillary
Finlay, Robert, Caricklane
Fleming, William, Camagh
Foster, James, Farnaloy
Freeland, Alex., Camagh
Freeland, Samuel, Camagh
Gibson, Wm., Drumacanver
Glasgow, Samuel, Drumgreenagh
Gormal, James, Drumgreenagh
Gormill, John, Drumgreenagh

Gray, John, Farnaloy
Grimley, Mrs. Eliza, Madden
Hawthorne, Sl., Derryhennett
Hughes, Edward, Camagh
Hughes, Francis, Farnaloy
Hughes, James, Madden
Hughes, John, Madden
Hughes, J., jun., Derryhennett
Hughes, Thomas, Curryhughes
Humphrey, David, Farnaloy
Huston, John, Farnaloy
Kane, Charles, Cavanagarvin
Kane, Joseph, T'glushkane
Kane, Samuel, T glushkane
Keenan, Jas. G., Cavanagarvin
Keenan, John, Tamlaght
Keenan, Joseph, Drummond
Keenan, Thomas, Drummond
Kelly, James, Dernalea
Kelly, Mrs. C., Tamlet
Kennedy, A., Tullyglushkane
Kennedy, W., Tullyglushkane
Lawson, John, Brootally
Lawson, Robert, Derryhennett
Lawson, William, Derryhennett
Loughlin, Michael, Madden
M'Ardle, Joshua, Tamlaght
M'Caghey, James, Lisglyn
M'Call, Mrs., Drumacanver
M'Call, Mrs. J., Drumacanver
M'Call, Nathl., Drumacanver
M'Call, Thomas, Lisglynn
M'Call, Wm. J., Farnaloy
M'Carten, John, Drumgreenagh
M'Carten, John, Farnaloy
M'Carten, Peter, jun., Farnaloy
M'Carten, Peter, Farnaloy
M'Cracken, David, Drumgreenagh
M'Creary, Robert, Derryhennett
M'Cree, John, Drummond
M'Crum, James, Drummond
M'Crum, Robert, Cavanagarvin
M'Culla, Thomas, Derryhennett
M'Cullough, John, Camagh
M'Elrath, Samuel, Farnaloy
M'Ilrath, Simon, Farnaloy

CUMING & SON,

Grocers, Bakers,

GRAIN, COAL & SEED MERCHANTS,

Egg & Butter Exporters.

FUNERAL UNDERTAKERS,

Markethill.

ROBERT SMALL,
Drapery, Hardware, Boot & Leather Warehouse,
MARKETHILL.
Agent for the White Star Line of Transatlantic Steamships.

JOSEPH MALLAGH,
Grocer, Provision, Grain and Seed Merchant,
AND EGG EXPORTER,
MARKETHILL.

MATILDA RICHMOND QUA,
DRAPERY, MILLINERY, AND DRESSMAKING ESTABLISHMENT,
MARKETHILL.
Hats and Bonnets altered to the Newest Shapes.
CHINA, GLASS AND DELF.

M'Kenna, George, Lisglynn
M'Kenna, Hugh, Tamlaght
M'Kenna, John, Creevekeeran
M'Kenna, John, Tamlaght
M'Kenna, Michael, Farnaloy
M'Keown, Patrick, Lisglynn
Mallan Francis, Farnaloy
Malon, Peter, Drumgreenagh
Marshall, J. C., Tullyglushane
Mills, James, Brootally
Mills, Robert, Brootally
Mitchell, John, Sheetrim
Mitchell, William, Sheetrim
Morgan, Bernard, Farnaloy
Morton, James, Drumacanver
Quinn, James, Brootally
Raverty, Henry, Madden
Rodgers, George, Sheetrim
Rogers, Alexander, Cavanagarvin
Rogers, William, Derryhennett
Smith, Hugh, Drummond
Smith, Patrick, Drumacanver
Stewart, Alexander, Dernalea
Sturgeon, James, Drumgreenagh
Teacy, James, Drumgreenagh
Teacy, James, jun., Drumgreenagh
Teacy, Mrs. Anne, Drumgreenagh
Teacy, Mrs. E., Drumgreenagh
Teacy, Nathaniel, Drumgreenagh
Treanor, Mrs. A., Farnaloy
Wilson, Mrs. J., Cavanagarvin

MARKETHILL.
Population 874 in 1881.

MARKETHILL is 8¾ miles, English, south-east from Armagh, by rail, and 5 miles, Irish, by road. Portadown lies to the north-east, about 9 miles, Irish, by road. Newry is 12¼ miles, English, to the south-east by rail. The main street of the village ascends to the summit of a hill, and there are two streets in the low ground. A great many well-built houses continue in a state of good repair. Markethill, like most of the other villages of the county, has been injured by the concentration of market interests in the larger towns. Armagh at one side, and Portadown at the other, draw away the cream of the produce. But for the enterprise of a few leading merchants the markets here would not be able to stand the competition referred to. Every Monday a small market is held for fowl, eggs and grain, and every Friday one for butter and eggs. On the 3rd Friday of every month a fair is held for cattle, sheep and pigs, on the Common, in the low ground, not far from the railway station. No tolls are levied in either markets or fairs. The land of the surrounding country is good, and in a high state of cultivation. Potatoes, oats and flax are the chief crops. Farmers still devote some attention to wheat, and most of them make a feature of dairying, and maintain a fair reputation for the quality of butter turned out. About 200 hand-loom weavers live in the neighborhood. Linen yarns are given out by manufacturers' agents in the village every Friday.

Lord Gosford is the owner of Markethill and vicinity. His castle, approached by an avenue at the head of the main street, stands in a richly planted demesne of 645 acres. The building of the castle was begun by Lord Gosford in 1820, and was not completed for nearly twenty years. It is in the Norman style, the walls being of county granite, from the Mullaglass quarries. Within the demesne there are several earthen forts of Danish construction, and many places pointed out as having been among the favorite resorts of Dean Swift, during the time of his memorable visit to Sir Arthur Acheson, in 1729. The Dean's writings under the *nom de plume* of " M. B. Drapier," had then been received with such admiration by the reading public of the United Kingdom, that medals were cast in commemoration. While enjoying the pleasure of this testimony to his greatness, he found an eminence now included in the demesne, which he called Drapier's Hill, and, with the sanction of Sir Arthur, decided to build a residence on it. Soon afterward he changed his mind, and gave the following reasons for doing so:

> " What intercourse of minds can be
> Betwixt the Knight sublime and me,
> If when I talk, as talk I must,
> It is but prating to a bust.
> Where friendship is by fate design'd
> It forms an union in the mind;
> But here I differ from the Knight
> In every point like black and white;
> For none can say that ever yet
> We both in one opinion met."

A poem concerning the Knight and Lady Acheson, written about the same time, will be found under the head of Hamiltonsbawn. H. Acheson, first of the family, received from James I. a grant of 1,000 acres in the parish of Mullabrack, now including Markethill. Also the manor of Coolemalish. Mr. Acheson built a stone " bawn," 140 feet long and 80 feet wide, protected by towers at four corners, and settled nineteen Scotch families. Sir James Douglas obtained a grant of 2,000 acres, and the manor of Cloncarney.

Sir A. Acheson, who succeeded him, built a castle for the protection of his settlers, and maintained 148 armed men for the king's service. The present town of Markethill was built around this castle. In the war of 1641 the castle was destroyed by the troops of Sir Phelim O'Neill, and a great deal of suffering inflicted upon the inhabitants of the village. The parish church of Mullabrack is situated at a distance of a mile from Markethill. It was rebuilt in 1830 at a cost of £1,787. Among the many monuments in the church-yard, the most interesting bears the following inscription :—" Under this marble slab are entombed the bodies of Abigail Black and Adam Black, her husband, the former of whom died at their residence in Monturg, October, 1813, after having preserved the respect of a numerous acquaintanceship during a life of 57 years. The latter died 27th February, 1821, aged 68 years. His strict honour and obliging disposition upon all occasions and other numerous virtues will long live in the recollection of a grateful people to whom he rendered many services. And they are here confidently recorded without fear of contradiction." A chapel of ease built at the head of the village has a tablet on the gable, which tells its history thus : " This tablet is erected by the parishioners of Mullabrack in grateful acknowledgment of the munificent gift of this chapel of ease by their rector, the Most Hon. and Rev. John De La Poer, Marquis of Waterford, on his retirement from the incumbency in 1859." The meetinghouse of the first Presbyterian church occupies a slight elevation near the railway station. It is surrounded by trees, and approached by an avenue from the Common. No date stone is visible, but there is no doubt this church was built for the use of the nineteen Scotch families settled in the vicinity after the Plantation of Ulster, 1609, under the protection of H. Acheson. Although it must have been repaired frequently since then, the original walls seem to have been retained. The second Presbyterian church stands at a short distance to the north-east. It formerly belonged to the Seceding Synod. There is also a Methodist church in the village. A library, established by the Dowager Lady Gosford, 25 years ago, has about 1,000 books and 60 members. It is managed by a committee of ladies. Mrs. James C. Wann is secretary. The Vicar's Cairn, referred to at page 31, lies to the west of Markethill.

Bakers : Cuming & Son, James Maguire

Bank, Belfast, agency every Friday

Blacksmiths : James M'Ilvenny, Samuel Patterson

Bootmakers : Samuel Campbell, Isaac Dickie, Michael M'Parland

Butter and Egg exporters : Miss S. J. Boyce, Cuming & Son, Josp. Mallagh

Carpenters : George Linden, James Lindsay, Thomas Wallace

Churches : C.I., Rev. John Maclaurin, LL.D., Methodist, Armagh Circuit ; Presbyterian, 1st, Rev. H. W. Morrow ; 2nd, Rev. Hugh M'Farlane ; Reformed Presbyterian, Ballylane, Rev. William M'Knight ; R.C., Rev. Patrick M'Williams, C.C.

Clog Maker : Robert Trimble

N

194

Coal Merchants : Cuming & Son, Joseph R. Sinton

Dispensary : Dr. Gilbert Marshall, Medical Officer. Attendance—Tuesday, Thursday, and Saturday, 10 a.m. to 1 p.m.

Committee :—Earl of Gosford, J.P., Gosford Castle, Markethill; George Gray, J.P., Glenanne, Markethill ; Alexander Small, J.P., Markethill ; Colonel Dobbin, J.P., Armagh ; James C. Wann, J.P., Markethill ; William Simpson, Killeen, Armagh ; William Byers, J.P., Mowhan, Markethill; Thomas Wynne, jun., Sandymount, Richhill ; Samuel Byers, J.P., Mowhan, Markethill ; Robert Black, Markethill ; Robert Dodds, Sagahan, Lisnadill ; William Cuming, Markethill ; Hugh Gass, Cladymore, Markethill ; Robert Small, Markethill ; Joseph Mallagh, Markethill

Meeting of Committee, second Thursday every month at noon

Wardens—John Scott, Lurgaboy ; John Vallely, Cladymore ; W. F. Sinton, Hamiltonsbawn ; James Gray, Enagh ; F. Shepherd, Lurgaboy ; William Marshall, Clady

Drapers : George Armstrong, Robert Black, Samuel Campbell, Misses A. and S. Gordon, Miss Matilda Richmond Qua, Robert Small

Emigration Agents : William H. Edwards, Robert Hampton, Robert Small

Estate Office : James C. Wann, J.P., agent

Fowl Exporters : Thomas Cassidy, Joseph Mallagh, Alexander Short, Edward Short

Glass, China, and Delf : Isaac Dickie, William M'Parland, Geo. Parr, Mrs. Mary Wilson

Grain Merchants : Cuming & Son, Joseph Mallagh

Grocers marked thus * retail spirits, † seed merchants: John Brann, Thos. W. Clements, Rt. Corkey, Lisdrumchor *, William Corkey †, Sl. Crawford, Cuming & Son,*† Miss My Edwards, William J. Green, Danl. Lemon, Cladymore*, Bd. McConnell*, Mrs Mt. Mackin*, Jas. Maguire, Joseph Mallagh†, Lewis Robinson*, James Ryan, Jos. R. Sinton, Dd. Wallace*, Jos. White, Mrs Mary Wilson

Hardware: George Parr, Lewis Robinson, Jos R. Sinton, Robert Small, David Torrens

Hotelkeeper: Rt. Hampton

Library: Mrs Wann, Secretary

Market: general, every Friday

Merchant Tailors : Rt. Small, David Wallace

News agents: Wm. J. Edwards, David Torrens

Petty Sessions last Monday of every month, Wm. H. Edwards, Clerk

Physicians : Gilbert Marshall, Joseph Pratt, J.P.

Postmaster and Stamp Distributer: Wm. Jas. Edwards

Railway Station: John Buchanan, Toll Collector

R. I. Constabulary: Jas. Latham, sergeant

Saddlers: Sl. Aston, Jno. Connor

Schools : National, Geo. Armstrong, Mrs. E. McCullagh (Markethill), Wm. Murray, Mullabrack, Miss Sarah Clements, Mullabrack

Spirit Retailers (see also grocers and hotel): Jas. Lindsay & Son

Undertakers: Cuming and Son, Lewis Robinson

Victuallers : Jno. Hughes, Rt. Hoye

Farmers & Residents

Acheltree, Michael, Markethill
Anderson, Hy., Manordogherty
Anderson, James, Monlurg
Anderson, Rd., Cornacrew
Armstrong, George, Markethill

Aston, John, Manordogherty
Black, John, Cabragh
Beatty, George, Tanaghmore
Burns, Alex., Brackley
Burns, James, Brackley
Burns, Joseph, Brackley
Dalzell, Geo., Maghnavery
Dobbin, Saml., Drumlack
Dougan, John, Carricklane
Callan, J., Shanecrackenbeg
Clarke, John, Brackley
Clarke, Saml., Brackley
Clarke, William, Brackley
Clelland, Hugh, Drumatee
Clements, Thos., Markethill
Conlan, James, Drumatee
Copeland, Robert, Manordogherty
Corkey, Wm., Coolmalish
Craig, John, Coolmalish
Cully, Alex., Brackley
Cully, Dd., Magherdogherty
Cuming, Miss, Markethill
Cuming, Wm., Markethill
Edwards, John T., Mullurg
Farrell, Robert, Corhammock
Flaville, Helen F., Mullurg
Fullerton, Alex., Tannaghmore
Fullerton, John, Tannaghmore
Fullerton, Samuel, Tannaghmore
Fulton, John, Ballymacawley
Gibson, Matthew, Corhammock
Gray, Hugh, Edenkennedy
Grant, Isaac, Lattery
Gray, James, Briandrum
Hanlon, James, Manordogherty
Hanna, David, Ballymacawley
Hosic, William, Dinnahorra
Hutchings, Rev. Hy., Lisnaget
Jackson, William, Corhammock
Johnston, Jas., Tannaghmore
Lambert, Jas., Mullaghbane
Lee, Mrs A., Lisnaget.
Lemon, Jos., Markethill
Lockhart, George, Lurgaboy
Loudan, William, Edenkennedy
Loughlin, James, Edenkennedy
Lowden, Saml., Briandrum
M'Anally, Chas., Markethill
M'Clean, John A., Drumshallen
M'Clinchy, Simon, Manordogherty

M'Crum, Wm., Shanecrackenbeg
M'Cullagh, Robert, Dinnahora
M'Cullough, T., S'crackenmore
M'Donnell, Robert, Edenkennedy
M'Mahon, Hugh, Manordogherty
M'Mullen, Robert M., Mullabrack
M'Mullen, William, Lurgaboy
M'Murray, William, Cornacrew
M'Murray, William, Mullabrack
M'Nally, Charles, Markethill
M'Roberts, William, Mullabrack
M'Stay, John, Mullurg
Maguire, Daniel, Mullybrack
Marshall, John, Cordrummond
Marshall, Mrs. T., Cordrummond
Marshall, Mrs. Mt., G'sdrummond
Marshall, William, Lattery
Moneypenny, Miss E., Markethill
Moneypenny, Wm., Markethill
Morton, James, Mullabrack
Murdock, Andrew, Corhammock
Murdock, Robert, Edenkennedy
O'Hagan, Francis, Lattery
O'Neill, Felix, Corhammock
Pillow, Richard, Mullaghbrack
Pillow, Robert, Mullurg
Porter, James, Lurgaboy
Pringle, James, Magherydogherty
Quinn, Joseph, Manordogherty
Quinn, Robert, Magherydogherty
Rush, Hugh, Tannaghmore
Scott, John, Lurgaboy
Sharp, John, Tanaghmore
Sheppard, Ferguson, Lurgaboy
Sheppard, Robert, Drumfergus
Sheppard, Samuel, S'crackenbe
Shields, George, Dennismullen
Shields, Samuel, Bryandrum
Small, Alex. (J.P.), Lattery
Small, John, Shanecrackenmore
Small, J. G., Shanecrackenmore
Spence, Henry, Garvagh
Spence, James, Drumatee
Spence, James, Retarnet
Spence, John Thomas, Mullabrack
Spence, Lewis, Drumatee
Steel, J. H., Carron
Taggart, Mrs. A., M'naverry
Thompson, David, Manordogherty
Torrens, Robert, Bryandrum

Torrens, William, Markethill
Tweedie, Samuel, Coolmillish
Wallace, Adam, Markethill
Wallace, Hugh, Bryandrum
Wallace, James, Mullabrack
Wallace, John R., Mullabrack
Wallace, William H., Cornacrew
Wann, James C. (J.P.), Markethill

Watson, John, Lurgaboy
Welsh, William, Coolmillish
Whiteside, James, S'crackenmore
Willis, William, Magherydogherty
Wilson, Daniel, Dennismullen
Wilson, James, Edenkennedy
Wilson, William F., Corhammock

MOWHAN.

MOWHAN is 2 miles south-east of Markethill and 7 miles south-east of Armagh. Markethill is the nearest railway station. There are 15 houses, including the post office. A small trout stream runs through the valley in which the village is prettily situated. The land of the district is fair for tillage and pasture. Oats, potatoes, and flax are the chief crops. Butter-making is almost confined to prints and "bricks."

Blacksmith : Robert McKenna
Churches : Presbyterian, Rev. John Entrican ; Reformed Presbyterian, Rev. Wm. McKnight
Corn and Scutch Mills : George Dougan. Tow Mill : S. and W. Byers
Grocer, Draper, &c. : Hy. G. Woods
Post M. : Henry G. Woods
School, National : Hy. Doherty

Farmers & Residents
Agnew, George, Killbracks
Agnew, John, Killbracks
Armstrong, James, Drumgane
Armstrong, James, Killbracks
Buchanan, James, Lurgyross
Byers, Samuel (J.P.), Mowhan
Byers, William, Mowhan
Carlisle, Alex., jun., Ballylane
Copeland, George, Killbracks
Cordner, William, Ballylane

Cowan, Arthur, Creenagh
Cromie, W. J., Drumalaragh
Dougan, George, Ballylane
Dougan, Samuel, Ballylane
Elliott, James, Killbracks
Gass, William, Ballylane
Gilmore, John, Killbracks
Jennings, Patrick, Derlett
Johnston, Hans, Ballylane
Kilpatrick, David, Crunaght
Kilpatrick, Thomas, Ballylane
M'Ewan, John, Derlett
M'Kean, Nicholas, Drumnagane
Mallaghan, Owen, Cladymore
Martin, James, Ballylane
Martin, John, Ballylane
Martin, Rev. John E., Derlett
Martin, Samuel W., Ballylane
Martin, Samuel, Ballylane
Martin, William, Ballylane
Mitchell, Mrs. Agnes, Drumnagan
Scott, Thomas, Derlett

Stevenson, Clarke, Ballylane	Thompson, Thomas, Kilbracks
Stevensohn, Robert, Drumgane	Whiteside, Samuel, Kilbracks
Taylor, Robert, Ballylane	Wilson, William, Kilbracks

JAMES * DEIGHAN,

General Merchant,

THE COMMERCIAL HOTEL AND POSTING ESTABLISHMENT,

MIDDLETOWN.

Departments :—

Groceries.	Farm and Garden Seeds·
Provisions.	Artificial Manures.
Bacon Curing.	Patent Medicines.
Wines and Spirits.	Stationery.
Hardware.	Paints, Oils, Colors and
Timber and Iron.	Varnishes.
Coal.	Funeral Undertaking.

PETER CORR,

COAL, IRON, TIMBER, PROVISION & SEED MERCHANT, GROCER, &c.,

ARTIFICIAL MANURES, OILS, PAINTS, & WINDOW GLASS,

MIDDLETOWN.

MIDDLETOWN.

Population 348 in 1881.

MIDDLETOWN is in the barony of Turanny, on the western border of the county, 8 miles, Irish, south-west of Armagh. Tynan, 4 miles north by east is the nearest railway station. The village consists of two principal streets, containing many well built houses. It is situated in a valley sourrounded by hills, none of which rise to a great height. The land of the district is good. Oats and potatoes are the chief crops. Flax and wheat are grown in a small way. Dairying is carried on to some extent by nearly every farmer. The butter is put up in squares, called "meskins." A market for butter and eggs is held every Thursday. There is a splendid markethouse, erected by the Trustees of Dr. Sterne's Charity, in 1829. Fifty years ago there were markets three times a week; for grain on Wednesday and Saturday, and for provisions on Thursday. The markets mainly served the purposes of a distillery established in 1831 by Mr. Matthew Johnston. The consumption of raw grain by it was 12,000 barrels per annum, and the output 80,000 gallons of whiskey. The failure of the distillery caused the discontinuance of the markets on Wednesday and Saturday. Dr. Sterne, Bishop of Clogher, bequeathed to trustees for benevolent purposes the village and eight townlands in the district parish, with five townlands in the adjoining parish of Donagh, County Monaghan. An Act passed by the Irish Parliament in 1772 incorporates the trustees. The market-house, school-house, dispensary and fever hospital were built for the benefit of the tenantry. Near the fever hospital, no longer used for its original purpose, an obelisk commemorates David Smith, M.D., 8 years its medical superintendent, died 1847. The school and dispensary are also given up. Brick manufacture is now the chief industry of the neighborhood. There is a large tract of blue clay which is being successfully worked. Middletown has acquired fame in the English markets as a centre for horse-finishing. There are two libraries in the village, each having a reading room attached. One was established about two years ago through the instrumentality of Miss Frances Irwin, and the other in 1887. Mr. James Deighan is chairman of the latter, and there are 64 members. The Convent of St. Louis was established about 6 years ago in a house left by the parish priest, since enlarged. It has a flourishing ladies' school, a school under the National Board of Education, and an Industrial School. Mrs. O'Donovan is the superioress. There are several ancient earthen forts in the neighborhood of Middletown, chief among which are Rathtrillick. Ardgonnell and Crifcairn Castles, strongholds of the O'Neill's, are described at page 33. Middletown used to have good fairs. They were given up some years ago.

Baker: Thos. M'Bennett

Blacksmiths: Thos. Agnew, Jas Finegan, Jas. M'Comb

Brick manftrs.: A. Burke, W. A. Bryans, Edw. Hughes, Jas. Hughes, Hy. Magee, Owen Sherry

Butter and Egg Shipper: Jas. Deighan

Carpenters: Jas. Hamilton, Rt. Harper

Churches: C. I., Rev. Alex. Irwin. Presbyn., Rev. D. Boyd.

R.C., Rev. Charles M'Evoy, P.P.;
Rev. B. O'Connor, C.C.
  Cooper: Jas. Ward
  Corn mills : Jas. Hughes, Jno.
Johnston
  Dispensary station : Dr. Rt. T.
Huston
  Drapers : J. and E. M'Namee,
Jos. Thompson
  Education: Convent, Ladies'
School, Mrs. O'Donovan, su-
perioress. National schools : Con-
vent, Rt. Jamison, Geo. Rowan
  Grocers : marked thus * retail
spirits, † hardware. ‡ seeds: Augus-
tine Burke*, Peter Corr †‡, James
Deighan*†‡, Wm. J. Graham*,
Jno. M'Carron, Jno. M'Quaide*,
Jos. Thompson, Patk. Treanor
  AUGUSTINE BURKE,
Tea, wine, provision and spirit
merchant, brick manufacturer,
farmer, and agent for the State
line of steamships to America
  Hotel keepers : Jas. Deighan,
W. J. Graham
  Library and Reading room : Jas.
Deighan, chairman ; Hy. Develin,
Thos. Agnew, secretaries ; F.
Donnelly, treas.
  Library and Reading room: Miss
Frances Irwin, Promoter
  Market : Thursday
  Petty sessions last Saturday of
every month : John Magrath, clerk
  Posting cars : Jas. Deighan
  Post. M.: Mrs. H. Johnston
  Process server : Hy. Craig
  R.I.C.: Sergt. O. M'Cabe
  Saddler : Thos. Harvey
  Scutch mill : A. W. Redmond
  Stamp distributor : Jas. Deighan
  Timber, iron and coal : Peter
Corr, James Deighan
  Undertaker : Jas. Deighan
  Farmers & Residents
Agnew, F., Middletown
Brians, Richard, Foyduff
Brians, W. A., Foyduff
Bryans, John, Drumgarron

Burke, Matthew (J.P.), Middletown
Campbell, Wm., Ardgonnell
Carroll, Bernard, Skerries
Carroll, Thomas, Skerries
Charleton, Sl., Tullyglush (Nevin)
Clinton, John, Ardgonnell
Cox, John, Reen
Daly, Hugh, Doogary
Davidson, Wm., Crievekeeran
Donnelly, Patrick, Drumgose
Drum, John, Coolkill
Farnan, John, Mullanary
Farrell, James, Doogary
Flanagan, James, Crossdall
Gaffney, Thomas, Carricklane
Gall, John, Ardgonnell
Gormell, Michael, Carricklane
Gormelly, James, Doogary
Graham, George, Crann
Gray, John, Creevekeeran
Gubby, John, Skerries
Hanlon, John, Creevekeeran
Hamilton, George, Crossdall
Harvey, Patrick, Rathcumber
Hawthorne, G., Tullyglush(Nevin)
Hughes, Bernard, Coolkill
Hughes, Christr., Reen
Hughes, Edwd., Drumgose
Hughes, James, Drumgarron
Hughes, James, Rathtrillick
Hughes, James, Drumakeen
Hughes, James, Knockbane
Hughes, James, Shantilly
Hughes, John, Hanslough
Hughes, John, Mullinary
Hughes, John, Shantilly
Hughes, Joseph, Rathcumber
Hughes, Michael, Drumgose
Hughes, Patrick, Rathtrillick
Hughes, Patrick, Kiltubrid
Hughes, Thomas, Bondville
Irwin, Misses, Annagold
Johnston, Wm., Doogary
Kelly, Christr., Creevekeeran
Kelly, Fr., Hanslough
Kirkpatrick, Matthew, Kiltubrid
Lappin, John, Crann
Lappin, John, Shantilly
Loughrane, Owen, Caricklane
M'Ardle, Bernard, Mullanary

M'Ardle, Francis, Rathcumber
M'Ateer, John, Creevekeeran
M'Bennett, Edward, Crossdall
M'Caffrey, Daniel, Rathtrillick
M'Carron, James, Middletown
M'Coombe, T., T'ybrick, Hamilton
M'Coy, Patrick, Doogary
M'Donnell, Felix, Carricklane
M'Garvey, William, Unshog
M'Grenan, Patrick, Foyduff
M'Keever, Patrick, Reen
M'Kenna, Francis, Unshog
M'Kernan, Charles, Drumaheen
M'Kernan, Francis, Drumaheen
M'Kerney, Henry, Crossdall
M'Nally, Francis, Kiltubrit
M'Nally, James, Kiltubrit
M'Naughtan, Ml., Drumgose
M'Parland, Matthew, Cavandoogan
M'Quade, Jas., Tullyglush (Nevin)
Mallon, Francis, Mullinary
Mallon, Ptk., Lislanley
Mallon, Patrick, Doogary
Mallon, Thomas, Doogary
Mallon, Thomas, Lislanley
Martin, William, Ardgonnell

Mooney, John, Cavandoogan
Mallon, Robert, Carricklane
Mooney, Terence, Crossdall
O'Neill, Henry, Tullyglush
Parks, John, Foyduff
Parks, Samuel, Carricklane
Potter, Robert, Skerries
Quinn, James, Hanslough
Reddock, Mrs. Glasdrummond
Rolstone, Robert, Shantilly
Rush, Daniel. Coolkill
Rush, John, Hanslough
Rush, Pr.. Tullyglush (Nevin)
Russell, William, Doogary
Sergeant, Mrs., Annarea
Stewart, James, Creevekeeran
Stewart, Robert, Hanslough
Thornton, John, Doogary
Todd, Samuel, Carricklane
Trainor, Patrick, Glassdrummond
Treanor, Thomas, Glassdrummond
Wade, Jas., M.D., R.N., J.P.
Wilson, Geo., Rathcumber
Wilson, Richard, Drumahane
Wilson, Samuel, Hanslough
Woods, James, Bondville

MOUNTNORRIS.

Trout Fishing.

OUNTNORRIS is a village of about 20 houses, 3 miles south-east of Markethill. Loughgilly, one mile, is the nearest railway station. The Cusher at this point is often good for brown trout, and attracts many anglers. The land of the district is of medium quality. Oats, potatoes and flax are the chief crops. A large part of the area is devoted to flax. Dairying is carried on to some extent. the produce being made up in "bricks." Mountnorris once had fairs. but none have been held for many years. The place owes its origin to the erection of a fortress by Lord Mountjoy during the rebellion of the Earl of Tyrone 1594-1603. At that time a morass, often containing a considerable amount of water, extended north to Poyntzpass, a distance of about 5 miles· It was called Loughgilly. The lough was removed by drainage. Mountnorris was named to compliment the commander, Gen. Norris. The fortress was one of the strongest in Ulster at the time of Charles I. He granted a charter for the maintenance of a college here, but Armagh having been regarded as a more suitable location, a transfer was made in favor of that city. See Royal School, page 81.

Brick mftr.: Sl. Girvin
Churches : Presbyterian, Rev. W. J. Lowe ; R.C., Rev. Thos. Donnelly, P.P.
Dispensary station : Dr. A. G. Young
Drapers : Mrs. A. Girvin, W. H. Magowan
Grocers : Miss M. Edgar, Mrs. A. Girvin, Mrs. E. M‘Cullough, W. H. Magowan
Post M.: Rt. Walker
Process server : Richd. Irwin
R.I.C.: Sergt. Jno. Latimer
School, Natl.: Hugh Morrison
Spirit retailer : none

Farmers & Residents

Aikens, John, Tullyherran
Boyle, Edward, Lisnalee
Clarke, Mrs., Steeple hill
Collins, John, Mountnorris
Feenan, Francis, Port hill
Hughes, William, Mountnorris
Gass, Mrs. Tullyallen
Girvan, R. J., Tullyherron
Girvan, S. G., Tullyherron
Hadden, John, Crankey
Halliday, John, Lisnalee
Harris, Henry, Lisnalee
Harron, Arcd., Tullyherron
Hutchinson, Wm., Mountnorris
Ingram, Thomas, Keadymore
Irwin, Arcd., Keadymore
Irwin, George, Keadybeg

Irwin, John, Keadymore
Irwin, Jos. J., Keadymore
Irwin, T., sen, Keadymore
Irwin, Wm., Keadybeg
Lockhart, Wm., Lisnalee
Lowe, Stephen, Lisnalee
M‘Clelland, James, Keadybeg
M‘Combe, Robert, Keadybeg
M‘Combe, Samuel, Keadybeg
M‘Corkill, Leonard, Mountnorris
M‘Court, Mrs. A., Port hill
M‘Cullough, Mrs., Tullyallen
M‘Dowell, Robert, Tullyallen
M‘Elroy, Hugh, Keadybeg
M‘Elroy, Hugh, Keadymore
M‘Murray, James Lisnalee
M‘Murray, William, Keadybeg
M‘Parland, Patrick, Tullyherron
M‘Pherson, Thomas, Lisnalee
Marshall, Gilbert, Portnorris
Marshall, Gilbert, Keadybeg
Magowan, Wm. H., Tullyherron
Mullins, David, Tullyherron
Qua, John, Mountnorris
Russell, Chr., Mountnorris
Russell, John, Mountnorris
Scott, John, Keadymore
Sleeth, Thomas, Tullyherron
Thompson, James, Lisnalee
Thompson, John, Lisnalee
Vallely, Neal, Cladymore
Walker, Robert, Mountnorris
Walker, Wm. J., Mountnorris

RICHHILL.

Population 595 in 1881.

ICHHILL is 4¾ miles by rail east by north from Armagh. The village is about a mile from the railway station. It is in the parish of Kilmore, and barony of O'Neilland west. The greater part of the houses are built on the side and top of a hill most appropriately named, insomuch that it commands a full view of a country rich in

COURSE LODGE, RICHHILL,

ESTABLISHED 1861.

A PRIVATE INSTITUTION FOR MENTAL AND NERVOUS INVALIDS.

EXCLUSIVELY for the RECEPTION of LADIES.

Resident Proprietors—JAMES and WILLIAM ORR.

Supervisional Management—The MISSES ORR.

Visiting Physician—HENRY FRAZER, M.D., L.R.C.S.I., Armagh.

Consulting Physician—ROBERT GRAY, L.K.Q.C.P.I., Armagh.

Full information and Forms of Admission on application.

pastures, plantations, orchards, and grain fields. The chief feature of attraction in the immediate vicinity is Richhill Castle, a stately turreted mansion, standing in a fine demesne. It was built by the Richardson family, and at present belongs to Col. Richardson. Mr. Henry Tate, J.P., is the tenant. Col. Richardson and Lord Gosford own the village and district. Richhill, at the beginning of the century, was one of the important linen markets in Ulster. The weekly sales averaged £2,600. After the opening of the railway between Armagh and Belfast, it began to decline as a market, and a great many of the hand-loom weavers moved away. Just now there are in the district from 200 to 300. Linen yarns are given to them by Portadown and Tandragee manufacturers. There is no market for produce held, and many years have passed since the repose of the village was disturbed by the holding of a fair. Two tanneries and a preserve factory are the chief industries. Oats, potatoes and wheat are the crops relied upon for rent-making. The Protestant Episcopalians (C.I.), Presbyterians, Methodists, Independents, Roman Catholics, and Society of Friends have places of worship.

COURSE LODGE.

THERE are ample facilities at Course Lodge for the successful treatment of mental diseases and nervous affections. It is situated in a beautiful district of country, sufficiently elevated to ensure good sanitary conditions, with the necessary seclusion to maintain perfect serenity. To these advantages are added well-shaded walks, bowered resting places, and a cozy tea house. Course Lodge was originally the private residence of Mr. James Orr, granduncle of the present proprietors, Messrs. James and William Orr. That was 80 years ago. It possesses the peculiar features of a quiet country home, and there is nothing in the surroundings to suggest a curtailment of liberty to the patient who is being gradually restored to sanity. In 1861 the late Mr. John Orr, father of Messrs. J. & W. Orr, converted Course Lodge to the purposes of an institution for mental and nervous invalids. Since then a large number of permanent cures have been effected. Lady patients only—of the higher class—are taken, and of these the institution is licensed to accommodate fifteen. A farm of fifty acres belonging to the Messrs. Orr, provides fruit, vegetables, milk, eggs and poultry in abundance. The preserves are all made on the premises. The patients rise at eight o'clock in the morning. Breakfast is served at nine o'clock, dinner at two o'clock, tea at six o'clock, and supper between eight and nine o'clock. Nine o'clock is bed-time. Nearly all the bread given to the patients is home-made, and of wheaten flour. A clergyman of some denomination—Church of Ireland, Presbyterian, Methodist, or Independent—visits the house once a week. Reading, music, draughts and chess, are the indoor amusements provided. The dietary adopted during preliminary treatment consists for the greater part of vegetables, milk, eggs and poultry. In the advances toward convalescence a building-up process is begun, in which beef, mutton and fish are freely used. Course Lodge is within half a mile of the village of Richhill, two miles of the Richhill Railway Station, and less than a mile from the railway station at Hamiltonsbawn. Numerous testimonials from medical men, including Dr. G. W. Hatchell, Commissioner of Lunacy, bear testimony to the fitness of Course Lodge for the object to which it is devoted, and to the kindly and judicious methods practiced by the proprietors.

RICHHILL DIRECTORY.

Blacksmiths : Thos. Gardner, Thos. M'Donagh

Cabinet makers : Wm. Connor, Joseph Towell

Churches, &c.: C. I., Rev. C. R. Williams ; Friends ; Independent, Rev. Dd. Sampson ; Methodist, Armagh Circuit ; Presbyterian, Rev. Geo. Gillespie ; R. C., Rev. Jos. Dunne

Coal and timber : Jas. Best & Sons, Wolsey Kane

Dispensary : Dr. Thos. A. Griffiths, Med. Officer; Attendance, Mon., Wed., and Frid., 10 to 11.30 a.m.

Committee—Earl of Gosford, J.P., Gosford Castle, Market hill ; John A. M. Cope, J.P., Drummilly ho., Loughgall ; John G. Winder, J.P., Armagh; Major J. H. Stronge, J.P., Hockley lodge, Armagh ; Colonel Dobbin, J.P., Armagh ; John Jackson, Richhill ; James Hobson, Kilmore, Richhill ; Jas. Best, Armagh ; Jacob Jenkinson, Armagh ; Moses Robinson, Grange O'Neiland, Loughgall ; Edward Reilly, Drummanmore, Armagh ; Thos. Wynne, jun., Sandymount, Richhill ; Jos. Robinson, Drumnahunchion, Richhill ; John Hall, Annaboe, Richhill ; Francis J. Best, Richhill

Meeting of Committee first Monday every month at noon

Wardens—John Albin, Rockmacreany ; Jacob Best, Richhill ; Dd. McClelland, Annahue ; Jos. Trouton, Mullylelish, Richhill

Drapers, Undertakers, &c.: Jas. Best & Sons, Wolsey Kane

Education : Ladies' School, Miss Bradshaw ; National Schools, Edw. Troughton, Miss J. Kendrick

Furniture Manufac. : Jos. Towell

Grocers : marked thus [*] retail spirits, [†] hardware, [‡] seeds. Jas. Best & Sons, †‡ ; Mrs. J. Ford,* ; W. J. Hoy,* ; A. Hutchison,* ; Jno. Jackson, Wolsey Kane, †‡ ; Robt. Magowan, Jos. Towell

Loan Fund : Jas. Best & Sons

Lunatic Asylum : Private (Ladies), Course lodge ; J. & W. Orr
Marine Store, &c.: Geo. Nesbitt
Postm. : Wolsey Kane
Preserve Manuf. : Lamb Bros., Fruitfield
R. I. C. : Sergeant Dd. Kane
Weighbridge, Wm. Best
Tanners : John Jackson, reps. of A. Hardy

Farmers & Residents

Albin, Chris., Rockmacraney
Albin, Jas., Rockmacraney
Albin, John, Rockmacraney
Albin, Robert, Rockmacraney
Albin, Thomas, Shewis
Albin, William, Rockmacraney
Allen, Samuel, Mulnasilly
Bell, William, Rockmacraney
Best, Fr. J., Richhill
Best, Jacob B., Richhill
Best, Wm. (P.R.C.), Richhill
Boyce, Elisha, Corcreevy
Bunting, Thos., Mullaletragh
Burke, James, Macantrim
Callaghan, Wm., Ballyleny
Carson, James, Ballynahinch
Cartmill, Mrs. L., Mullaletragh
Chambers, Alex., Mullalelish
Chambers, L., Mullalelish
Clement, John, Tullygarden
Clinton, Nicholas, Tullygarden
Cranston, John, Ballyleny
Donaldson, Jas., Drumnahuncheon
Finnegan, John, Drumnahuncheon
Forker, James, Mulladry
Forker, Samuel, Ballyleany
Fullerton, John, R'macreaney
Gardner, John, Liskyborough
Gowdy, James, Ballygroobany
Greer, H. Mullalelish
Greer, Jas. (Wee), Mullalelish
Greer, Miss, Ballynahinch
Greer, Mrs., Ballynahinch
Greer, Wm., Richhill
Guy, John, Tullygarden
Halligan, Wm. J., R'macreaney
Hardy, Charles, Richhill
Hardy, Mrs., Woodlawn
Hardy, T. H., Woodlawn

Harker, Miss, Ballyleaney
Hayes, Robert, Drumnahuncheon
Heatley, Jas., jun., Ballynahinch
Heatley, Philip, Ballynahinch
Henderson, Samuel, Cavan
Hardy, Charles, Richhill
Hewitt, Atkinson, Mullaletra
Hewitt, John, Mullaletra
Hewitt, Ios., Ballynahinch
Hewitt, Mark, Mullaletra
Hewitt, Robinson, D'huncheon
Hewitt, Wm., Mulladry
Hill, John, Corry
Hutchinson, Alex., Turcarra
Hutchinson, James, Ballynahinch
Hutchinson, John, Ballynahinch
Hutchinson, John, Liskyboro'
Hutchinson, Rd., Liskyboro'
Irwin, James, Cavan
Irwin, John, Crewcat
Irwin, Johnson, Shewis
Irwin, William, Crewcat
Irwin, William, Shewis
Jackson, Edward, D'huncheon
Jackson, John, Richhill
Jenkinson, Abraham, Cloughan
Johnston, John, Rockmacreany
Johnston, John, Liskyboro'
Johnston, Joseph, Mecantrim
Jones, James, Ballyloughan
Kane, David Wolsey, Richhill
Kane, Wolsey, Richhill
Kelly, James, Turcarra
Kelly, Thomas, Turcarra
Lamb, Charles B., Fruitfield
Lamb, Rd. H., Fruitfield
Logan, George, Ballynahinch
Loney, Thomas, Crewcat
Loney, Thomas, Liskeyboro
Long, Moses, Cloughan
M'Alister, Geo., Drumard Jones
M'Alister, Jas., Cavan
M'Alister, Wm., Drumard Jones
M'Clatchy, James, Mullalelish
M'Clatchy, Rd., Ballynahinch
M'Cune, Wm., Mullalelish
M'Gowan, Thos., Tullygarden
M'Quillan, J., Drumnahuncheon
Mackey, Joseph, Richhill
Major, Singleton, Liskeyboro

Murray, Francis, Turcara
Orr, Gibbins, Macantrim
Orr, James, Course lodge
Orr, William, Course lodge
Person, Isaac, D'huncheon
Person, John, Mullaletragh

Person, Joseph, Shewis
Person, Robert, Crewcat
Person, Sl., Drumard Jones
Pierson, John, Tullygarden
Proctor, James, Richhill
(Continued on opposite page.)

Redmond, A. W., Maynooth
Redmond, D. W., Ballyleny
Reid, John, Ballyleny
Riddall, Walter, Richhill
Robinson, Joseph, D'huncheon
Rountree, John, Mullaletragh
Running, W., Mullinasilla
Scott, Francis, Cloughan
Sinton, John, Greenmount
Sinton, Thomas, Greenmount
Spence, Samuel, Annareagh
Spence, Thomas, Ballyleny
Steenson, John, Ballynahinch
Stothers, George, Cavan
Tate, Hy. (J.P.), The Castle
Todd, James, Drumnahuncheon
Troughton, J., sen., Mullalelish
Troughton, J., jun., Mullalelish
Troughton, Jos., sen., Mullalelish
Troughton, Jos., jun., Mullalelish
Troughton, Thos., Drumard Jones
Troughton, T., sen., Mullalelish
Troughton, T., jun., Mullalelish
Walker, James, Mulladry
Weir, Mark, Mullaletragh
Weir Thomas, Corcreevy
Williamson, W., Rockmacreaney
Wilson, Edw., Mullalelish
Wilson, James E., Ballyleny
Wilson, J. H., Mullalelish
Wilson, Jones, Mullalelish
Wilson, Joseph, Mullalelish
Wilson, Robert, Corry
Wilson, Singleton, Richhill
Wilson, S., jun., Mullalelish
Wilson, Wm., Ballyleny
Wynne, T., jun., Sandymount

TARTARAGHAN.

ARTARAGHAN is 9 miles north-east of Armagh, and 4 miles north-east of Loughgall. The land is stiff and heavy, but when properly treated yields good crops of potatoes, wheat and oats. A great many hand-loom linen weavers live in this district, cultivate small farms, and are fruit-growers in a modest way.

Churches: C. I., Rev. Nicholas H. James ; Presbyterian; R. C., Rev. F. Byrnes, P.P.

Dispensary : Dr. Geo. Dougan, Medical Officer. Attendance Tuesday and Friday

Committee—Right Hon. Lord Lurgan, Brownlow house, Lurgan ; John Sinnamon, Derryanville, Portadown ; J. Crockett, Legany, Portadown ; John M'Clelland, Derrylard, Tartaraghan ; John M'Clure, Milltown, Portadown ; James Carrick, Foymore, Portadown ; Samuel Woodhouse, Drumlellum, Portadown ; Richard Robinson, Diviney, Portadown ; George Carter, Derryall, Portadown ; Wm. M'Adam, Cloncore, Tartaraghan ; Wm. Robb, Derrybroughas, Portadown ; George Baxter, Breagh, Tartaraghan ; Henry Sinnamon, Clonamola, Portadown ; W. Forsythe, Derrymattry, Portadown ; James Mercer, Breagh, Portadown ; Thomas John Hall, Derrycorey, Portadown ; Thomas Atkinson, Ballyfodrin, Portadown ; Thomas Woodhouse, Derrinraw, Portadown

This Committee meets in the Town Hall, Portadown, on the First Saturday in each month, at Two o'clock p.m.

Post Master : Jas. Conlin

School, Natl. : Thos. Matchett

Farmers & Residents

Allen, Richard, Clonmacash
Arklow, Jno., Carnagolamore
Baxter, George, Breagh
Benson, John, Carnagolamore
Benson, William, Carnogolamore
Boyce, John, Breagh
Boyce, Mrs. M., Breagh
Conlon, John, Clontilew
Conn, Joseph, Clonmacash

Conn, Mrs. M., Clonmacash
Conn, Thomas, Cloncarrish
Conn, T. W., Clonmacash
Creely, Mrs. E., Tartlogue
Hamill, Daniel, Breagh
Johnson, Mrs. M., Tartlogue
Lavery, Edward, Carnagolamore
Lavery, Patrick, Carnagolamore
Lester, John, Breagh
M'Conville, William Breagh
M'Fall, Thomas, jun., Breagh
Matchell, Mrs. E., Breagh

Mercer, James, Breagh
Mercer, William, Breagh
Milsop, David, Breagh
Mulholland, Ptk., Carnagolamore
Obre, Edw. S., Clontilew
Platt, George, Clonmacash
Telford, Thomas, Cloncarish
Waugh, George, Carnagolamore
Williamson, James, Tarthlogue
Williamson, William, Breagh
Wilson, J. J., Carnagolabeg
Wilson, Thomas Breagh

TASSAGH.

ASSAGH is a beautifully situated village of a few houses, in the valley of the Callan, 5½ miles south of Armagh, and 2 miles north-east of Keady. The Redford Linen Co., Limited, of Redford, Moy, Co. Tyrone, have a branch here for the manufacture, by power-loom. of buckrams, hollands, etc., and for beetle-finishing and dyeing. Employment is provided for about 70 people. The land of the district is fair. Oats, potatoes and flax are the chief crops. Considerable interest attaches to the burial ground at the foot of the village. It was originally laid out for the use of the Culdean Priory of Armagh. The Culdees were secular priests serving in the choir of the ancient cathedral of St. Patrick. Their President officiated as Precentor. The Priory occupied a site in Castle Street, and was largely endowed. In the reign of Charles I. the revenues appear to have been received by the Archbishops. In 1625 its endowments were made over to the Vicars Choral of Armagh. While excavating in the graveyard at Tassagh, 1824, a massive gold ring was found. It contained a large emerald in a rich setting.

Blacksmith : John O'Hanlon
Churches : Presbyterian, Rev. David M'Clelland ; R. C., Rev. P.Corr,P.P.,Rev. F. M'Niece,C.C.
Corn Mills : Mrs. B. Boyd, Henry M'Farren
Grocers : (*) are spirit retailers, Miss Ann Cullen, Mrs. N. Cunningham,* Mrs. N. M'Cartan*
Linen Manufacturers, buckrams, and hollands, Redford Linen Co., Limited
Postmaster : John Wilson
Schools, National : Joseph Lilley, Balleen ; Bd. M'Veigh, Granemore
Scutch Mills : Thomas Ferguson, Henry M'Farren, John Phœnix

Farmers & Residents

Allen, Robert G., Killyfaddy
Atkinson, John, Tassagh
Barcroft, T. M., J.P., Dundrum House
Blackley, John, Darkley
Birch, John, Ballibrolly
Blackley, Robert, Tassagh
Cassidy, John, Tandragee
Connory, John, Granemore

Conroy, Michael, Granemore
Conroy, John, Granemore
Conry, John, jun., Keady
Corr, James, Granemore
Corr, Peter, Granemore
Corry, John, Tassagh
Courtenay, David, Tassagh
Crookshanks, J. R., Killyfaddy
Cruikshanks, Robt. J., Killyfaddy
Cullan, Patrick, Tassagh
Cunningham, Mrs., Killyfaddy
Cunningham, Robert, Killyfaddy
Cunningham, William, Killyfaddy
Donnelly, Henry, Granemore
Dunleavy, Henry, Ballinagalliagh
Ferguson, Thomas, Balleer
Fleming, George, Corkley
Flemming, William, Corkley
Garvey, Bernard, Balleer
Gordon, Adam, Tassagh
Gordon, Andrew, Tassagh
Gordon, Andrew, Dundrum
Gorman, Michael, Ballybrolly
Gordon, George, Dundrum
Hanley, William, Corkley
Hanlon, Hugh, Ballybrolly
Hughes, Henry, Granemore
Hunter, James, Killyfaddy
Johnston, Frank, Tullybrone
Johnston, Thomas, Killyfaddy
Keenan, Owen, Granemore
Lappen, Charles, Cabragh
M'Ardle, Patrick, Granemore
M'Cann, James, Balleer
M'Cardle, Peter, Granemore
M'Clung, James, Killyfaddy
M'Clung, Maxwell, Killyfaddy

M'Clung, Samuel, Killyfaddy
M'Cabe, James, Darkley
M'Cormick, John, Darkley
M'Kinstry, Edward, Broughan
Maggeniss, Hugh, Ballybrally
Merry, James, Darkley
Merry, John, Darkley
Miskelly, Rev. James, Darkley
Moffatt, John, Ballybrawley
Moffett, Robert, Broughan
Moffatt, Thomas, Killyfaddy
Moore, John, Tassagh
Moore, John, Darkley
Murphy, John, Granemore
Nugent, Edward, Granemore
Nugent, Hugh, Corkley
Nugent, Thomas, Balleer
Nugent, Thomas, Broughan
Nugent, William, Tassagh
Paxton, William, Granemore
Phœnix, John, Glenburn
Porter, William, Corkley
Quinn, Arthur, Balleer
Quinn, Bernard, Broughan
Quinn, Patrick, Broughan
Quinn, Thomas, jun., Broughan
Quinn, Thomas, sen., Broughan
Quinn, Thomas, Broughan
Reany, Robert, Balleer
Reid, Joseph, Balleer
Short, Patrick, Tassagh
Smith, Samuel, Granemore
Stephenson, William, Ballybrolly
Trodden, James, Broughan
Trodden, Terce., jun., Ballybrolly
Valvelly, Michael, Darkley
Warmington, Joseph, Balleer

TYNAN.

YNAN is a village in the parish of same name, 7 miles south-west of Armagh, by road, and the same distance by rail. The land consists of a rich loam, much of it being on a limestone basis. The village is pleasantly situated upon an eminence surrounded by hills and richly planted demesnes. Originally, the parish of Tynan was of wide extent, and included the district parishes of Killylea and Middletown. Tynan Abbey, the residence of Sir John Calvert Stronge, Bart. is the place of greatest interest in the neighborhood. It

O

is open to the public. In the splendidly wooded demesne there are two crosses, one plain, standing on an arch over a well, is found to the right of the avenue leading to Caledon. It is about 7 feet high. A sculptured cross stands in one of the streets of the village. The ancient Irish name of Tynan was *Tuidhnedha*. Dr. O'Donovan, in the *Annals*, refers to it as being mentioned in O'Clery's Irish Calander at the 28th of August, as the Church of St. Uindic. In Pope Nicholas's Taxation, 1291, the parish of Tynan is enumerated as belonging to the Culdee Priory of Armagh, and it continued to be so held for some time after many of the religious houses had been dissolved.

Tynan has a library in connection with the Church of Ireland. The members only pay a subscription each of 1s. a year. A steam tramway runs from the Tynan Railway Station up the Clogher Valley via Caledon. Oats, potatoes and flax are the chief crops in the parish.

The rural post office of Derryhaw is served from Tynan. Its principal farmers will be found named under the Tynan list of Farmers and Residents.

Blacksmith : Willliam Gordon

Carpenter : John Gaskin

Churches : C.I., Rev. Robert J. Shaw, Rev. George H. La Nauze; Methodist, Armagh Circuit; Presbyterian, Rev. Thos. Irvine ; R.C., Rev. Charles McEvoy, P.P.

Corn and Scutch Mill : John Magrath

Dispensary : Dr. Robert T. Huston, Medical Officer. Attendance : Wednesday and Saturday, 11 a.m. to 1 p.m. Committee : Sir Calvert Stronge, Bart., J.P., Tynan Abbey, Tynan ; Earl of Gosford, J.P., Gosford Castle ; St. J. T. Blacker-Douglas, J.P , Elm Park ; Major Tenison, J.P., Portnelligan ; Henry B. Armstrong, J.P., Killylea ; Colonel Dobbin, J.P., Armagh ; Colonel Simpson, J.P., Ballyards House, Armagh ; Joseph Marshall, Cappy, Tynan ; John McNamee, Middletown ; James Deighan, Middletown ; John Gamble, Lisagally House, Killylea ; John Gillespie, Lislooney, Tynan ; John Knipe, Derrydarragh, Killylea ; Francis M'Allister,

Dartan, Killylea ; Cornelius Hughes, Dartan House, Killylea ; James Mills, Brootally, Killylea ; Matthew Burke, J.P., Middletown ; A. St. George, Woodpark, Tynan ; Wm. Gamble, Derryhaw, Killylea.

Meeting of Committee, first Saturday, every month, at noon. Wardens : Robert Mills, Brootally ; George Hamilton, Crossdall ; Charles M'Aleavy, Raws ; Hugh J. Robinson, Lisdrumbrughas ; Robert McCullagh, Kilcreevy-Etra ; James McAree, Lislooney ; Thomas Orr, Tynan ; Major Bond, J.P., Bondville.

Education : Erasmus Smith's School, Thomas Orr ; Infant School (Lady Stronge), Miss R. Murray ; National, Miss M. Ross, Tynan ; John Corr, Manooney.

Grocers : Dd. Callaghan ; Chas. Holmes.

Library : Lending

Petty Sessions, Monthly : John Magrath.

Post M.: Miss S. E. Murray

Railways : Great Northern, Charles Kenny. Toll Collector,

Clogher Valley Steam Tramway
  R.I.C.: Sergt. Richard Martin
Farmers & Residents
Allen, Joseph, Kennedies
Anderson, John, Breaghy
Armstrong, James, Cortynan
Bond, Major E. W., Bondvill
Brownlee, John, Mullen
Brownlee, Thomas, Tynan
Bunting, Taylor, T'hamilton
Busby, Archibald, Enagh
Busby, Robert, College Hall
Clarke, John, Breaghy
Couser, W. J. Mullen
Craig, Nathl., Breaghy
Dixon, Thomas, Drumhillery
Donaldson, Thomas, College Hall
Erskine, Mrs., Cooey
Finlay, Samuel, Drumhillery
Gallagher, Miss E., Tynan
Gillesple, John, Lislooney
Gillespie, Robert John, Coolkill
Glass, Wm. R., Tynan
Gordon Nixon, Cooey
Greason, James, Mullen
Grey, Samuel, Dillay
Hamilton, James, College Hall
Hamilton, Robert, Kennedies
Hamilton, William, College Hall
Henderson, Francis, Lisglinn
Henderson, William, Cortynan
Holmes, Charles, Tynan
Hustin, George, Mullin
Huston, Mrs. C. J., Tynan,
Kirker, Thomas, Tynan
Lawson, Robert S.J., Breaghy
Little, Wm., Breaghy
Little, Wm., jun., Breaghy
Livingston, Henry, College Hall
Lyons, Alex., Cavanapole
M'Aleavey, James, Breaghy
M'Aleavey, Wm., Breaghy
M'Aree, James, Lislooney
M'Clelland, James, Mullan
M'Clelland, John, Mullen
M'Clintock, Mrs. C. C. B.,
  Fellow's Hall
M'Cormick, Thos., Tynan
Marshall, Jos., Tynan

Marshall, Thos., sen., Drumgoliff
Mills, Wm., Tynan
Moffatt, Thos., Breaghy
Murray, Benjn., Tynan
Peel, John, Kennedies
Piper, Hugh, Cortynan
Robinson, Rt., sen., Cortynan
Robinson, Rt., jun., Cortynan
St, George, Acheson, Woodpark
Scroggy, Mrs., Cortynan
Scroggy, T. J., Cortynan
Stitt, Miss E., Tynan
Stronge, Sir J. C., Tynan Abbey
Tennison, Major W. C., J.P.,
  Portnelligan
Todd Francis, Cavanapole
Wilson, George, Cooey
Woods, Alex., Cavanapole

DERRYHAW, TYNAN.
Caldwell, Sl., Derryhaw
Cassidy, Francis, Balteagh
Cassidy, John, Balteagh
Cassidy, Thomas, Balteagh
Carberry, Thomas, Balteagh
Clarke John, Breaghy
Clarke, Matthew, Derryhaw
Crawford, R. J., Derryhaw
Daly, John, Derryhaw
Devlin, Francis, Dillay
Gamble, William, Derryhaw
Gray, Alexander, Dillay
Gray, Samuel, Derryhaw
Hamilton, George, Breaghy
Henderson, John, Derryhaw
Henderson, Robert, Derryhaw
Hughes, John, Woodpark
Irwin, David, Dernalea
Irwin, Thomas, Dernalea
Irwin, William, Balteagh
Loughlin, John, Derryhaw
M'Clatchy, John, Balteagh
M'Grane, James, Derryhaw
M'Ilvanny, Henry, Dernalea
Reid, John, Derryhaw
Reid, Ralph, Dernalea
Steele, John, Derryhaw
Wilson, James, Balteagh
Woods, Francis, Dernalea

WHITECROSS.

 HITECROSS is a rural post office, 11½ miles south-east of Armagh, and 6 miles west by north from Newry. Loughgilly 3 miles to the north-east, is the nearest railway station. The Bessbrook and Newry electric tramway is 4 miles. The land of the district is fair. Crops : oats, potatoes and flax. A considerable area is usually devoted to flax. Whitecross is also a good butter-making district. An interesting feature of the neighborhood is Crilly's Cave, on the farm of Mr. John Crilly. It is about 5 feet high, lined with field stones. One of the finest springs in the county is on the farm of Mr. James Cunningham.

Bakers : Deighan Bros.

Blacksmith : H. Kernon

Butter and Egg Exporters : Deighan Bros

Churches : C.I., Rev. Jno. Finlay Presbyterian, Rev. James Meeke ; R.C. Rev. Thomas Donnelly, P.P., Rev. Patrick Montague, C.C.

Corn Mills : Thos. Scott, P. G. Synnott

Drapers : Deighan Bros,

Estate Agent : P. G. Synnott, J.P.

Grocers : Marked [*] retail spirits, Deighan Bros*, Mrs. Margaret Markey*, William R. Nesbitt*

Post M. : James Deighan

Scutch Mills : Edw. Boyle, Ml. Boyle, Rd. Garland, Patk. Loughlin, Mrs. Mt. Markey, Thos. Scott, P. G. Synnott

Farmers & Residents

Adams, John, Lisadian

Barron, Irwin, Lisadian

Bell, John, Drumnahoney

Birch, William, Drumcrow

Boyle, Patrick, Corlet

Burke, John, Carrickanany

Canning, Denis, Aughincurk

Canning, Matthew, Aughincurk

Cannon, Charles, Aughincurk

Cooney, Henry, Aughincurk

Cooney, Thomas, Aughincurk

Corkey, Isaac, Aughincurk

Coulter, Alexander, Cavanakill

Copeland, Isaac, Drumcrow

Cowan, Anthony, Cavanakill

Cowan, Arthur, Cavanakill

Cunningham, Owen, Ballintemple

Deighan, Patrick, Carrickgallogly

Dolloghan, Patk., Drumnahunshion

Donnelly, Henry, Drumhariff

Doyle, L., Drumnahunshion

Edgar, John H., Drumhoney

Elliott, David, Rathcarbery

Elliott, John, Lisadian

Elliott, John, jun., Lisadian

Elliott, Thomas, Lisadian

Farrell, Bernard, Carnagat

Finegan, Bernard, Ballintemple

Garland, Patrick, Greyhillan

Gray, James, Lisadian

Hadden, Thomas, Greyhillan

Hamilton, John, Outleckan

Harper, William, Lisadian

Harpur, William, jun., Lisadian
Harrison, Mrs. E., Drumhoney
Haughian, Edward, Ballintate
Henning, James, Cloghinny
Hunter, Moses, Cloghinny
Kearney, John, Lisadian
King, Andrew, Drumcrow
King, John, Lurgana
King, Joseph, Cavanakill
King, Joseph J., Drumnahoney
Lamph, Felix, Cladybeg
Loughran, Lawrence, Tullyagh
M'Comb, Samuel, Greyhillan
M'Guire, Michael, Keadybeg
M'Kee, Thomas, Lisadian
M'Keown, Francis, Ballintate
M'Parland, Daniel, Cavanakill
M'Parland, John, Corlat
M'Parland, John, Corlat
M'Parland, Mrs. M., Cavanakill
M'Shane, John, Tullyah
Maguire, Thomas, Keadybeg
Markey, Michael, Drumnahoney
Markey, Patrick, Tullyah
Morgan, Michael, Lisadian
Murphy, Mrs., Grayhillan
Murphy, Mrs. S., Corlat
Murphy, Peter, Grayhillan
Nesbitt, James, Drumcrow
O'Brien, William, Cavanakill
O'Hare, James, Cavanakill

Patterson, James, Lisadian
Patterson, James, Lurgana
Patterson, John, Cavanakill
Patterson, John, Drumhariff
Patterson, Jno., Drumnahunshion
Patterson, John, Lurgana
Patterson, John, Outlacken
Patterson, Mark, Lurgana
Patterson, Samuel, Cavanakill
Quinn, Daniel, Greyhillan
Robb, James, Drumhoney
Robb, Samuel, Drumnahoney
Robb, William, Drumhoney
Robb, William J., Drumnah
Savage, Henry, Outlacken
Savage, Mark, Outlacken
Shiels, Patrick, Drumcrow
Simpson, John, Ballintate
Sinclair, Thomas, Lisadian
Synnott, Parker G. (J.P.) Lurgana
Toner, Michael, Drumcrow
Wallace, James, Lisadian
Wallace, John, Rathcarberry
Wallace, John, Rathcarberry
Wallace, Robert, Rathcarberry
Watson, Thomas, Corlat
Whelan, John, Drumnahoney
White, William, Enagh
Williamson, John, Drumnahoney
Young, Dr. Alex. G., Sandymount

WOODVIEW.

WOODVIEW is a rural post office 2¼ miles east by north from Armagh, on the way to Portadown. In the vicinity is Castledillon, the residence of Capt. George De La Poer Beresford. D.L., and Hockley Lodge, of Major James H. Stronge, J.P., both beautifully situated.

Grocer: G. M. Running
Postmaster, G. M. Running

Farmers & Residents

Allen, William, Altaturk
Bradford, William, Mullaghbane
Birch, James, Ternascobe
Bridget, Thomas, Ternascobe
Brooks, James, Ternascobe
Burch, William, Mullyloughran
Connor, Joseph, Cloughan

Cornwall, William, Mulnasilly
Deacon, David, Altaturk
Deacon, George, Ternascobe
Deacon, John G., Altaturk
Dacon, Thomas, Altaturk
Davidson, Richard, Cloughan
Davidson, Samuel, Mullyloughran
Edgar, David, Rathdrumgran
Hamilton, David, Ternascobe
Henderson, James, Ternascobe

Herron, James, Ternascobe
Hutchinson, George, Mullinasilly
Jenkinson, John, Mullinasilly
Kearney, Samuel, Mullyloughran
M'Cann, Thomas, Mullyloughran
Macartney, Robert, Cloughan
M'Combe, Robert, Mullinasilly
M'Cullagh, John, Ternascobe
M'Gill, John, sen., Mullinasilly
M'Gowan, Thos., Mullyloughran
M'Kenna, John, Ternascobe
M'Kiggen, John, Mullinasilly
M'Loughlan, Robert, Ternascobe

Mallon, Michael, Mullinasilly
Mallon, William, Mullinasilly
Mears, George J., Cloghan
O'Hare, John, Mullaghbane
Platt, William J., Ternascobe
Redpath, Samuel, Mullyloughran
Rice, James, Mullabane
Scarr, James, Ternascobe
West, John, Ternascobe
West, William, Mullyloughran
Wiley, Samuel, Mullinasilly
Wiley, William, Mullinasilly
Wright, Robert, Mullinasilly

SUB-POST OFFICES
IN THE MOY DISTRICT.

LETTERS addressed to residents of a sub-postal district should bear the name of the head office thus : Maghery, Moy. Moy is on the Armagh border, in the County Tyrone. Residents of the County Armagh named as follows, receive their letters from its post office :

Bond, Robert, The Argory
Clarke, Joseph, Corr
Clarke, Wm., Corr
Clarke, Wm., jun., Corr
Davison, Geo., sen., Canary

Goodlatte, A. R., Salem Lodge
Goodlatte, Wm., Salem Lodge
Murray, Henry, Canary
Sinclair, Simon, Canary

BENBURB.

BENBURB, County Tyrone, is 3 miles south-west of Moy, and 6 miles east by north from Armagh. Residents of the County Armagh named as follows, receive their letters from its post office :

Armstrong, John, Eglish
Bennett, John, Corr
Browne, Charles, Corr
Campbell, Francis, Edenderry
Conlan, Ml,, Tullymore-otra
Connolly, Thos., Tullymore-otra
Donnelly, Jos., Eglish
Finnegan, J., Tullymoreagowan
Finnegan, T., Tullymoreegowan
Hodge, R., Tullymore-otra
M'Anallen, James, Eglish
M'Anallen, Luke, Corr
M'Anallen, M., Laraghshankill
M'Anallen, T. Tullymore-otra

M'Gahan, J., sen., Tullymore-otra
M'Gahan, J., jun., Tullymore
M'Gahan, J., Tullymore-otra
M'Kee, Hugh, Tullymore-otra
Oak, John, Corr
Reynolds, T., Carrickaness
Shanks, John, Carrickaness
Sherry, James, Corr
Stewart, W., Tullymore-otra
Sweeney, James, Carrickaness
West, Mrs., Glenaul house
White, P., Maydown
Wilson, James, Edenderry

BLACKWATERTOWN.

Population 183 in 1881.

LACKWATERTOWN is 2 miles to the south of Moy, and 4 miles north by west from Armagh. The village consists of one long street, and has many houses, the style of which suggests better days. The Blackwater and Ulster Canal pass close to the village. Fifty years ago the population was almost three times greater than at present. The canal was not then finished. Blackwatertown was an important centre for the distribution of general merchandise. Vessels of 50 tons burden were able to navigate the Blackwater, and took from here large quantities of grain and potatoes. Stores, still in existence, tell the story of "the good old days." This year, owing to a misunderstanding with the railway company, the Ulster Canal is being used largely by merchants of Armagh. The land of the district of Blackwatertown is good. Oats, potatoes and flax are the principal crops. Some remains exist of the fort which was celebrated in the Rebellion of Hugh O'Neill, Earl of Tyrone, 1594-1603. It was toward Blackwatertown that the English Army, under Gen. Bagnall, was marching, 1598, when intercepted by O'Neill and O'Donnell, and defeated at the Yellow Ford, midway between Armagh and Blackwatertown. See pages 15 and 67.

Baker: Felix Fox

Blacksmiths: T. Fox, A. Quinn

Churches: Methodist, Charlemont Circuit; R.C., Rev. Ml. Coyne, P.P.

Coal mt.: Jas. M. Beattie

Dispensary : Dr. Samuel M. Fergus, M.O. Attendance, Wednesday and Saturday 10 a.m. to noon. *Committee*—Sir J. Calvert Stronge, Bart., J.P., Tynan Abbey, Tynan; J. W. M. Bond, J.P., D.L., Drumsil House, Armagh; J. A. M. Cope, J.P., Drumilly, Loughgall; James Orr, J.P., Cranagill, Loughgall; Robt. Gillespie, J.P., Armagh; Robert Clarke, J.P., Charlemont; Moses Gillespie, Culkeeran, Killylea; George Rice, Armagh; Thomas Gilpin, Tullyrone, Moy ; John Trotter, Mullyleggan, Blackwaterown; John S. Riggs, Armagh; Jacob Orr, J.P., Cranagill, Loughgall; John Crothers, Blackwater-town; George Matthews, Glenaul House; William James Clarke, Corr and Dunavally, Charlemont; W. H. Addey, Allistragh, Armagh. Committee meets 2nd Monday every month at 11 a.m. Wardens —Robert Allen, Corr and Aughintarragh; Brown Rolston, Aughinlig; Joseph Frazer, Blackwatertown. William Crozier, Tullymore-Etra. Thomas M'Cabe, Foyar ; John Frazer, Killymaddy; James Magill, Mullynure ; Sinnamon Noble, Lisnafeedy ; Joseph Alderdice, Charlemont.

Grocers : (*) retail spirits : Jas. M. Beattie, Thos. Hagan *

Post M.: Miss E. Campbell

R.I.C.: Sergt. Dougan

School, National : Dl. Campbell, Miss M. Mackay

Ulster Canal : Cornelius Devlin, toll collector

Farmers & Residents.

Allen, James, Mullenarry
Atkinson, Edward, Annamoy
Atkinson, John, Annamoy
Atkinson, William, Annamoy
Beattie, John, Tiregarty
Brannigan, John, Creaghen
Burton, Charles, Ballycullen
Callan, Irwin, Drumcullen
Cappagh, Alex., Mullyleggan
Connolly, Thos., B'watertown
Corrigan, Robert, Annamoy
Donnelly, Peter, Kilmore
Finn, John, Kilmore
Finn, Michael, Mullanary
Frazer, Joseph, B'watertown
Garland, Edward, Mullanary
Garvey, James, Mullanary
Heagerty, Dl., B'watertown

Hughes, Peter, Mullanary
Kelly, James, Drumcullen
Kingsborough, Rev. R., Black-watertown
M'Anespe, John, Drumcullen
M'Glone, James, Mullanary
M'Glone, Peter, Kilmore
M'Grann, Patrick, Drumcullen
M'Keough, John, Drumcullen
Mackle, John, Annahagh
Maguire, Cornelius, Mullanary
Murphy, John, The Glen
Murphy, P. J., Tirgarve
O'Neill, Felix, Kilmore
Toner, Patrick, T'gowan
Trotter, Hamilton, Mullyleggan
Trotter, John, Mullyleggan
Walker, Wm., jun., B'watertown

CHARLEMONT.

Population 247 in 1881.

CHARLEMONT is really not a sub-post office. It is an independent village, but the authorities do not think it necessary to appoint a post master, as the Blackwater only divides it from Moy, and connection is formed by a substantial stone bridge. Charlemont is 6 miles north by west from Armagh. The land of the district is good. Oats and potatoes are the chief crops. Nearly all the farmers plant a little flax and devote some attention to butter-making, in lumps. Charlemont was at one time a place of considerable importance. Lord Mountjoy, Lord Deputy in 1602, built a castle here to protect the bridge from the O'Neill's, and made a name for it by cutting down his own (Charles Mountjoy) to *Charlemont.* In 1641 the castle was taken by stratagem and the governor, Lord Caulfield, put to death. The circumstances in which he was surprised will be found detailed, with a description of the castle, at page 33. Charlemont was incorporated as a borough by James I., 1613. Provision was made in the charter for the election of a portreeve and 12 burgesses. The inhabitants all became freemen. The portreeve was elected annually by the burgesses, and the burgesses were elected by the freemen and held office for life. Two representatives were elected to serve in the Irish Parliament, until the Union. Lord Charlemont received £15,000 from the Government as compensation for the disfranchisement of the borough. Barracks at Charlemont were occupied by two companies of the Royal Artillery until 1858. After the withdrawal of the troops, the Government sold the barracks to Lord Charlemont. A gold ring and a gold cross, with a setting of precious stones, were dug up in the vicinity nearly 60 years ago. The ring was supposed to have belonged to Sir Teague O'Regan, commander of the garrison under James II., in 1690.

Blacksmith : Jas. Henry, v.s.
Carpenter : John Boyle
Churches : C.I., Rev. John Watson ; Methodist, Rev.Wm. Conlin, Rev. W. L. Coade, Rev. Robt. Kingsborough
Draper : Miss Kenny
Fort : Wm. Henderson, keeper
Gas works : Lord Charlemont, owner ; 8/4 per 1000 feet
Groceries, seed, and hardware : Joseph Alderdice
Process Server : Thos. Johnston
Schools : Ladies', the Misses Smart ; National, John Devine, Spirit retailers : Mrs. M. A. Gedge, Wm. G. Herron, John Kelly, Patrick O'Hagan

Tinsmith : P. Doherty

Farmers & Residents.

Bennett, John, Aghinlig
Campbell, James, Keenaghan
Clarke, Robert (J.P.), Charlemont
Dickson, Mrs., Charlemont
Gilpin, Thomas, Keenaghan
Grimason, Thomas, Charlemont
Heagerty, Thomas, Aghinlig
Heather, Jn. (P.S.C.), Charlemont
Kerr, Cornelius, Keenaghan
Kilpatrick, John, Keenaghan
M'Kay, Robert, Corr
Mallon, Michael, Keenaghan
Marshall, George, Keenaghan
Millar, William, Corr
Myles, George, Corr
Powell, William, Charlemont

MAGHERY.

Fishing.

MAGHERY is a rural post-office 8¼ miles north-east of Moy and 11 miles north by east from Armagh. It is beautifully situated on the southern shore of Lough Neagh, and is a favorite summer resort for excursionists and tourists. Derrywaragh Island has the necessary romantic features to attract sightseers and help to amplify the pleasures of a day's outing. Facilities for fishing and shooting are first-rate. Many of the natives of the district are fishermen. A few dealers ship pollen and trout to England. Verner's Bridge is the nearest railway station, 4 miles. A large number of the residents in the district are hand-loom weavers. The land, for the greater part, is boggy. Good crops of oats and potatoes are produced by heating the bog. The process is described at page 37.

Churches : C. I., Rev. M. A. Holden ; Methodist, Charlemont | Circuit ; R. C., Rev. F. O'Brien, P.P., Rev. P. Hughes, C.C.

Fish Exporters : F. Campbell, N. M'Alinden, William Ross

Grocers,* sells spirits : James Fulton, Derrylilah, William Ross, Maghery*

Post Master : William Ross

School, National : Danl. Campbell

Farmers & Residents.

Abraham, Robert, Derryane
Anderson, John, Derryane
Baxter, Henry, Maghery
Breslin, Lewis, Maghery
Brown, George, Derrylileagh
Campbell, Chas., jun., Maghery

Campbell, Mrs. A., Maghery
Campbell, Mrs. Margt., Maghery
Hughes, John, Derryane
Jackson, Thomas D., Derryane
M'Anulty, Patrick, Maghery
M'Garry, Mrs., Derryane
M'Kee, Mrs. A., Maghery
M'Kelvey, John K., Maghery
Magee, James, Maghery
Magee, John, Derrylileagh
Mawhinney, Joseph, Derryane
O'Donnell, Richard, Maghery
Verner, Mrs. A. J., Derryadd
Verner, William J., Derryane

TULLYRONE.

Fishing.

TULLYRONE is a village of about 14 houses, 3 miles east by north from Moy, and 6 miles north by east from Armagh. Verner's Bridge, 1 mile, is the nearest railway station. Tullyrone is prettily situated in a valley through which a new cut from the Callan runs. In this some brown trout, pike, eels, and perch are found. The cut is about 2 miles long. It starts from the old Callan at Greenhall, 1 mile from Loughgall, and joins the Blackwater at Verner's Bridge. The land is fair for oats, potatoes, and wheat. A small space only is devoted to flax. About 200 hand-loom weavers live in the district. Most of them cultivate small farms. A large earthen fort continues to exist at Derryscollop, on the farm of Mr. William Martin.

Blacksmith : Robert Davidson
Carpenter : James Donnelly
Grocers (*) Spirit retailer : Geo. M'Clelland,* Johnson Lightbody
Post M. : George M'Clelland

Farmers & Residents.

Blevins, John, Derryscollop
Campbell, Collough, Tullyrone

Campbell, Mrs. R., Tullyrone
Cherry, Robert, Derryhirk
Cherry, Thomas, Derryhirk
Cooke, William, Copney
Cunningham, Jn., Derrymagowan
Downey, Mrs. E., Herk
Downey, James, Derryhirk
Downey, William, Derrycorry s

Emerson, John, Derryscollop
Emerson, Thomas, Derryscollop
Fox, James, Tullyrone
Gilpin, George, Tullyrone
Gilpin, James A., Derrycorry s
Gilpin, Richard, Derrycorry
Gilpin, William V., Copney
Hall, George, Copney
Hall, Jeremiah, Copney
Hyde, Francis, sen., Copney
Hyde, Francis, jun., Copney
Irwin, Andrew, Derrycorry s
Irwin, Christopher, Tullyrone
Lawson, John, Tullyrone
Lightbody, Isaac, Tullyrone
M'Call, George, Tullyrone
M'Kittrick, Mrs. M., Tullyrone

Marshall, Mrs. J., Derryscollop
Martin, Robert, Derryscollop
Martin, William, Derryscollop
Matchett, William, Copney
Murray, George, Derrymagowan
Murray, Patrick, Derrymagowan
Murray, Richard, Derrymagowan
Potts, Robert, Derrycorry N
Reid, Nathaniel, Tullyrone
Reid, William, Tullyrone
Rowe, George, Tullyrone
Rowe, William, Tullyrone
Sinclair, T. W., Tullyrone
Thompson, John, Copney
White, Mrs. E., Tullyrone
White, Thomas, Tullyrone

VERNER'S BRIDGE.

ERNER'S BRIDGE is a rural post office and railway
station 4 miles, Irish, north by east from Moy, 8 miles,
Irish, north by east from Armagh, and 8 miles, Irish,
north-west from Portadown. The railway station is
about a mile from the post office. Over 200 hand-loom weavers
live in the district. They are employed by manufacturers of
Lurgan and Bessbrook. The land of Verner's Bridge is, for the
most part, rather poor. Potatoes, oats, and wheat are the principal crops. Church Hill, a fine residence, was occupied by Sir
William Verner, Bart., until his death in 1886. His wife, Lady
Verner, lived in it until her death this year. Neither had attained
the age of 40.

Blacksmith: Jas. Haughey
Churches: Methodist, Charle-
mont Circuit ; R.C., Dean Burns,
P.P.
Draper: Jno. Gilpin
Grocers, (*) sells spirits: Dl.
Finn, Jno. Gilpin*
Post M.: John Gilpin

Railway station: Wm. H. West,
toll collector
Schl. Natl. Miss L. W. Hyde
Farmers & Residents.
Campbell, John, Derrylee
Carr, Mrs., Clontyclay
Cassidy, Mrs., Clontyclay
Coyne, Felix, Clontyclay

Dynes, Arthur, Clontyclay
Dynes, Patrick, Clontyclay
Finn, Daniel, Clonmore
Finn, Miss, Clonmore
Finn, Mrs., Clonmore
Fox, Francis, Clonmore
Fox, John, Clontyclay
Fox, Patrick, Clonmore
Fullerton, Mrs., Clontyclay
Hamill, E., Clonmore
Hamill, John, Clonmore
Haughey, J., Clonmore
Hayes, Geo., Clontyclay
Hayes, James, Clontyclay
Hayes, John, Clonmore
Hayes, Thomas, Clonmore
Hayes, W. J., Clonmore
Hynes, David, Cronkill
Hynes, Thomas, Cronkill
Jackson, John, Clonmore
Jackson, William, Mullenakill N
Kelso, T., Derryhubbert E
Kerby, Jos., Cronkill
M'Clusky, Mrs., Clonmore
M'Culla, Rt., Verner's Bridge
M'Kee, Mrs., Clonmore
Mullan, Fr., Clontyclay
Mullen, Wm., Mullenakill N
O'Neill, John, Clontyclay
Smith, Rt., Derrylee
Vallelly, John, Clonmore

SUB-POST OFFICES.

IN THE DUNDALK DISTRICT.

LETTERS addressed to residents of a sub-postal district should bear the name of the head office, thus : Silverbridge, Dundalk.

FORKHILL.

Population 177 *in* 1881.—*Fishing.*

FORKHILL is 4½ miles north north-west from Dundalk, on the road to Armagh. It is in the barony of Upper Orior, close to the Louth border. A fertile valley stretches north and south from this point for several miles. Oats, flax and potatoes are the principal crops. In good times the farmers of the district are able to live comfortably. There has been a small increase in the population of the village within a period of 50 years. The old fairs are still kept up, and the houses have a prosperous appearance. Capt. Granville Alexander, an extensive property owner here, has lately spent from £6,000 to £7,000 improving his fine residence, Forkhill House. The demesne is open to the public, and is much frequented by excursion and pic-nic parties. A trout-lake, containing between 8 and 10 acres, romantically situated, affords good sport for anglers. Capt. Alexander reserves nothing but the game. Forkhill River is also good for trout. There is a great deal in the vicinity of Forkhill to attract tourists. Slieve Gullion, rising to a height of 1,893 feet above the level of the sea, is about a mile north of the village. A large cairn on the top is believed to have been the burial place of Cualgue, a Milesian chief, who was slain in battle at the foot of the mountain. The poet Ossian made this battle the subject of a poem, in which Cualgue is referred to. A small lake near the cairn is among many interesting objects. Then there is the view than which the county affords nothing finer. In the townland of Shean, about a quarter of a mile from Forkhill, there are foundations of an ancient priory. They were discovered not long ago by men digging in a field. In Urney, ½ a mile distant, there is a fragment of the ruin of an old church. In Forkhill churchyard, one of the curiosities is the grave of Michael Locke, a yeoman of 1798. He died a few years ago at the age of 115.

Blacksmith : Owen Dooley

Churches: C. I., Rev. Thos. H. Royce ; Methodist, Dundalk circuit ; Roman Catholic

Corn and scutch mills : Thos. W. Brooks, Thos. O'Neill

Drapers : John S. Johnston, Jas. Smith, Wm. Smith

Education : Jackson's Charity, Hy. Barber, Mrs. Barber, Mrs. Locke ; National School, Bd. McGinness

Grain mercht. : Thos. Brooks

Grocers, marked thus * sell spirits † hardware, ‡ seeds : John S. Johnston, Jas. M'Namee*, Bd. Smith*, Jas. Smith†‡, W. Smith†‡

Hotel : Jas. M'Namee

Petty Sessions, 2nd Wednesday in each month : Jas. Smith, clerk

Post Master and Stamp distributor : Jas. Smith

Process server : Rd. Gracy

R.I.C.: Sergt. Jas. Belford

Farmers & Residents.

Alexander, Capt. Granville H. J. (D.L.) Forkhill house

Balmer, Richard, Carrickasticken

Brooks, Robert C., Forkhill

Brooks, T. W., Forkhill

Burns, Hugh, Forkhill

Burns, Patrick, Carrive¡

Carlisle, John, Shean

Coburn, Ml., Forkhill

Cunningham, James, Tievecrom

Cunningham, P., Tievecrom

Feagan, Ml., Longfield

Haughain, Bernard, Shean

Hearty, Terence, Tievecrom

Hughes, James, Longfield

Johnston, J. (J.P.), Carrickbreda ho

Johnston, John S., Shean

Locke, Thomas, Shean

M'Cann, Mrs. C., Shean

M'Coy, Patrick, Shean

M'Elroy, P., Carrickasticken

Murdock, A., Carrickasticken

Murdock, Joseph, C'sticken

Murphy, Bernard, Shean

Murphy, Hugh, Carrickasticken

Murphy, Ml., Longfield

Murphy, Mrs., Longfield

Murdock, Samuel, C'sticken

O'Neill, J., Carrickasticken

O'Neill, Thomas., Shean

Rafferty, Mrs. Cath., Shean

Shields, Jas.,

Smith, Bd., Carrickasticken

Smith, Mrs. J., Apple Lodge

Toal, Owen, Carrickasticken

BALLSMILL.

 ALLSMILL is a village of about 10 houses, 5 miles, Irish, from Dundalk, and 4 miles, Irish, east of Crossmaglen. It lies within a ¼ of a mile of the Louth border, and is only a mile from the famous Roche's

Castle. A small lake, partly planted around, is one of the immediate attractions of Ballsmill. Glassdrummond Lake, about six acres in area, is a mile distant on the way to Crossmaglen. This has a wooded island in the centre like a *crannoge*. Ballsmill has one fair each year, in May. It used to have fairs also in February and December, but they have been discontinued for a long time. The land of the district is good. Potatoes, oats and flax are the chief crops.

Dispensary : Dr. Jno. Wilson
Grocers : Patk. Finnegan, Jno. Lowe
Post M.: Jno. Lowe
School, Natl. : Ml. M'Donnell, Mary Smith.
Scutch and corn mill : John Johnston, Woodvale
Spirit retailer : none

Farmers & Residents.
Brannigan, Mrs. M., Tullydonnell
Devitt, Owen, Glassdrummond

Fegan, Mrs. A., Tullydonnell
Jeffers, Rd., G'drummond
Johnston, J., (J.P.), Woodvale
Kirk, Thos., G'drummond
Kelly, Mrs. B., Tullydonnell
Kelly, Mrs. E., Tullydonnell
Lynch, Patk., G'drummond
M'Gahan, Thos., G'drummond
M'Ginn, Thos., G'drummond
Murphy, Ptk., G'drummond
Mynes, Ptk., G'drummond

MULLAGHBAWN.

ULLAGHBAWN is a village of about 20 houses in the parish of Forkhill, 6 miles, Irish, north north-west from Dundalk. It is situated in a valley flanked by Slieve Gullion and the Forkhill Mountains. The land is good. Oats, potatoes and flax are the chief crops. Some of the farmers devote attention to dairying.

Blacksmith : Bd. Lappen
Church : R. C., Rev. Jas. M'Namee, c.c.
Dispensary : Dr. Jos. M'Dowell
Draper : Rt. Wright
Grocers, marked thus (*) sell spirits : Mrs. Ann Bennett, Mrs. Sarah Kearns, Felix M'Coy*, Rt. Wright
Post M. : Rt. Wright
School, Natl. : P. M'Creesh
Scutch mill : Rt. Wright
Spirit retailer (see also grocers) : Mrs. Cathn. O'Hanlon.

Farmers & Residents.
Carberry, Edward, Shanroe
Collins, Peter, C'nagavna
Crawley, T., Carrickaldreen

Daly, John, Aghadanove
Donnellan, John, Cashel
Garvey, B., Tullymacreeve
Hanlon, Patrick, Mullaghbawn
Jeffers, Saml., Aghadanove
Keenan, Mrs. B., Mullaghbawn
M'Coy, Felix, Carrickaldreen
M'Coy, Ml., Aghadanove
M'Coy, T., Tullynacreeve
M'Dowell, Dr. Jos., Shanroe
M'Gill, Jas., Carricknagavna
M'Keown, Felix, Aghadanove
M'Keown, John, Aghadanove
M'Keown, Terence, Aghadanove
M'Parland, J., Carricknagavna
M'Parland, Mrs. M., Lattherget
Magee, Patrick, Carrive
Magennis, Ml., Levallymore

Morgan, Mrs. P., Lathberget
Morgan, Mrs. M., Lathberget
Muckian, Ptk., Mullabawn
Murcan, Jas., Carrickaldreen
Murcan, Owen, Tullynacreene
Murphy, E., Carricknagavna
Murphy, Ml., Carricknagavna
Murphy, Ml., Maphonet
Murphy, Ml., Tullnacree

Murphy, Ptk., jun., Mullaghbawn
Murphy, Stpn., Mullaghbawn
O'Hanlon, Mrs., Lathberget
O'Hanlon, Patrick, Mullaghbawn
Quinn, P., Carricknagavana
Shevlin, E., Mullaghbawn
Smith, Edward, Lathberget
Smith, Mrs. S., Mullaghbawn
Smith, Peter, Mullaghbawn

BERNARD CARRAGHER,
General Merchant,
POST OFFICE, SILVERBRIDGE.

DEPARTMENTS :—Groceries, Provisions, Wines and Spirits, Seeds,
Artificial Manures, Hardware, Funeral Undertaking.

SILVERBRIDGE.

SILVERBRIDGE is a village of about 15 houses, on the Cully Water, between 7 and 8 miles, Irish, north north-west of Dundalk, 3 miles, Irish, east by north from Crossmaglen, and 5 miles, Irish, north-east of Culloville, the nearest railway station. The land of the district is fair in the valley, but it soon rises to lofty heights and becomes poor. Potatoes and flax are the principal crops. Most of the farms are small.

Beer retailer: Jno. Grant
Blacksmith : Hy. M'Namee
Corn mill: Jos. Malone
Grocers: Bd. Carragher, Jno.
Carragher, Ptk. Faughey, Mrs. E.
M'Court, Ml. M'Geough, Ml.
Murphy, Jas. Stokes
Post M. : Bd. Carragher
R. I. C. : Sergt. Jno. Lochhart
School, Natl. : P. F. Grant
Scutch mills : Jas. M'Cullough,
Jas. Stokes
Spirit retailer : Bd. Carragher
Farmers & Residents.
Burns, Samuel, Dorsey
Crilly, Patrick, Dorsey
Grant, Owen, Cashel
Grant, Patrick, Carrive
Hanratty, Mrs., Cashel
Hughes, Hy Carrigans

Johnston, Jas., Ummerimore
Johnston, Mrs. B., Ummericam
Loughran, James, Dorsey
Loy, John, Dorsey
Loy, Mrs. B., Dorsey
M'Antear, Mrs. B., Aughenduff
M'Court, Mrs. T., Aughenduff
M'Creesh, F., Ummerimore
M'Culloch, John, Carnally
M'Dermott, Patrick, Dorsey
M'Gorman, Laurence, Dorsey
Martin, Mrs. A., Cashel
Martin, Mrs. M., Cashel
Mullen, Ml., Silverbridge ho
Murchan, P., Ummericam (Ball)
Murchan, Mrs. M., Cashel
Murphy, Anthony, Carrive
O'Hare, Thomas, Carnally
Stokes, James, Carrigans

Edward Rodden,

THE OLD ESTABLISHED

Woollendrapery and Manchester Warehouse,

Tea, Wine and Spirit Store,

TANDRAGEE.

WM. KILPATRICK,

Manufacturer of Linen

AND

LINEN HANDKERCHIEFS,

CABRA GROVE,

TANDRAGEE.

TANDRAGEE.

Population 1,592 in 1881.—Trout-fishing.

TANDRAGEE compares favorably with the most beautifully situated towns in Ireland. The main street, which runs up the side of a hill, is broad, and the houses for the greater part are large and well built. With one exception the churches occupy favorable sites on the side of the hill, and help to relieve the regularity of the other buildings. The exception is the Church of Ireland, and this crowns the summit at one point, in line with the Castle at the other. Tandragee is in the barony of Lower Orior, and parish of Ballymore, within a mile and a half of the County Down border. The Belfast Junction Railway and Newry Canal run close to the dividing line. It is about an Irish mile from the town to the railway station. On the way, the road crosses the Cusher, a trout stream affording good sport for anglers. Tandragee is 82 miles from Dublin, 30½ miles from Belfast, and 5½ miles south by east from Portadown, by rail. There is a great deal of good land in the neighborhood. Oats, potatoes and flax are the chief crops. The town owes its origin to the

P

O'Hanlons, descendants of the Collas, Princes of Argial, whose exploits are described at page 119. They built a strong castle where the present Castle of Tandragee stands, and dominated the surrounding country until deprived of power and possessions by James I., as a punishment for having taken part in the rebellion of O'Neill, Earl of Tyrone, 1594-1603. Soon after O'Neill and O'Donnell had escaped to Rome, 1607, the Plantation of Ulster was begun, and Tandragee was given to Sir Oliver St. John. He rebuilt the castle, and the settlers upon his "portion" built the town, which speedily began to flourish. Rights for markets and fairs were granted by the King. In the war of 1641 the O'Hanlons endeavored to repossess themselves of their ancestral estates. They captured and destroyed the castle. Sir Oliver was shot through the head with a bullet while directing the defence. Viscount Mandeville, 50 years ago, rebuilt the castle with stone from a quarry at Tullyhue, in the parish. It is maintained in excellent condition, and even from the ramparts commands a view of surpassing loveliness. At the foot of the hill a small stream winds most picturesquely through the demesne. It is crossed by the avenue which, in the gradual ascent from the lower part of the town, produces charming scenic effects. A steep avenue, giving a more direct connection, is called "The Dark Walk," for the reason that it passes between two rows of great lime-trees, growing so close to each other as to almost shut out the light. The Duke of Manchester is the owner of Tandragee and district.

Next in interest to the Castle is the Church (C.I.), which was also built by Sir Oliver St. John. In the war of 1641 it met the same fate at the hands of the O'Hanlons. It was rebuilt in 1684, and again in 1812. On the last occasion the skull of Sir Oliver was exposed to view, and identified by the bullet-hole. Two transepts were added in 1849. While the work was in progress the skull of Sir Oliver was again taken from the vault. It was stolen shortly afterward, and retained for three days. On the morning of the fourth it was found wrapped in paper, inside the church-yard wall, having been thrown over during the previous night. Thomas Best, deceased, a carpenter employed by the contractor, told a thrilling story to the Sexton, Archibald Annett, still in office. He said that on opening the St. John vault he saw an erect object resembling the form of a woman. It crumbled to dust on being touched with his rule. The supposed sudden death of a lady, who came on a visit to Tandragee a long time ago, is associated with the discovery by the carpenter. Interment was made in the St. John vault ; in accounting for the erect object many persons were led to believe that she was buried alive, and on returning to consciousness was literally frozen to the spot near the door.

Among the mural tablets in the Church, one shows that Tandragee did not escape the ravages of the cholera in 1832-3. It was erected to the memory of " William Loftie, J.P., under whose fostering care, as agent for 35 years, Tandragee flourished, and the estate and tenantry congenially prospered. On his resignation of this arduous agency, it was proposed by many tenants, who could well appreciate a faithful pattern of genuine uprightness, to cheer his declining years with some token of cordial affection and respect, but alas, the malignant cholera denied them the grateful opportunity, and in sorrow they substitute this humble but sincere tribute to his memory." Died November 7th, 1833, aged 62 years. The burial place of the Mandeville family is at Kimbolton. The other churches of the town include those of the Presbyterian, Methodist, Baptist, and Roman Catholic denominations. The Christians, sometimes called Plymouth, and sometimes Exclusive Brethren, also have a meeting house. In the first half of the century, Tandragee was the centre of an extensive linen industry, and had a great market every Wednesday. In the season the sale of flax alone averaged over £6,000 a week. There were also departments for linen and general produce in which the sales averaged over £2,500. A monthly fair was likewise a great success. Now the market exists for a few people who sell roll butter. The patent for fairs has been long a dead letter. The linen industry in the town and district is still important, but of the people employed, about 3,000, the greater part live elsewhere. One flax spinning mill in town has about 600 workers. It is owned by the Messrs. Sinton, who employ about 700 at their factory at Laurelvale. Mr. William John Turtle, of Mullavilla House, employs about 1,000 hand-loom linen weavers, belonging to various places, and Mr. William Kilpatrick, of Cabra Grove, about 500.

James I. failed to incorporate Tandragee, but it is said that he intended to do so. The inhabitants, by petition to the Lord Lieutenant, were brought under the Towns Improvement Act in 1863. The valuation of property then was: houses, £2,160 10s.; lands, £744 12s. 3d.; total, £2,905 2s. 3d. In 1888 the total valuation was £3,741 14s. A rate for general purposes of 5d. in the £ covers all expenses. There are 26 gas lamps, lighted at a cost of £36 11s. 9d. in 1887. Out of this the bill for gas alone was £30 4s. 6d. The town has a pretty good sewerage system. Pumps in the streets supply water for domestic and other purposes. A Lawn Tennis Club, referred to at page 51, and a Gun Club, described at page 41, are established on a firm basis.

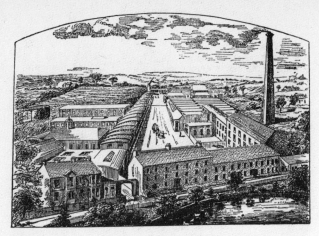

LAURELVALE.

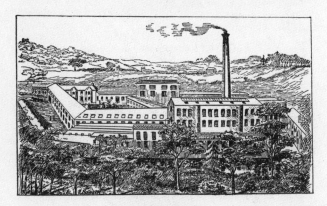

TANDRAGEE.

THOMAS SINTON,

Linen Manufacturer and Flax Spinner,

LAURELVALE,

TANDRAGEE.

LAURELVALE, TANDRAGEE AND KILLYLEICH.

AT the time of his demise, in 1887, Mr. Thomas Sinton was conducting a manufacturing business of a most extensive character at Laurelvale, the yarns for which were spun in mills at Tandragee and Killyleigh, Co. Down. He began his career at Laurelvale about thirty-five years ago, naming the place himself. The property consists of about 150 acres. Of this over four acres are covered by the buildings seen in the illustration. In these there are 350 looms, driven by two steam engines of 180 horse power indicated. Water for condensing purposes is provided from a lake to which a small stream is directed from Glenoran stepps. This enhances the attractions of tastefully planted pleasure grounds, facing the family residence near the factory. The manufactures from the Laurelvale looms include superior heavy linens and sheetings, Nearly 700 people are employed here. Yarns are given out to cottage weavers to the number of 1,500 in the counties of Armagh and Down, to be woven into heavy household linen, and cambric and linen handkerchiefs. The mill at Tandragee, also illustrated, was acquired by Mr. Sinton 18 or 19 years ago. Previous to that time it was owned by the Tandragee Spinning Company. It spins for the heavy end of the trade, and there are employed in it about 600 people, chiefly females. The splendid mill at Killyleigh, Co. Down, was taken by Mr. Sinton in 1885, and conducted under the style of Thomas Sinton & Sons. Linen yarns of the finest grade are spun there, the work-people employed numbering over 500. The business at Laurelvale and mill at Tandragee continue to be carried on under the name of Thomas Sinton. The proprietors are his sons, Messrs. Maynard, Arthur, Thomas and Frederick Sinton. Laurelvale is situated at a distance of a mile and a half from Tandragee, and three and a half miles from Portadown Railway station, the shipping point for all the manufactured goods. The Belfast office of the firm is at 3 Linen Hall Street.

WILLIAM JOHN TURTLE,

MANUFACTURER ∴ OF ∴ LINEN

AND

LINEN HANDKERCHIEFS,

MULLAVILLA HOUSE,

TANDRAGEE.

TANDRAGEE DIRECTORY.
——— :o:———
BUSINESS BRANCHES, PUBLIC BODIES,
PROFESSIONS, &c.
[Arranged alphabetically. Names not mentioned here should be sought
in the County Directory, page 53.]
——— :o:———

Bakers: Hy. Aston, Geo. Davidson, Jas. O'Hare

Bank, Belfast : Thomas B. Powell, mgr. ; H. Hayes, cashier ; John A. Pentland, act.

Bootmakers (shops), Peter Kinney, Thos. Harvey

Timber Mercht.: Thos. Mathers

Churches, &c. : Baptist, Rev. John Taylor ; C.I., Rev. Wm. McEndoo; Christians ; Methodist, Rev. Jas D. Foster; Presbyterian, Rev. Alex. R. Foy ; R.C., Rev. Jas. Donnelly, P.P.

Coal merchants: John Anderson, Seth Jelly, Jas. O'Hare, Jas. Whiteside, Dd. Williamson

Dispensary: Dr. Jas. Taylor, M.O.

Drapers: Geo. Crothers, Miss M. Gillis, Sl. McCallan, Rt. Meredith, Jas. Purdy, Miss O'Hare, Edward Rodden, Jas. Taylor, Miss A. Qua

Emigration Agt.: Rt. Emerson

Estate office: Capt O'Brien, agt.

Gas Co.; Thos. H. White, J.P., chairman; John J. Mayes, mgr.; 7/6 per 1,000 feet

Glass and Delf, &c.: Hy. Baxter, Mrs. S. Loughran, Mrs. D. McWhinney, Jas. Whiteside

Grain merchants : Seth Jelly

Grocers marked thus [*] retail spirits, † hardware, ‡ seeds : Jno. Anderson, Sl. J. Barr†, George

Dickson‡, Rt. Emerson†‡, Philip Hughes, Seth Jelly‡, Mrs. S. Loughran*, Sl. McCallan, Mrs. S. McIlroy, David McDonald, Jas. McMurray, Jno. McMurray, Miss Mt. Maginnis, Thos. Maginnis†, Thomas Mathers*, Rt. Meredith, Thos. Nesbitt, Jas. O'Hare‡, Edward Rodden*, Jas. Whiteside†, Dd. Williamson

Gun Club, Mandeville: Viscount Mandeville, President ; Thomas Dickson, Secretary; Wesley Watson, treasurer

Hotel Keepers. * spirit license: Jas. Dinsmore*, Geo. Davis, sen.

Miller (corn) : T. H. White

Manufacturers : Linen, Wm. Kilpatrick, Cabra Grove ; Thos. Sinton (Laurelvale, Weaving, Tandragee, flax spinning), Wm. John Turtle, Mullavilla House

News agent : Geo. Davis

See also stationers, &c.

Painters : Jos. Greenway, Wm. M'Cullough, Jno. Matthews

Petty Sessions, 2nd Tuesday of every month, Rt. Emerson, clerk

Physicians: Jas .Taylor, Jas. H. Wallace

Plumbers and tinsmiths : Henry Baxter, J. J. Mayes

Post Mistress and stamp distributor : Mrs. D. M'Whinney

Process server : James M'Callen

Railway station : J. Livingston, toll collector

R. I. C. : Sergt. William Power

Saddler : Thomas Greer

Schools, Ladies': Miss Moore ; National : Robt. Ross, Miss F. Harvey, Jas. Devlin, Mrs. L. Rice

Solicitors : Edward D. Atkinson and Son

Spirit retailers : see also grocers, Bernard Byrne, James Dolaghan, John Hagan, Mrs. J. Harcourt, Mrs. E. Quinn

Stationers, &c. : Miss Ellen M'Henry, Miss S. M'Cullough, Mrs. D. M'Whinney

Town Commissioners : James O'Hare, chairman ; E. D. Atkinson, solicitor ; Saml. J. Barr, Geo. Crothers, Jas. H. Wallace, Bernard Burns, George Dickson, Jas. Purdy, Robert Meredith, Robert Trotter, town clerk ; Archibald Annet, collector of rates

Victuallers : Bernard Burns, Robert Gamble, Bernard M'Cann

Watchmaker : Robt. Stirling

Farmers & Residents.

Abbreviations, sub-offices : C—Clare ; L—Laurelvale

Adair, Alexander, Ballyshielbeg, C
Adaire, Henry, Mullaglass
Adams, William, Brackagh ho
Adams, William, jun., Brackagh
Adair, Henry, Corenagh
Alexander, Thomas, Cargans
Alexander, Thos., jun., Corlust, C
Alexander, William, Corlust, C
Allister, Robt., Drumnamather, C
Anderson, Thomas, Cargans
Anderson, William, Mullaglass
Annet, David, Cargans
Annet, James, Mullahead
Annet, John, Cargans
Aston, Thomas, Lisbane
Atkinson, John, Ballyshielbeg, C
Atkinson, John, Broomfield, C
Babe, Charles, Tamnaghvelton, L
Balance, George, Mullaglass
Balmer, John, Cargans
Bell, Benjamin, Drumart ho
Bennett, George J., Cargans
Bennett, Robert, Tullyhugh
Best, Mrs., Ballymore
Black, William John, Lisbane
Blacker, James, Brackagh
Blacker, John, Mullahead
Bridget, Wm. J., Drumnamather, C
Brown, Robert, Cargans
Cahey, Moses, Ballyshielbeg, C
Caghy, Hugh, Drumnaleg
Campbell, James, Lisavague, L
Christie, Wm. J. Mavemacullen, C
Clarke, Thomas, Athol cottage

Cloughley, Moody, Mullaglass
Cloughley, John, Teemore
Coburn, James, Moodage
Coburn, Jn., Corn mills, Moodage
Cochrane, William, Moyrourkan, C
Collen, Thomas, sen., Tandragee
Collen, Thos. junr., Ballynock
Corr, James, Clare
Cousins, Thos., Mavemacullen, C
Crawford, Rev. A.——
Cromie, David S., Tullymacann
Cromie, James P., Clohoge
Crossan, Patk., Drumnamather, C
Cullen, Thomas, jun., Ballyknock
Cummins, Thomas, Mullahead
Davis, George, Tullyhugh
Davidson, Robert H., Prospect ho
Dermott, Lawrence, Brackagh
Dermott, Thomas, Brackagh
Donnelly, Patrick, Cloghoge, C
Ewings, Robert, Cargans
Fegan, W. H.——
Ferguson, Hugh, Drumart, C
Ferguson, Jas., Drumnamather, C
Ferguson, Ths., Drumnamather, C
Ferris, George, Ballyshielmore, C
Ferris, John, Cabragh
Ferris, William, Tullyhugh
Finigan, James, Lisavague, L
Finn, William, Lisavague, L
Frazer, W. J.——
Fullerton, Robert, Moyrourkin, C
Gamble, John, Ballylisk
Geddis, David, Cargans
Geddis, Wm., Ballyknock
Gough, Hy., Unshinagh
Gough, William, Brackagh
Gillespie, John, Lisavague, L
Gillespie, Wm., Lisavague, L
Gillis, Jos., T'dragee
Gillis, Wm., M'coomore, C
Gippin, R. L.——
Glass, Nath., Lisavague, L
Goold, James, Tullyhugh
Gracey, Daniel, Ballyknock
Gracey, John, Mullahead
Gracey, Robert, Tullyhugh
Gracey, Thomas, Ballymore
Graham, Jos., Maymacullen. C
Graham, Rt., Druminure, C

Graham, Wm., Ballyshielmore, C
Greenaway, Geo., Moyrourkan
Greenaway, James, Cargans
Greenaway, N., Drumnamather, C
Greer, John, Lisavague, L
Greer, Rd., B'shielmore, C
Greer, Saml., asst. co. surveyor
Greer, Thomas, Druminure, C
Hackett, John——
Hake, Archbd., Cargans
Hake, James, Cargans
Hale, Samuel, Lisbane
Hamil, Wm., Unshinagh
Hamilton, G. jun., B'shielmore
Hamilton, H., B'shielmore, C
Hamilton, J., B'shielmore, C
Hamilton, John, Cloghage
Hamilton, J., jun., B'shielmore
Hanlon, James, Unshinagh
Harden, Henry, Corernagh
Harden, R. J., Harrybrook, C
Hardy, Mrs. Anne,——
Hare, John, Brackagh
Hare, Thomas, Mavemacullen, C
Harvey, Jeremiah, Tullyhugh
Henry, James, Corlust, C
Hodgens, A., jun., Brackagh
Hodgins, Wm., Brackagh
Horner, J., jun., Tamnaghvelton
Irwin, John, Ballymore
Irwin, Thos., Brackagh
Irwin, Wm., senr., Brackagh
Johnston, Sl., Cargans
Joyce, Andrew, Brackagh
Joyce, George, Brackagh
Joyce, Ralph, Brackagh
Joyce, Valentine, Tamnaghmore
Joyce, Wm., Brackagh
Kelly, Thos, Ballyshielbeg
Kerr, John, Ballylisk
Kerr, William, Unshinagh
Kilpatrick, Wm., Cabragh grove
King, John, Lenelea, C
Kirkland, Wm., Druminure, C
Lavery, Bernard, Cordrain
Leggett, Sl., Tullyhugh
Lewis, J. Mavemacullen, C
Livingstone, Isaac, Tullyhugh
Loftie, Hy. (C.E.) T'dragee
Loftie, Misses, T'dragee

Loughran, Edward J., Tandragee
Loughran, Rev. M., P.P., T'velton, L
Loy, Michael, Moodoge
Lynas, Wm., Lisavague, L
M'Call, Crozier, Lenalea, C
M'Clean, Wm., Clohoge
M'Cormick, Arthur, land steward
M'Creight, Wm., Derryallen
M'Clelland, W., Mavemacullen, C
M'Cullough, Alex., Mullintur
M'Cullough, Alex., Tullymacann
McCune, Mrs. L.,——
M'Cutcheon, W. John, Ballyargan
M'Grane, Peter, Tam'velton, L
M'Henry, Miss, Market sq
M'Intyre, Millar, Mullahead
M'Kee, James, Mavemacullen, C
McKelvey, Miss,——
M'Mahon, Robert, Clare
Maddock, Henry, clerk, Tandragee
Magennis, Charles, Mullahead
Magennis, Charles, Tullyhugh
Magennis, John, Ballymore
Maginness, Edward, Mullahead
Manchester, Duke of, The Castle
Mandeville, Viscount, The Castle
Marks, John, Drumnaleg
Mason, H., Ballyshielmore, C
Mason, Thomas, Cloghoge
Matchett, G. A., Tullyhugh
Mathers, Francis, Drumart
Mathers, John, Ballymore
Mathers, Seth, Mullahead
Mitchell, B., Ballyshielmore, C
Moffit, John, Tannaghmore, C
Molony, The Misses,——
Monaghan, John, Cargans
Moneypenny, James, Cordrain
Moore, Mrs.,——
Morrison, T., Tamnaghvelton
Muldrew, John, Teemore
Muldrew, William, Teemore
Murphy, H., Tamnaghmore
Murphy, J., Drumnaglontagh
Napier, John, Mullaglass
Neil, William, Mullahead
O'Hanlon, E., Unshinagh
O'Hanlon, Hugh, Drumart, C
O'Hare, D., Drumnaglontagh
Overend, David, Tullyhugh

Overend, John, Brackagh
Patterson, J. M'C., Ballyshielbeg, C
Porter, Alex., Corenagh
Porter, James, Moyrourkin, C
Prichard, J., Tamnaghmore
Prichard, J., Mullavilly
Pringle, George, Corenagh
Purdy, Hugh, Ballyargan
Purdy, W. J., Ballyargan
Qua, Francis, Cordrain
Qua, Jas. M'Clelland, Ballyargan
Quinn, James M., Marlacoomore, C
Rea, Jas., Lisavague L
Redpath, Jas., Cargans
Redpath, Thos., Cargans
Redpath, Wm., Cargans
Reany, John, Ballymore
Reid, Wm., Marlacoobeg, C
Rice, F., Cloghoge, C
Ross, Mrs., Mullaglass
Shevlin, John, Mullaghglass
Shields, John, Tandragee
Sinton, Arthur, Laurelvale
Sinton, Corry, Ashtrees
Sinton, David, Brackagh
Sinton, Fredk., Laurelvale
Sinton, James, Drumnamather, C
Sinton, John, Tamnaghmore
Sinton, Maynard, Laurelvale
Sinton, Mrs., Laurelvale
Sinton, Thomas, Laurelvale
Sinton, William, Tamnaghmore
Sinton, W. H., T'naghmore ho, L
Smith, Thomas, Cargans
Snodden, E., Drumnamather, C
Snodden, T., Maymacullen, C
Snodden, W., Maymacullen, C
Somerville, James, Drumnaleg
Steenson, Alex., Moyrourkan, C
Stewart, J. A., Moyrourkin, C
Stewart, Rev. J., Clare
Suliot, Miss, Ballymore House
Taylor, George, Ballymore
Taylor, John, Ballymore
Taylor, Mrs., Tandragee
Taylor, Robert, Ballymore
Taylor, William, Cordrain
Thompson, Joseph, Clare, C
Thornton, David, Tamnaghvelton
Toal, George, Brackagh

Trotter, Robert, Commissioner for taking Affidavits, Tandragee
Turtle, James, Mullavilla house
Turtle, Wm. John, Mullavilla ho
Vance, David, Cordrain
Vance, James, Cordrain
Wardell, J. B., Laurelvale
Whan, Rev. R. J. W., M'macullen, C
White, Miss M., Ballymore ho
White, T. H. (J.P.), Orange hill ho
Whitten, Robert, Drumnaleg
Whitten, Wm., Drumnamather, C
Whitten, Wm., Marlacoomore, C
Williamson, J., Moodage
Williamson, Robert, Moodage
Willis, George, Drumnamather, C
Willis, James, Marlacoolbeg, C
Wilson, David, Ballyshielbeg, C
Wilson, John, Ballylisk
Wolfe, Rev. E. J., Mullavilly
Wolsey, James, Marlacoomore, C
Woods, John, Cargans
Woods, Charles, Lisnakea
Wright, George, Ballylisk
Wright, Henry, Ballylisk
Wright, James, Mullavilly
Wright, Thomas, Teemore
Wright, W., Unshinagh

SUB-POST OFFICES

IN THE TANDRAGEE DISTRICT.

LETTERS addressed to residents of a sub-postal district should bear the name of the head office, thus : Clare, Tandragee. Clare is a rural post office 2 miles south by west from Tandragee. The names of the principal farmers and residents of the district are given in the list of Farmers and Residents under the head of Tandragee. Laurelvale is a mile and a half west by north from Tandragee. It is described and illustrated at pages 228-9. The names of the farmers and residents will be found under the head of Tandragee.

ELEVEN LANE ENDS.

ELEVEN LANE ENDS is a rural post office in a beautiful country, 3 miles, Irish, from Tandragee, 8 from Portadown, 2 from Markethill, and a mile and a half, Irish, from the Loughgilly railway station. The land of the district, which is of average quality, belongs to the Commissioners of Education. Oats, potatoes, and flax are the chief crops. Many of the farmers engage in dairying, and make up butter for market in "bricks" and firkins.

Brick Manuftr. : Rt. J. Haire
Grocer, Hardware, &c. : Thomas Haire
Post M. : Thomas Haire

Farmers & Residents.

Bittles, David, Carran
Brown, Robert, Carran
Brown, William, Carran
Cole, Acheson, Carran
Cole, Isaac, Brackagh
Cromie, Wm. J., Mullinary
Dermott, Daniel, Mullinary
Flack, Hugh, Brackagh
Geddis, William J., Mullinary
Kenny, Michael, Mullinary
Kenny, Peter, Mullinary
M'Creery, John, Mavemacullen
M'Creery, Joseph, Mavemacullen
M'Creery, Samuel, Mavemacullen
M'Mahon, George, Mullinary
M'Mahon, James, Mullinary
M'Mahon, Mrs. S., Mavemacullen
Muldrugh, John, Corlust
Purdy, Charles, Corlust
Purdy, John, Corlust
Purdy, William, Corlust
Shaw, William, Carran
Shields, Thomas, Brackagh
Slaven, Mrs. Mavemacullen
Steel, David, Carron
Steele, John, Brackagh
Toner, John, Brackagh
Walker, J. M'Cartney, Corlust

SUB-POST OFFICES
IN THE NEWRY DISTRICT.

ꟼETTERS addressed to residents of a sub-postal district should bear the name of the head office, thus: Fathom, Newry. Fathom is a rural post office over 2 miles south of Newry. The names of the principal residents are included in the following list of persons receiving their letters direct from Newry. Carriers from the Newry post office deliver letters on the " walk " down. Ballybot, although in the County Armagh, forms a part of the Parliamentary Borough of Newry, and is described, and the names of the residents given in the Newry department of my BOOK OF COUNTY DOWN :

Agnew, Robert, Kilrea
Alderdice, David, Mullaglass
Barcroft, Henry, The Glen
Best, John, Mullaglass
Boyd, James, Skegatilled
Boyle, Michael, Newtown
Brown, John, Mullaglass
Clarke, James, Fathom
Clark, Patrick, Ellis's holding
Close, M. A., Drumbanagher
Courtenay, Patrick, Corrinshigo
Cronin, Patrick, Fathom lr
Cruikshanks, James, Corrinshigo
Doran, James, Lissummon
Eakin, Wm., Fathom
Ewart, John, Tullyhappy
Ford, Rev. J. M., Goragh
Gillow, Alexander, Demoan
Gordon, Wm., Demoan
Gourlay, Samuel, Derrywilligan
Halliday, John, Carnbane
Hollywood, Capt. James, Fathom
Hollywood, Capt. M., Fathom
Hollywood, Owen, Fathom
Kearney, James, Cloghoge
Kelly, Peter J., Heath hall
Larkin, Michael, Newtown
Little, James, Altnaveigh
Little, Joseph, Altnaveigh
Little, Robert, Altnaveigh
Lockhart, Henry, Lett
Lockhart, William, Altnaveigh
M'Connell, W. J., Carrievemaclone
M'Court, Patrick, Killyboda
M'Coy, Bernard, Fathom
M'Cullagh, David, Altnaveigh

M'Cullagh, James, Altnaveigh
M'Cullough, Wm., Carrickbrack
M'Dermott, Hugh, Corrinshigo
M'Elherron, Michael, Tullyhappy
M'Evoy, Hugh, Cloghoge
M'Evoy, Michl., Ellis's holding
M'Evoy, Ml., jun., Ellis's holding
M'Ewen, William, Demoan
M'Ewen, Wm., Killabodagh
M'Ginty, Peter, Killybodagh
M'Keown, John, Altnaveigh
M'Knight, John, Cloghoge
M'Knight, Michael, Fathom lr
M'Knight, Wm., Carnabane
M'Loughlin, Terence, Greenan
M'Mahon, Jas. (J.P.), Bellevue
M'Parland, John (P.M.), Fathom
M'Watters, James, Corrinshigo
Mallin, Luke, Derrybeg

Marmion, Patk., Carrievemaclone
O'Hara, Hugh, Carnagat
O'Neill, Arthur, Fathom
O'Neill, James, Fathom
O'Neill, Patrick, Fathom lr
Quinn, Terence, Newtown
Rantin, Thomas Mullaglass
Rogers, Wm., Carnagat
Sands, Hugh, Cullentra
Sloan, Patrick, Goragh
Sturgeon, Robert, Latt
Thompson, Henry, Carnagat
Thompson, John, D'willigan
Thomson,Hy.(J.P.),Altnaveigh ho
Trusdale, John, Derrywilligan
Waddell, Isaac, Lisdrumgullion
Wallace, John, Corrinshigo
Wallace, Robert, Lisnalee
Whiteside, Wm., Goragh

BESSBROOK.

Estimated population 3,500 in 1887.

BESSBROOK is situated in the barony of Upper Orior, 2½ miles north-west of Newry by road, and 3 miles by electric railway. It occupies the side of a hill, from the summit of which the range of view includes the Mourne Mountains, and the County Down as far as the hill of Rathfriland. In the building of Bessbrook the streets and places were laid out so that all the advantages of high eleva-tion might be secured without any of the troublesome drawbacks arising from steep descents. As a social experiment this town has been much talked about, and frequently described in print by enthusiastic visitors. The enterprise which gave it birth was initiated by the Richardson family in 1845. They had plenty of land and water, and the requisite capital to carry out a scheme intended to be of great magnitude. A beginning was made by the purchase and re-building of the first power flax spinning mill in Ireland. A few scattered houses and the residence of Mr. J. Nicholson, then represented Bessbrook. It was not classed among the villages of the County.

The various stages of development are recorded in the next chapter. In a period of 43 years the manufacturing interests had necessitated the erection of from 600 to 700 houses for the accommodation of factory and mill-workers. To provide con-stant employment for these people and, at the same time, attend to their social well being taxed the energies of the Messrs.

Richardson and their partners. Although the proprietary interest belonged to members of the Society of Friends there was no attempt to make Bessbrook a settlement for persons of that denomination. The moral teachings which have prominence in the Society were responsible for putting into practice the theory that the happiness of a community may be secured without public houses. In the course of time it came to be a settled belief that by ruling out the publican the services of the pawn-broker and policeman could also be dispensed with. In short, it may be said that the town is governed under an unwritten law, the main feature of which is the exclusion of the three P's. It is not easy for a stranger to examine all the points for and against the system in vogue at Bessbrook, but this much can be said truthfully, that the inhabitants are well domiciled, and have a thrifty appearance. Each house has a garden containing an eighth of an acre, and when the tenant enters into possession he is required to sign an agreement which contains certain stipulations in regard to the keeping of fowl and pigs, so that they may not be found in the quarters occupied by the family or in the yard. He can have a pig-stye and fowl-run in the garden if he pleases. Another binding clause places him under obligation to send his children to school until they are old enough for mill-work. In 1885 a Town Hall was built at an expense of £2,600, from a design by Mr. W. J. Watson, Architect, Newry. It is a handsome granite structure, and has a spacious assembly room and reading room and library. The working people elect their own committee of control, and appear to enjoy the benefits of the institution. The Company provides gas, and maintains Co-operative Stores for the supply of provisions of all kinds, including milk, butter and beef, but, as there are private business houses in town, and perfect freedom is accorded in the matter of trading, the suspicion of monopoly is avoided. The attractions of Newry may also be easily reached by the Electric Railway. This was opened in October, 1885, and in 1886 carried 97,668 passengers. Electric power is generated at Millvale, one mile from Bessbrook, by a 62-horse turbine. The road is owned by a separate Company, the stock-owners in which are nearly all stock-owners in the Bessbrook Spinning Company, Limited (see page 23). Excellent granite is quarried by the Spinning Company in the vicinity of the town, where there are also extensive polishing works.

Maghernaghely, or the hill of prayer, overlooks Bessbrook, and is the point from which the most charming view is obtained. It had a religious house early in the Christian Era. Some of the foundations existed at the time of the plantation of Ulster by James I., 1609. Henry McShane O'Neill received a

BESSBROOK SPINNING COMPANY, LTD, BESSBROOK

New York Agents: Messrs. RICHARDSON, SONS, & OWDEN, Ltd., 84 Franklin Street.

life interest in 1000 acres, 12 townlands, including Maghernaghely, part of the O'Hanlons country. At his death Sir Toby Caulfield came into possession, and built a "bawn" on Maghernaghely. It is said that he used the stones of the ancient abbey of Killeavy with great liberality in completing the work. There are extensive remains of the "bawn," some portions of the walls being fully 14 feet high, and partly covered with ivy. "Bawn" is derived from the Irish *Bo-dhun*, and means a cow enclosure or cow fortress.

The Protestant Episcopalians (C.I.), Presbyterians, Roman Catholics, Methodists, and Friends have places of worship, some of them in their architectural outlines helping to relieve the uniformity of the workers' houses. The land of the district of Bessbrook is good for pasture and tillage, until it rises to stony heights. Oats, potatoes and flax are the principal crops.

THE BESSBROOK SPINNING CO., LIMITED.

THE fine linens and cambrics woven by the looms of the Bessbrook Spinning Co., Limited, are known and appreciated in most of the countries of the world. The history of the Company must, therefore, be regarded as possessing considerable interest. A family named Pollock had a modest woollen industry at Bessbrook at the end of the last century, and owned the lands of the immediate vicinity. Mr. Joseph Nicholson succeeded the Pollocks by purchase, and erected the first power flax spinning mill in Ireland. It was destroyed by fire in 1845. Soon afterward the Richardson family bought Bessbrook. They put up a new mill on a much larger scale, near the site of the old one. From that time building operations were carried on at intervals until Bessbrook assumed the proportions of a populous town, one spinning mill alone having 22,000 spindles, and one weaving factory from 500 to 600 looms. A hand-loom weaving factory occupies the spot where the Pollock woollen mill stood. Here the methods of "the good old days" for the production of superfine linens, are still preserved. A green for yarn-bleaching by a particular process, is also maintained. Works of the Company, in addition to those mentioned, extend for over a mile along the River Bess, between Camlough and Newry. At Mount Caulfield there are two mills—one for spinning, and the other for beetle-finishing. At Deramore a mill for granite polishing and flax scutching. At Millvale there are two mills, one for scutching and the other for generating power for the electric tramway between Bessbrook and Newry. At Craigmore there is a weaving factory containing 160 power looms. Steam and water are used for driving purposes. There are nine steam engines giving an aggregate indicated power of 1,400 horse. Six turbines and four breast wheels give a united power of 412 horse. Camlough is the source of the Bess. It receives the surplus after supplying the domestic requirements of Newry. About 3,500 people are employed at Bessbrook. A branch at Lurgan is used for preparing and distributing linen yarns to between 800 and 1,000 cottage weavers. The Dromalane spinning mill at Newry, described in the Book of County Down, has 7,200 spindles, and from 300 to 400 work-people. Over 4,500 receive employment in the County Armagh, and a record of the interests of the Company will be found also in the Book of Antrim. For many years, until 1876, when the Bessbrook Spinning Co., Limited, was organized, the vast business which I have briefly outlined was conducted by Mr. John G. Richardson and his partners, Messrs. James N. Richardson, jun., Mr. John F. Harris, and Mr. Henry Barcroft.

Bakers: J. & L. Dale, S. Sinton
Churches: C. I., Rev. A. L. Forde; Christians; Friends; Methodist, Rev. Samuel Allen; Presbyterian, Rev. Thomas Cromie; R. C., Rev. James Grimes, c.c.
Dispensary: Dr. Charles Clarke
Drapers: Miss Margaret Barr, General stores, John Harland, Thos. O'Hare, Mrs. Frances Pearson
Electric Railway, John G. Richardson, chairman; Herbert Harrison, secretary and manager
Glass, China, &c., Michl. Boyle
Grocers: Cinnamon Brothers, Wm. Crouch, Hugh Dale, J. and L. Dale, General stores, John Harland, Thos. O'Hare, Edward Shimmons, Samuel Sinton, John Wilson
Hotel, Temperance, Alex. Weir
Linen manufacturers, flax spinners, bleachers, &c.: The Bessbrook Spinning Co., Ltd
Physicians: Charles Clarke, Hy. G. Gray, Millvale, Joseph Lightburne, Millvale
Post M. : Michael Boyle
Quarry owners: Bessbrook Spinning Co., Ltd
Schools, National : John Harding, Miss S. Thorpe, Bessbrook; Miss Sarah Quinn, Maghernahely
Town hall, Library, and Reading room, T. Hanna, caretaker

Victuallers: The Farm, Chas. M'Call, Daniel O'Hare

Farmers & Residents
Auterson, George, Mullaglass
Auterson, John, Haytown
Barron, Wm., Eshwary
Bell, Joseph, Springhill
Best, John, Cloghinny
Best, Robert, Cloghrea
Best, Thomas, Cloghinny
Bowes, James, Derrymore
Boyle, Edward, Drumhariff
Boyle, Michael, Drumhariff
Bradley, Bernard, Drummond
Brown, Jas. R. H., Mullaglass
Brown, John, Mullaglass
Brown, Samuel, Maytown
Burns, Francis, Eshwary
Chambers, Wm., Mullaglass
Cardwell, L. B., Carrickbracken
Cartmill, Samuel, Divernagh
Cartmill, Thomas, Mullaglass
Crawford, Henry, Derrybeg
Crilly, John, Maghernahely
Dale, James, Clogharevon
Darcy, Peter, Tullywinney
Davies, Wm. (J.P.), Farm Yard
Davis, Edwin, Bessbrook
Dillon, Wm., Tullyhappy
Donnelly, Patrick, Cloghrea
Ewart, Thomas, Divernagh
Fisher, Joseph R., Bessbrook
Flynn, Thos. M. H., Bessbrook
Freeburn, John, Clogheraven

Freeburn, Joseph, Clogheraven
Gilbert, Henry, Bessbrook
Gourley, John, sen., Divernagh
Graham, James, Divernagh
Graham, John, Tullywinney
Graham, Robert, Derrywilligan
Graham, Samuel, Tullywinney
Gray, Edward W. A., Mullaglass
Greene, Wm. E., Divernagh
Hanlon, Mrs., Maghernahely
Hardy, John, Derrymore
Harris, John F., The Cottage
Harris, Wm., The Cottage
Harpur, Robert (J.P.), Divernagh
Harrison, Mrs., Divernagh
Hill, Mrs., Derrymore
Ingram, Robert, Divernagh
Kearney, Patrick, Divernagh
Lefevre, Gustave, Bessbrook
Lemon, W. H. G., Derrywilligan
Livingston, Archbd., Mullaglass
Livingstone, John, Maytown
M'Anulty, Arthur, Drumhariff
M'Clelland, Wm., Mullaglass
M'Clenchan, John, Clogharivan
M'Cormick, John, Divernagh
M'Keown, Ed., jun., Tullywinny
M'Keon, Felix, Maghernahely

M'Keown, Felix, Tullywinney
M'Keown, John, Drumhariff
M'Keown, Michael, Drumhariff
M'Keown, Patrick, Drumhariff
M'Knight, Stewart, Derrybeg
Maffit, Thomas, Drumhariff
Magennis, Edward, Drumhariff
Martin, Robert, Maghernahely
Murphy, Archibald, Mullaglass
O'Hare, Patrick, Tamnaghbane
Pedlow, Robert, Bessbrook
Pringle, Alexander, Derrymore
Reynolds, Edwin D., Derrymore
Rice, James, Enagh
Richardson, Jas. N., M'tcaulfield
Richardson, John G., Woodhouse
Rogers, R. S., Tullywinny
Rogers, Wm., Tullywinny
Smith, James, Enagh
Taylor, Robert, Derrywilligan
Thompson, Wm., Divernagh
Thorp, John, Bessbrook
Torley, James, Carrickcloghan
White, Daniel, Divernagh
White, Henry, Divernagh
Williamson, A. W., Millvale
Williamson, Wm., Divernagh
Wonfor, Wm.. Clogharevan

Q

CLONTIGORA.

LONTIGORA is a rural post office, 4 miles south by west from Newry, and 2 miles north of Flurrybridge. The land is stony, and not easily cultivated. Oats and potatoes are the chief crops.

Post Master: James M'Guigan

Farmers & Residents.

Boyle Denis, Clontigora
Clarke, Cornelius, Clontigora
Clarke, John, Clontigora
Clarke, Mrs. C., Fathom
Clark, Patrick, Clontigora
Hanlon, Terence, Clontigora
Kinney, Edward, Killeen
Loughran, Mrs. S., Fathom
M'Donnell, Arthur, Clontigora
M'Donnell, Mrs. Bt., Clontigora
M'Keown, Philip, Clontigora
M'Namee, Joseph, Clontigora
M'Nulty, Mrs. E., Killen
M'Nulty, Mrs. S., Killen
Mathers, James, Clontigora
Matthews, James, Clontigora
Matthews, John, Newtown
Mullan, Patrick, Killeen
Murphy, Lawrence, Killeen
Murphy, Patrick, Clontigora
Sloan, Thomas, Killeen

DRUMANTEE.

RUMANTEE is a village of 10 houses, 6 miles, Irish, south-west of Newry, and 4 miles, Irish, north-west of Dundalk. It is at the head of the beautiful valley of the Forkhill river, and within a short distance of the foot of Slieve Gullion. Some of the land of the district is good, and the rest rocky. A fine Roman Catholic Church occupies the highest point in the village, and is seen for miles around. It was built in 1870.

Blacksmith: Patrick Groogan
Carpenter: John Campbell
Church: R. C., Rev. B. Donnellan, C.C., Rev. P. Gogarty, C.C.
Grocers : George M'Aleavey, Terence M'Aleavey
School, National: Bernard Larkin, Mrs. Mary Fegan

Farmers & Residents.

Begley, Michael, Carrickbroad
Begley, Patrick, Carrickbroad
Begley, Patrick, Drumantee
Boyle, Michael, Drumantee
Brennon, Patrick, Drumantee
Cahoon, James, Drumantee
Downey, Mrs. M., Drumantee
Dunn, James, Drumantee
Fegan, John, sen., Tievecrom
Finnegan, Daniel, Foughill Otra
Finnegan, Owen, Foughill Etra
Finnegan, Peter, Foughill
Gallagher, Charles, Drumantee

Hanratty, James, Cloghinny
Harvey, James, Drumantee
Kelly, Owen, Slievegullion
M'Crink, Francis, Drumantee
M'Crink, Patrick, sen., Drumantee
M'Nabb, Patrick, Drumantee
M'Shane, Arthur, Tievecrom
M'Shane, Bernard, Slieve Gullion
M'Shane, E., Tievecrum
M'Shane, Patrick, Drumantee
M'Shane, Patrick, Tievecrom
Morgan, John, Drumantee
Mulholland, Charles, Drumantee
Mulholland, Patrick, Drumantee
Mulholland, Thomas, Drumantee

Murphy, Arthur, Carrickbroad
Murphy, Owen, Cloghinny
Murphy, Owen, Drumantee
Murphy, Thomas, Carrickbroad
O'Hare, F., Drumantee
O'Hare, Bernard, Slieve Gullion
O'Hare, Michael, Drumantee
O'Hare, Mrs. A., Drumantee
O'Hare, Mrs. Mary, Drumantee
O'Hare, Patrick, Drumantee
O'Rorke, Patrick, Foughill Otra
Rice, Laurence, Foughill Etra
Rice, Thomas, Foughill Etra
Stanley, Hugh, Drumantee
White, Michael, Foughill Etra

FLURRYBRIDGE.

FLURRYBRIDGE is a picturesquely situated village, on the border of Armagh and Louth, over 5 miles south by west from Newry, on the way to Dundalk. The village is divided by the Flurry River. One part is called Jonesborough, and the other Flurrybridge. To the postal authorities the name Flurrybridge covers both. Lord Carlingford and the Jones representatives are the proprietors of the village and district. Fairs were held at Jonesborough down to about 20 years ago, but none since. Some of the land of the neighborhood is fair, some rocky, and some boggy. Oats and potatoes are the chief crops. The Castle of Moyre Pass, described at page 33, is 3 miles to the north-west.

Blacksmith: H. M'Kinley
Carpenter: John Walker
Churches: I.C., Rev. J.R. Scott;
Presbyterian, Rev. Samuel L. Harrison; R. C., Rev. Thomas J. Murphy, P.P.
Grocers: Owen M'Manus, Mrs. Neary, Mrs. J. O'Neill
Post M.: Mrs. S. Morton
R. I. C.: Sergeant Patrick Boylan

School, National: John Murphy, Mrs. Kate Keegan
Spirit retailer: Samuel M'Comb
Farmers & Residents.
(See also Book of County Louth by George Henry Bassett.)
Barrett, Richard, Foughill Otra
Campbell, John, Foughill Otra
Dick, James, Edenappa
Jordan, Peter, Edenappa
Scott, Rev. J. R., Edenappa

JERRETSPASS.

JERRETSPASS is a rural post-office, on the Dow border, between 4 and 5 miles north by west from Newry, and 1 mile from the Goraghwood Railway Junction. The land of the district is good for pasture and tillage.

Blacksmiths : Robert Loughlin, John Shannon

Carpenter : William Porter

Churches : C. I., Rev. Henry Taylor, Rev. James M. Ford ; Presbyterian, Rev. Robt. R. Lindsay, Rev. Alfred Hamilton ; R. C., Rev. Charles Quinn

Corn and Scutch Mill : Nathl. Henry

Grocers : David Gordon, John Hughes.

Post Master : John M'Laughlin

Railway Junction (Goraghwood) Robert Lewis, toll collector

Quarry owners, Goraghwood : John Robinson & Son

Schools, National : John Gilmore, Anne M'Donnell, Henry Fenn

Spirit retailer : James Porter

Farmers & Residents.

Agnew, Robert, Serse
Bell, John, Serse
Best, James, Latt
Buchanan, James, Tullyhappy
Buchanan, Stewart, Lett
Buchanan, William, Cloghinny
Clarke, George, Goragh
Clarke, George, Lissummon
Clarke, John, jun., Derrywilligan
Clarke, Samuel, Goragh
Clarke, Thomas, Goragh
Connolly, Bernard, Lett
Copeland, Joseph, Tullyhappy
Doran, Patrick, Lissummon
Douglas, Gawn, Latt
Ewart, John, Tullyhappy
Finch, Alexander, Demoan
Gordon, Hugh, Serse
Gordon, John, Serse
Gordon, Samuel, Serse
Gracey, Joseph, Tullyhappy
Hawthorne, Hugh, Tullyhappy
Henry, John, Kilrea
Henry, William, Kilmonaghan
Irvine, James, Cloghinny
Irwin, Robert, Goragh
Kearns, David, Tullyhappy
Kearns, Samuel, Tullyhappy

Kelly, Robert, Kilrea
Kelly, William, Knockduff
Kerr, Francis, Serse
Lisgow, William, Mullaglass
Lockhart, Edward, Kilmonaghan
Lockhart, John, Knockduff
Lockhart, Robert, Tullyhappy
Lynch, Daniel, Skegatilleda
Lynch, James, Kilrea
Lynch, John, Lisummon
M'Caffery, Dr. Hugh, Lissummon
M'Caffery, Hugh, Lissummon
M'Cartney, George, Serse
M'Cartney, Wm., Tullyhappy
M'Comb, David, Drumbanagher
M'Murray, William, Jerrettspass
M'Wheter, John, Tullyhappy
M'Whirter, John, Goragh
Mooney, James, Lissummon
Mooney, Michael, Kilrea
Morton, Thomas, Drumbanagher
O'Hagan, Thomas, Lissummon
O'Hare, John, Lissummon
Patterson, W. J., Tullyhappy
Porter, Jobn H., Cloghinny
Porter, John, jun., Goragh
Porter, Joseph, Kilmonaghan
Porter, Robert, Latt
Porter, William, Kilrea
Poyntz, George, Serse
Rafferty, Charles, Lissummon
Rantin, Thomas, Tullyhappy
Reid, Isaac, Serse
Reid, Thomas, Serse
Revill, Joseph, Tullyhappy
Revill, Nathaniel, Tullyhappy
Rice, David, Lissummon
Robinson, Thomas, Demoan
Ross, W. G., Tullyhappy
Thompson, Alex., Knockduff
Thompson, Benjamin, Knockduff
Wallace, Hugh, Tullyhappy
Whigham, Joshua, Lett
White, John, Demoan
Whiteside, John, Drumbanagher
Whiteside, Robert, Demoan
Whiteside, Robt., Drumbanagher
Whiteside, Thos., Drumbanagher
Wilson, Samuel, Skegatilda
Wilson, Samuel, jun. Skegatilda

KILLEAVY AND MEIGH.

KILLEAVY is a village of 8 houses, known locally as Meigh, 4 miles south by west from Newry. The land of the district is of medium quality in some parts, and in others boggy and stony. Killeavy Castle, residence of Mr. Joseph Bell, is charmingly situated at the foot of Slieve Gullion. Mr. Joseph Foxall, over 60 years ago, planted a considerable portion of the mountain, and his successor, Mr. Powell Foxall, continued the example until a large tract had been covered. Much of the plantation higher up has been removed. There are some remains of a nunnery close to Slieve Gullion, the walls of which were quarried by Sir Toby Caulfield to build his " bawn " at Bessbrook, which see. The nunnery is said to have been founded by St. Monenna, sister of St. Patrick. Her death is recorded by the Annalists as having occurred in 517.

Blacksmith : Thos. Connellan
Carpenter : Ml. McKeever
Churches : C.I., Rev. Thos. G. Irwin ; R.C., Rev. Thos. Hardy, P.P., Rev. Francis Carlon, C.C.
Dispensary: Dr. Thos. Mulligan
Grocers : Patrick M'Nally, Mrs. Cath. O'Hagan
Post M. : Patrick Lee
Process server : John Turner
School, National : Jas. Gallen, Miss B. Johnston
Spirit retailer : Mrs. M. Connellan

Farmers & Residents
Bell, Joseph, Killeavy castle
Boyle, John, jun. Aghyalloge
Burns, Thos., Aghadavoyle
Byrne, Peter, Ballymacdermott
Colgan, Henry, Aghyalloge
Fearon, Mrs. M., T'bawn
Ford, Thomas, Ballintempel

Hanlon, Mrs. S., Seafin
Haughey, Mrs. B., Meigh
Hoey, John, Seafin
Larkin, Bernard, Seafin
Loughrin, Owen, Ballymacdermott
M'Conville, Patrick, Clonlum
M'Donnell, Anthony, Aghyalloge
M'Ginnis, Wm., Clonlum
M'Kernan, John, Aghyalloge
M'Nally, James, Ballinliss
M'Nally, Patrick, Meigh
M'Parland, Edward, Seafin
M'Sherry, Neal, Seafin
Maginness, James, Clonlum
Mallin, Thomas, sen., Meigh
Mallin, Thomas, jun., Meigh
Mallon, E., Ballymacdermott
Mallon, Stephen, Seafin
Murphy, Thomas, Adavoil
O'Hare, John, Ballintemple
Paul, Robert, Adavoil
Toal, Mrs. A., Ballintemple

POYNTZPASS.

Population 343 in 1881.

POYNTZPASS is situated on the side of a hill 8 miles, Irish, north by west from Newry, and 4 miles, Irish, south of Tandragee. It is a station on the Belfast Junction Railway, between Dublin and Belfast. The land of the district has been much improved during the last

50 years by drainage, etc. Oats and potatoes are the principal crops. The farmers also grow some flax, and make a feature of dairying. There are good cattle fairs, and a market, established over a year, is held every Friday, for fowl, butter, and eggs. A few hand-loom weavers live in the village, and employment is given to the surplus female population, at hem-stitching, by manufacturers belonging to other places. Poyntzpass was once the north-eastern extremity of a morass which began at Mount-norris. In the vicinity there were extensive earthworks, called Tyrone's Ditches. Hugh O'Neill, Earl of Tyrone, in his rebellion against Queen Elizabeth, 1594-1603, made a strong-hold here. During the period when the O'Hanlons and the Magennises ruled portions of Armagh and Down, the " Pass " connected their territories. The present name was given to it in recognition of a feat of arms performed by Lieutenant Poyntz of the English army. At the head of a comparatively small force he captured the " Pass " in a hand-to-hand struggle with a superior number of O'Neill's troops. A grant of 500 acres, in the barony of Lower Orior, was included in the reward he received for this service.

POYNTZPASS DIRECTORY.

Blacksmiths : Bernard Conlan, P. Mooney, Dd. Moody

Carpenters : Robt. Hunter, J. M'Murray, Wm. Moody

Cattle dealers : J. and J. Little, Hugh O'Hare

Churches : C. I., Rev. C. F. Archer ; Presbyterian, Rev. Thos. Irwin ; Presbyterian Reformed, Rev. Geo. Laverty : R.C., Rev. John M'Donald, c.c.

Corn and scutch mills : Wm. B. Bennett

Dispensary : Dr. W. R. M'Dermott

Drapers : Wm. Griffith, Geo. W. M'Kelvey, Misses. J. and M. Sheilds, Miss Eliza Ward

Grocers marked thus (*) retail spirits ; (†) hardware); Ml. Canavan (spirit grocer only), Edward Griffith †, Geo. Hare, Wm. Kelso, Robt. M'Kelvey, Mrs. Agnes Mann *, Patrick O'Hare, Patrick Quinn †, Thos. Rice *

News Agents : James Bell, Ml. Canavan, Mrs. M. A. Dargan, Marcus Searight

Nursery : Mrs. A. Mann

Petty Sessions first Monday every month ; Robt. Emerson, Tandragee, clerk

Physicians : Jos. Davis, Wm. R. M'Dermott

Post M. : Geo. Hare

Process server : Wm. Baird

Railway station : Jere. Davidson, T.C.

R.I.C. : Sergt. J. H. Blair

Schools, National : James Watson, 1 ; Arch. M'Veigh, 2

Spirit retailers, see also grocers : Jas. Bell, Mrs. E. Rice, Marcus Searight

Victuallers : Ml. M'Guill, Patk. Quinn

Farmers & Residents

Acheson, Jos., Crewmore
Acheson, R. J., Crewmore
Acheson, Wm. B., Crewmore
Alexander, Col. Wm. J., Brannock
Alexander, Mrs. G., Brannock
Andrews, Hugh, Ballynaleck
Atcheson, Jas., sen., Crewmore
Atcheson, Jas., jun., Crewmore
Barber, Wm. J., Lisnagree
Bell, Mrs. L., Acton
Bennett, Wm. B., Poyntzpass
Bennett, Mrs. I., Poyntzpass
Bittles, Jacob, jun., Cullentragh
Blacker, Francis, Aghantaraghan
Boardman, John, Crewbeg
Boyce, John, Druminargle
Boyd, Thos., Druminargle
Calvert, Wm., Brannock
Campbell, Chas., jun., Tanyokey
Christy, Geo., Ballyreagh
Clarke, Hy., jun., Aghantaraghan

Clarke, James, Carrickbrack
Clarke, Thomas, Corcrum
Cole, Isaac, Crewmore
Cole, James, Carrickbrack
Close, J., Aughantaraghan
Connor, Bernard, Corcrum
Crothers, Alex., Lisraw
Crothers, Geo., Lisraw
Cunningham, Rt., Rathconville
Cunningham, John, Rathconville
Denny, Aaron, Ballyreagh
Denny, Joseph, Tullylinn
Derry, Hugh, Corcrum
Dillon, John, Rathconville
Douglas, David, Rathconville
Fegan, Samuel, Ballenan
Ferguson, Alex., Ballyreagh
Finch, Henry, Tannyokey
Fisher, Charles, Tullynacross
Gillow, John, Ballynalack
Gillow, Joseph, Ballynalack
Goodfellow, Mrs. C., B'nagreagh
Gracey, John, Druminargle
Hall, George, Aghantaraghan
Hanlon, James, A'taraghan
Hanna, James, Ballynalack
Hazley, F., Aghantaraghan
Hazley, Samuel, A'taraghan
Henry, Robert, Ballynalack
Henry, Thomas, Tannyokey
Hunter, Aaron, Tullynacross
Hunter, John, Glassdrummond
Hunter, Wm., Ballyreagh
Hutcheson, James, Crewmore
Hutchinson, T., Crewmore
King, Mrs. E., Ballyreagh
Kinnel, James, Carrickbrack
Lamb, John, Federnagh
Lamb, Robert, Federnagh
Leggett, —, Aghantaraghan
Liggett, Thos, Ballynagreagh
Little, James, Federnagh
Little, John, Tullynacross
Little, J., Aghantaraghan
Lundy, Ferguson, Carrickbrack
M'Clelland, Mrs., Crewmore
M'Clelland, R. S., Crewmore
M'Clelland, Thomas, Ballynaleck
M'Conville, James, Ballydoherty
M'Dermott, Wm. R., Poyntzpass

M'Donnell, Hugh, Tullynacross
M'Donnell, John, Tullynacross
M'Dowell, John, Lisnagree
M'Elroy, Robert, Lisnagree
M'Elroy, Thos., Corcrum
M'Guill, James, Federnagh
M'Guill, James, Poyntzpass
M'Guinness, I., Aghantaraghan
M'Mullen, Mrs. E., Ballyrea
M'Mullan, Thomas, Ballyreagh
M'Murray, R. J., Crewbeg
M'Nally, Hugh, Corcrum
M'Parland, John, Shaneglish
Madden, John, Federnagh
Mighau, Hugh, Lisnagree
Monaghan, James, A'taraghan
Moody, David, Lisraw
Murray, John, Corcrum
Neill, Michael, Lisraw
Nelson, John, Crewbeg
Nicholl, Mrs., Cornair
O'Hare, H., Aghantaraghan
Porter, James, Ballenan
Porter, Thos., Carrickbrack
Quinn, Felix, Lisnagree

Qua, John, Rathconville
Qua, William, Federnagh
Rafferty, Patrick, Lisnagree
Reid, Rev. W., Crewmore
Savage, Rev. Alex., Cullentra
Shields, Saml., Lisnagree
Smith, Wm., Crewbeg
Stephenson, Archibd., Rathconville
Stephenson, S., Rathconvil
Strain, David, Crewmore
Stratton, James, Demoan
Turner, Robert, Crewbeg
Turner, William, Tannyokey
Watson, Wm., Tanyokey
White, John, Ballyreagh
Whiteside, John, Corcrum
Wiley, D., Ballynagreagh
Wiley, Wm., Tanyoky
Williamson, Jos., Aghantaraghan
Williamson, Jos., Poyntzpass
Williamson, Rt., Shaneglish
Woods, Wm. J., Ballynaleck
Wright, Fr., Aghantaraghan
Wright, J., Aghantaraghan
Wright, Sl., Ballyreagh

SUB-POST OFFICES

IN THE DISTRICT OF CASTLEBLAYNEY.

LETTERS addressed to residents of a sub-postal district should bear the name of the head office, thus : Camlough, Castleblayney. The following residents of County Armagh receive their letters from Castleblayney :

Hunter, Andrew, Cortanty | Verner, Robert, Derryane

ALTNAMACHIN.

Trout Fishing.

ALTNAMACHIN is a rural post-office on the border of County Monaghan, 3 miles, Irish, south-west from Newtownhamilton. It is within sight of a trout stream called the County Water, referred to at page 43. The land of the district is fair, and the chief crops are flax, oats and potatoes.

Blacksmith : Jas. Lutton
Beer license : Mrs. Mary Lutton
Church : Presbyterian, Rev. Rt.
J. Tweed
Grocers : Thos. J. Gray, Wm. Magill

Post M.: Mrs. M. Lutton
School, National: Miss L. Megaw, Skeriff; Sl. Adair, Cortamlet; Sl. Lockhart, Mulladuff
Scutch mills: Mrs. S. Clarke, David M'Kee

Farmers & Residents.
Allen, James, Altnamachin
Allen, Samuel, Cortamlet
Bell, James, Tullyvallen
Blackwood, George, Ballynarea
Blackwood, John, Ballynarea
Carsewell, William, Altnamachin
Caswell, John, Altnamachin
Clarke, James, Cortamlet
Clarke, Mrs., Cortamlet

Clarke, Robert, Cortamlet
Clarke, Samuel, Cortamlet
Clarke, Wm., Cortamlet
Clarke, Wm., jun., Cortamlet
Gordon, Thos., Altnamachin
Hughes, Robt., Altnamachin
Hughes, Wm., Altnamachin
Jenkins, James, Altnamachin
Lennon, Owen, Agincurk
Lyons, John, Altnamachin
M'Mahon, Mrs., Altnamachin
M'Quilly, Mrs., Altnamachin
Sheridan, Edward, Ballynarea
Steenson, James, Tullyvallen
Tremble, Wm., Altnamachin

BELLEEK.

BELLEEK is a village of 21 houses, in the barony of Lower Fews, 3 miles, Irish, east of Newtownhamilton, 5 Irish, west of Newry, and 13, Irish, south-east of Armagh. Loughgilly, 3½ miles, Irish, to the north-east, is the nearest railway siation. It is pleasantly situated on the side of a hill, and the land surrounding is fair when not rocky. The principal crops are oats, potatoes and flax. Buttermaking is carried on to some extent. Lord Gosford is the landlord. During the rebellion of Hugh O'Neill, Earl of Tyrone, 1594-1603, his chief ally, O'Donnell, besieged a barrack garrisoned at this place for Queen Elizabeth, and having compelled its surrender gave no quarter to the vanquished.

Churches: R.C., Rev. Thomas Donnelly, P.P., Rev. T. Montague, C.C.
Draper: Thos. M'Genney
Grocers and spirit retailers: Thomas M'Genney, John O'Hare
Post M.: Thos. M'Genney
R.I.C.: Sergt. John O'Grady
School, National: Mrs. M. M. Campbell
Scutch mill: John Markey
Spirit retailer, see also grocers: Bernard M'Ardle

Farmers & Residents.
Andrews, H. S., Carrowmannon
Andrews, Wm., Carrowmannon
Bennett, John, Carrickgollogly

Burns, Ml., Carrowmannon
Bennett, Patrick, Carrowmannon
Carroll, Peter, Belleek
Cowan, Francis, Cavanakill
Crilly, John, Dorsey M'Donald
Crilly, John, Carrickanany
Crilly, Lawrence, Cavanakill
Kernaghan, John, Outlacken
King, Alex., Outlacken
King, Andrew, Outlacken
King, James, Outlacken
King, Sl., Carrowmannon
King, Wm., jun., Outlacken
M'Ardle, John, Carrickanany
M'Ardle, Mrs. Ml., Carrowmannon
M'Comb, Alex., Outlacken
M'Conville, Mrs. E., T'gallahan

M'Conville, Mrs. M., Carromanon
M'Conville, Jas., Carrowmannon
M'Cresh, Mrs. A., T'gallahan
M'Cresh, Mrs. C., T'gallahan
M'Cresh, Mrs. M., T'gallahan
M'Cresh, Mrs. R., T'gallahan
M'Cresh, Owen, Tullyogallaghan
M'Cresh, Thos., Tullyogallaghan
M'Dermott, John, Carrowmannon
M'Dermott, P., Carricknagavana
M'Donnell, Alex., Drumnahunshin
M'Elroy, Ml., Carrowmannon
M'Gee, John, Ummerinvore
M'Geeney, Jas., Dorsey M'Donnell
M'Geeney, Ml., Dorsey M'Donald
M'Geeney, Thos., Carrowmanon
M'Geeney, Thos., jun., Belleek
M'Knight, Mrs. S., Carrowmanon
M'Parland, Edward, Outlacken
M'Parland, James, Belleek
M'Parland, Mrs. A., Carromanon
M'Parland, Patk., Carrickgallogly
M'Shane, James, Belleek
M'Verry, Fr., Drumilly
M'Verry, James, Belleek
M'Verry, John, Carnacally
M'Verry, Michael, Belleek

M'Verry, Owen, Belleek
M'Verry, Patrick, Carrowmanon
M'Verry, Peter, Carrowmannon
Magee, Mrs. M., Ummerinvore
Markey, James, Belleek
Markey, Michael, Belleek
Markey, Ml., Tullyogallaghan
Mitchell, Jas., Dorsey M'Donald
Mullan, James, Tullyogallaghan
Mullan, John, Belleek
Murphy, James, T'donnell Gage
Murphy, John, Tullyogallaghan
O'Callaghan, Owen, Belleek
O'Hare, A., Carrickgallogly
O'Hare, Mrs. E., Carromanon
Patton, Geo., Carrowmannon
Patton, Geo., Carrickananny
Patton, Mrs. Mt., Carromanon
Patton, Wm., Carrickananny
Preston, Wm., Carrickgollogly
Robb, Alex., Belleek
Robb J., Carrowmannon
Ross, J., Carrowmannon
Spires, James, Belleek
Walsh, Mrs. M., Carrowmanon
Walshe, Thos., Carrowmannon
Watson, Mrs. A., Carrowmanon

CAMLOUGH.

Population 192 *in* 1881.

CAMLOUGH is 3 miles, Irish, west of Newry, on the direct road to Newtownhamilton. The nearest station is Bessbrook, Belfast Junction Railway, a mile and a half. Its chief importance is derived from a fair held on the third Monday of every month, which is usually good for cattle, and improving for horses. With few exceptions the houses are well-built, and maintained in good condition. Mr. John G. Richardson owns the estate. For the most part the land of the district is light and rocky. Oats, potatoes and flax are the chief crops. Camlough, the crooked lake, is situated less than half a mile above the village. It is a handsome sheet of water, a mile and a half in length. In winter, at deepest point, it is 55 feet. The requirements of Newry for domestic and other uses are supplied from this, on terms fully described in my BOOK OF COUNTY DOWN. According to the provisions of the Act of Parliament, the Bessbrook Spinning Company, Limited, for power purposes, may draw from the lake 19 feet 6 inches of water. That in 1887 came to 750,000,000 gallons. "This," said Mr. Henry Bancroft, to whom I am indebted for the information, "was equal to the entire yield of petroleum for the same year."

Auctioneer: Jos. T. Cardwell
Bakers: Peter Boyle, Jno. Doyle, Ml. Murphy
Churches: R.C., Rev. Chas. Quinn, P.P., Rev. P. Quinlan, C.C.
Corn and scutch mill: Jno. Doyle
Dispensary: Dr. Jos. Lightburne
Grocers: John Doyle, Thos. Rafferty
Post M.: Ml. Sheeran
R.I.C.: Sergt. McKinney
Schools, Natl.: Peter McParland, Mrs. S. McParland
Spirit Retailers: Peter Boyle, Rt. Clancy, Mrs. E. Collins, Jno. Doyle, Ml. Murphy, Thomas Rafferty

Farmers & Residents.

Aiken, Jas., Carrickbracken
Barry, Ml., Camlough
Boyle, Bd., Ballynaleck
Boyle, John, Ballynaleck
Boyle, Ml., Ballynaleck
Burns, Ptk., Lissraw
Boyle, Peter, Cross
Burns, L., Duburren
Byrne, Thos., Carrickcloghan
Callaghan, Jos,, Liseraw
Cardwell, J. T., Cross
Cartmill, David, Divernagh
Collins, Bd., Carrickcruffen
Collins, Jos., Camlough
Conlan, Rev. P., C.C., Keggall
Cosgrove, D., Drumilly
Cosgrove, J., Eshwary
Crilly, Colin, Carrickcroppan
Crilly, Ml., Carrickbracken
Crilly, Mrs., Carrickbracken
Crilly, Ptk., Maghernahely
Collins, Edward, Derrybeg
Darcy, Anthony, Liseraw
Doyle, L., Carrabane
Doyle, Peter, Carrickcruppen
Eakin, J., Carrickbracken House
Elliott, Rt., Drumhariff

Fagan, Ml., Drumilly
Fearon, Dl., Carrickbracken
Fearon, John, Drumilly
Fearon, Patrick, Deburren
Garvey, Stephen, Aghmakane
Graham, Geo., Drumilly
Graham, Rt., Tullywinney
Graham, W., Tullywinney
Hanlon, John, Eshwary
Hanlon, Terence, Eshwary
Harrison, James, Tullywinny
Hughes, John, Liseraw
Kane, John, Drumilly
Kerr, Patt, Keggall
King, John, Sturgan
Larkin, Ml., Keggall
Lewers, Mrs., Tullywinney
Lowe, John, Carivekeeny
Lowe, Mrs., Carrickbracken
M'Cullagh, Geo., Tullywinney
M'Donnell, James, Tullywinney
M'Elroy, James, Sturgan
M'Glade, Patrick, Sturgan
M'Grath, Peter, Liseraw
M'Keown, John, Liseraw
M'Keown, Owen, Liseraw
M'Keown, Patrick, Drumilly
M'Keown, Peter, Eshwary
M'Parland, Luke, Tullyagh
M'Parland, Ml., Cross
M'Parland, Peter, Deburren
M'Quaide, Berd., Carrickloughan
M'Quaide, Mrs., Carrickcruppen
M'Shane, Mrs. M., Kegghall
M'Shane, Mrs. Mary, Cross
M'Shane, Mrs. Mt., Cross
M'Keown, Bernard, Liseraw
Maginnis, Felix, Liseraw
Maginnis, John, Aghmakane
Maginnis, Owen, Aghmakane
O'Hare, Mrs. M., Ashwary
O'Hare, Mrs., Ashwary
O'Neill, Hugh, Derrymore
O'Toole, John, Deburren
Quinn, Patrick, Liseraw

OWEN McARDLE,

Family Grocer,

TEA, WINE, SPIRIT & PROVISION MERCHANT,

NORTH STREET,

CROSSMAGLEN.

COMMERCIAL HOTEL
AND
POSTING ESTABLISHMENT,
CROSSMAGLEN.

HENRY LENNON,
Proprietor.

The Commercial Hotel is situated within a mile of some of the finest angling places in Ireland. Salmon and Trout fishing. First-rate Duck, Widgeon, Snipe and Plover shooting to be had in the Crossmaglen district. Fishing and Shooting rights free to all comers.

☞ Cars attend at Culloville Railway Station on notification by wire or postal card.

Rogers, Wm., Liseraw
Smith, James, Carrickloghan
Sands, John, Sturgan
Smith, Ml., Carrickloghan

Smith, Thos., Carrickloghan
Toal, James, Drumilly
Torley, Bd., Carrickcroppan
Williamson, Jno., Eshwarry

JAMES McCONVILLE & CO.,
CROSSMAGLEN.

Departments : Groceries, Provisions, Plain & Fancy Baking, Wines and Spirits, Farm Seeds, Artificial Manures, Funeral Undertaking.

☞ **FLAX SCUTCHING MILLS.**

JAMES BEGLEY,
FAMILY GROCER,
TEA, PROVISION & LEATHER MERCHANT,
CROSSMAGLEN.
Agent for Manufacturers of Hemstitched and Embroidered Handkerchiefs.

CROSSMAGLEN.

Population 872 in 1881.—Trout-fishing.

CROSSMAGLEN is in the barony of Upper Fews, at the southern extremity of the County. The City of Armagh is 16 miles, Irish, to the north. Culloville, on the border of Monaghan, 2 miles, Irish, to the south-west, is the nearest railway station. The chief feature of the town is a broad square, fronted by well-built business houses. In this a market is held every Friday for butter, eggs, fowl, and for grain and grass-seed in season. The supply of grass-seed is usually quite large. A fair is also held on the first Friday of every month for cattle, sheep, pigs and horses. No tolls are charged, but there is a market house where a small fee is paid for weighing. Crossmaglen depends for prosperity almost entirely on the results of the agricultural operations in the surrounding country. In some parts of the parish of Creggan, in which the town is situated, the land is good. There is a considerable amount of bog, and a large area is rocky. Oats, potatoes and flax are the principal crops. Flax is relied on to a great extent by the farmers as a rent-making crop. Dairying is also done extensively. There are lead mines at Cregganduff and Tullydonnell in the vicinity of Crossmaglen, but they have not been worked for 14 or 15 years. Plenty of slate is also found in the parish, but it is not used. The water supply of the town

PHILIP McARDLE,

FAMILY GROCER,

Tea, Wine, Spirit & Provision Merchant

CROSSMAGLEN.

FRANCIS SHORT,

WHOLESALE & FAMILY GROCER,

Tea Importer,

WINE, SPIRIT AND PROVISION MERCHANT,

AND CAR PROPRIETOR,

CROSSMAGLEN.

☞ Agent for the **Allan** and **Warren** Lines to America.

Exporter of Butter and Eggs.

is drawn from a pump in the Market Square, and, as evidence of its purity, it is said that when the cholera raged in Ireland, 1832-3, not a case occurred at Crossmaglen. Between 600 and 700 females of Crossmaglen and district receive work at embroidery and hemstitching through resident agents for manufacturers.

Ample facilities are afforded for fishing and shooting. The Fane, a fine salmon river, is within a mile and a half, and the Creggan, an excellent trout river, within a mile. In addition to these there are 18 lakes, the furthermost not more than 3 miles. All are stocked with trout, and open to be fished without either "leave or license." (See page 41.) Duck, widgeon, teal and snipe are abundant. Lough Ross, within an Irish mile of Crossmaglen, has beautiful surroundings. An island almost in the centre, is one of the attractive features. Mr. James Hanratty, J.P., owns most of Lough Ross, which is one of a chain of 16 lakes winding most picturesquely between cultivated hills from the vicinity of Cullyhanna toward Castleblayney. There are several curious earthen forts to interest the antiquary. Along the Creggan river the scenery is charming. The parish church, a fine edifice, is on the eastern bank, about three-fourths of a mile from town. It was built in 1758. In the grave yard attached visitors are shown a memorial slab bearing the name of Daniel O'Neill, and a representation of the hand which denotes the O'Neills of Ulster.

The people of Crossmaglen are fond of sport; grey hounds are kept by several of the merchants. Hares are easily found. The custom is to go out with about four dogs and slip off two at a hare.

A branch of the Gaelic Athletic Association, called the "Red Hand of Ulster," has been in existence for nearly a year, and is in a flourishing condition.

Auctioneer: P. Fitzgibbon

Bakers: Jas. McConville & Co., Ptk. McConville, Peter McNamee, Hugh Morris

Bank, Belfast: Wm. E. Rogers, Mgr., John Porter Borough, Cash.

Blacksmiths: E. McArdle, Ml. McArdle, Jas. Morgan

Butter Mt.: F. Short

Carpenters: Ml. Grant, Ml. Malone

Churches: Rev. Fdk. W. Austin, Methodist, Castleblayney Circuit; R.C., Rev. Ptk. McGeeney, P.P., Rev. Jas. Loughran, C.C., Rev. Ptk. Quinn, C.C.

Dispensary: Dr. B. A. Palmer, J.P.

Drapers: John Boyle, Hugh Corr, Mrs. Kate Coyne, Jas. Hanratty, M. and E. McShane

Egg Exporters: John Hughes, Francis Short

Emigration Agents: Jno. Hughes Francis Short

Fowl Buyers: Jas. Martin, Jas. Martin, jun., Ptk. Martin, Peter Rush

Grain Merchants: Jas. Hanratty, Martin Kearney, Hy. Lennon

Grocers, marked thus [*] retail spirits, † hardware: Jas. Begley,

John Boyle, Hugh Corr, John Donaghy, Jas. Duffy*, Misses T. and M. Foley*, Nicholas Hale*, John Hannon, Thos. Laville*, Henry Lennon*, Owen McArdle*, Philip McArdle*, Jas. McConville and Co.*, J. McCormack, Bd. McEneaney, Ml. McEneaney†, Hugh Morris, Thomas Morris†, Francis Short*

Hotel and Posting Establishment: Henry Lennon

Lamps, &c.: Wm. Brown

Markets: Ptk. Fitzgibbon, clerk and weighmaster

Marine Stores: Patrick Barker, Patrick McQuillan

Newsagents, &c.: Patrick Fitzgibbon, Jno. Hannon, Dl. Magill

Petty Sessions first Saturday after the first Friday every month. James Smith, Clerk

Post Master and Stamp Distributor: Hugh Corr

Process Server: Patrick McEvoy

R.I.C.: Sergeant Edward Monaghan

Saddler: John Hughes

Schools, Natl.: P. Garvey, Miss E. McArdle, Miss A. Hanratty

Scutchmill: James McConville and Co.

Sewing Agents: James Begley, John Donaghy

Solicitor: Wm. R. Corr

Spirit Retailers, see also Grocers: Richard Craige, Francis Hanratty, Martin Kearney, Owen McGowan, Owen Ward

Tinsmiths: White and Sons

Undertakers: James Duffy, James McConville & Co., John McCormick, J. M. Morris

Victuallers: Thomas McAntee, Peter McQuillan

Farmers & Residents

Bailey, Mrs., Drumlogher
Beatty, Wm., Creggan
Begley, John, Cregganbane
Boyle, James, Urker

Brown, Alex., Cloghoge
Brown, Mrs., Crossmaglen
Brown, Thomas, Cloghoge
Burns, Owen, Annagad
Cunningham, Patk., Creevekeeran
Carragher, Fr., Crinkill
Carragher, Mrs., Tullyard
Daly, Michael, Carron
Devine, Peter, Cregganduff
Donaghy, Henry, Clarbane
Donaghy, James, Corliss
Donaldson, James, Cloghoge
Donaldson, Wm., Cloghoge
Ellis, Mrs. Ann, Crossmaglen
Gartland, Owen, Annagad
Gilmore, Eleazer, Liscolgat
Grant, James, Corliss
Grant, John, Carron
Hale, James, Crossmaglen
Hale, Joseph, Crossmaglen
Hale, Richard, Crossmaglen
Hanratty, Felix, Crinkill
Harvey, James, Drumboy
Harvey, John, Drummuckavall
Harvey, Owen, Drummuckavall
Harvey, Patrick, Drumuck
Hughes, Peter, Shieland
Jackson, David, Liscolgat
Keenan, John, Anagad
Laverty, Owen, Culloville
Lavery, Patrick, Cregganbane
Lennon, James, jun., Clonalig
Loy, Bernard, Kiscolgat
Loy, Owen, Moybane
M'Alister, J., Lurgancullenboy
M'Cabe, Henry, Teer
M'Cabe, Patrick, Teer
M'Clean, Wm., Cregganduff
M'Conville, James, Teer
M'Conville, Michael, Loughross
M'Coy, Michael, jun., Moybane
M'Conville, Patk., Crossmaglen
M'Creesh, Patrick, Corliss
M'Creesh, Thomas, Ballynacarry
M'Donnell, Thomas, Corliss
M'Elroy, James, Corliss
M'Elroy, Patrick, Drummuckavall
M'Eneany, Owen, Drummuckavall
M'Entegart, James, Liseraw
M'Guinness, Henry, Monugh

M'Keown, John, Drummuckavall
M'Keown, Owen, Drummuckavall
M'Mahon, Ardle, Monaguilla
M'Mahon, Owen, Ballinacarry
M'Manus, Thomas, Crinkill
M'Nulty, Bernard, Creevekeeran
M'Nulty, Patrick, Creevekeeran
M'Nulty, Terence, Anamar
M'Nulty, Thomas, Monugh
M'Shane, James, Carron
M'Shane, Owen, Carron
M'Shane, Owen, Liseraw
M'Shane, Patrick, Cornahove
M'Veigh, Patrick, Carron
Mallon, Michael, Loughross
Morgan, Patrick, Cornonagh
Morris, Bryan, Creevekeeran
Murphy, Bernard, Clonalig
Murray, Patrick, Cregganbane
Murtagh, E., sen., Cregganbane
Murtagh, E., jun., Cregganbane
Nugent, Bernard, Drumboy

Nugent, James, Crinkill
O'Neal, John, Drumboy
Paul, James, Creggan, lr
Rogers, Peter, Cornahove
Scott, Alexander, Creggan lr
Scott, John, Creggan lower
Scott, Thos., Creggan up
Scott, Thos. (Lr.), Creggan up
Shiels, Patrick, Urcher
Shevlin, Peter, Anagad
Short, Patrick, Cregganbane
Sleeth, Samuel, Creggan lr
Sleith, Thomas C., Creggan lr
Slieth, Joseph Hen., Creggan lr
Stephenson, John, Crossmaglen
Toner, John, Corrinure
Toner, Loughlin, Corrinure
Wallace, Robert, Creggan up
Walsh, Hugh, Creggan up
Wilson, George, Culloville
Wilson, John, Culloville
Woods, Peter, Tullyard

CARNAGH.

CARNAGH is a rural post-office in the barony of Turanny, 4 miles north by west from Keady. The land of the district is good. Oats, potatoes and flax are the chief crops. Dairying is carried on to a considerable extent.

Blacksmith : Rt. Dalzell
Grocers: Rt. Dalzell, Mrs. Sarah McCall
Post M: Mrs. S. McCall
R.I.C.: Sergt. Ml. O'Toole
School, Natl.: Ellen McClure
Farmers & Residents.
Allan, J., Tievenamara
Argue, R. A., Kilcam
Conn, Rt., Carrickaduff
Conn, Rt., Crossnenagh
Connolly, Ml., Tievenamara
Connolly, P., jun., Tievenamara
Conroy, Patrick, Drumherney
Curry, John, Carrickaduff
Curry, John, Tievenamara
Dalzell, T., Tievenamara
Feehan, Fr., Kilcam

Hill, Robert, Kilcam
Hughes, Bd., Crossnenagh
Hughes, Edward, Carrickaduff
Hughes, Edward, Tievenamara
Hughes, James, Drumherney
Irwin, Thomas D., Curryhugh
Irwin, W. A., Carnagh House
Keating, Dl., Clay
M'Ardle, Thos., Kilcam
M'Carron, Ptk., Tievenamara
M'Clure, Thos., Drumnahovill
M'Wharter, David, Carrickaduff
Mallon, James, Carrickaduff
Mallan, Peter, Drumherney
Nesbitt, Allen, T'namara
Nesbitt, J., sen., T'namara
Nesbitt, J., jun., T'namara
Nesbitt, John, Crossnenagh

R

Powell, Robert, Tievenamara	Seymour, Sl., Crossnenagh
Rooney, Andrew, Clay	Strahan, Robert, Kilcairn
Rush, Ml., Crossnenagh	Turner, Joseph, Carrickaduff
Seymour, John, Drumnahaville	

HUGH CONNELL,

General Merchant,

POST OFFICE, CULLYHANNA.

DEPARTMENTS:

Groceries.	Wines and Spirits.
Provisions.	Artificial Manures.
Seeds.	Hardware.
Bakery.	Timber and Iron.

EXPORTER OF EGGS.

CULLYHANNA.

CULLYHANA is a village of about 20 houses, 3½ miles, Irish, south of Newtownhamilton, and an equal distance north by east from Crossmaglen. Representatives of the late T. P. Ball, and Col. Synge, own part of the district, and the tenants have acquired the other part (Freeduff) under Lord Ashbourne's Purchase Act. The land is uneven in quality, some being very good, and some very bad. In the valley of the Cullyhanna, otherwise the Creggan River, below the village, a great deal of damage is done by floods. Oats, potatoes, and flax are the chief crops. A patent was granted to provide for the holding of fairs, but it has been a dead letter for more than twenty years.

Baker : Hugh Connell	R. Drysdale ; R. C., Rev. A
Blacksmith : Ptk. Leonard	O'Toole
Churches : Presbyn., Rev. R.	Draper : Felix Kelly

Grocers : Hugh Connell, John Hanlon, Jno. M'Mahon
Post M. : Hugh Connell
R. I. C. : Sergt. Edwd. Crossen
School, Natl. : P. Murray
Scutch mill : Rd. Palmer
Spirit retailer : Hugh Connell (two licenses)

Farmers & Residents

Bellew, Ml., Mulladuff
Bellew, Mrs. A., Kiltybane
Black, James, Lisleitrim
Black, Wm., Lisleitrim
Blacker, Edward, Dorsey
Boyle, Bernard, Tullynawall
Boyle, James, Tullynawall
Bradley, David, Freeduff
Callaghan, Patrick, Drumlogher
Carragher, James, Skeriff (T)
Carragher, John, Cullyhanna (Big)
Carragher, Mrs. B., Cullyhanna
Carragher, Mrs. B., Skeriff
Carragher, Mrs. M., Skeriff up
Carragher, Ptk., Tullynawall
Carragher, Philip, Ballynarea
Carty, John, Cregganduff
Carragher, M., sen., Skerifftrueman
Carragher, Ml., Skerifftrueman
Carragher, Owen, Tullynawall
Carragher, Rd., Skerifftrueman
Carragher, T., Cullyhanna (Big)
Crozier, Mrs., Tullyvallen
Cully, John, Creggan up
Donaldson, Mrs., Cloghoges
Donaldson, Mrs. A. B., Tullynavall
Donaldson, John, Cloghoge
Donaldson, Jos., Cloghoge
Donaldson, Thos., Cloghoge
Donaldson, Wm., Cloghoge
Donnelly, Arthur, Tullynavall
Donnelly, Peter, Tullynavall
Duffy, Patrick, Dorsey
Durnin, J., Skerifftrueman
Durnin, P., Cullyhanna (Big)
Garvey, Owen, Dorsey
Goodfellow, Sl., Cullyhanna (Big)
Hanna, Crozier, Sheetrim
Hearty, Ml., Cregganduff
Henry, David, Dorsey
Johnston, Alex, Cloghoge.

Johnston, John, Cloghoge
Kelly, Mrs. E., Drumlogher
Kelly, Mrs. E., Tullyvallen
Kelly, Mrs. J. Tullyvallen
Largey, Michael, Cloghoge
Larkin, Terence, Cregganduff
Lennon, Francis, Cullyhanna (B)
Lockhart, Sl., Mulladuff
Loughran, Patrick, Cregganduff
Loughran, Patrick, Dorsey
Louth, John, Tullynavall
M'Birney, Dd., jun., Mulladuff
M'Birney, Samuel, Mulladuff
M'Birney, Wm. J., Mulladuff
M'Clean, Wm., Cloghoge
M'Cooey, Ptk., sen., Drumlogher
M'Cooey, Patrick, Drumlogher
M'Creesh, Peter, Tullynavall
M'Gaw, J., Skerifftichburn
M'Geough, Peter, Sheetrim
M'Ginnis, Mrs. M., Dorsey
M'Ginnis, Mrs. M., Sheetrim
M'Mahon, Hugh, Sheetrim
M'Mahon, John, Cullyhanna lr
M'Mahon, John, Sheetrim
M'Mahon, Patrick, Lisletrim
M'Nancy, John, Skerifftrueman
M'Nulty, Bernard, Sheetrim
M'Nulty, Hugh, jun., Drumlogher
M'Shane, Hugh, Drumlogher
Mackin, Felix, Dorsey
Mackin, Joseph, Tullynavall
Mackin, Patrick, Tullinavall
Mackin, Redmond, Dorsey
Moley, Michael, Dorsey
Moore, Mrs., Tullyvallen
Morrison, John, Creggan lr
Nelson, Samuel, Freeduff
O'Hanlon, Peter, Cullyhanna
Quigley, Bernard, Dorsey Hearty
Quigley, Edward, Dorsey
Quinn, Edward, Dorsey M'D
Quinn, John, Cullyhanna lr
Quinn, John, Dorsey M'D
Quinn, Patrick, Cullyhanna (lr)
Quinn, Peter, Cullyhanna (lr)
Ronaghan, Edward, Camly Ball
Savage, Ptk., Skerifftrueman
Sheridan, Bd., Skerifftichburn
Sheridan, Michael, Ballynaare

Toner, Chas., Cullyhanna (Big) | Wiley, Wm., Mulladuff
Wiley, Geo., Dorsey

STEPHEN M'CANN,

𝔊rocer, 𝔓rovision 𝔐erchant and 𝔈gg 𝔈xporter,

LISLEA.

LISLEA.

LISLEA is a rural post office 4½ miles, Irish, west of Newry, and 6 miles, Irish, south-east from Newtown-hamilton. It is situated in the valley of a river which passes through Forkhill. Slieve Gullion rises on the eastern side and on the western a height known to the natives as The Burren Mountain. The Misses Quinn of Newry own the district. In the valley the land is fair. Oats, potatoes and flax are the chief crops. One of the disadvantages experienced by the inhabitants is the danger from mountain floods. They come rapidly and sometimes carry away grain in stook.

Blacksmith : Bd. O'Neill
Church: R.C., Rev. Chas. Quinn
Grocer, &c.: Stephen M'Cann
Post M. : Stephen M'Cann
School, Natl : Ml. M'Parland, Mrs. T. Byrne
Scutch mill : L. Donnelly

Farmers & Residents.

Crawley, Thomas, Levallymore
Curtis, J., A'loughmullin
Donnelly, Mrs. B., Doctors Qrs.
Donnelly, Peter, Lislea
M'Cann, Stephen, Lislea
M'Parland, Francis, C'galliagh
M'Parland, James, Ballard
Murphy, P., jun., Doctor's Qrs
Murphy, Terence, Lislea
Quinn, Bernard, C'galliagh
Ward, Mrs B., C'gallion
Ward, Mrs. S., Doctor's Qrs

NEWTOWNHAMILTON.

Population 898 in 1881.

NEWTOWNHAMILTON is in the barony of Upper Fews, 9 miles, Irish, south by east from Armagh, and 8 miles, Irish, west of Newry. It is situated on rising ground, and favorably impresses the stranger entering from either Armagh, Newry, or Castleblayney. There are three good streets in the town and a large square. The houses are well built and maintained in excellent condition. A free market is held every Saturday for butter, eggs, and fowl, and a fair on the last Saturday of every month for cattle, sheep, pigs and farm horses. Hiring fairs are held on the last Saturday of May and the last Saturday of November. A few hand-loom linen weavers live in the town. Resident agents for handkerchief manufacturers give out work to be hemstitched and embroidered. It is estimated that about 1,500 of the female residents of Newtownhamilton and district receive employment in this way. Within half a mile from the Armagh direction the land is good, and it is nearly all good toward the Monaghan border. Oats, potatoes and flax are the chief crops—a great deal of flax. It is also a fair grass country, and the farmers make a feature of dairying. A cave was found in a field belonging to Mr. William Warmington, at the edge of the town, about 18 years ago. The roof is high enough to allow a man of medium height to stand erect in it. At a distance of about a quarter of a mile from the main thoroughfare there is an excellent chalybeate spring, on the farm of Mrs. Maguire. One of the features of Newtownhamilton is the parish church (C.I.), built in 1870, at a cost of £2,500. It is a handsome edifice of black stone, with a tower. The old church, unroofed, is retained as a monument. Mr. William Warmington collected the money to pay for the new church. The late Rev. Alexander Hamilton Synge, father of the present landlord, gave the site and a subscription of £50. One of the Hamilton family was the founder of Newtownhamilton in 1770. At the time of the Plantation of Ulster, 1609, attempts were made to build towns at Blackbank, and Johnstown Fews in the parish, but both failed. Barracks were built with castellated flankers, to protect the settlers. The garrisons were maintained by the Government until Newtownhamilton began to flourish, and it then became head-quarters of the soldiers. The barracks speedily went to ruin, and at present there are only small remains. Lead mines were worked in the parish a long time ago, when wood was to be had in sufficient abundance to be used profitably for smelting purposes.

Auctioneers: Sl. Andrews, Alex. M'Clean, Felix M'Parland

Bakers : Peter Hughes, John M'Donnell, Mrs. Ann Maguire, Wm. Warmington

Bank, Ulster : Agency Saturday

Blacksmiths : C. Lutton, Andw. M'Kenna, Arthur M'Kenna, Alex. Masterson, John Whisker

Carpenters : Wm. Belshaw, Jas. Johnston, Wm. M'Bride, Robert M'Cullough

Cattle shippers : Edward Markey, Jas. Paxton, Wm. Paxton

Churches, C. I. : Rev. Rt. J. Ballard ; Presbyterian, Rev. Dd. Jamison ; R. C., Rev. F. Kearley

Coopers : Matt. Hall, Frank Murphy

Corn and scutch mills, † corn only, ‡ scutch only : Dd. Caswell†, Mrs. Clarke, John Irwin‡, Palmer, Wm. Warnock

Dispensary : Dr. Jas. A. Swann

Drapers : John Caraher, Mrs. Mt. W. Gass, Thos. Irwin, John M'Kee, Miss E. Mills, James Smith

Grocers, marked thus * retail spirits, † hardware, ‡ seeds, § delf, ‖ leather : Jas. Bailie, Jas. Bradley§, Mrs. Mary Burns§, Miss Eliza Burton†, Patk. Canning, Francis Cosgrove†, Patk. Cosgrove*, Hugh Crozier*‡, Jas. Devine*, John Drake‖, Patton Farley†‡ ‖, John Hawthorn*, Alex. M'Clean*, Mrs. Mt. M'Coey, Thos. M'Murray, Felix Mackin*‡, John Maguire, Mrs. Anne Maguire*, Mrs. Anne Markey*†‡, Sl. Mason, John Moffatt‖, Adam G. Morris*, John Morris, Jonathan Nesbitt*†‡, Mrs. Ann Paxton*, James Rafferty*, Misses Stinson

Nail makers : Jno. Burns, Ml. Slane

Petty sessions, 2nd Monday every month: Wm. H. Starr, clerk

Posting Car Owners: Patrick Cosgrove, John Hawthorn, John McCulla, Adam G. Morris

Post M : Mrs. Mt. W. Gass

R.I.C. : Sergt. John Knox

Process Server : Dd. Mitchell

Schools Nat. : Alex. Burns, Thos. Mackin, Henry Rusk

Sewing Agents : Thompson Cooke, James Neill, Wm. Trodden

Spirit retailers (see also grocers) :

Saml. Andrews, John Caraher,
Thos. Irwin, Andrew Loughead,
Wm. McClean, Edward McCourt,
John M'Culla, Felix McParland,
Mrs. Bridget Martin, Mrs. Anne
Murphy, Mrs. Anne Simpson
  Tinsmith : Neil Rice
  Undertakers : Thos. Irwin,
Adam Morris
  Victuallers : John Cook, Wm.
Cook, Frank McKeown, Peter
Murphy

Farmers & Residents.

Ardis, Dd., Tullyvallen
Ardis, Mrs., Dungormley
Ardis, Rt., Tullyvallen
Bailie, Caleb, Armaghbrague
Bailie, Jos., Armaghbrague
Bailie, Rt. Tullyvallen
Bailie, Wm., Tullyvallen
Belshaw, John, Tullyvallen
Blackwood, Sl., Cortamlet
Black, W. G., Tullyvallen
Boyd, Geo., Tullyvallen
Boyle, Thomas, Tullyvallen
Bradshaw, Wm., Camly (McC.)
Burns, Alex., N'hamilton
Burke, Francis, Cavanakill
Carragher, James, Tullyvallen
Carroll, John, Tullyvallen
Caswell, T. D., Tullyvallen
Conn. Andrew, Tullyvallen
Conn, James, Ballintemple
Conn, Robert, Tullyvallen
Cooke, Alex., N'hamilton
Coon, Andrew, Tullyvallen
Cooney, John, Knockavannon
Cowan, Patrick, Cavanakill
Craig, David, Camly (M'C.)
Craig, James, Camly (M'C.)
Crozier, James, Tullyvallen(M'C.)
Cunningham, P., Knockavannon
Dawson, Geo., Camly (M'C.)
Dawson, Wm., Camly (M'C.)
Donaldson, David, Tullyvallen
Donaldson, W., Knockavannon
Donaldson, W., Tullyvallen
Donnelly, J., Tullyvallen (M'C.)
Falloon, James, Tullyvallen
Falloon, John, Camly (M'C.)

Fenix, John, Ballintemple
Finegan, Ml., Knockavannon
Finlay, Rev. John,
Finnegan, Peter, Ballintemple
Frazer, Alex., Callintemple
Frazer, Alex., Ballintemple
Frazer, James, Ballintemple
Frazer, James, N'hamilton
Garland, Hy, Ballintemple
Garland, Mrs. C., Tullyett
Garvey, Henry, Tullyvallen(T.E.)
Garvey, John, Camly (Ball)
Garvey. John, Tullyallen
Garvey, Thomas, Tullyallen
Glover, Alex., Tullyvallen
Graham, John, Tullyvallen
Grimes, John, Tvllyvallen
Hadden, David, Cladybeg
Haire, James, Tullyvallen
Hanaway, Ptk, Cortamlet
Hanaatty, L., Tullyvallen T. E.
Harrison, John, Camly (Ball)
Harrison, Samuel, Camly (Ball)
Hawthorne, Andrew,Ballintemple
Hawthorne, Jas, Ballintemple
Hawthorne, Thos, Ballintemple
Hayes, Francis, Dorsey (M'D.)
Hayes, Michael, Dorsey (M'D.)
Henderson, Rt., Tullyvallen
Henry, James, Tullyvallen
Henry, Robert, Tullyvallen
Heron, George, Tullyvalllen
Heron, W., Tullyvallen
Herron, Dobbin, Cladybeg
Hogg, Thomas, Ballintemple
Hughes, John, Camly M'C
Hughes, Robert, Tullyvallen
Hughes, Wm., Camly, M'C.
Hyde, Wm., Ballintemple
Jenkins, Miss M., Tullyvallen
Johnston, Andrew, Knockavannon
Johnston, Geo., Ballintemple
Johnston, Isaac, Ballintemple
Johnston, James, Ballintemple
Johnston, John, Ballintemple
Johnston, Thos., Knockavannon
Johnston, Wm., Ballintemple
Johnston, Wm. J., Ballintemple
Keenan, Arthur, Ballintemple
Kelly, Peter, Tullyvallen (M'C)

Kiniston, C., Camly (McC)
Lennon, Terence, Dorsey
Loughead, Jos., Ballintemple
Lowe, Ml., Knockavannon
Loy, Philip, Dorsey (McD)
M'Alister, Jas., Tullyvallen
M'Anliss, Alex., Tullyvallen
M'Anliss, James, Tullyvallen
M'Ardle, John, Camly (McC)
M'Birnie, David, Tullyvallen
M'Clean, Alex., Ballintemple
M'Clean, Hugh, Tullyvallen
M'Connell, Alex., Tullyvallen
M'Connell, Jas., sen., Tullyvallen
M'Connell, John, Tullyvallen
M'Connell, Nevin, Tullyvallen
M'Court, Edward, N'hamilton
M'Court, Terence, Knockavannon
M'Crea, John, Cortamlet
M'Crea, Wm., Cortamlet
M'Cully, Patrick, Tullyvallen
M'Elwain, J., Carrickacullion
M'Evoy, J., Tullyvallen (T.E.)
M'Ginn, Thos., Tullyvallen
M'Grath, Ptk., Aughincurk
M'Kee, Andrew, Cortamlet
M'Kee, James, Tullyvallen
M'Kee, Ter., Tullyvallen
M'Keown, Dr. Arthur, Harrybrook
M'Kenna, Arthur, N'hamilton
M'Lenaghan, J. W., Knockavan
M'Manus, Jas., Camly (Ball)
M'Murray, Rt., Knockavannon
M'Parland, Arthur, Ballintemple
M'Shane, Jas., Tullyvallen
M'Shane, J., Tullyvallen, (H.W.)
Mackin, Arthur, Dorsey McD
Mackin, C., Dorsey (Mullaglass)
Mackin, Patrick, Dorsey McD
Mackin, T., Dorsey (Mullaglass
Mackin, Thos., N'hamilton
Marshall, Sl., Tullyvallen
Meeke, James, Tullyvallen
Meek, Wm., Tullyvallen
Melvin, Samuel, Tullyvallen
Mooney, J., sen., N'hamilton
Mooney, John, jun., Tullyvallen

Mulholland, J., Knockavannon
Mulligan, Hugh, Altnamackin
Murphy, James, Tullyvallen
Murphy, Ptk., Tullyvallen
Nugent, John, Tullyvallen
O'Hare, Mrs. C., N'hamilton
O'Neill, J., Ballintemple
O'Neill, Ter., Tullyvallen
Palmer, Rd., Roxboro'
Parr, James, Tullyvallen
Patterson, James, Tullyvallen
Pepper, John, Tullyvallen
Preston, John, Cortamlet
Preston, Wm., Camly (Ball)
Quigley, John, Camly (Ball)
Quinn, Patrick, Camly (McC)
Rafferty, John, Tullyvallen
Reaney, Archibd., Camly (Ball)
Redmond, Thomas, Cortamlet
Shannon, Sl., Tullyvallen
Shannon, Wm., Tullyvallen
Shaw, John, Tullyvallen
Slane, J., Knockavannon
Stephenson, James, Tullyvallen
Strain, John, Tullyvallen
Synnott, M. S. (D.L.), Ballymoyre
Synnott, M. S., jun., Ballymoyre
Synnott, P. G. (J.P.), Lurganagh
Thompson, Geo., Camly (McC)
Thompson, Jas., Tullyvallen
Thompson, John, Cortamlet
Thompson, Thos., Tullyvallen
Tierney, Denis, Tullyvallen
Toner, Denis, Corrinure
Toner, John, Maytone
Toner, John, Dorsey (McD)
Treanor, Thomas, Tullyvallen
Warmington, Jas., Tullyvallen
Warmington, W., Tullyvallen
Watson, Henry, Ballintemple
Watson, W., Ballintemple
Watters, James, Tullyvallen
West, Mrs., Tullyvallen
Whiteside, Geo., Drumcrow
Whitten, Geo., Ballintemple
Wilson, James, Camly (McC)
Wilson, John, Camly (McC)

PORTADOWN.

Estimated population, 10,000 *in* 1888.

PORTADOWN is pleasantly situated on the Bann, 87¼ miles north by west from Dublin, 25 miles south by west from Belfast, 10½ miles north-east from Armagh, and 5 miles south-west from Lurgan. It is an important junction in the system of the Great Northern Railway, embracing the counties of Armagh, Antrim, Down, Monaghan and Tyrone, and si the chief port on the canal between Newry and Lough Neagh. The ground rises high enough at both sides of the river to afford a great many beautiful sites for villas, and the wealthy residents, in recent years, have taken advantage of them to such an extent, as to greatly enrich the picturesque features of the outskirts. From the manufacturing point of view Portadown comes next to Lurgan. In its weaving and hem-stitching factories, and spinning mills, employment is given to over 3,000 people, and it is the centre of a district in which there are upward of 2,500 cottage-weavers. As a market for general produce it ranks with the foremost towns in the North of Ireland. The great market is held every Saturday, and although several inclosed places are specially provided for conducting transactions incident to sale and purchase, there is an overflow of odds-and-ends that has a fascination for the country people, the effect of which is quite amusing. A prominent figure in the overflow is the vendor of second-hand clothing. In style, manner and get-up he is intensely dramatic, and with every article offered, goes through a form sustained by speech and gesture to a most artistic climax. Traveling shooting-galleries, shows on wheels, dancing maidens, and venerable acrobats, in a modest way, second the efforts of the clothing artist. The warehouse windows, and the side-walks in front, on such occasions are dressed in bright colors. Indeed, nothing seems to be left undone in order to make the day one of genuine pleasure as well as of business.

The residents of Portadown have considerable taste. This fact soon becomes manifest to the stranger in going through the streets. Most of the buildings are well constructed and sightly, and the places of worship, in architectural outlines and internal decoration, are very much above the average. Societies for mental and physical culture exist in proportion to the requirements of the population, and there is a public park, purchased and laid out by subscription, in which the people are familiarized with the beauties of Nature.

WILLIAM PAUL & SON,

DRAPERS, &c.,

PORTADOWN.

EXCELLENT QUALITY,

LARGE VARIETY,

MODERATE PRICE.

OUR MILLINERY, DRESSMAKING & TAILORING DEPARTMENTS

Are distinguished for Style and Superior Workmanship.

In every direction from Portadown the formation of the country is favorable to agricultural operations. The land is generally good. Potatoes, oats, and flax are the principal crops. Dairying is not carried on as largely as it was ten years ago, but it still receives attention. A great many of the farmers find fruit-growing a valuable aid to income. Apple-orchards are abundant, especially toward the west, facing Loughgall. In the season it is not uncommon to find 200 loads of apples on one Saturday in Portadown.

BEFORE AND SINCE THE ENGLISH CONNECTION.

BEFORE the power of England became supreme in the County Armagh, the district of Portadown was in possession of the M'Canns. They were subordinate to the O'Neills, and had a stronghold which commanded the passage of the Bann, and gave name to the place, *Port-ne-dun*, port of the dun or fortress. In those days the wealth of chieftains was measured by the number of cattle in their herds. Payments of consequence, such as tribute to the kings, ransomes, etc., were made in cattle. Cattle were also used as a means of barter. The country of the M'Canns was well adapted for grazing purposes, and no doubt was largely used in this way. At the time of the Plantation of Ulster, 1609, James I. granted an extensive " portion " of land here to William Powell. In 1625 this was confirmed to Prudence Obins and John Obins. They formed a settlement with 14 English families, and built a fine mansion in the Elizabethan style, with turreted corners. It was called a castle, and its chief approach was by way of the thoroughfare now known as Castle Street. The People's Park was a part of the demesne, and the nursery of Messrs. Samuel McGredy & Son, Woodside, was the site of at least a portion of the mansion. A few years ago, during the progress of an excavation in the grounds devoted to rose cultivation, a vaulted passage was discovered. It runs into the People's Park, and is 6 feet high and 4 feet wide. A few green oaks mark the parts known as the Castle Gardens. One at the gate entering the Park, a short distance below the nursery, is in a wonderful state of preservation, and really worth seeing, especially by those interested in arboriculture. The Yeomanry Barrack stood at the opposite side of the road from the nursery, now the residence of Mr. Seth Robb.

During the war of 1641, directed by the Confederate Parliament at Kilkenny, terrible scenes were enacted at Portadown Bridge. Captives taken by Sir Phelim O'Neill were brought

J. & J. ACHESON & CO,
POWER LOOM
Linen Manufacturers,
PORTADOWN.

J. & J. ACHESON,
CHEMISTS AND DRUGGISTS,
PORTADOWN.

J. & J. ACHESON,
Wholesale and Family Grocers,
PORTADOWN.

J. & J. ACHESON,
Preserve Manufacturers,
PORTADOWN.

J. & J. ACHESON,
SEED MERCHANTS,
PORTADOWN.

from various parts of the country, and drowned in the river, those escaping the water being killed as they reached the shore. After Col. Owen Roe O'Neill had assumed command of the "Catholic Army of the North," he took prompt measures to put a stop to the horrors which had been sanctioned by his predecessor. Imprisoned families were released, and the strife conducted more in accordance with ideas of chivalry. At the trial of Sir Phelim in Dublin, 1652, a supernatural element was introduced. One of the witnesses, wife of Captain Price, testified that she was present at Portadown Bridge, when the form of a woman rose out of the water, and cried, "Revenge, revenge, revenge." Col. Owen Roe O'Neill was also there, and by his directions a Catholic priest questioned the apparation in English and Latin without eliciting a reply. A Protestant clergyman from the English army, specially sent for, addressed it on another occasion, and the words, "Revenge, revenge, revenge," were repeated. It was said that for some time the heads and forms of men and women were frequently seen at the same place. The trial ended in the conviction of Sir Phelim O'Neill, and he was put to death.

Portadown is owned by the Duke of Manchester. From the time of the Obins settlement progress was slow until the introduction of the linen industry at the beginning of the century. In 1819 the population numbered 900. In 1831 it had increased to 1,591, and in 1881 to 7,850. At present it cannot be far from 10,000. Portadown is a district parish, and was confined to the barony of O'Neilland West, on the western side of the Bann, until 1840. Its boundary was then extended to the barony of O'Neilland East, taking in Edenderry, in the parish of Seagoe. The principal thoroughfare of the town is united to Edenderry by a fine stone bridge. A few of the factories, the gas works, railway station, and many of the handsome private residences are on the same side. Soon after the passing of the Act to provide for the lighting, cleansing, and watching of towns, 1829, Portadown took advantage of it. The inhabitants lost no time in petitioning the Lord Lieutenant to be brought within the scope of the Towns Improvement Act of 1854. On the 8th of January, 1885, the Commissioners elected under it held their first meeting. They were: John Obins Woodhouse, chairman, Thomas Averell Shillington, William Langtry. William Paul, Thomas Harden Carlton, John Wilson, David Thornton, David Wilson Irwin, John Watson, John James Marley, James O'Hanlon, William Montgomery, David Ferguson, and William John Dawson. Of the entire number three only survive : Messrs. James O'Hanlon, David Thornton, and William Montgomery. No change has been made in the town

boundary since 1840. It includes the whole townland of Tavanagh, Corcrain, from Tavanagh and Clounagh to Pound Lane, thence to a point next to Corcrain Bridge, to the Dungannon Road, the Ballybay River, to the drain passing under Castle Island Bridge, continuing by the drain across the Bann, taking in Edenderry to the Lurgan Road, "and by the ditch outside Mr. Carlton's garden to the bogs, and from the end of said ditch, in a straight line, to the River Bann, at the point where the *mearing* between Edenderry and Levaghery meets at the river." This year, 1888, the Local Government Board has been asked to sanction a further extension of the boundary from " Lurgan Road to Seagoe Turns, and from Quarry's Turns to end of Quarry's property on Killicomain Road, and from Annagh Bridge, on Tandragee Road, to south end of James Totten's property on same road." This would bring in that portion of the townland of Edenderry not included in the boundary of 1840, and the whole townland of Annagh. The object is to get jurisdiction over a district in which new villas and other dwellings have been erected, so that the occupiers, by contributing to the taxes levied by the Commissioners, may share in the benefits of public lighting, cleansing, and sewerage.

The town was brought under the provisions of the Sanitary Act of 1874, and continued under the Amended Act of 1878. In 1857 the valuation of property within the boundary was £5,210 10s., and the rate for general purposes 1s. in the £. In 1862 the valuation was £7,066 5s., and the general purposes rate 1s. The progress of the town between 1862 and 1870 is marked by an increase in the valuation to £14,163 15s., more than double, while the rate for general purposes continued the same. In 1876 the valuation was £15,162 5s., and the rate for general purposes that year was only 11d. in the £. The valuation in 1886 was £17,510 15s., and the rate for general purposes 1s. In 1887 the valuation was £17,679 10s., and the rate for general purposes 1s.

MARKETS & FAIRS, WATER SUPPLY, SEWERAGE SYSTEM, GAS, PUBLIC LAMPS, VOLUNTEER FIRE BRIGADE.

EVERY Tuesday in the season a market is held for the sale of flax ; grain is sold on Wednesday and Saturday ; hay and straw on Wednesday ; grass-seed on Wednesday from August to October ; and on Saturday fowl, eggs, butter, and pork. A retail market for potatoes and vegetables is held every day. On Saturday a retail market for butcher's meat is also held. The pork market is improving;

T. MORRISON,

Select Family Grocer,

Tea, Coffee, Provision and Seed Merchant,

MARKET ST. & WILLIAM ST.,

PORTADOWN.

PLAIN & FANCY BISCUITS, JAMS, JELLIES, PICKLES, SAUCES,
ETC.

it averaged from 350 to 400 dead pigs per week until May of
this year, but this number promises to be largely increased in
the near future, for the reason that two firms, extensively
engaged in curing, have recently been established in the town.
A market for sucking pigs, in carts, is held every Saturday. The
fowl market is good, but not up to what it was when conducted in
the open street. There is a first-rate wholesale potato market that
seems to increase in importance every year. The Duke of Manchester had a patent for markets and fairs, but no tolls were
collected. In 1878 the Town Commissioners secured a lease
of his right for 999 years, and have expended about £6,000 in
providing market places, erecting suitable buildings, walls, etc.
The money was procured partly from the Board of Works at 3½
per cent., repayable, principal and interest, by instalments, in
30 years, and partly from private lenders at 4 per cent. The
charges in the markets at present are, pork, including weighing
and porterage, 2d. per pig ; pigs on foot 1d. each ; pigs in cart,
young, ½d. each ; butter, including weighing, 10lbs. and under,
½d., over 10lbs. and up to 20lbs., 1d., over 20lbs, 1½d. ; eggs,
any quantity not exceeding 50, ½d., exceeding 50, and not exceeding 100, 1d., every additional 50 or fraction of 50, ½d. ; geese
and turkeys 4d. per dozen, all other poultry and game 2d. per
dozen ; potatoes, turnips, carrots or mangel-wurzel, 2d. per load,
including weighing, 1d. per bag up to 6—no charge above 6 ;
cabbage 1d. per load ; fruit, 1d. per load, bag, basket or barrow,
½d. ; hay and straw, including weighing, 2d. per load ; grass-
seed 1d. per bag ; no charge on grain. The market-places are
situated as follows :—Pork and grass-seed, entrance West-street ;
pigs on foot and young pigs in cart, entrance Woodhouse-
street ; butter, eggs and fowl, entrance Mandeville-street ; potatoes, turnips, cabbage, etc., wholesale, in Market-street and
High-street, north side ; fruit, in High-street, south side ; hay
and straw, in Church-street and Market-street ; retail market
for potatoes, vegetables and fruit, entrance from William-street ;
fish, every day in High-street, north side. The receipts from
tolls average about £675 per annum, and the expenses about
£560. When the debt is paid off it is expected that a considerable reduction can be made in the tolls, after contributing
toward repairs of side-walks, etc., in the immediate vicinity of
the markets. As usual there are two opinions regarding closed
market-places. Many of the merchants prefer the old system
of crowding everything into the streets, but the majority believe
that it is better for the interests of the town, and for every one
concerned, to have things so arranged that they may be con-
trolled without confusion.

A good cattle fair is held in the fair green, entered from

S

JOSEPH DOUGLAS

(Late AVERELL, SHILLINGTON & SON),

PORTADOWN,

DOES EVERY DESCRIPTION OF

Ladies' & Gents' Outfitting and General House Furnishing.

Wedding Outfits and Mourning Orders specially and promptly attended to.

Good Value for Ready-money in every department.

UNDERTAKING.

**Hearses, Mourning Coaches, Coffins, and Funeral
Requisites of every kind supplied on the shortest
notice and most favorable terms.**

JOSEPH DOUGLAS,
36 HIGH STREET, PORTADOWN.

Shillington-street, on the 3rd Saturday of each month. Attempts have been made a few times to establish a horse fair, but without success. A toll of 2d. on cows, 1d. per calf, yearling, etc., is charged in the fair green. In 1887 the total amount derived from this was £94 10s. 8d. About seven acres are embraced in the fair green and market-places. A hiring fair is held on the 1st Wednesday every 3rd month.

Water for domestic purposes still continues to be drawn from street pumps, of which there are 23. At the bridge there is a pump, not included in this number, used specially for soft water. How to procure a first-rate supply of potable water is a question which has been under consideration for some time. One scheme proposes to utilize Marlacoo Lake, between 4 and 5 miles south by west from Portadown. The estimated cost of this would be £21,350. Another scheme makes Slieve Croob, County Down, the source for a supply equal to the requirements of Waringstown, Banbridge, Dromore, Downpatrick and Seaford, all in the county Down; and of Lurgan and Portadown in Armagh. The proportion of expense to Portadown would be £21,000.

Since 1878 a great deal has been done toward providing a perfect sewerage system. From £1,200 to £1,400 has been spent in this work. The money is repaid by each district at the rate of 2d. in the £. Owing to the high elevation of the town, the facilities for discharge of matter are excellent.

In January, 1887, the Portadown Gas-Light Co. held its Forty-first Annual Meeting, and declared a dividend at the rate of five per cent. per annum on the paid-up capital stock, and a bonus of 20s. per share, free of Income-tax. A table prepared by the Secretary, Mr. George Kinkead, shows the amount of gas sold each year since 1849 to private consumers. In 1850 the amount was 612,225 cubic feet at 10s. per 1,000 feet, total £153 18s. In 1853 it was 1,077,700 cubic feet at 8s. 4d., total £449 0s. 10d.; in 1863 it was 3,095,200 cubic feet at 7s. 6d., total £1,160 14s. 8d.; in 1873 it was 5,680,100 at 7s. 6d., total £2,130 0s. 9d.; in 1883 it was 8,503,200 at 5s., total £2,125 16s.; and in 1887 it was 9,965,300 cubic feet at 5s. per 1000 feet, total £2,491 6s. 6d. At the Forty-first meeting it was decided to supply the gas for the 130 public lamps, by meter, at 4s. 2d. per 1,000 cubic feet, the Town Commissioners undertaking to do the lighting, cleaning, extinguishing, and repairs of pillars and fittings.

A Volunteer Fire Brigade, organized under the auspices of the Town Commissioners, is capable of effective work in emergency. Mr. Thomas Shillington, secundus, is Captain, and Mr. John Acheson, Lieutenant. There are twelve volunteers. Two manual engines and a fire escape are maintained. The engine-house is in William-street.

MONYPENY & WATSON,

Linen Handkerchief Manufacturers,

Machine Hemstitchers

And Preparers of Yarn.

Factory—CORNASCREBE,

PORTADOWN.

Office and Warehouse:

10 JAMES'S STREET SOUTH,

BELFAST.

MANUFACTURING AND OTHER INDUSTRIES, THE
CARRYING TRADE, NEWRY CANAL, LOUGH
NEAGH, AND LAGAN NAVIGATION, BANN
DRAINAGE, LOSS BY FLOODING.

ITHIN a comparatively short period, a change has been made in the methods of manufacture at Portadown which threatens very soon to dispense entirely with the services of hand-loom weavers. Twenty years ago over 4,000 of these industrious hard-working people lived in the town and district. Good authorities agree that the number at present is not above 2,500. The young people are not following the occupation of their fathers to an appreciable extent, and a great many of the families have emigrated. The power-loom has been resisted as long as possible, but it has latterly been coming into fashion here with a rush. There are four large factories now in operation, giving employment between them to upward of 2,000 people, the majority of whom are females. Messrs. Watson, Armstrong & Co., J. & J. Acheson & Co., Castle Island Linen Company, and Grimshaw & McFadden. Flax and Tow Spinning : Messrs. D. Graham & Co., provides employment for about 400. Hemstitching by machinery has latterly come to be quite a promising feature of the industries of town and district. Between 500 and 600 people are employed as a beginning. Those partly engaged in it are Messrs. Thomas Dawson, Andrew J. Lutton & Son, Hamilton Robb, William Cowdy, John Malcolmson, Samuel Wilson, R. & W. Stewart & Co., John Gilbert, and Monypeny & Watson, at Cornascrebe. Messrs. Spence, Bryson & Co. are hemstitchers by hand. All those mentioned are linen manufacturers by hand-loom, and give employment in the aggregate to nearly 6,000 cottage-weavers of the Portadown and other districts of Armagh, and of the counties of Antrim, Down, Derry and Tyrone. Messrs. Thomas Kernaghan, Portadown, John Montgomery & Sons, Derryvore, Robert Reid & Son, Tarson, and James Irvine Annett, Riverside, are also linen manufacturers by hand-loom. The number of weavers they employ is included in the calculation. It is necessary to explain that the same weavers are not exclusively employed by any one manufacturer. Yarn-boiling and preparing are also done at Portadown. Pork-curing has become an important branch of industry this year. A distillery consuming 3,000 tons of malt,

here and oats, and a brewery, once flourished in the town, but are no longer in existence.

The carrying trade between Portadown, Newry and Belfast *via* the Newry Canal, Lough Neagh and Lagan Canal, is still successful. The Newry Canal joins the Bann about an Irish mile south-east of the town, and continues the navigation system to Lough Neagh, 7 Irish miles. The Lagan Canal also joins Lough Neagh, so that vessels up to 70 tons burden may go from Belfast to Newry by way of Portadown. It takes one day to go to Newry from Portadown, light, and two days with cargo, going or returning. Freights, consisting of coal, grain, timber and general merchandize, are usually brisk enough to make the trade profitable for four individual boat owners, and four firms of boat owners. The tolls on the Newry Canal are 6d. per lock per boat, light, and 1s. 6d. with cargo going into Newry, and 2s. per lock, with cargo, returning. There are 13 locks. Nearly all the masters of boats share profits with the owners. About a third of the number live with their families on board the boats. The competition is so keen that there is no opportunity to exact high rates. Between Belfast and Portadown the trade is quite large. Boats up to 85 tons burden are towed by steamer from the Lagan Canal through Lough Neagh to Portadown. The toll is 9½d. per ton cargo; nothing on register. At one time Portadown had direct communication by boat with Scotland and Wales. Belfast is now the limit.

A Bill before Parliament this year, 1888, provides for the dredging, deepening and widening of the Lower Bann, for improving its channels, the construction of sluices at some of the weirs, and the removal of obstructions. It resulted from the appointment of a Royal Commission which sat in Portadown, last year, with the view to the collection of testimony showing the injury caused to occupiers of farms along the Upper Bann and its tributaries by flooding. This year, 1888, it is estimated that 4,000 acres, within the area referred to, were flooded, and that the loss caused thereby aggregated £20,000. The Bill provides that a sum of £65,000 shall be expended in order that the summer level of Lough Neagh may be perpetually maintained. This it is believed can be effected by the works contemplated in the Lower Bann. The proposal of the Government is that £45.000 only of the grant shall be repaid, which sum is to be levied upon the lands in the catchment area of Lough Neagh, including the towns of Portadown and Lurgan. Some anxiety has been felt lest the navigation between Lough Neagh and Portadown may be impaired by the reduction to summer level, but it is believed that care will be taken to safeguard this valuable interest.

PEOPLE'S PARK, TOWN HALL, BUILDING IM-
PROVEMENTS, BANKS, LOAN AND BUILDING
COMPANIES, YOUNG MEN'S INSTITUTE, PUB-
LIC LIBRARY.

HE People's Park consists of about twenty-one acres in what may, at no distant day, be the centre of the town. The land was secured in 1871 from the Duke of Manchester on lease for 999 years, at £32 18s. 3d. per annum, less half Poor-Rates. The amount spent in laying it out, legal fees, etc., came to £1,365 6s. 10d. A moiety of the old loan fund represented £250 14s. The rest was made up from the proceeds of bazaars and by subscription, leaving a balance due of £170. The cost of maintenance is met by sale of the grass and by letting to foot-ball and cricket clubs, and for athletic sports, lawn tennis, etc. Whatever deficit there may be is covered by subscription from residents. Messrs. Averell Shillington, J.P., Thomas Shillington, J.P., Thomas Shillington (2), Charles Johnston, J.P., Joseph Acheson, J.P., George Kinkead, Benjamin Robb, and John Grew are trustees, and Mr. James Boyle, secretary. A handsome artificial pond, some stately forest trees and yews, are among the attractions. The Corcrain river runs through on the way to join the Bann, and pleasant walks are carried along its banks.

Portadown is to have a new Town Hall presently. The old one, which is partly represented in the illustration of Messrs. William Paul & Son's business premises, was sold in August of this year 1888, to Mr. Thomas Shillington, J.P., for £1,540. The Town Commissioners, after paying off a mortgage of £240, will have a substantial balance with which to begin the erection of the new building. This will have a suitable assembly room for dramatic and musical entertainments of a high order, in addition to the needful accommodation for Commissioners' meetings, offices for Town Clerk, etc.

Building improvements in the business quarter of the town have been carried on extensively during the past few years. Nearly every street has had an increase in the number of houses.

Portadown is well supplied with banks. There are branches of the Bank of Ireland, Belfast Bank, and Ulster Bank. It has also the Portadown Discount Company, Limited, the Portadown Loan Company, and the Portadown Building and Investment Company, Limited.

The Young Men's Institute is situated in Edward Street. It was established in 1883 under the Limited Liability Act, upon a capital of £1,000, in 1,000 shares of £1 each. Five shares were

GENERAL HOUSE-FURNISHING ESTABLISHMENT,

PORTADOWN.

HUGH WALLACE,

WHOLESALE AND RETAIL HARDWARE MERCHANT,
WATCHMAKER AND JEWELLER.

Furniture neatly and promptly repaired by competent Workmen on the premises.

Oils, Paints, Colours and Varnishes; Carpenters' and Joiners' Tools of every description.

Room-papers and Stationery; Carpets, Oil Cloths and Hearth-rugs; Grates, Fenders and Fire Irons.

paid in full, and 12s. 6d. per share on 780. With the amount thus procured, and a loan of £740 17s. at 4 per cent., building and other expenses were met. The accommodation includes library, reading-room, class rooms, and an assembly room large enough to seat 200 people. At the rear there are two well-appointed ball courts. About fifty members pay 5s. a year each. Mr. John Acheson is Chairman, and Mr. William Weir, Secretary.

A part of the Young Men's Institute is occupied by the Public Library, at a fixed rent. The library was established in 1872. Trustees appointed for the purpose then received an equal share of £500, and accrued interest, from trust funds of the old Portadown Loan Fund. This was supplemented by donations, etc. The library contains over 2,200 volumes, including in the various sections, history, science, philosophy, natural history, poetry, biography, travels, and general literature. The subscription is 5s. a year, and there are 130 members. A reading-room, well supplied with newspapers and periodicals, is managed in connection with the library. Books are lent out for two weeks, subject to renewal. The trustees are Messrs. C. F. Wakefield, George Kinkead, A. Shillington, J.P. ; Charles Johnston, J.P. ; and Arthur Thornton. Mr. Charles Johnston, J.P., is president, Mr. Hugh Anderson, vice-president, Mr. George Kinkead, treasurer, Mr. James McKell, secretary, and Mr. William Hunter, librarian.

MUSICAL SOCIETY, ROMAN CATHOLIC YOUNG MEN'S ASSOCIATION, LAWN TENNIS, CRICKET AND FOOTBALL CLUBS, ATHLETIC CLUB, BICYCLING, PORTADOWN ROWING CLUB.

THE Portadown Musical Society is organized on a firm footing, and is doing an excellent work. It was founded by Mr. Henry Shillington, C.E., and he continues to be its conductor.

About 10 years ago the Roman Catholic Young Men's Association was established. Its house is in William Street. There are 150 members in good standing. The subscription is 1s. a quarter. A reading-room, plentifully supplied with newspapers and magazines, is the chief feature. Mr. James Grew is president, Mr. Robert Cullen, vice-president, Mr. John Reynolds, secretary, and Mr. D. Fitzpatrick, treasurer.

Lawn tennis has been a popular game at Portadown for many years, but there was no established club until 1881. In that year the initiative was taken in the matter by Messrs. Charles

Johnston, James McFadden, J. B. Atkinson, W. H. Atkinson, and William Jones. There are now about 40 members, of whom 15 are ladies. The subscription for gentlemen is 10s., and for ladies 5s. per annum. Mr. Wm. H. Atkinson is secretary, and Mr. James McFadden, treasurer. The ground is at Tavanagh. Four grass courts are laid down, and there is room for two more.

The Portadown Cricket Club was established about 10 years ago. It has 40 members, who pay a subscription of 10s. a year each. The club ground is in the People's Park. There are some good players among the members.

A junior foot-ball club (Rugby), consisting of 30 members, has been in existence for over two years. The subscription is 2s. 6d. per season, and the ground in the People's Park.

The Portadown Athletic Club was organized in 1884. Sports are held annually, in August, under its auspices. The track is in the People's Park, and is said to be the second best in Ireland. About £70 is usually expended in prizes, and the programme consists of 15 "events." Members of the club pay an annual subscription of 10s. The management of the sports in 1887 devolved on a committee consisting of Messrs. James Grew, chairman, John Crummie, secretary, D. T. Gillespie, treasurer, J. C. Stanley, D. W. Walker, and J. Doak.

Bicycling is very popular at Portadown, but there has been no attempt, thus far, to form a club. A race for cyclists is always included in the programme of the sports, and several of the local men enter.

A rowing club has been established for about eleven years. There are 40 members paying a subscription of 10s. each. A boat-house was erected at a cost of £70, on the Edenderry side of the Bann. Three regattas have been held since the foundation. At present scratch races only are rowed. Fifteen boats are in use, 9 racing and 6 pleasure

---

CHURCH OF IRELAND AND METHODIST CHURCHES, MONUMENTS, &c.

THE Church of Ireland occupies the most prominent site at Portadown. It faces Market Street and High Street, and is flanked by Church Street and West Street. Many structural changes have been made since the erection in 1823. The original outlay was about £1,300, consisting of a gift of £831 from the old Board of First Fruits, and a loan of £461 from the same body. The style of architecture was early English, with square battlemented pinnacled tower. In 1885 the most important part of the edifice was remodeled, and the seating capacity enlarged by the addition of

transepts. The church is now cruciform, and the main roof groined. In the aisles, the roof-timbers are exposed, and harmonious effects produced by staining. The chancel is exceedingly chaste in design and detail. The pews are fitted in pitch pine, and the floor laid with encaustic tiles. A beautiful pulpit, constructed of Caen stone and marbles of Connemara, Cork, and Kilkenny, a lectern, with carved oak eagle, and a fine organ, are among the striking attractions. The church was reopened in 1886. Over £4,000 was spent upon the new work, and in remodeling the old. A mural tablet in the southern transept commemorates Alexander Bredon, M.D., who for thirty-four years discharged the duties of public officer in the district. Rev. Canon Augustine Fitzgerald, D.D., is rector of Portadown, the Rev. Robert M'Cracken, curate, and Mr. W. Archbutt Taylor, As. Mus. T.C.L., organist.

Portadown is the great stronghold of Methodism in the County Armagh. The principal church is in Thomas Street. It is a spacious edifice, and has a handsome portico, supported by four great pillars with Corinthian capitals. In the interior a gallery resting on thirteen ornamental pillars, runs all round. The front is tastefully ornamented, the pulpit is mahogany, and the Communion rails of the same wood. Over the pulpit there is a fine organ. The pews are modern and painted in oak. Several mural tablets commemorate prominent Wesleyans, and make a most interesting historical record. One erected by trustees of the church is to the memory of Thomas Shillington, who died in 1830, at the age of 63. "He was the nursing father of Methodism in this town and neighbourhood for nearly forty years." The next to Thomas Averell Shillington, J.P., who died in 1874, aged 74. "Erected by fellow townsmen in grateful remembrance of his public spirit and private virtues, and of the many valuable services rendered by him in promoting the progress of Portadown, and the true welfare of its inhabitants." The third, under the galleries, tells its object thus : "As an enduring record of his social virtues and Christian character this monument is inscribed by his fellow citizens to the memory of William Paul, of Portadown." Died 1857, aged 65.

Set into the wall, above one of the galleries, a tablet bears this inscription : " Rev. Adam Averell, M.A., a clergyman of the Established Church, President of the Primitive Wesleyan Methodist Society, 1818 to 1841. Died at Clones, 1847, in the 93rd year of his age." It was originally erected in the Donegall Street Primitive Methodist Church, Belfast. At the taking down of that edifice in 1887, the tablet, for family reasons, was brought to Portadown. The present Methodist Church was erected in 1860, and with the school-house attached, and minister's residence, cost about £5,000. The old church at the opposite side of the street, higher up, was built in 1832. It is now used for commercial purposes. The senior minister, Rev. Andrew Armstrong, appointed by Conference this year, was stationed at Portadown when the old church was in use. Rev. Robert Jamison, and Rev. Randal C. Philips are the associate ministers, and Mr. Henry Shillington, C.E., is organist.

The Primitive Methodist Church is in Mary Street. It is a small, plain-gabled building, and dates from 1860. Rev. John Taylor is minister.

PRESBYTERIAN CONGREGATIONS, CHRISTIANS, SALVATION ARMY, ROMAN CATHOLIC CHURCH AND CONVENT, BURIAL PLACES.

THERE are two congregations of Presbyterians, one belonging to the first church, in Bridge Street, Edenderry, and the other to the Armagh Road Church.

The Edenderry Church has a handsome gable front, supported on two large Corinthian columns. It was built in 1857. The interior appointments are appropriate ; seatings and pulpit in pitch pine, and the ceiling in stained pine. The gallery is carried around on three sides, with front of ornamental iron rails. In 1822 the original church was built. It stood further back from the street, on the site afterward occupied by the school-house. Near it was the tomb of the Rev. J. W. G. Dowling, erected by the congregation whose minister he had been for many years, although he died at the age of 38, in 1838. Rev.

T

A. J. BURNETT,

General Draper,

MILLINER & DRESSMAKER,

HIGH STREET,

PORTADOWN.

AGENT FOR THE AMERICAN AND LONDON SCIENTIFIC SYSTEM OF DRESS-CUTTING.

HENRY BALFOUR,

SAUSAGE SKIN MANUFACTURER,

PORTADOWN.

W. J. Macaulay is the present minister. The Armagh Road Church has been built about 21 years. It is a handsome edifice, of black stone with freestone dressings. The interior is fitted in good taste; seatings in pitch pine, modern style. The church and manse stand in well-kept grounds. Rev. Robert Jeffrey is minister.

The Christians, originally known as Plymouth Brethren, assemble for worship at the Victoria Hall, David Street. A strong foothold appears to have been made by the Salvation Army. It has extensive barracks in Edward Street, built about four years ago.

The Roman Catholic Church is a large cruciform edifice, situated in William Street. It has a high battlemented pinnacled tower, and altogether is quite imposing. The interior is rich in embellishments, and the effects harmonious and well calculated. Among the most noticeable features are the high altar, the Virgin's altar, and the pulpit, all in sculptured Caen stone, relieved by different colored Irish marbles. As a work of art, the high altar is really meritorious. The roof of the church is stained, and there is a spacious gallery at the eastern end. A fine stained chancel window deserves mention. Very Rev. Laurence, Canon Byrne, is parish priest. His curate is Rev. P. Slevin.

Next to the Roman Catholic church there is a Presentation Convent, founded about five years ago, through the instrumentality of Canon Byrne, who unselfishly gave the parochial residence so that it might be brought into immediate use by the nuns. A ladies' boarding school and infant school, under the National Board, are carried on under the supervision of Mrs. Harbison, the superioress.

Four burial places are used by the residents of Portadown. Seagoe is nearest to the town, less than a mile from the boundary, and is under the authority of the Lurgan Board of Guardians. All denominations inter in it. A fragment of the ruin of the ancient church, ivy-covered, still remains. At Drumcree, within a mile from town, there are church-yards for Roman Catholic and Protestant burials. There is also an ancient ground at Mullavilly, about 3 miles distant.

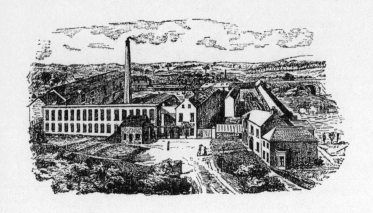

DAVID GRAHAM & CO.,

FLAX AND TOW SPINNERS

PORTADOWN.

MESSRS. DAVID GRAHAM & CO.

MESSRS. DAVID GRAHAM & CO.'S spinning mills are so situated as to be seen from all trains either entering or leaving Portadown, and are well calculated to impress the stranger with the importance of the town from the manufacturing point of view. The history of the mills dates from 1852. During that year Messrs. Wilson, Irwin & Co. put up a building two storeys and an attic in height, and 135 feet long, for flax and tow spinning. The capacity was for 2,000 spindles. Stimulated by the activity in the linen trade, produced by the American War, they erected a second building 160 feet long, in 1865. It was two storeys high, fire-proof, and so constructed that it can be raised to five storeys if necessary. The ceilings are lofty, and the rooms well ventilated. Very extensive stores are in use for flax, tow, and other materials. The number of spindles was increased to 5,000. In 1872 the Portadown Linen Co., Limited, purchased the interest of Messrs. Wilson, Irwin & Co., and worked the concern in connection with their weaving factory at Tavanagh. Four years later, Messrs. David Graham & Co. purchased the mills from the Portadown Linen Co., Limited, and began at once to renew the machinery, and increased the number of spindles to 8,000. The land under premises measures a little over 3¼ acres, in the heart of the town. Messrs. David Graham & Co. have considerably extended the buildings since their advent. A private residence, standing in handsome grounds, and approached by a tastefully planted avenue from Castle Street, is a pleasing feature of the improvements which they have made. The raw material spun by Messrs. David Graham & Co. for the greater part is of Irish growth. Flax from Belgium and Holland are also used. The yarns made are chiefly prime warp for both damask, heavy linen and cambric, and are purchased by the principal manufacturers of Ulster and the Continent. The engines, a beam and a horizontal, are capable of driving up to 430 horse power. About 400 workers are employed. Owing to the central position of the mills these are enabled to go to their own home for meals. Those who are too young to work more than half time, have excellent facilities for attending school. The mills are connected by a siding with the Great Northern Railway. Mr. David Graham and Mr. Robert Graham constitute the firm of Messrs. David Graham & Co.

◁Thomas Dawson▷

LINEN & CAMBRIC HANDKERCHIEF
MANUFACTURER AND BLEACHER,
STEAM WINDER,
YARN BOILER AND PREPARER,
MACHINE HEMSTITCHER, &c.,

CORCRAIN HOUSE.

PORTADOWN.

MR. THOMAS DAWSON.

R. THOMAS DAWSON'S enterprise at Corcrain House, has been in a state of active development since 1872. In May of that year he became owner in perpetuity. Linen manufacturing by hand-loom was begun here in 1840 by Mr. Joseph Druitt. He became lessee of Corcrain House, the handsome residence now occupied by Mr. Dawson, and built the stores and offices in connection with his trade, thirty of the workers' houses, and the porter's lodge seen in the illustration. Mr. Dawson, since his accession, has made considerable alterations and extensions, including the erection of a hemstitching factory. He also added departments for yarn boiling, preparing, and winding. About 400 hand-loom weavers are employed in the manufacture of linen and cambric handkerchiefs, about 60 inside and 30 outside hands in connection with the hemstitching factory, and from 20 to 30 in the yarn boiling and preparing departments.

Steam machinery was also introduced by Mr. Dawson. The buildings are principally of stone and slate. Belfast is Mr. Dawson's market. Corcrain House, grounds, factory and premises embrace over fifteen statute acres. The grounds are tastefully planted and laid out. Trees of many varieties flourish in them. Among those in greatest perfection are beech, ash, birch and oak. There are some choice specimens of Portuguese and common laurel, Irish yew, holly—common and variegated—and a splendid array of rhododendrons.

Corcrain House is within the town boundary. It is about three quarters of a mile from the Railway station. The Corcrain river bounds the property on the west, and the Great Northern Railway on the north.

THE WOODSIDE NURSERY.

THE WOODSIDE NURSERY consists of about sixteen acres, and occupies the site of the famous Castle Gardens of Portadown. They were converted to nursery purposes by the late Mr. Francis Grant, about fifteen years ago. Messrs. Samuel McGredy and Son bought the property from the trustees of Mr. Grant, nine years since. Mr. Samuel McGredy has had a life-long experience in nursery work and landscape gardening. Some of the finest private places in Ulster have been laid out from his designs, and under his personal supervision. Messrs. Sl. McGredy and Son have at present five glass houses, each 95 feet in length, and a dozen frames for bringing forward young stock. Pansies and violas are a speciality. For specimens of these, the firm received highest award at the Show of the Royal Horticultural Society, Dublin, in 1887, and wherever else exhibited. Rose culture is the great feature of their labors. The stock for sale in 1888 exceeded 60,000. They were awarded first prizes for roses at Douglas, Isle of Man, in 1886 and in 1887, first prize and cup at Glasgow in 1886, first prize at the Royal Horticultural Society's Show, Dublin, in 1887, and first prizes at Greenock, Glasgow, Edinburgh, and elsewhere in Scotland in 1886. The cultivation of fruit trees is still another of the specialities. During the Autumn of 1887-8, over 25,000 apple trees were sold at the Woodside Nursery. Conifers and ornamental shrubs take up a large space. As many as 50,000 rhododendrons are often purchased by one buyer. Dahlias and gladioli receive a large share of attention at the hands of Messrs. Samuel McGredy & Son. The water supply is procured from the River Bann.

IMPERIAL HOTEL, PORTADOWN.

THIS LONG ESTABLISHED HOTEL has now been much enlarged by the addition of new Premises, and fitted with every requisite for the convenience and comfort of Commercial Gentlemen and Visitors. The Hotel 'Bus attends the Arrival and Departure of Trains. Posting, &c. WILLIAM HALL, Proprietor.

W. J. REDMOND,

PLAIN and FANCY BAKER,

CONFECTIONER & FAMILY GROCER

1 and 2 CHURCH STREET,

PORTADOWN.

PORTADOWN DIRECTORY.

—:o:—

BUSINESS BRANCHES, PROFESSIONS, PUBLIC BODIES, &c.

—:o:—

[Arranged Alphabetically. Institutions, etc., not mentioned here should be sought in the Portadown Alphabetical Directory, and in the County Directory, page 53.]

—:o:—

AUCTIONEERS.
Chapman, Robert, William st
Cooper, Joseph, Woodhouse st
Fordyce, James, Thomas st
Locke, George A., Woodhouse st
Pentland, J. S., West st

BABY LINEN.
Brown, Mrs., Woodhouse st
Dickson, Mrs., Market st
Maconachie, Mrs. M., Bridge st
Sinnamon, Mrs. M., High st
Wortley, Thos., Woodhouse st

BAKERS.
Anderson, Walter, Mandeville st
Courtney, Clement, West st
Grimason, S., Lurgan rd
M'Kell, James, Market st
M'Shane, Patrick, Bridge st
Mitchell, Wm., High st
Redmond, William J., Church st
Stanley Brothers, High st
Wright, Robert, West st

BANKS.
Bank of Ireland, High st., T. D. Atkinson, agent; A. S. Gore, sub-agent; J. J. Loughlin, cashier
Belfast Bank, High st., George Kinkead, mgr.; Edward Harpur, cashier; James Malseed, act

Ulster Bank, High st., Hugh Anderson, mgr.; D. T. Gillespie, cashier; Jas. Harper, acct.

BILLPOSTER.
Major, M. J., Woodhouse st

BLACKSMITHS.
See also Coachbuilders.
Gallagher, Charles, Railway st
Montgomery, James, Edgarstown
Mooney, Edward, Obins st

BOAT BUILDER.
Sherman, Thomas, Bridge st

BOOTMAKERS
who have shops.
Donaghy, Patrick, High st
Hoy, Joseph, High st
Jeffers, John, Market st
Jenkinson, Wm. J., West st
M'Conville, John, Bridge st
Pentland, Edward, High st
Stanley, Wellington, High st
Tate, John, High st
Trimble, Mrs. S., West st

BUILDERS.
Bright Brothers, Bridge st
Collen Brothers, Hanover st
Cullen, Robert, Hanover st
Lutton, Richard, Carlton st
Reid, Wm., Edward st

JOSIAH PEEL,

𝔓harmaceutical 𝔠hemist, 𝔇ruggist,

SEED MERCHANT, &C.,

HIGH STREET, PORTADOWN,

AND

THOMAS STREET, ARMAGH.

Prescriptions Carefully Compounded from the Purest Drugs.

Patent and Proprietary Medicines.	Garden & Farm Seeds.
Horse and Cattle Medicines.	Dog Biscuits by the Celebrated Manufacturers.
Toilet Requisites.	Oil Cake, Cattle Spice, etc.
Paints, Oils, Colors and Glass.	Artificial Manures.

JAMES WALSH,

NURSERYMAN & FLORIST,

DRUMCREE,

PORTADOWN.

Rose & Fruit Tree grower in all the leading varieties

Roses, Apples, Pears, Plums, Cherries, Apricots, Peaches, Raspberries, Strawberries, Gooseberries & Currants.

The Public will find it advantageous to visit the Drumcree Nursery

Whitten, Wm., William st
BUILDING AND INVESTMENT CO., LTD., THE PORTADOWN.
Office, Hanover street, Wm. J. Paul, J.P., chairman ; R. J. Grimason, secretary

BURIAL PLACES.
Drumcree, Church of Ireland, Drumcree ; R. C. Church-yard, Mullavilly old Church-yd. ; Seagoe Church-yard

BUTTER EXPORTERS.
Benson, John, Scotch st
Harvey, J. and J., Mahon cottage

CABINET MAKERS
Wallace, Hugh, Woodhouse st
Wright Joseph, Woodhouse st

CANAL BOAT OWNERS.
Acheson, J. and J., Castle street
Bright Brothers, Bridge street
Caddell, Samuel, Francis street
McClatchey, Robert
Monaghan, Laurence, Castle st
Robb, Benj. and Hamilton, jun. (carrying Co.), Edenderry
Robb, Seth, Woodside
Shillington, T. A. & Son, Castle st

CARRIER, FURNITURE.
Wright, Joseph, Woodhouse st

CHANDLERS.
Richardson Brothers, High st

CIVIL ENGINEER.
Shillington, Henry, Bridge street

CHURCHES, MEETING HOUSES, &c.
Christians—Victoria hall, David street
Church of Ireland—St. Mark's, Rev. Augustine Fitzgerald, D.D.; Rev. Robert McCracken, Curate
Methodist—Thomas street, Rev. Andrew Armstrong, Rev. Robert Jamison, Rev. Randall C. Phillips
Methodist (Primitive)—Mary st, Rev. John Taylor
Presbyterian, 1st, Edenderry— Rev. W. J. Macaulay ; Armagh road, Rev. Robert Jeffrey
Roman Catholic—William st—

Very Rev. Laurence Byrne, P.P.; Rev. P. Slevin, C.C.
Salvation Army—Edward st

CLOG MAKERS.
Donaghy, Patrick, High street
Scarborough, W. L., Woodhouse st
Trimble, Mrs. S., West street

CLOTHIERS (Old and New).
Cooney, John, West street
Rafferty, F., Woodhouse street
Woods, John, Woodhouse street

CLUBS, &c.
(See Portadown Descriptive.)

COACH BUILDERS AND SMITHS.
Atkinson, John, Mary st
Locke, Wm. J., Woodhouse st
McConnell, James, William st

COAL MERCHANTS.
Bright Bros., Bridge street
Robb, Seth, Castle street
Shillington, T. A. & Son, Castle st
The Portadown Carrying Co

COFFEE ROOMS.
Atkinson, Miss, Market street
Rodgers, Woodhouse street

CONVENT, PRESENTATION.
William street, Mrs. Harbison, Superioress

DINING ROOMS.
Anchor, Bridge street, John Mulholland, manager

DISPENSARY.
Carleton street, Dr. William Stewart, J.P., Medical Officer. Attendance—Monday, Wednesday, and Friday
Committee—Thos. Shillington, J.P.; Thomas Armstrong, J.P.; Averell Shillington, J.P.; Joseph Acheson, J.P.; Charles Johnston, J.P.; John C. Fulton, J.P.; John Collen, J.P.; William J. Paul, J.P.; John Macoun, William Hall, Wm. Orr, John Malcolmson, James Maginnis, David Ruddell, John McNally, Richmond Pepper, Wm. John Calvert, John Lutton, Robt. White, Watson Walker, William Robinson, Samuel Carrick

Committee meets on the first Monday in every month at 11 o'c

DRAPERS.

Anderson, Robert, Church street
Burnett, A. J., 43 High street
Corbett, Robert, Market street
Dickson, Mrs. Wm., 23 Market st
Douglas, Joseph, 36 High street
Fleming, Joseph, High street
Hosey, John, 28 Market street
Paul, Wm. & Son, 46 & 48 High st
Richardson Brothers, 2 Market st

DRUGGISTS.

Acheson, J. & J., Market st
Peel, Josiah, High st
Richardson Bros., High st

EDUCATION.

LADIES' SCHOOLS.

Alexandria — High st., Miss Mary A. W. Kinkead
Convent — William st., Mrs. Harbison
—— Miss Stewart

NATIONAL SCHOOLS.

Armagh rd.—J. Omelvena, B.A.
Church st. (Duke's)— William Doherty, B.A., Miss Major
Curran st.—Chas. M'Dermott
Edenderry—John Bell, M.A.
Montague st.—Mrs. Mullan
Thomas st.—Jas. N. Jamison
Union st.—Miss E. J.. Flavell
William st Convent—Mrs. Harbison

EMIGRATION AGENTS.

Boyle, James, Meadow lane
Cooper, Joseph, Woodhouse st
Fearon, John, Woodhouse st
Grew, John, High st
Livingston, John G., Bridge st
Locke, George A., Woodhouse st
Pentland, John S., West st
Walker, John, Castle st

ESTATE (MANCHESTER).

Agent : Captain O'Brien, J.P., Tandragee

ESTATE (LURGAN).

Agent : Claude Brownlow, J.P., Lurgan

FIRE BRIGADE (VOLUNTEER).

Engine house, William st.—Thos. Shillington, Secundus, Captain ; John Acheson, Lieutenant

GAS LIGHT CO., PORTADOWN.

Works, Lurgan Road.
George Kinkead, Secretary
James Nisbet, Manager

GLASS, CHINA & DELF.

Hegan & Co., Mandeville st
Livingston, Henry, West st
Livingston, John, G., Bridge st
M'Broom, Isaac, High st
Rountree, John, High st

GRAIN MERCHANTS.

† Seed.

Clow, James & Co., Castle st
†Grew, James & Co., Bridge st
Johnston, James, Edenderry
†Loughran, Patrick, Mary st
†M'Conville John, West st
†Robb, Benjamin, Thomas st
†Shillington, T. A. & Son, Castle st

GREEN GROCERS.

Connolly, Peter, West st
Downey, Wm., West st
Hanratty, Mrs. M., William st
Loney, Mrs. A., William st
M'Knight, Christy, William st

GROCERS.

Marked thus (*) retail spirits, (†) seed merchants

†Acheson, J. & J., Market st
Anderson, George, West st
Alexander, John, Woodhouse st
Anderson, Robert, Market st
Baxter, W., Castle st
Courtney, Clement, West st
Craig, Henry, Obin st
Devers, Wm. J., 24 High st
*Doogan, Thomas, Woodhouse st
Frizelle, William, 6 West st
Fulton, John & Sons, Church st
Gardiner, Thomas, Bridge st
Gibson, John & Co., 29 Market st
†*Grew, M., High st
Guinness, George, 8 West st
†Hewitt, Wm., 29 West st

†*Jeffers, I. & J., Market st
Joyce, Mrs. J. E., West st
Kernaghan, Thos., Woodhouse st
Levingston, Henry, West st
Livingston Bros., Bridge st
Locke, George, 12 Woodhouse st
London & Co's. Tea Co., High st
†M'Broom, Isaac, High st
M'Ilveen, Wm J., 18 High st
M'Kell, James, Market st
*Matchett, Benjamin, Edgarstown
Miller, Robert, Obins st
Milligan, Edward, 10 West st
Mitchell, Wm., 3 High st
*Morgan, L. J., 3 West st
Morrison, Robert, Woodhouse st
†Morrison, Thomas, 12 Market st
†Peel Josiah, 2 High st
Preston, Francis W., Church st
Redmond, William J., Church st
Reynolds, A., Bridge st
Richardson Bros., 17 High st
*Ripley, Mrs. My., Clounagh
Rountree, John, High st
Ruddell, Henry, West st
†*Sheil, P. J., Woodhouse st
Stanley Bros., 27 High st
†Thornton, A., Thomas st (wholesale only)
Thornton, David, 42 High st
Walker, John, Castle st
Watson, James, Devon lodge
Wilson, Samuel, Bridge st

HARDWARE.

Bright Brothers, Bridge st
Carrick, Samuel, West st
Collen Bros., Hanover st
Davidson, John, Woodhouse st
Hegan & Co., Mandeville st
Paul, Robert, Market st
Shillington. T. A. & Son, Castle st
Walker, John, Castle st
WALLACE, HUGH, Woodhouse st

HAY AND STRAW EXPORTERS.

Coburn, J. and Son, Edenderry
Cosgrove, Hugh, William st
Frizelle, Henry, Woodhouse st

HIDES AND SKINS.

M'Cahey, Joseph, Woodhouse st

HOTELS.

Temperance. (*)

*Albert, Castle st
*Frazer's, Church st
*Hall's, Woodhouse st
IMPERIAL, High st
QUEEN'S, High st

IRON FOUNDERS.

Bright Brothers, Bridge st

LEATHER & BOOT UPPER MERCHANTS.

Hegan & Co., Mandeville st
Hoy, Joseph, High st
Rigby, Fredk. & Co., West st
Tate, John, High st

LOAN COMPANIES.

The Portadown Discount Co., Ltd., Meadow lane. Wm. Paul, John C. Fulton, J.P., directors; W. H. Atkinson, solicitor; James Boyle, secretary
The Portadown Loan Co., Woodhouse st., Thomas Shillington, J.P., chairman; George Kinkead, secretary; James Wightman, manager

Manufactures.

HANDKERCHIEF MANUFACTURERS.

Linen, Cambric, &c.

Cowdy, Wm., Thomas st
Dawson, Thomas, Corcrain ho
Gilbert, John, Seagoe
Lutton, A. J. and Son, Edenderry
Malcolmson, John, Windsor ter
Monypeny & Watson, Cornascrebe
Reid, Robert & Son, Tarson ho
Robb, Hamilton, Edenderry
Spence, Bryson & Co., Meadow le
Wilson, Samuel, Alma ter

HEMSTITCHERS (Machine).

Cowdy Wm., Thomas st
Dawson, Thomas, Corcrain ho
Gilbert, John, Seagoe
Lutton, A. J. and Son, Edenderry
Monypeny & Watson, Cornascrebe
Spence, Bryson & Co., Meadow le

LINEN MANUFACTURERS.

Bleachers. (*)

Acheson, J. & J. and Co., Castle st
Annett, Jas. Irvine, Riverside
Carter, Thomas, Derryall
Grimshaw & M'Fadden, Armagh rd
Kernaghan, Thos., Woodhouse st
Lutton, A. J. & Son, Edenderry
Montgomery, Jn. & Sons, Derryvore
Reid, Robert and Son, Tarson
Robb, Hamilton, Edenderry
Stewart, R. and W. & Co., Bridge st
The Castleisland Linen Co.
Watson, Armstrong & Co. R'way st

SPINNERS, FLAX AND TOW.

Graham, David and Co , Castle st

MARINE STORES.

Bond, James, Obin st
M'Guigan, Stephen, Obin st

MARKETS.

General market, Saturday;
straw and hay, Wednesday ; grain,
Wednesday and Saturday ; flax,
Tuesday; fowl, eggs, butter and
pork, Saturday ; grass-seed, Wednesday

MARKET PLACES.

Mandeville st., Market st., William st and Woodhouse st

MERCHANT TAILOR.

See also Drapers.
Ross, J. H., 24 Market st

MILLERS (Corn).

Clow, James & Co., Castle st

NEWS AGENTS.

See Stationers.

NEWSPAPERS.

Portadown and Lurgan News and Tenant Farmers' Gazette,
Thomas st., Saturday, 1d., S. Farrell.

The Advertiser, Mandeville st ,
Thursday, gratis, Wm. Reid

NURSERYMEN.

M'Gredy, Saml. & Son, Woodside
Walsh James, Drumcree

PAINTERS.

Lamb, John, Castle st
Magee, James, West st
Wright, Joseph, Woodehouse st

PAWBROKERS.

Gardiner, Thomas, West st
Hazelton, Charles, Woodhouse st
Hewitt, Holt M., West st
Hunter, William, Bridge st

PETTY SESSIONS.

2nd and 4th Mondays every
month, J. Searight Atkinson, LL.D.,
clerk

PHOTOGRAPHER.

Murray, J., Woodhouse st

PHYSICIANS.

Clarke, George, Bridge street
Dougan, George, Millicent ter
Hadden, Wm. H., Thomas street
Heron, Samuel, Bridge street
Stewart, Wm., Alten place

PLUMBERS, &c.

Cochrane, William, Thomas street
Cooper, William, Bridge street

PORK CURERS.

McCammon and Sprott, Castle st
Shemeld, A. & Co., West street
Thompson, A. G., Market street

POSTING CAR OWNERS.

Annesley, J., Chapel street
Burns, Hugh, Woodhouse street
Burns, Jno., Woodhouse st
Dickson, James, Castle street
Grew, M., Queen's Hotel
Hall, William, Imperial Hotel
Locke, George, Woodhouse st
Lutton, John, Baltylum
Sinnamon, D., Woodhouse st
Wilson, Mrs., Bridge street
Wilson, Samuel, Bridge street
Wortley, Thomas, Woodhouse st
Wright, Joseph, Woodhouse st

POST OFFICE.

Market street
Frank I. O'Hanlon, J.P., Post
Master; Joseph Williams, supervising officer
Edenderry Receiving Office,
Robt. McKeown, P.M.

POTATO DEALERS.

Flavell, Thomas, William street
Scott, John, William street

POTATO EXPORTERS.

Allen, Richard, Castle street

U

Conn, Thomas, Obins street
Cosgrove, Hugh, William street
Frizelle, Henry, Water street
Grew, James and Co., Bridge st
Honeyford, James, Woodhouse st
POULTERERS.
Corr, George, William street
McCourt, P., Obins street
PRESERVE
MANUFACTURERS.
Acheson, J. and J., Market st
PRINTERS, JOB.
See Newspapers.
PROCESS SERVERS.
John Lecky, William J. Cooke
PROVISION CURERS.
See Pork Curers.
PROVISIONS.
See Grocers.
PUBLIC PARK.
Entrances: Castle street, Obin
street, and The Walk.
Trustees: A. Shillington, J.P.;
Thomas Shillington, J.P.; Thos.
Shillington; Chas. Johnston, J.P.;
Jos. Acheson, J.P.; Geo. Kinkead,
Benj. Robb, John Grew. James
Boyle, Secretary; Robert Bullock,
Keeper.
RAILWAY, G.N.
T. Johnston, Toll Collector.
S. Mears, goods agent
REED MAKERS.
Boyd, James, David street
McKinley, Mrs. S., Carrickblacker
road
Neill, Robert, Bridge street
Neill, Wm., Edenderry
Wallace, John, Bridge street
ROPE AND TWINE
MANUFACTURERS.
Logan, Henry & Son, Carrick-
blacker road
R.I. CONSTABULARY.
Barracks, Bridge street, Eden-
derry, Obins street, Edward street
James Bonis, D.I.
Patrick McBrien, H.C.
SADDLERS.
Bell, John, Market street

Dickson, Wm., Market street
Ferris, Joseph, Woodhouse street
SAUSAGE SKIN
MANUFACTURER.
Balfour, Henry, Clounagh
SAW MILLS.
Bright Brothers, Castle st
Collen Brothers, Hanover st
Shillington, T. A. & Son, Castle st
SEED MERCHANTS.
See also Grain merchants Grocers
M'Cammon and Sprott, Castle st
Peel, Josiah, High st
SOLICITORS.
Atkinson, W. H. (E. D. Atkin-
son and Son,) Coroner for North
Armagh, Commissioner for taking
acknowledgment of deeds by mar-
ried women for county Armagh,
Agent for the Scottish Widows',
the British Empire Life Assurance
Co., the Railway Passengers Acci-
dental Insurance Co., and the
Phœnix Fire office, Solicitor for
the Portadown Building and In-
vestment Co., Ltd., and the Por-
tadown Discount Co., Ltd., Tho-
mas st
Carleton, Atkinson and Sloan,
Church st
Harris, Henry J., Church st
Farrell, Arthur T., Thomas st
Thompson, James, agent for the
Scottish Provincial Assurance Co.,
Fire and Life, William st
Wright, Wm. H., High st
SPIRIT RETAILERS.
See also Grocers. (*)
Aldred, Mrs. Mary, Woodhouse st
Berwick, Jas., Obins st
Brankin, John, Obins st
Byrne, Charles, Market st
Byrne, John, Woodhouse st
Byrne, Joseph, Market st
Grew, John, High st
Hendron, Mrs. E., Woodhouse st
Johnson, Thomas, Railway Station
Joyce, Mrs. Jane E., West st
Kelly, Mrs. Margt., Woodhouse st
M'Clatchy, Mrs. A., Bridge st

M'Conville, Henry, West st
M'Conville, John, West st
M'Corry, Hugh, Market st
M'Kinley, Archbd., Bridge st
Mulligan, Timothy, High st
O'Hanlon,Felix, High st
Robinson, Jos., Drumnahuncheon
Slowey, Patrick, West st
Stevenson, Thomas, Woodhouse st
Thornton, Arthur, High st
Woodhouse, Wm., Woodhouse st
Wright John, High st

STAMP DISTRIBUTOR.

Frank I. O'Hanlon, J.P., Post-master

STATIONERS.

(†) Newsagent only.

Allen, Mrs. E., High st
†Hoey, Joseph, High st
Wallace, Hugh, Woodhouse st
Waugh, D. W., High st

TIMBER MERCHANTS.

Bright, Brothers, Bridge st
Collen Bros., Hanover st
Shillington, T. A. & Son, Castle st

TEACHERS' SOCIETY.

Portadown and Lurgan.

J. Watson, chairman

TOWN COMMISSIONERS.

William Hall, chairman; Dr. George Dougan, ex-chairman; Wm. John Paul, J.P.; Arthur Thornton, John Rountree, John Geo. Livingston, James Grew, Archibald M'Kinley, John Lutton, John Richardson, Wm. Mitchell, Wm. Henry Atkinson, solicitor; Samuel Carrick, Wm. John Locke, Joseph M'Caghey

Robert M'Clatchey, town clerk and executive sanitary officer; Dr. Wm. Stewart, J.P., consulting sanitary officer; Henry Grimason,

Town Constable and Sanitary sub-officer; Edward Dougan, weigh-master; Shambles; Thomas Russell, weighmaster, general market

UNDERTAKERS.

Douglas, Joseph, High st
Grew, M., High st
Wilson, Mrs. E., Bridge st
Wright, Joseph, Woodhouse st

VICTUALLERS.

Campbell, John, Market st
Foy, Robert, Woodhouse st
Hughes, Charles, Market st
Hughes, Edward, Market st
Loughran, Edward, Woodhouse st
M'Corry, Hugh, Market st
Totton, James, Market st
Totton, Mrs., Market st

WATCHMAKERS.

Carrick, Samuel, West st
Gray, David, West st
WALLACE, HUGH, Woodhouse st

YOUNG MEN'S INSTITUTE, LIMITED.

Edward st., John Acheson, chairman; Wm. Weir, secretary

Reading-room, library, &c., Wm. Hunter, librarian; James M'Kell, hon. secretary

YARN MERCHANTS.

Capper, Adam, Bridge st

YOUNG MEN'S ASSOCIA-TION.

Roman Catholic, Wm. st., James Grew, president; D. Fitzpatrick, treasurer; John Reynolds, secretary; Charles M'Shane, caretaker

YOUNG MEN'S ASSOCIA-TION, PORTADOWN.

John Bell, chairman; T. D. Gillespie, secretary; Hugh Hegan, treasurer

PORTADOWN ALPHABETICAL DIRECTORY.
——:o:——
FARMERS AND RESIDENTS.
——:o:——

For names not found here, see Portadown Business Branches, &c., and Portadown Sub-Post Offices.

Abbreviations, Sub-Post Offices included in this list : B'corr—Ballynacorr; B'hill—Battlehill; Crab—Crabtree lane; D'ville—Derryanville; D. C.—Derryhale Corner ; Mul—Mullantine ; S' st—Scotch st.

Acheson, Geo., Church st
Acheson, John, Dunavon
Acheson, Rev. J., Windsor ter
Alexander, T., Artabracka, Mul
Allen, Rd., Ballybegan
Anderson, Abm., Cornascrebe
Anderson, James, Derryhale c
Annesley, Geo., Ballinteggart
Annesley, G., Portmore st
Armstrong, John, Eden hall
Armstrong, T. (J.P.), Eden hall
Armstrong, Thos., jun., Eden hall
Armstrong, Wm. F., Eden hall
Atkinson, E., Derryanville
Atkinson, James, Seagoe lr
Atkinson, John B., Church st
Atkinson, Miss. Millicent ter
Atkinson, R., Ballyfodrin, S' st
Atkinson, Wm., Derryall
Atkinson, W. (P.M.), Crabtree le
Atkinson, Wolsey R., Eden villa
Bailey, Mrs., Hanover st
Beattie, James, Cornascrebe
Bell, David F., Mandeville st
Benson, George. Farra, S' st
Benson, John, Ballynagone
Benson, T., Drumhariff, S' st
Best, John, Balteagh
Best, Robert, Killycomain
Black, G., Drumard P, B'hill
Black, H., Drumard P, B'hill
Blacker, V., Drumnevin, S' st
Boyce, J., T'lasson, C'roll
Boyce, James, Bocambra
Boyd, Edward, Battlehill
Boyd Mrs., Carleton st
Boyle, James, Drumcree
Bradshaw, James, Breagh
Brankin, Felix, Selshion
Brankin, Michael, Derrycaw

Bready, Miss, Church st
Bredon, Mrs., Millicent ter
Brogan, J., Drumnasoo, Mul
Brown, Wm. (P.M.), Ballynacorr
Brownlee, T., Drumnasoo, Mul
Bright, Geo., Bridge st
Bright, W. H., Bridge st
Bryson, John B., Carleton st
Bullick, Ralph, Mountain view
Bullick, Samuel, Drumnagoon
Bullick, Thomas, Drumnagoon
Burrell, T., Artabracka, Mul
Byrne, James, Woodhouse st
Byrne, Rev. F., Selsion
Caddell, W. J., Ballynacorr
Calvert, George, Breagh
Calvert, James, Drumnacanvey
Calvert, Wm. J., Ballymacrandle
Campbell, George, Breagh
Campbell, Willian, Annagh
Campbell, William, Ballyworkan
Carleton, Miss, Church st
Carr, Joseph, Baltylum
Carrick, J., Richmount, S' st
Carrick, Thos., Richmount, S'st
Carrick, Wm., Derryanville
Carter, George, Derryall, Crab
Carter, John, Derryall, Crab
Carter, T., Derryall, Crab
Chapman, D., B'teggart, B'hill
Chapman, Eliza, Battlehill
Chapman, J., Battlehill
Chapman, J., Mulladry, Mul
Chapman, J. (P.M.), Battlehill
Chapman, Mrs., D'huncheon, B'hill
Chapman, Mrs. A., C'root, B'hill
Chapman, Robert, Ballinteggart
Chapman, Thomas, Battlehill
Cheetham, George, Edward st
Church, Wm. J., Ballyworkan

Cinnamon, George, Kilmagamish
Clayton, Charles, Clounagh
Clayton, Edward, Clounagh
Clayton, Thomas, Derryanville
Clayton, Thomas, Drumnakelly
Clow, Wm. M., Carleton st
Cochrane, Robert, Cornascrebe
Collen, John (J.P.), Killicomain ho
Collen, Jos., Ashton villa
Collen, Richard, Oakfield
Collins, John, Seagoe up
Conn, F., Ballymacgeown, S' st
Conn, Rt., Kilmoriarty, Mul
Conn, T., Farra, S' st
Conn, Thos., Breagh
Conn, William, Drumnakelly
Conn, Wm., jun., Baltylum
Conn, Wm., jun., Drumnakelly
Cook, John, Concullentrabeg
Cook, John, Levaghery
Corbett, Rev. E. St. J., Mulladry,
　Mullantine
Costello, James, Ballynacorr
Coulter, Samuel, Tarsan, B'corr
Coulter, William, Tarsan, B'corr
Courtney, Archibd., Ballinteggart
Courtney, John, Selshion
Courtney, John, Ballynagowan
Cox, John, Derryhale corner
Cox, Mrs. M., Fruithill, D c
Cranston, Wm., Drumnasoo, Mul
Cregan, Arthur, Corcullentramore
Cregan, Wm., Ballinteggart, B'hill
Crockett, John, Legany, S' st
Crockett, Thos., Diviney, S' st
Crosbie, Wm. J., Drumnakelly
Crosby, Wm. J., Mahon
Crummie, J., Artabracka, Mul
Cullen, James, Ballyworkan
Curry, George, Clonroot, B'hill
Curry, Robt., Clonroot, B'hill
Davidson, Alex., Ballygargan
Davison, Henry, Ballygargan
Davison, Joseph, Ballygargan
Dawson, Rev. Abhrm., Seagoe, L
Dawson, Thomas, Corcrain ho
Dawson, William J., Corcrain ho
Devlin, Bernard, Derrymattry
Devlin, Edward, Muckery
Devlin, Henry, Muckery, Crab

Devlin, John, Ballynagowan
Devlin, John, Derrycaw
Dickson, J., T'lasson, Clenroll
Dickson, J. (P.M.) Mullantine
Dickson, Mrs. Margt., Clenroll
Dickson, Mrs., Lisnisky, Clenroll
Dillon, Samuel, Canagolabeg, S' st
Dilworth, Robert, Lisnisky
Dixon, James, Mullantine
Dixon, John, Artabracka
Dixon, John, Tamnifiglasson
Dixon, Samuel, Ballygargan
Dobson, G., Ballinteggart, B'hill
Doherty, Wm., Kilmoriarty, Mul
Doyle, John, Kingarve, S' st
Doyle, Richard, Derryhale, Mul
Doyle, William, Kingarve, S' st
Dugan, David, Derryvane
Duke, Thos., Drumnasoo, Mul
Dunbar, Ruth, Crabtree lane
Dynes, Samuel, Derrymattry
England, Henry, Knocknamuckly
England, Thos., Knocknamuckly
Fearon, James, Artabracka Mul
Fergus, Mrs., Bridge st
Ferguson, D., Bridge st
Ferguson, John, Clounagh
Ferguson, John, jun., Clounagh
Ferran, Bernard, Mulladry, D c
Ferrin, John, Cornascrebe
Fforde, John, jun., Mullantine
Flavell, James, Corbrackey, D'ville
Fleming, Miss M., Battlehill
Forbes, John, Crabtree lane
Forbes, Robert, Drumnakelly
Ford, James, Mullantine
Ford, William, Mullantine
Forde, David, Mullantine
Forsythe, George, Kilmagamish
Forsythe, John H., Ballintaggart
Forsythe, Rev.J.H.,Vinnecash,Mul
Forsythe, Robert, Derrymattry
Forsythe, William, Derrymattry
Foy, Rev. Edward, Drumcree
Frackleton, William, Clenroll
Fulton, J. C. (J.P.) Church st
Furphy, Mary, Derryanville
Garvey, Joseph, Coharra, S' st
Garvey, Patrick, Annagora, S' st
Gennett, Robert, Ballintaggart

Geough, John, Mulladry, Mul
Gibson, James, Crabtree lane
Gibson, Miss S., William st
Gibson, Richard, Lylo
Gibson, T. D., Res. Magistrate
Gibson, William, Ballyworkan
Gilbert, Jthn., Ballynacorr
Gilbert, Richard, Ballynacorr
Gilbert, Stephen, Mulladry, Mul
Gilbert, William A., Seago up
Gillespie, Henry, Derryletiff, S' st
Gillespie, William, Roughan, S' st
Gilpin, Andrew, Drumnagoon
Gilpin, John, Balteagh
Gilpin, Thomas, Clenroll
Gilpin, Wm. J., Tamnifiglasson
Glass, Samuel, Mulladry, Mul
Gough, William, Bridge st
Gracey, Robert, Balteagh
Gracey, Robert, T'lasson, C'roll
Graham, David, Castle st
Graham, Francis, Cornascrebe
Graham, John, Derryhale c
Graham, John, Cushenny, S' st
Graham, Robert, Castle st
Graham, Thomas, Derryhale c
Green, James, Ballynaghy
Greer, James, Mullalelish, D c
Greer, John, Mullalelish, D c
Greer, J. W., Church st
Greer, Thomas, Ballybreagh D c
Greer, William, Ballybreagh D c
Greer, William, 41 High st
Grew, James, Alma terrace
Grew, John, High st
Gribben, Daniel, Artabracka
Gribben, Francis, Artabracka
Gribben, James, Artabracka
Grimes, David, Drumheriff, S' st
Grimshaw, H., Kilmoriarty, Mul
Grimshaw, Wm., Kilmoriarty, Mul
Guy, Robert, Derryvore, B'corr
Guy, Mrs. M. A., Carlton st
Haddock, Mrs , Baltea, Clenroll
Hall, C., Artabracka, Mul
Hall, Charles, Derrycorry
Hall, Jas., Clonroot, B'hill
Hall, Mrs., Hanover st
Hall, Wm. (C.T.C.) High st
Halligan, John, Derryhale c

Hamill, Thomas, Mullantine
Hamilton, William, Seagoe lower
Hampton, E., Clonroot, B'hill
Hampton, J., Drumard P. B'hill
Hampton, S., Drumard P. B'hill
Harbinson, Thomas, Cornascrebe
Harcourt, James, Ballyworkan
Hare, Moses, Derryhale c
Hare, W. J., Derryhale c
Harrison, Sl., Muckery, Crab
Harrison, S. J., Muckery
Hart, Gabriel, Ballymageown
Hart, James, Drumard Primate
Heaney, W., Drumnacanvey
Henon, Miss I., Ballynacor
Henry, J., Carleton st
Henry, Mrs., William st
Henry, Ptk., Ballyworkan
Henry, Robt., Hanover st
Hewitt, Geo., Clonroot, B'hill
Hewitt, J., Clonroot, B'hill
Hewitt, John, Ballintaggart
Hewitt, Jthn., Clonroot, B'hill
Hewitt, J., jun., Clonroot, B'hill
Hewitt, Mark, Battlehill
Hewitt, Mrs., Clonroot, B'hill
Hewitt, Mrs., Dromard P. B'hill
Hewitt, Rt., Clonroot, B'hill
Hewitt, R., jun., Clonroot, B'hill
Hewitt, Thos., Battlehill
Hewitt Wm., Ballintaggart
Hewitt W. J., Clonroot, B'hill
Hobson, Rt., Mullantine
Holmes, John, Killycomain
Honeyford, B. jun., C'muckly, S'st
Honeyford, J., C'muckla, S'st
Honeyford, John, Drumgoose
Honeyford, Rd., Ballyfodrin, S'st
Honeyford, Rbsn., Ballintaggart
Honeyford, T., Ballyfodrin, S'st
Hopps, Robert, Clenroll
Hopps, William, Crossmacugley
Hughes, Mrs., K'mena, Clenroll
Hunniford, David, Ballintaggart
Hunter, David R., Artabracka
Hyde, Robert, Tumblekeny S'st
Hyde, Thomas, Foybeg
Ingram, Thomas, Drumgoose
Jackson, Alex., Corcullentrabeg
Jennett, George, Breagh

Johnston, Chas. (J. P.) Beechcote
Johnston, John, Woodhouse st
Johnston, Jno. (P. M.) Clenroll
Johnston, M., K'mena, Clenroll
Johnston, Mrs. L., Unshena S'st
Johnston, Samuel, Roughan S'st
Johnston, T., Canoneill, S'st
Jones, John, Ballyworkan
Jones, John, Corbracky
Jones, Ralph, Derryvane
Jones, William, Corbrackey
Kane, Jno., Ballinarry, B'corr
Keegan, William, Timakeel, S'st
Keiron, J., Artabracka, Mul
Kelly, John, Ballynagone
Kelly, Thomas, Battlehill
Kingsboro', H., Drumalis, S'st
Lappin, Alex., Cornascrebe
Larmer, W., D'macfall, D'ville
Lawson, George, Mullantine
Leckie, John, Ballyworkan
Leckey, John, Battlehill
Leckie, Thomas, Ballyworkan
Leitch, Rev. A., Drumcree
Lindsay, William, Ballintaggart
Loughead, James, Derryhale c
Loughead, Joseph, Derryhale c
Loughran, Mrs., Artabracka, Mul
Love, David, (P. M.) Scotchstreet
Love, James, Timakeel, S'st
Love, John, Roughan, S'st
Love John, Timakeel, S'st
Love, Joseph, Roughan, S'st
Love, J. G., Carnagolabeg, S'st
Love, R , Timakeel, S'st
Love, Wm., Drumheriff S'st
Lutton, Jno., Bridge st
Lutton, Robert, Baltylum
Lutton, W. J., Breagh
Lynas, Robert, Tarsan, B'corr
Lyness, Jas., Carne, B'corr
M'Adam, Joseph, Drumenagh
M'Adam Wm. J., Drumenagh
M'Anally, H., Derryletiff, S'st
M'Anally, J., C'ullentramore
M'Broom, I., D'huncheon, B'hill
M'Cabe. Robert, Ballynacorr
M'Caghley, W., Derryvore, B'corr
M'Callan, James. Cornascrebe
M'Cannon, Hugh W., Annagh

M'Cann, Edward, Clenroll
M'Cann, James. Selshion
M'Cann, Mrs. Mj., Derrymacfall
M'Cann, William, Ballyhannon
M'Cann, W., Kingarve, S'st
M'Cann, Wm., Muckery
M'Cann, Wm., Muckery, Crab
M'Carrison, Robert, Portmore st
M'Cleery, Amelia, B'nacorr
M'Clelland, Wm., Drumgoose
M'Connelle, Clarke, Marlacoomore
M'Connell, Richard, Selshion
M'Conville, Anthony, Cornascreeb
M'Cooe, James, Anagora, S'st
M'Creery, J. G., Kilmgamish Crab
M'Creery, William, Muckery Crab
M'Crory, John, Ballinacorr
M'Cullagh, Isaac, Timakeel, S'st
M'Cune, John, Ballybreagh, D. c.
M'Donnell, Alexander, Annagh
M'Fadden, James, Carleton street
M'Geown, H., Ballinarry, B'cor
M'Geown, J., Ballinarry, B'corr
M'Geown, J., Drumnagoon, B'corr
M'Geown, John, Tamnificarbet
M'Grane, P., Artabracka, Mul
M'Gredy, Sl., sen., The Walk
M'Gredy, Sl., jun., The Walk
M'Ilroy, Miss, Bridge street
M'Kenna, Ross, Anagora, S'st
M'Kenny, Joseph, Muckery Crab
M'Kenzie, Archbd., Seagoe house
M'Kenzie Brothers, Seagoe house
M'Kenzie, James, Bridge street
M'Keown, Fr., Derryletiff, S'st
M'Knight, William, Ballinacorr
M'Loughlin, Mrs., Carleton street
M'Murray, Ar., Crossmacaughley
M'Murray, James, Ballynaghy
M'Murray, J. H., Ballynaghy
M'Murray, W., Crossmacaughley
M'Ormond, Miss E., Clenroll
M'Shane, Chas., Drumhariff, S'st
M'Shane, Francis, Ballynagowan
M'Shane, Patrick, Anoagora, S'st
M'Sherry, John, Ballygargan
Magee, William, Breagh
Maginnis, James, Ballymacrandle
Magown, William, Artabracka
Maitland, James, Lisnamintry

Major, John, Church street
Mallow, A., Kilmoriarty, Mul
Mallagh, Benjn., Corcullentrabeg
Marlay, Miss, Bridge street
Marlay, Thomas, Castle street
Marley, Thomas, Castle street
Matchett, Francis, Derrycaw
Matchett, James, Derryanville
Matchett, James, Drumcree
Matchett, John, Derryanville
Matchett, Richard, Derryall, Crab
Mathers, David, Derrycorey
Mathers, Francis, D'neskin, Crab
Mathers, Joseph, D'neskin, Crab
Mathers, Richard, Muckery
Maxwell, William, Derryhale c
Maze, James, Levaghery
Maze, S., Knocknamuckly
Metcalf, William, Seagoe L
Milsop, William, Teague
Mitchell, J., Drumard P., B'hill
Mitchell, W., Drumnasoo, Mul
Monroe, Henry, Levaghery
Montgomery, J., Derryvore, B'corr
Montgomery, John, Seagoe upper
Montgomery, Mrs., Clonroot, B'hill
Montgomery, Mrs., Curglass, S'st
Montgomery, Robert, Annagh
Montgomery, Stewart, Lylo
Montgomery, Thomas, Derrycorey
Montgomery, Thos., Derryanville
Montgomery, W., Ballynagowan
Montgomery, W., Battlehill
Montgomery, William, Seagoe lr
Morgan, James, Castle street
Morris, Henry, Ballynagowan
Morris, James, Ballynagowan
Morrison, Thomas, Derryhale c
Morrow, George, Ballyworkan
Morrow, Isaac, Ballyworkan
Morrow, Richard, Canoneil, S'st
Morrow, Thomas, Canoneil, S'st
Mulholland, Edward, Coharra, S'st
Mulholland, Henry, Richmount
Mulholland, John, Ballymageown
Mulholland, P., jun., Coharra, S'st
Mullan, R., Drumheriff, S'st
Mullin, H., Drumheriff, S'st
Murphy, Daniel, Ballyworkan
Murphy, Patrick, Mahon

Murray, David, Drumnakelly
Murray, J., Ballinarry, B'corr
Murray, M., Drumnasoo, Mul
Nelson, George, Ballyhannon
O'Connor, Patrick, The Rockery
O'Hanlon, F. I. (J.P.), Market st
Orr, William, Church street
Parker, W., Artabracka, Mul
Patterson, David, Drumnakelly
Patterson, John, Cornascrebe
Paul, David G., Erindale
Paul, W., High street
Paul, W. J. (J.P.), High street
Pentland, D., Durmnakelly
Pentland, John, Drumnakelly
Pentland, Thomas, Ballyworkan
Pentland, William, Drumnakelly
Pepper, Richmond, Ballyworkan ho
Porter, David, Seagoe lr
Porter, George, Seagoe lr
Porter, Henry, Seagoe lr
Porter, John, Ballymagowan
Porter, John, Seagoe lr
Porter, Thomas, Corbrackey
Porter, Thomas, Derryanville
Preston, J. J., Clonroot, B'hill
Ramsey, James, Drumnagoon
Rea, Thomas, Clenroll
Reeves, William, Battlehill
Reid, Capel W., Tarson ho., B'corr
Reid, Geo., Derrykeeran, D'ville
Reid, John, Seagoe lower
Reid, J. F., Imperial hotel
Rice, Arthur, Artabracka
Richardson, Henry, Market st
Richardson, John, High st
Richardson, Thomas, Derrymattry
Ripley, Thomas A., Clounagh
Robb, Hamilton, Edenderry ho
Robb, H. jun., Edenderry ho
Robb, Seth, Woodside ho
Robb, Wm., Derybroughas, D'ville
Robinson, David, Drumheriff, S'st
Robinson, Dawson, Tamnificarbet
Robinson, George, Cushenny S' st
Robinson, George, Devinney, S' st
Robinson, John, Ballyhannon
Robinson, John, West st
Robinson, Joseph. Annakerra, S' st
Robinson, Robert, Divinney S' st

Robinson, Samuel, Roughan, S' st
Robinson, Thomas, Devinney, S' st
Robinson, Thomas, Scotch st
Robinson, T., T'lasson, C'roll
Robinson, Thos., Tamnifiglasson
Robinson, William, Artabrackagh
Robinson, William, Ballyhannon
Robinson, William, Lisnamintry
Robinson, William, Lylo
Rountree, Charles, Derryhale c
Rountree, Jones, Mulladry, D c
Rountree, Robert, Mulladry, D c
Rowland, B. G., Ballynacorr
Ruddell, David, Ballynacorr
Ruddell, George, Tamnifiglasson
Ruddell, Henry, Ballinteggart
Ruddell, John, Ballinteggart
Ruddell, H., Ballinteggart, B'hill
Ruddell, John, Battlehill
Ruddell, John, Clonroot, B'hill
Ruddell, John, B'teggert, B'hill
Ruddell, Mrs., L'nisky, Clenroll
Ruddock, R., Divinney, S' st
Russell, John, Ballynagowan
Russell, Robert, Crossmacaughley
Russell, Samuel, Farra, S' st
Russell, Thomas, Bridge st
Russell, William J., Farra, S' st
Rutledge, James, Drumlisnagrilly
Savage, Roland, Clonmartin
Scott, Charles, Scotch st
Shillington, A. (J.P.) Alta villa
Shillington, T. (J.P.) Tavanagh ho
Shillington, Thomas, Alta villa
Sinnamon, John, Derryanville
Sinnamon, Mrs. R., Wentworth ho
Sinton, B., Ballinteggart, B'hill
Sinton, Jacob, Annagh
Sloan, A. G., Solicitor, Alma ter
Sloan, H , Corbrackey, D'ville
Sloan, James, Mahon
Smith, James, Baltylum
Smith, John M., Baltylum
Smith, M., Artabracka, Mul
Sommerville, Simon, Ballyhanon
Spears, Henry, Derrybroughas
Spence, John, Hacknahay
Spence, L., Drumnagoon, B'corr
Spence, Thomas, Hacknahay
Spence, Thos. H., Bridge st

Sprott, Saml., Carleton st
Stanley, Chas., Derryhale c
Stanley, John, Derryhale c
Stanley, John, Annagh ter
Stanley, J., Edgarstown
Stanley, J., Mulladry, Mul
Stanley, Mrs., B'teggart, B'hill
Steen, Leo James, West st
Steen, Rt., Corcullentragh
Stevenson, I., Derryhale c
Stevenson, Thos., Selshion
Stewart, Wm., Artabracka
Stothers, J., Roughan, S'st
Stothers, J., Derryletiff, S'st
Stothers, W., C'golabeg, S'st
Sturgeon, A., D'huncheon, B'hi l
Symington, Wm., Glenroll
Taggart, D., Ballybreagh, Dc
Tate, Dawson, jun., Drumcree
Tate, Dorothy, Crabtree lane
Tate, Samuel, Derryall
Taylor, James, Derryvane
Taylor, John, Tamnificarbet
Taylor, J., D'macfall, D'ville
Taylor, Rd., D'macfall, D'ville
Taylor, Rt., D'macfall, D'ville
Taylor, Thomas, Derrycorry
Taylor, W. A. (A. Mus.), Millicent terrace
Thompson, John, Cornascreeb
Thompson, Robert, Ballinteggart
Thompson, R. (P.M.), Deryanvill
Thornton, James, Foybeg
Tiffany, James, Scotch st
Tiffany, J., Timakeel, S'st
Todd, Sl., Derryletiff, S'st
Todd, Thos., Roughan, S'st
Totton, Mrs., Carleton st
Trevors, John, Ballymagowan
Trotter, Miss, Hanover st
Trouton, Robert, Bocombra
Troughton, Thos., Corbrackey
Trouton, W., Anakera, D'ville
Tuft, James, Drumagoon
Tudor, W., Derryhale c
Twinem, C., Derryvore, B'corr
Twinem, Chas., Tarson, B'corr
Twinem, Jas., Ballynacorr
Twinem, Leonard, Ballyhannon
Twinem, Mrs., K'mena, Clenroll

Twinem, Robert, Knockmenagh
Twinem, T., Moyraverty, C'roll
Twinem, Wm., Lylo
Twinem, Wm., Ballyhannon
Twyble, Wm., Tamnificarbet
Uprey, James, Ballyhannon
Vaughan, Jas., West st
Von Stieglitz, Baroness, Carrick-
  blacker
Wakefield, C. F., Corcrean villa
Wakefield, E. T., Cloncore ho
Walker, John, Seago, l
Walker, Watson, Seagoe up
Warnock, Samuel, Derrycorey
Walker, Samuel, Levaghery
Watson, Alex., Cornascreeb
Watson, James, Devon lodge
Watson, John, Killycomain
Watson, W. J., Edenderry
Waugh, Jos., Selshion, S'st
Webb, James, Clenroll
Weir, Joseph, Ballynaghy
Weir, W., Kilmoriarty, Mul
Wetherall, H., C'braky, D'ville
White, F., Ballybreagh, Dc
White, J., B'breagh, Dc
White, Robert, Bocombra
Whittle, Adam, Scotch st
Whitley, J., D'huncheon, Mul
Whitley, Mrs. W., Curglas, S'st
Whitten, James, Drumnamather
Willis, George, Drumnamather

Willis, S. W., Victoria ter
Wilson, James, Ballymacrandle
Wilson, James, Lisnisky
Wilson, John, D'neskin, Crab
Wilson, J., Lisnisky, Clenroll
Wilson, Moses, Derryvane
Wilson, Samuel, Edenderry
Wilson, Thomas, Seagoe upper
Wilson, W., Mulladry, Dc
Woolsey, B., Kilmoriarty, Mul
Woodhouse, S., Drumlellum, S'st
Woodhouse, A., Drumlellum, S'st
Woods, Stewart, Derrybroughas
Workman, J., Richm., S'st
Workman, Miss E., Scotch st
Wright, Francis, Maghon
Wright, James, Artabrackagh
Wright, Jas., Clenroll ho
Wright, James, Drumnakelly
Wright, Jas., Derryhale c
Wright, J., jun., Mulladry, Mul
Wright, John, Artabrackagh
Wright, John, Baltylum
Wright, Joseph, Artabrackagh
Wright, Mrs. M., Battlehill
Wright, Sl., Drumnakelly
Wright, Thos., Ballyworkan
Wright, W., Corbrackey
Wright, W., sen., Artabracka, Mul
Wright, W., jun., Artabracka, Mul
Young, Mrs., Parkmount

SUB-POST OFFICES
IN THE PORTADOWN DISTRICT.

LETTERS addressed to residents of a sub-postal district should bear the name of the head office, thus : Diamond, Portadown. The names of the principal farmers and residents of the rural post office districts of Ballynacorr, Battlehill, Clenroll, Crabtree Lane, Derryanville, Derryhale Corner, and Scotch-street are included in the alphabetical list of Farmers and Residents of Portadown. The object of this consolidation is to prevent, as far as possible, the confusion which might arise by reason of the fact that delivery is made direct from Portadown by rural carriers on the way to the several places mentioned. Ballynacorr is 4 miles from Portadown, Battlehill 2½ miles, Clenroll 2½ miles, Crabtree Lane 3 miles, Derryanville 3¼ miles, Derryhale Corner 4 miles, Mullantine 2 miles, and Scotchstreet 3 miles.

W. & S. MERCIER,

FLOUR & CORN MILLERS

AND

SPECIALISTS in the MANUFACTURE of FOOD PRODUCTS,

MOYALLON,

GILFORD,

COUNTY DOWN.

GILFORD.

GILFORD is in the County Down, less than 4 miles, Irish, south-east of Portadown. The post-office at Moyallon, which is nearer to the Armagh border, is served from Gilford. Farmers and residents of Armagh, who receive their letters by way of Gilford, are named in the following list :

Bell, William, Knock
Black, George, Knock
Davidson, Alex., Ballygargan
Davison, John, Ballygargan
Dickson, John, Ballygargan
Hunter, William, Knock
Maginness, Robert, Ballydonaghy
Maginnis, William, Ballydonaghy
Mayes, Thomas, Knocknamuckly
Mercier, Samuel T., Drumlin house
Patton, John, Ballydonaghy
Richardson, J. G., Moyallen
Rogers, J. H., Ballygargan
Vaughan, Thomas, Moyallen

MESSRS. W. & S. MERCIER.

IF the millers of Ireland were to follow the example of Messrs. W. & S. Mercier, the competition of American flour manufacturers would not be so severely felt. For some years past the efforts of this firm have been marked by that intelligence and spirit of enterprise by means of which large fortunes have been made in other countries. For more than two years they have been manufacturers of wheat Semolina. Hitherto the Semolina prepared from Indian corn has been extensively used. Their Semolina "contains in a granulated form the richest and most nutritious elements of pure wheat, and is valuable as a food for infants and children, as well as in the various forms of puddings, cakes, etc.," recipes for which are provided on the wrappers of tins. It is nearly two years since they began the manufacture of Oat Flour, and their brand is now in use, by invalids and others, at hydropathic and health resorts generally throughout the United Kingdom. Messrs. W. & S. Mercier, as flour millers, employ the latest improvements in roller machinery. They also make Indian Meal— coarse and fine. The flour mill, stone and slate, was erected in 1839, and the steam mill, brick stone and slate, in 1864. All the buildings are fire-proof, and are connected by a bridge, as seen in the illustration.

Water and steam are employed for driving purposes, both producing about 250 horse power. The mills are situated in the Bann valley, close to the Armagh border, and within a hundred yards of the Newry Canal. A tramway, built by Messrs. W. & S. Mercier, runs from their premises to the canal, which gives them the advantage of direct communication by water with Belfast and Newry. The railway station for Gilford and Tandragee—Madden—is distant about a mile and a quarter, and Portadown is three miles.

AHOREY.

 HOREY is a rural post-office 4½ miles, Irish, south-west of Portadown, and 3 miles south-east from Richhill. The land of the district is good for pasture and tillage. Oats, potatoes and flax are the chief crops. Dairying is caried on to a considerable extent, and many of the farmers make a feature of fruit-growing.

Church, Pres.: Rev. Jas. Forsythe
Post M. : James Davidson

Farmers & Residents.

Anderson, James, Ahorey
Anderson, John, Ballybreagh
Anderson, Mrs. E., Burn cottage
Anderson, Thomas, Mullalelish
Ballentine, Wm., Ballyloughan
Best, James Hunter, Ballyloughan
Best, Joseph, Ballyloughan
Best, Richard, Ballyloughan
Best, Richardson, Ballynewry
Bridget, Joseph, Ballybreagh
Brown, David, Mullalelish
Brown, Wm., Ballyloughan
Carson, Henry, Ballyloughan
Carson, Robert, Ballyloughran
Cherry, Robert, Corry
Davidson, William, Ballybreagh
Douglass, Robert, Ahorey
Foster, Joseph, Ballyloughan
Francis, Thomas, Ballynewry
Goudy, James, Corry
Greenlee, James, Ballynewry
Greer, James, Ballybreagh
Greer, John, Ahorey

Hart, Morris, Ballyloughan
Hoey, Thomas, Ballyloughan
Holland, Wm., Ahorey
Holland, Wm. J., Ahorey
Hutcheson, F. G., Ballyvalley
Jackson, Moses, Ballybreagh
Jeffrey, Isaac, Ahorey
Lewis, John, Ahorey
M'Clean, James, Ballynewry
M'Cune, David, sen., Ballyloughan
Marshall, William, Ballyloughan
May, S. J., Ballyloughan
Mulligan, Peter, Ballynewry
Patterson, Thomas, Ahorey
Quinn, Joseph, Ballynewry
Quinn, Mrs. Mt., Prospect hill
Quinn, William, Ballynewry
Ross, George, Ahorey
Ross, William, Ballynewry
Sherry, Robert, Ahorey
Singleton, Daniel, Ballynewry
Watson, Thomas, Ballyloughan
Wiley, Alexander, Legavilly
Williamson, Robert, Ahorey
Wilson, Nicholas, Ahorey
Wynne, Thos., jun., Sandymount

ANNAGHMORE.

ANNAGHMORE is a station on the Great Northern (Ulster) Railway, 6¼ miles, English, west by north from Portadown, and 7 miles, Irish, north by east from Armagh, by road. The distance by rail is 18 miles, English. Mr. John A. M. Cope, J.P., Drumilly, Loughgall, is the landlord. The land of the district, when not boggy, is heavy, and not easily cultivated. Potatoes, wheat and oats are the principal crops. There is an extensive tract under bog. and the inhabitants cut and save a great deal of "turf" for market. The road to Armagh, at all seasons of the year, suffers from the constant traffic of turf-carts. Turf is also sent to Moy and Richhill. A large amount of bog-deal is found in the peat, and sold for fire-lighting. Occasionally pieces of oak turn up. They are mostly utilized for fencing purposes. Nearly all the houses of Annaghmore are built of the heavy native clay. When dry it is very hard, and resists the action of the weather for a long time without cracking. Most of the inhabitants of Annaghmore are small farmers and cottage weavers. Nearly every house has two or three looms. Linen manufacturers of Portadown and Lurgan send agents every week to take in webs and give out yarns. Many of the cottagers are also fruit-growers in a modest way, and many also make a feature of sending butter to market in lump. Lough Neagh is 3½ miles from Annaghmore. Some of the fish dealers ship pollen and trout from here to Liverpool.

Carpenter : Robert M'Neill
Churches: C.I., Rev. Thomas Kingsborough ; Methodist. Cranagill, Rev. James Orr ; R.C., Rev. Patrick Hughes, C.C.
Drapers: Felix Devlin, Jas. Duffy
Grocers : marked thus (*) retails spirits: Mrs. C. Deighan, Felix Devlin, Mrs. M. Devlin, James Duffy, Thomas J. Hall*, Wm. J. Mullin
Post M.: Patrick Doherty
Railway station : Patk. Doherty, toll collector
R.I.C. ; Sergeant L. Toolan
School, Nat.: James M'Gurrin

Farmers & Residents.
Conn, John, Derrycorr
Devlin, Felix, Annaghmore
Fearin, Daniel, Eglish
Gallagher, James, Annaghmore

Gilpin, John, Annaghmore
Gilpin, Robert, Annaghmore
Greenaway, Francis, Deerycoose
Greenaway, Francis, Derrycorr
Greenaway, Geo., Derrycorr
Hall, John, Derrycorr
Hall, Mrs., Drumnott
Jackson, John, Derrycorr
Locke, Mrs., Derrycorr
Loney, Joseph, Annaghmore
M'Keown, Mrs. M. T., Annaghmore
M'Keown, Terence, Annaghmore
M'Niece, Thos., Annaghmore
Martin, George, Derrycoose
Matchett, Thomas, Derrycorr
Palmer, Wm. jun., Annaghmore
Smith, William, Derrycoose
Willis, George, sen., Derrycoose
Willis, George, Derrycorr

DIAMOND.

DIAMOND, a village of a few houses, in the barony of O'Neilland West, is about 4¾ miles to the west of Portadown. The post-office, which is also a parochial school-house, supported by Mrs. Cope, of the Manor, Loughgall, is three quarters of a mile nearer. Potatoes, beans, oats and wheat are the chief crops of the district. The land is heavy and difficult to manage. Apple-orchards are numerous, and in good seasons—when fruit is not too abundant—farmers find them valuable aids to income. "The Diamond," as it is generally called, is interesting mainly as the scene of a battle fought September 21st, 1795. For some years previously the County Armagh was greatly disturbed. Among the Protestants an organization was formed, which was known as "The Peep-o'-day Boys," and the Roman Catholics had an organization known as "Defenders." In order to prevent conflicts of a bloody nature, an Infantry Volunteer Corps was embodied at the City of Armagh in July, 1788, under command of Captain Joshua McGeough. The uniform consisted of green jackets, nankeen small clothes, white waistcoats, round hats, and black plumes. It numbered 70, and was speedily increased to 100 by a contingent raised at Derrycaw, under the auspices of Mr. Thomas Clogher. Lord Charlemont, who had accepted command of the first volunteers raised, addressed a letter to the new corps in the following month of the same year, in which he exhorted the men to observe two principles—"Defence of the country against invaders, and the preservation of internal peace and good order." To put an end to the animosity between Protestants and Roman Catholics he wrote : "I do solemnly exhort my friends and fellow soldiers thoroughly to divest themselves of all such criminal prejudices, and to consider their fellow subjects of every denomination as their countrymen and brethren." Assemblages of Peep-o' day Boys and Defenders were prevented by the Volunteers at various places, but at "The Diamond" they came together without interference, and the Defenders were defeated. A few were killed, and several wounded. Residents of "The Diamond" at present talk about the battle with as great an appearance of interest as if it had occurred in their day. "The Diamond House" was a much frequented inn during the 18th century. It was kept by James Winter, and it seems Mr. Winter was not friendly to the Defenders. As a consequence they made him a midnight visit, and having spread his supply of flour and meal upon the floor, spilled all the whiskey and beer upon it. To this was added broken glass taken from the windows. "The Diamond House" is now owned by Mr. John Watt, but within sight of it there is a

neat cottage occupied by Misses Jane and Margaret Winter, of
the fourth generation of Winters since 1788. In the kitchen
window at the back of the house there are two small panes of
glass of the old bulls-eye pattern. These they point to as
having been rescued from the "mortar." Close to the
door of the Winter Cottage a root of shamrock, of the four-
leaved variety, so difficult to "find," has spread until it covers
the pavement for several yards—perhaps insuring to the occupants a continuance of peaceful days and nights, the sort of
"good luck" which was denied to their progenitor.

Blacksmith : J. M'Gall
Church, C.I. : Rev. D. M'Ferron
Post M. : Richard Lindsay
School, Parochial : Rd. Lindsay

Farmers & Residents.
Allen, Ephraim, Grange lr.
Allen, Richard, Grange lr.
Atkinson, William, Cusheny
Blacker, John, Cusheny
Blacker, William, Cusheny
Blacker, Wm. J., Cusheny
Collen, Thos., Faughart
Curran, Patrick, Cusheny
Dalzell, John, Grange lr.
Dick, Edward, Grange lr.
Ford, James, Kilmoriarty
Gardner, Robert, Tullymore
Graham, David, Cusheney
Hughes, Mrs., Grange lr
Kells, Thomas, Grange lr
Lindsay, Alex., Grange lr
M'Coo, Matthew, Annagora
M'Fadden, James, Grange lr
M'Fadden, John, Grange lr
M'Keever, Jas., Faughart
M'Keever, John, Grange lr
M'Keever, Mrs. J., Faughart hill
M'Murray, John, Grange

M'Quade, Mrs. M., Tullymore
Mears, John, Grange lr
Moor, John, Grange lr
Newport, James, Grange lr
Quinn, Daniel, Cusheny
Quinn, James, Grange lr
Quinn, Mrs., Cusheny
Redmond, Johnston, Grange lr
Ruddock, James, Grange lr
Ruddock, Richard, Grange lr
Ruddock, W. J., Grange lr
Russell, John, Grange lr
Stewart, Marshall, Ballytrue
Taylor, Edward, Grange lr
Taylor, John, Grange lr
Taylor, Richard, Grange lr
Taylor, Robert, Grange lr
Taylor, Samuel, Grange lr
Troughton, Christr., Grange lr
Troughton, Jacob, Corglass
Troughton, John, Grange lr
Watt, John, Diamond house
Weir, John, Grange lr
Weir, Robert, Grange lr
Whiteside, Thomas, Kilmoriarty
Williamson, James, Grange lr
Winter, Francis, Diamond
Winter, Misses J. & M., Diamond

SCARVA.

SCARVA is a village in the County Down, divided from
Armagh by the Newry Canal. It is 3½ miles south-
west of Banbridge, and a station on the Great Northern Railway. A full description is given of it, and of
the celebrated "Danes' Cast," in my BOOK OF COUNTY DOWN.
Residents of the County Armagh named as follows, receive their
letters from the Scarva post-office :

X

Black, Edward, Aughlish
Black, John, Aughlish
Clarke, Andrew, Aughlish
Cole, Alexander, Aughlish
Cole, Andrew, Monclone
Crothers, Andrew, Aughlish
Crozier, Thomas, Monclone
Ferrin, Edward, Terryhoogan
Girvan, Mrs., Druminargal
Greenaway, David, Mullaglass
Greenaway, T., jun., Mullaglass
Hake, Edward, Aughlish

Hudson, William, Monclone
Johnston, John, Monclone
Jones, James, Aughlish
Jones, William, Aughlish
Liggett, John, Mullaghglass
M'Birney, David, Mullaghglass
Mathers, W. H., Mullaglass
Plunkett, John, Terryhoogan
Smith, John, Shanelish
Whiteside, George, Mullaghglass
Whitten, Charles, Monclone

THE BIRCHES.

THE BIRCHES is a rural post-office and Petty Sessions district, 6 miles north-west of Portadown. Colonel Stanley, Mr. Edward S. Obré, Mr. Charles Stanley, Lord Charlemont, Capt. William Brown, and Mr. A. T. Wakefield are the landlords. A clump of birches growing near the road, a short distance below the post office, suggests the appropriateness of the name given to the neighbourhood, the greater part of which is a partly cultivated bog. Birches grow naturally in this region. Mr. Thomas Palmer informs me that the entire bog was a birch forest 70 years ago. The roots are now found in cutting peat. Good crops of potatoes and oats are produced in the boggy land by means of a process known as "heating." Turf fires are lighted around the parts about to be planted, and kept up until sufficient warmth is generated to force vegetation. Hot ashes are also spread upon the surface. By treatment of this kind a better crop of oats is secured than is yielded by the richest loam lands. Without "heating," oats will not average eighteen inches in height. Some of the landlords have objected to the heating process on the ground that it is using up the surface of the bog. A proposal was made to induce the tenants to pay 5s. an acre extra for the privilege, but they did not seem to relish the idea.

Church, Methodist, Portadown Circuit.
Draper: Thos. Palmer

Grocers. Marked thus [*] retail spirits: Jos. Jackson, Clonmacate; Richard Jackson, Clonmacate;

John McClure, Derryaugh*; John Matchett, Ballynarry*; Thomas Palmer, The Birches; Jno. Wethered, Milltown

Hardware and Seed: Thomas Palmer, The Birches

Petty Sessions, 1st Monday every month, Thomas Palmer, clerk

Post M.: Thomas Palmer

R.I.C.: Sergeant, Chas. Feeney

School, Nat.: Christr. Boyce

Farmers & Residents.

Bell, David, Derrykeevan
Boyce, William, Drumaliss
Campbell, Joseph, Derrylard
Carrick, David, Foymore
Carrick, James, Foymore
Carrick, Thomas, Derrykeevan
Cassells, Mrs. M., Cloncore
Connolly, Patrick, Derrinraw
Carrick, William, Derrykeevan
Cullen, Daniel, Derrinraw
Donnelly, James, Derrylard
Farquhar, Robert, Derryaugh
Fawcett, A., Derrinraw
Fearon, Bd., jun., Derrinraw
Ferrin, Bd., sen., Derrinraw
Ferrin, Michael, Derrinraw
Fox, William, Derrinraw
Fulton, James, Derrylileagh
Gardener, Henry, Foymore
Gilmore, James, Derrykeevan
Hendron, Joseph, Derrykeeran
Hume, Robert, Derrylard
Hyde, George, Breagh
Jackson, Moses, Ballinary
Jackson, Richard, Clonmacate
Jackson, Thomas, Ballinary
Kilpatrick, Mrs. M., Ballinary
Kingsborough, Henry, Breagh
Leeman, John, Derrykeevan
M'Adam, Thomas, Derryaugh
M'Adam, Wilson, Cloncore
M'Adam, Wm. H., Cloncore
M'Anally, John, Derrykeeran
M'Causland, John, Derrykeevan
M'Clelland, John, Derryadd
M'Clelland, John, Derrylard
M'Clure, James, Derryaugh

M'Conville, William, Cloncore
M'Cullagh, Aaron, Drumlellum
M'Cullagh, Seth, Drumlellum
Mackall, Edward, Derrykeeran
Mackall, Henry, Derrykeeran
Mackall, Mrs., Derrinraw
Magee, Henry, Clonmacate
Martin, John, Ballinary
Matchett, John, Ballinary
Matchett, Joseph, Derrycaw
Matchett, Joseph, Gallrock
Matchett, Richard, Derryall
Matchett, Richard, Clonmacate
Mathers, John H., Derrykeeran
Mathers, Joseph, Derryneskin
Matthew, Samuel, Ballinary
May, James, Drumlellum
May, Richard, Drumlellum
Moore, John, Ballynary
O'Hanlon, Mrs. C., Ballinary
Robinson, J., Druminallyduff
Sinnamon, Henry, Clonamola
Smyth, Joseph, Ballinary
Smyth, Thomas, Derrylileagh
Stevenson, Mrs. L., Cloncore
Sullivan, James, Derrylard
Sullivan, Thomas, Derrylard
Sullivan, Wm. F., Cloncore
Todd, Joseph, Clonmacate
Todd, Robert, Foymore
Todd, Wm., Druminallyduff
Todd, William, Foymore
Trotter, Richard, Foybeg
Troughton, Richard, Derrycaw
Troughton, Robert, Derrycaw
Turkington, Samuel, Ballynary
Uprichard, Charles, Clonmacate
Wakefield, C. S., Cloncore ho.
Wakefield, Edw. T., Cloncore ho.
Walsh, Mrs. A., Derrinraw
Weatherall, Jno., Derrykeeran
Weatherall, Richard, Derrykeeran
Weatherhead, Jno., Derrylard
Wilson, Wm. D., Cloncore
Woods, Loftus, Ballynary
Woodhouse, T. A., Derrinraw
Wright, George, Derrykeevan
Wright, Wm., Derrykeevan

LURGAN.

Estimated population over 14,000 in 1888.

LURGAN is in the barony of O'Neilland East and parish of Shankill, 20 miles south-west of Belfast, 92½ miles north of Dublin, 5 miles north-east of Portadown, and 15½ miles north-east of Armagh. It is surrounded by a good farming country, and most favorably situated for communication with the centres of commercial activity. The lines of the Great Northern Railway bring it into direct connection with Dublin and Belfast, and at a distance of less than two miles, by means of a cut from Lough Neagh, an opportunity is afforded for participation in the benefits of the Lagan and Newry Canals. With the single exception of Belfast, no town in Ireland has increased in population and wealth so rapidly as Lurgan. The population in 1851 was 4,651. In 1881 it was 10,135, and there is good reason to believe that it is now far on the way to 15,000. This progress is entirely due to the development of the linen industry, initiated by William Waring, M.P., during the reign of Queen Anne, 1702-14. The most interesting fact in connection with the progress is that it does not seem to have been retarded by the great wave of depression which swamped so many promising enterprises elsewhere. During the last few years wonderful strides have been made in Lurgan. Several new streets have been added. Indeed it is calculated that within three years over 200 houses have been built for the accommodation of working people alone.

Handsome dwellings for well-to-do residents, factories, warehouses, and school-houses are included in the descriptive particulars of the aggregate outlay in bricks and mortar. Some of the churches have been remodeled, and the Great Northern Railway Company, to keep pace with the march of improvement, has erected a large goods store. It is worthy of remark, as a most instructive feature of the building operations, that a considerable number of the smaller houses belong to working men, built for homes, and paid for out of their own savings. At every side of the town expansion has been the order of the day, but to the stranger, there is quite enough in view from the railway station to give an exalted idea of Lurgan enterprise. Brownlow Terrace, Victoria Street, Princess Street and Sunnyside had no existence a very short time ago. Now they form a substantial contribution toward the work of extending the town to the edge of Lough Neagh, about a mile and a quarter. As a market for agricultural produce, Lurgan is improving. Transactions are conducted in the principal thoroughfare, which is broad enough to give room for a large number of people without seriously interfering with the ordinary traffic. Associations for mental and physical culture are numerous at Lurgan. The walks and drives in every direction lead to places of interest, and bring into sight much scenery of a charming nature. In summer Lough Neagh invites with a magnetic power that cannot be resisted, and its exhilarating breezes do a great deal to maintain a respectable standard of health and vigor particularly among the working people.

BEFORE AND SINCE THE ENGLISH CONNECTION.

BEFORE the arrival of the English the broad acres forming the present parish of Shankill were used as grazing pastures for cattle. The formation of the country was such that it afforded no desirable point for a great stronghold. The O'Neill's dominated the territory in which it was included. After Hugh O'Neill, Earl of Tyrone, had fled to Rome in company with O'Donnell, his principal ally, 1607, Shankill was forfeited to the Crown with the possessions of the O'Hanlons, at Tandragee, and those of other Armagh chieftains who had contributed to swell the forces under his command during the Rebellion against Queen Elizabeth, 1594-1603. In the Plantation of Ulster by James I., 1609, William Brownlow received a "portion" of the forfeited lands containing 2,500 acres. He immediately took steps for the settlement of a number of "well disposed" English families, and

The Newest Styles & Best Value for Ready Money

IN

Millinery and Mantles,	Boots, Shoes and Slippers,
Shawls, Stays and Skirts,	Gloves, Hosiery & Shirts,
Ribbons, Laces & Flowers	Blankets and Flannels,
Velvets, Silks & Dresses,	Carpets, Room Papers,
French Merinoes & Prints,	Tailoring, &c.,

AT

"The Arcade," LURGAN.

REBURN & COMPANY

Invite an Inspection of their Goods, which, for Style and Quality,
combined with Moderate Prices, cannot be excelled.

founded Lurgan. A census of 1619 shows that 42 houses had been built. For 20 years the town continued to grow in comparative peace. Soon after the Parliament of Kilkenny began to make its power felt in Ulster, 1641, the troops of Sir Phelim O'Neill seized Lurgan and destroyed it. While engaged in this work they used for garrison purposes a small church which had been erected by the settlers, and subsequently burned it also. Two fine mansions, belonging to Mr. Brownlow, were reduced to ashes. During the Cromwellian period the inhabitants had not recovered from the effects of the O'Neill visitation. They made no sustained attempt to rebuild the town until the advent of Charles II. Encouraged by the hope of permanent security under his reign, Mr. Brownlow stimulated his people to exertion, and things had begun to assume a favorable aspect when the war of the Revolution broke out. The then Mr. Brownlow was opposed to James II., and declared an outlaw. About the same time the town was again destroyed. After the Battle of the Boyne, 1690, had decided the war in favor of William, Prince of Orange, the prospects of Lurgan soon became brighter than they had been at any time since the Plantation. King William granted a patent for markets and fairs, and the inhabitants of the town and surrounding country, having devoted themselves earnestly to the cultivation of the land, these rights soon proved valuable. When the Princess Anne, daughter of James II., succeeded to the throne, 1702, William Waring, M.P. introduced the manufacture of diapers, and to the interest aroused by the instruction personally given by him may be attributed the fact that Lurgan has reached the present stage of prosperity.

TOWN GOVERNMENT, VALUATION, SEWERAGE SYSTEM, PUBLIC LICHTING.

FOR many years the town was governed by Commissioners, appointed under the 9th of George IV. cap. 8. The lighting and cleansing clauses only were taken advantage of. When the Towns Improvement Act came into force in 1854 the people of Lurgan were among the first to petition the Lord Lieutenant to be permitted to participate in its benefits. The old Commissioners, on September 4, 1854, appointed a committee, consisting of Messrs. Hancock, Paul, May, Conn and Macoun to consider the propriety of preparing the petition. The Bill had only received the Royal Assent on the 19th of the previous month. On the 2nd of October a report was made in favor of the Act, and a memorial, signed by Lord Lurgan, Chairman, on behalf of the Com-

JAMES JOHNSTON,

Porter, Ale

and Beer Brewer

and Maltster,

MARKET STREET

— AND —

UNION STREET,

LURGAN.

missioners, was forwarded to Dublin Castle. The next step was an order from the Lord Lieutenant to take the sense of the ratepayers upon the subject. A meeting was accordingly held at the Town Hall, 14th December, 1854. On the motion of Mr. James Malcolm, father of Mr. James Malcolm, D.L., seconded by Mr. Francis Watson, the Act was adopted in its entirety, and by a unanimous vote. The result having been made known to the Government, an election of 15 Commissioners was ordered. It was held January 13th, 1855, and choice made of Lord Lurgan, John Hancock, J.P., Samuel Rogers, John Hazlett, James Armstrong, Arthur Donnelly, William Murray, Charles Magee, Joseph Murphy, John Gilbert, George Lockhart, James Malcolm, John Johnston, W. W. Paul, and John Ross. Of the number, Messrs. Joseph Murphy, J.P., W. W. Paul, and John Ross are the only survivors. Five Commissioners go out of office every third year. The election takes place on the 15th of October. Mr. William Sear was appointed Town Clerk. He was succeeded by Mr. Hamilton Rankin, and Mr. Rankin by Mr. Thomas Lutton. Messrs. Sears and Rankin were also Town Surveyors. The office of Town Surveyor is now separate, and is held by Mr. William James O'Neill, C.E. When Mr. Sear was Town Clerk and Surveyor, although the estimated population was 5,650, the work he had to do could not have been regarded as laborious. His salary was only £40 a year, and in consideration of this he was obliged to provide the Commissioners with an office for meetings, etc.

In the first year of the Government under the new Act, 1855, names were given to the streets, and recorded on panels at the corners, and arrangements made for connecting the town with the outer world by means of the electric telegraph. The rate for general purposes in 1856 was 8d. in the £. This produced a total of £231 14s. 10d. In 1868 the valuation of the town was £14,467, and the rate for general purposes 10d. Ten years later the valuation was £16,052 15s., and the rate for general purposes 1s. 8d. In 1888 the valuation was £19,770 10s., the rate for general purposes 3s. 0d., and a sanitary assessment of 6d. in the £.

The Commissioners began without delay to establish a system of sewerage that would keep the town in good sanitary condition. In 1855 the North East sewer was built. This gave accommodation to 397 houses. A flushing apparatus was added in the following year, at a cost of £950, toward which Lord Lurgan subscribed £250, and the necessary water from the lake in his demesne. The town was divided into four drainage districts in 1857, the property-owners in each to be assessed sepa-

rately, according to the amount of money expended in new works. The Town Commissioners at present are in debt to the extent of nearly £6,000. Most of this was spent on sewers. The discharge is at Lough Neagh. Upward of £4,000 out of the £6,000 was advanced by the Board of Works, at 3½ per cent. repayable, principal and interest, in a given period. The remainder represents loans from private persons, to whom the highest rate of interest paid is 5 per cent.

In 1857 the town was lighted by 62 gas lamps. This number was increased to 87 in 1861, to 145 in 1882, and to 177 in 1888. The contract with the Gas Company is in effect that a payment of £1 6s. each is made for lamps used up to midnight, and £2 6s. per annum each for those maintained at full pressure all night. The Commissioners pay a special rate of 3s. 11d. per 1,000 feet for lighting half a dozen or more large lamps and the great church-clock.

WATER SUPPLY, FIRE DEPARTMENT, BURIAL BOARD.

EVER since 1854 there has been a " Water Question." Several eminent engineers have had "schemes" for meeting the difficulty, but the supply continues to be drawn from street-pumps.

In 1887, the driest season for many years, the scarcity was so great that the subject began to be more seriously discussed, and during the present year, 1888, a Committee of the Commissioners, consisting of Messrs. R. Mathers, J.P., Claude Brownlow, J.P., Robert Hazelton, and John M'Caughey, was appointed to confer with the Town Commissioners of Portadown and other places as to the desirability of adopting a scheme to make a reservoir at Loughislandreavy. An effort was made in 1859 to have the necessary service provided by a private Company. The capital stock was fixed at £10,000 in 1,000 shares at £10 each. Lord Lurgan sent in his name for 200 shares ; but, notwithstanding the stimulus which his example should have caused, only half the capital was subscribed, and the project fell through. But for the trouble to come to a decision regarding the source, the matter would have been settled long ago. Lough Neagh is only two miles from the centre of the town, and a great many persons believe that it could be utilized for a first-rate service. A great many also believe that the majority of the people could never be induced either to drink, or use for cooking purposes, water which receives the sewage of Lurgan and of several other populous towns. Schemes for utilizing Lough Neagh have been reported as follows :—By Mr.

James Thompson, C.E., Edinburgh, 1857, to supply 180,000 gallons per day to a height of 174 feet, at a cost of £8,668. By Mr. Robert Young, C.E., 1871, to supply 347,000 gallons per day to a height of 196 feet at a cost of £10,507. By Mr. Wm. J. O'Neill, C.E., 1887, to supply 560,000 gallons per day to a height of 196 feet at a cost of £16,424. Mr. Henry Smyth, C.E., in 1887, proposed to supply by gravitation from Slieve Croob, in conjunction with the service to other towns, 500,000 gallons per day at a cost of £34,345. The Diamond Rock Boring Company (Artesian scheme) proposed, 1888, to make a 4 inch trial bore to a depth of 300 feet, if necessary, "on the understanding that if they do not, previous to that depth being reached, find sufficient water to warrant going on with the boring, they shall only be paid 7s. per foot ; but if they find enough they shall receive 12s. per foot for actual depth bored. If they have to go down say 300 feet or less (total, 600 feet), they will say with regard to this next 300 feet, or less, a price of 10s. per foot if unsuccessful, and 16s. per foot if successful. If the test bore reveals the presence of sufficient water, they shall be pleased to quote for the permanent boring and for pumping, tackle, engine, &c."

Dr. S. Agnew sent a sample of Lough Neagh water for analysis to Prof. Hodges, Belfast. The professor says :—

"The water had no remarked smell; color slightly yellowish ; microscope showed numerous organisms and water fleas. Total solid matters per Imperial gallon, 16·80 grains, consisting of mineral and saline matters, 6·30 grains ; Organic and volatile matters, 10·50 grains ; Chlorine in chlorides, 1·40 grains ; one million parts yield—free ammonia, 0·080 parts ; albuminoid ammonia, 0·140 parts.—JOHN F. HODGES, M.D., F. Inst. C, &c.

"Remarks—The sample of water contains an excessive amount of nitrogenous matter, and unless filtered would be unfit for domestic use.—JOHN F. HODGES."

A Fire Department is maintained by the Town Commissioners, but its efficiency cannot be brought to a high standard until there are hydrants giving power to send a stream of water over the largest building, as at Armagh. Mr. John Long is Superintendent, and Mr. James Dunwoody, who also fills the position of Town Constable, is Deputy Superintendent. He receives a salary for the latter-named office of £2 a-year, and £1 extra for every fire attended. Mr. Long receives £10 a-year. Seven firemen are paid £2 a-year each, and when on active duty 3s. 6d. each for first hour, and 2s. each for every succeeding hour. The engine in use was presented by Mr. James Malcolm, D.L.

The Town Commissioners were created a Burial Board under the 19th & 20th of Victoria. They have jurisdiction over all the cemeteries used by the residents. The old Shankill church-yard, within the town, is still used. It has many interesting monuments, and the Mausoleum of the Brownlow family. The Roman Catholics inter around the site of the old chapel. It was first opened for the purpose in 1824, and became so full that more ground was added by Lord Lurgan in 1857. The burial ground of the Society of Friends is at the back of the Meeting House in High Street. The Presbyterian ground is at the back of the First Church in High Street. A new cemetery, one mile from town, was laid out in 1865, at a cost of £300. It is situated in the townland of Monbrief, and consists of 4 acres, bought from Lord Lurgan.

MARKETS AND FAIRS.

MARKET for the sale of grain, grass-seed—in the season—pork, fowl, butter, eggs, hay, straw, potatoes, turnips, etc., is held every Thursday. Until about 1846 the market was on Friday. It was then considered good policy to make an alteration, so that there might be no clash with Belfast, especially as nearly all the linen manufacturers and merchants in Ulster assemble there on that day. Lord Lurgan owned the patent for markets and fairs, but under his jurisdiction no tolls were charged in either, except for weighing. In 1858 the Town Commissioners, by desire of Lord Lurgan, exercised general supervision over the markets, but made no alteration in the procedure regarding tolls. Negotiations were opened between the Town Commissioners and Lord Lurgan for the purchase of the patent in 1882, and on the 17th of November, 1884, he transferred his title in consideration of £2,000. The market-house was included, and the value of this was assessed at £1,000. The Town Commissioners had been making many improvements, and were about to tear down the market-house to widen Market Street. Lord Lurgan had been using the upper story as an office, and prevailed upon the Commissioners to let it stand, and accept him as tenant at £55 a year. The grass-seed market has become a great feature, and there has been a noticeable improvement in the pork market. Thus far the transactions in every department have been conducted in the open streets, preference for locality only being made for convenience in weighing. On Saturday there is a market for fresh meat, etc., and as the working hours in the factories are short, there is usually almost as much life and motion as on Thursday. During the three years ending in

ADAM HEWITT,

IMPORTER OF

English, Scotch and Welsh Coals,

EDWARD STREET,

LURGAN.

DEPOT:

Great Northern Railway Station, LURGAN.

GRAHAM BROTHERS,

General Merchants,

58 CHURCH PLACE,

LURGAN.

DEPARTMENTS—*Groceries* (*Wholesale and Family*);
Italian Warehouse Goods;
Irish and American Provisions: Pork-curing;
Flour, Meal, Bran, Oil Cake, Linseed Meal, etc., etc.;
Ironmongery; House Furnishing Hardware.

BUTTER AND EGGS A SPECIALITY.

1888, the receipts for weighing have averaged £244 per year, but the expenditure has been in excess. The charges for weighing have not been changed for over 30 years. No bye-laws have yet been drawn to be submitted for approval to the Local Government Board. A movement, initiated some time ago, culminated in a petition to the Local Government Board, December, 1887, by the Town Commissioners, as the Urban Sanitary Authority, for a provisional order under the Public Health Act, 1878, to enable them to put in force the provisions of the Land Clauses' Acts for the acquisition of houses and lands as the site of a market for butter, eggs, fowl and fish, and an approach by means of a new street, with good buildings on each side. An advance of £6,000 was asked as the probable cost of carrying out the scheme. In addition to providing necessary accommodation for markets, it was expected that a substantial sanitary improvement would be effected by the removal of an inhabited lane from 5 to 6 feet wide, and only 2½ feet at the entrance. It was believed that the ground left, after providing for the approach to the markets, would be worth more than the amount expended upon the entire undertaking. The Local Government Board sent down Mr. Cotton, one of its engineers, who held an inquiry, and reported that the project " appeared to be far more for a new street under Section 38 of the Public Health Act, 1878, than for a market under Section 103 of that Act. And, furthermore, the expenditure out of the proposed loan of £6,000 would be almost three times more for the works connected with the new street than for providing the market, which appeared by the advertisement to be the main object of the scheme." Having taken this view of the matter the Local Government Board declined to accede to the request, but without prejudice to any further proceedings that may be taken in furtherance of the object in view. In a letter dated 18th May, 1888, on this subject, Mr. Thomas A. Mooney, clerk to the Local Government Board, concludes as follows : " If the Sanitary Authority see fit to publish fresh advertisements and notices in September, or October, or November next, describing fully and accurately the purposes in respect of which the lands are proposed to be taken, and their intention to make a new street, the Board will be willing to give the subject their prompt attention, and re-open the inquiry to receive evidence in the case."

A minority of the Town Commissioners have expressed disapproval of the scheme in a resolution from which I make this extract: "Wishes to thank the Local Government Board for having, in the prudent and judicious exercise of its powers, protected the ratepayers of Lurgan from the imposition of an uncalled-for,

Y

unpopular, and absurd outlay of £6,000—an expenditure the direct result of which would be to gratify the designs of an interested few, without conferring any corresponding benefit on the many by whom it would have to be borne—to have deformed our ample market arrangements and to have opened our ethereal enterprise (without regard to physical and scientific defects), the commencement of which would have launched the town into protracted litigation, and the completion of which would inevitably have entailed a remodeling and extension of the original scheme, and an enormous waste of the public rates, against the will of the ratepayers, and without the remotest prospect of any future advantage to the town in general." A monthly fair for cattle and pigs, on the second Thursday of every month, is held in the streets, also. At an inquiry instituted in June, 1888, by the Royal Commission on Markets and Tolls, Mr. Thomas Reburn, chairman of the Town Commissioners, testified that on market days which are also fair days, a great deal of confusion often occurs in the streets owing to the cattle, pork, butter, and sundry other articles being exposed in one place.

TOWN HALL, MECHANICS' INSTITUTE, COURT HOUSE, ROYAL IRISH CONSTABULARY, UNION WORKHOUSE, GAS WORKS.

THE Town Hall is an extension of the Mechanics' Institute from the corner of Market Street and Union Street. It was built in 1868, at a cost of about £2,300. The Assembly Room has a seating capacity for 800 people, and a platform, but no scenery. Use is made of it extensively for concerts, dramatic performances, bazaars, etc. The rent is £1 for first night and 15s. for every succeeding night. The site of the Town Hall was leased at £60 a year from the trustees of the Institute, who contributed £1,000 toward the expense. The police barrack adjoining the Town Hall, in Union Street, belongs to the Commissioners, and is rented at £36 a year, which sum deducted from the £60 paid to the Mechanics' Institute trustees, reduces their liability to £24 a year. The amount realized by letting the Assembly Room should more than cover this, so that the maintenance of the Town Hall is really not much of a tax on the people. In January, 1858, the Mechanics' Institute was opened, but there was a ceremony of inauguration on the 6th of March, 1859, in which the chief figure was the Lord Justice of Appeal. The Institute was intended to be of great benefit to the community. It had a good library, reading-room, school of design, and rooms for evening classes.

MAGEE'S WINE & SPIRIT STORES,

Billiard Rooms and Posting Establishment,

UNION STREET,

LURGAN.

Carriages, Covered Cars, Brakes, &c.,
ON SHORTEST NOTICE.

*Arrangements for Wedding Parties
a special feature.*

(JOHN MAGEE.)

Magee's Wine and Spirit Stores,

WILLIAM STREET,

LURGAN.

(HUGH MAGEE.)

Magee's Wine and Spirit Stores,

EDWARD STREET,

LURGAN.

(THOMAS MAGEE.)

The building, which has a handsome front and clock tower, cost £1,400. A bazaar, held by Lady Lurgan, in conjunction with the ladies of the town and neighborhood, realized enough to pay for the library. There was a membership of 400 to begin, and things looked well for a long run of prosperity. The School of Design proved to be a little in advance of the time, and was eventually closed, but the other features are still maintained. There are 200 members at present. Mr. James Johnston is Chairman of the Committee of Management, Dr. S. Agnew, secretary, and Mr. Courtney Johnston, treasurer. The library contains about 1,500 books, and the reading-room is supplied with the leading daily and weekly newspapers, reviews, and popular magazines. Five shillings a-year pays for the use of the reading-room, and ten shillings for the reading-room and library. A billiard-room is one of the features. Members have to pay so much for each game. Chess, and kindred games, may be played without charge. By a special arrangement, in the event of failure, the Institution becomes the property of the Town Commissioners, and they are required to keep it up in accordance with the ideas promulgated at the time of the foundation.

The Court-House is situated in William Street. It is well appointed, and has convenient offices' for the Petty Sessions Clerk, Mr. Frederick W. Magahan. A hewn-stone building, at the opposite side of the street, used to be the bridewell, but it has not been occupied for some time. Under the system of concentration, all the prisoners are sent to Her Majesty's Prison at Armagh. Lurgan is the head of a police district, and has barracks in Union Street, Edward Street, Queen Street, and High Street, and will soon have one in North Street. In 1840 the Union Workhouse of Lurgan was built. It stands in handsomely laid out grounds at the corner of Union and John Streets, and has a farm of three acres cultivated by the inmates. Notwithstanding the fact that the town is supplied with water from street springs, at the time of my visit, March 20th, 1888, there was not one fever patient in hospital, and I was informed by the clerk, Mr. James Donaldson, that none had been admitted for about 12 weeks.

Lurgan received the advantages of gas-light in 1848. The works are in William Street, and seem to be maintained in excellent condition. They are owned by the Lurgan Gas Light and Chemical Company, Limited. Although a dividend at the rate of 7½ per cent. was paid in 1887, the rate to the general consumers was only 3s. 11d. per 1000 feet. There are 23 shareholders, Mr. Saml. A. Bell, J.P., is chairman, Mr. Frederick W. Magahan, secretary, and Mr. Thomas Tallentire, manager

FITZSIMONS & COY.,

Drapers and Silk Mercers,

59 MARKET STREET,

LURGAN.

Our Stock is selected with the view of always having on hand the Newest London and Paris designs.

A special Buyer from this house visits the leading Markets in time to procure the Latest Novelties for each Season.

DEPARTMENTS-

Drapery.	Mantles,
Hosiery.	Flannels.
Haberdashery.	Blankets.
Millinery.	Woollens.
Dress.	Ready=made Clothing.

Tailoring a Feature.   Cut, Style, Fit and Finish Guaranteed.

OUR MOTTO—"**Small Profits and Quick Returns,**"

and engineer. In addition to the gas, the Company manufactures sulphate of ammonia.

BROWNLOW HOUSE AND DEMESNE, THE LURGAN ESTATE, LOUGH NEAGH—NAVIGATION SYSTEM, CURATIVE EFFECT OF WATERS—BOAT CLUB, LURGAN RIFLE ASSOCIATION.

BROWNLOW HOUSE, the residence of Lord Lurgan, is beautifully situated within a few minutes walk from the centre of the town. It is in the Elizabethan style of architecture, and was built in 1836 by the Right Hon. Charles Brownlow. It was called Lurgan House until Mr. Brownlow was raised to the peerage. Freestone, imported from Scotland, was used in construction. Part of the mansion which existed previous to 1836, and was at that time joined to the new edifice, still continues in habitable condition. The demesne consists of about 350 acres, including an artificial lake of 53 acres. In this there are trout, tench and bream. The feeding sources of the lake are rivulets from the County Down. Part of the overflow helps to flush the town sewers, and the other part turns the corn mill of Mr. Robert M'Climond, in North Street. The demesne is splendidly planted. It is open to the public every day, and serves the purposes of a park without any cost to the ratepayers. Lord Lurgan has offered to sell his estate to the tenants, under the provisions of the Ashbourne Land Purchase Act, on the following terms:—For lands in the Electoral Division of Lurgan, 18½ years' purchase; for holdings in the Electoral Division of the Moyntaghs, 16½ years' purchase; and for the remainder of the estate (excluding town of Lurgan, building ground, &c.), 18½ years' purchase. Lord Lurgan has done a great deal to stimulate building operations in the town by giving long leases. Many handsome villas have been erected along the road leading to Lough Neagh, owing to this liberal policy. There is a side-walk all the way from the town, and on the edge of the lough there are seats. The side-walk was constructed by the county over three years ago. A cut from Lough Neagh, at Kinnego, is nearly 300 yards in length. It was made about the year 1863. In winter it has a depth of from 12 to 15 feet of water, and in summer from 7 to 8 feet. Lighters, from 60 to 100 tons burden, come in here with coal. Mr. William John Green owns 4 vessels of this class. The captains, as a rule, live on board with their families. After paying all expenses Mr. Green divides the net profits with them. The lighters are towed from Ellis's Cut, the Lagan Canal con-

nection with Lough Neagh, at a fixed rate of 6s. each, with cargo, and 3s. light. The toll on vessels from Belfast to Kinnego, is 9d. per ton cargo ; nothing on register. Coal and grain are the principal freights.

Kinnego Bay is good for pollen, and is "worked" by a few fishermen. Duck and widgeon shooting is to be had in the vicinity. There is no hindrance to either shooting or fishing. At one time Lough Neagh was very much frequented by invalids. Its waters were regarded as a "sure cure" for scrofulous affections, and rheumatism. The treatment consisted of bathing and drinking. In summer pleasure boats are numerous on the lough. Four belong to the Lurgan Boat Club, which also owns 4 practice gigs, 2 "fours" and 2 "pairs." The club was established in 1877, and has a good boat-house at Kinnego. About 30 members pay 10s. a year each. Mr. James H. Clendinning is secretary, and Mr. Patrick M'Geown, treasurer. The funds show a balance to credit.

Rifle shooting is an amusement engaged in by about thirty of the residents. The Lurgan Rifle Association was established in 1886. Members pay an entrance fee of 10s. and an annual subscription of 10s. each. Mr. George Greer, J.P., chairman of the association, gives free ground for a range at Woodville. Mr. James Johnston is vice-chairman, Mr. Thomas Watson, secretary, and Mr. Thomas Faloon, treasurer. Committee meetings are held at the Mechanics' Institute, and the practice days are Wednesday and Saturday. A team tried conclusions with the Carrickfergus Club in 1887, and won by one point. Mr. James Johnston, in 1886, presented a Challenge Silver Cup, to be won three times in succession by one member, 200, 500, and 600 yards. It weighs 40 ozs. Mr. Thomas Watson gave a Challenge Shield. The Martini-Henry is the rifle used by the members. The four highest scores in 1888, at 200, 500 and 600 yards, were made by Messrs. James Gorman, Thomas Faloon, Patrick M'Geown, and George Fleming.

CHURCH OF IRELAND, BELLS, CLOCK, CHANGE RINGERS, SHANKILL BUILDINGS, YOUNG MEN'S CHRISTIAN ASSOCIATION, Y.M.C.A. OF THE WORLD, GIRLS' FRIENDLY SOCIETY.

URGAN has one of the finest Protestant Episcopal churches in the County Armagh. It is situated in the middle of Church Place, and its graceful freestone spire is identified in the view of the town for miles around. The style of architecture is decorated Gothic, and the

chief material in consruction black stone, with freestone dressings. Ornamental iron railings inclose a tastefully laid out space, encircling the edifice. The interior of the church, as a whole, is in keeping with the exterior. Three arches, supported on freestone pillars at each side, divide the nave from the aisles. There are three galleries, one in each of the aisles, and one over the principal entrance, used for the choir, and for the organ, an excellent instrument, presented by Mr. James Malcolm in 1863. The seatings are in pitch-pine, and have a capacity for a congregation of from 800 to 900. Some fine memorial windows, in stained glass, help to embellish the chancel. One, on the south side, representing Faith, Hope and Charity, was erected as a tribute of affection from his son Charles, 2nd Baron, in 1853, to Charles 1st Baron Lurgan, who died in April, 1847, aged 52. The principal window, by Meyer, of Munich, consisting of three lights, was presented by the late Mr. Francis Watson, of Lake View, in 1873. The largest light, 28 feet high, has full length figures of the Apostles Mark and Luke, and the others, 22 feet each, of Matthew and John. Tablets in the vestibule indicate that the church was built in 1725, and rebuilt in 1863. Bequests are also noted in the same place, as follows :—1763, William Lee, interest of £100 for the poor ; 1794, Joseph McVeagh, interest of £300 for decayed housekeepers ; 1821, Jacob McCann, interest of £350 for the poor ; 1843, Thomas English, interest of £200 and £100 each to the rector and Presbyterian Minister, to be distributed among the poor of the parish annually. The painting and decoration of the church, a noticeable feature, were done at the expense of Mr. George Greer, J.P., Woodville. An object of curious interest is the baptismal font, bearing date 1684, used in the first house of worship erected by the settlers. The re-building of the church, etc., cost over £8,000. Very Rev. Theophilus Campbell, Dean of Dromore, is rector, and the curates are Rev. Robert Forde and Rev. Jos. S. Carolin. Eight bells, by John Taylor & Co., Loughborough, were put up in the tower, 1877, and a splendid 4-dial clock, by Gillett and Bland, Croydon, in 1878. The amount spent on both, £1,500, was raised by public subscription, through the instrumentality of Mr. James Ussher, solicitor. The clock is lighted by the Town Commissioners, and is a great convenience to the community. One of the bells was paid for by the ladies, and another by the children of the parish, numbering thousands. The largest individual subscription was given by the late Mr. William Watson, of New York, £200. All but four of the subscribers were residents of the parish. As a result of the purchase of the bells, the Lurgan Society of Change Ringers was organized in 1878. It has eight members, and is conducted

ISAAC BULLICK & CO.,

Manufacturers and Bleachers

OF

LINEN CAMBRIC HANDKERCHIEFS,

PLAIN, PRINTED AND EMBROIDERED,

MANUFACTORY & WAREROOMS at LURGAN,

Salerooms,

11 CHICHESTER STREET, BELFAST,

AND

11 & 12 GOLDSMITH STREET, LONDON, E.C.

TELEGRAPHIC ADDRESS—"Embroidery, Lurgan."

by Mr. William Neill. The Shankill Buildings, Coffee Palace, opposite the church, cost £1,500. Mr. Ussher took the initiative in raising this money also, and the rent paid by the tenant, Mr. James Dickson, goes to the Parish Fund.

The Lurgan Young Men's Christian Association, a branch of the Y.M.C.A., of London and the world, was established about two years ago. It has 58 members, who pay an annual subscription of 2s. 6d. each. A 7 years' lease was taken of a new house in Union Street this year, 1888. Mr. William Mahaffy is President, and Mr. Hugh Ross, and Mr. George Parke, secretaries.

In the Church of Ireland Young Men's Society there are 100 members. Mr. James Malcolm, D.L., is president, Mr. Hugh Livingston and Mr. Charles W. Neill, secretaries, and Mr. Robert Mathers, J.P., treasurer. It has a debating class, the members of which pay 1s. each per session. An extra charge of 4s. a quarter is made for the use of the reading-room. The Society was established about twenty years ago.

A branch of the girls' Friendly Society was established in October, 1887. At the first meeting, on the 11th of the following month, over 200 girls presented themselves for membership. This number was increased to 360. Weekly meetings are held, at which instruction is given in reading, writing, spelling, and plain and fancy needlework. One meeting in the month is devoted to Bible teaching, music, and readings. The Dean of Dromore, Very Rev. T. Campbell, is president.

PRESBYTERIAN CHURCHES, MILLAR MONUMENT, METHODIST CHURCHES, "TALKING MAN" AND JOHN WESLEY, BAPTIST CHURCH, FRIENDS, CHRISTIANS, SALVATION TEMPLE, ROMAN CATHOLIC CHURCH, ST. JOSEPH'S CONVENT, ST. VINCENT'S PATRONAGE.

THE first Presbyterian Church, situated in High Street, is a structure of considerable dignity, with a handsome portico. The interior is spacious, and tastefully appointed. There are three galleries, supported on fluted pillars with Ionic capitals. It is about 200 years since the congregation was formed. The Meeting House originally was at the opposite side of the same street, further down. The present church was opened in 1827. About 300 families belong to it. The Rev. Hamilton Dobbin was minister until 1844. He was succeeded by the Rev. Thomas Millar, who was killed

W. R. NELSON & CO.,

Manufacturers and

Bleachers of Linen,

AND CAMBRIC HANDKERCHIEFS,

AND LAWNS,

LURGAN.

~~~~~~~~~~

Warehouse—3 Bedford St., BELFAST.

LONDON AGENCY:

11 Lawrence Lane, CHEAPSIDE,

And at Manchester and Glasgow.

~~~~~~~~~~

TELEGRAPHIC ADDRESS—"Nelson, Belfast."

in the Trent Valley Railway accident, 1858, in the 39th year of his age. A monument facing the Court House, corner of William Street and Charles Street, was erected by "a grateful public, sensible of their deep obligation and desirous to perpetuate the memory of a good citizen, an affectionate friend, and a faithful minister of the gospel." The Rev. Mr. Millar's successor was the Rev. L. E. Berkeley, first convener of the Sustentation Fund in connection with the Presbyterian Church in Ireland. He died in 1878, and his remains are interred in the cemetery at the back of the church. Rev. Thomas M'Afee Hamill is the present minister.

At the corner of Hill and James' Streets there is another Presbyterian church. It is in the Gothic style of architecture, and dates from 1862. The chief material used in construction is black stone with freestone corners. The interior is large and tastefully fitted throughout. Rev. J. G. Clarke, now of Athy, Co. Kildare, was in charge of the congregation at the time the church was built. Rev. Charles W. Kennedy is the present minister. There is a handsome manse situated in the outskirts of the town, toward Portadown.

Methodism in Lurgan dates from the period of John Wesley, 1767. It is recorded that he was entertained here by Mr. Miller, father of Joseph Miller, M.D., a man of great inventive genius. At that time he had completed a mechanism in the form of a man, which repeated several sentences in a full and distinct voice. It called the hour, "Past twelve o'clock. O how the time runs on!" to the admiration of Mr. Wesley. The secret of construction died with Mr. Miller. The Methodist Church, situated in High Street, was erected in 1826, and completely remodeled in 1888, at a cost of about £800. The interior is fitted and wainscoted, for the most part, in pitch pine. One of the improvements was the raising of the ceiling two feet. There are three galleries. Two interesting mural tablets commemorate Rev. John Armstrong, 60 years in the ministry, born 1788, died 1875, and John Johnston, who was distinguished for "deep and long tried love of the cause." Died 1834. The site of the church was purchased from Mr. George Chapman. Rev. Thos. Pearson and Rev. E. Decourcey are the present ministers. A second church, belonging to the Methodists, is situated in Queen Street. It was built in 1856 by the Primitive Wesleyans, and continued in use by them until the Union. Rev. William Maguire is the present minister.

In Union Street a small Baptist congregation has worshipped for about eight years in a hall owned by Mr. Charles Baird. It was remodeled and enlarged this year, 1888. Rev. F. J. Ryan is the minister.

The Friends have a Meeting House off High Street. It occupies a secluded place, and is a plain building. The date is 1696. Repairs were made in 1839. About 100 members constitute the society here.

The Christians, once known as Plymouth Brethren, have had a hall in Union Street for about 10 years. A Temple was erected in Union Street about four years ago, by the Salvation Army.

Previous to 1800 the Roman Catholics had no place of worship in Lurgan. Mass was celebrated in a shed in the townland of Tanaghmore, North, about a mile from town. Mr. Brownlow in the year named gave an old mill at "the Dougher," outside the boundary, and it was remodeled to suit the purposes of a chapel. In 1829, Charles, 1st Baron Lurgan, gave a site in North Street, upon which a handsome church was erected, and dedicated in 1833 by the Most Rev. Dr. Blake, Bishop of Dromore, and enlarged in 1885 so as to give seating accommodation for 2,500 worshippers. It is a cruciform edifice of black stone with granite dressings. There are three galleries. A mural tablet commemorates the Very Rev. Wm. O'Brien, D.D., P.P., builder of the church. He died in 1870, aged 74. A fine stained window in the chancel has, among other figures, one of the Apostle Peter, patron saint of the church. The parish priest at present is Rev. Arthur J. Finnigan, and the curates Rev. M. B. McConville, and Rev. P. P. Campbell.

St. Joseph's Convent, Sisters of Mercy, situated in Edward Street, was founded about 22 years ago. It has schools under the National Board of Education for girls, infants (boys and girls), for ladies, and an industrial school, opened in 1888, and certified for 50 females. The buildings are large, and occupy part of four acres, most of which is embraced in a beautifully laid out garden at the rere. Mrs. O'Hagan is superioress.

St. Vincent's Patronage, under the management of priests and brothers of St. Vincent de Paul, was established in October, 1882, at the request of the Rev. James M'Kenna, P.P. The premises occupied, include a large house, three storeys and basement, in Church Place, and about 6 acres of land. Library, reading, recreation and billiard rooms for the young men of the town, free night schools for the working classes, and a day school for boys, in which the charge is £1 a year each, are the principal features of the Patronage. Those who use the library and reading, and billiard room pay 5s. a year. It cost nearly £4,100 to found the institution. Of this £3,000 was subscribed by the Congregation in France, and the remainder in the United Kingdom. Very Rev. Emile Piché is Superior, and Rev. D. F. Desmond, Director.

Z

James Glass & Co.,

Manufacturers and Bleachers of

Linen & Linen Cambric Handkerchiefs

OF EVERY DESCRIPTION.

~~~~~

Manufactory at LURGAN.

OFFICE AND WAREHOUSE:

BEDFORD ST., BELFAST.

~~~~~

NEW YORK: 335 BROADWAY.

LONDON: 8 MILK STREET.

MANCHESTER: 37 PICCADILLY.

GLASGOW: 145 QUEEN STREET.

PARIS: 4 RUE D'HAUTEVILLE.

COLLEGE, MUSICAL AND MUSICAL AND DRA-
MATIC SOCIETIES, EASTER TUESDAY SPORTS,
HORSE-JUMPING, DRIVING AND TROTTING,
FLOWER SHOW, LAWN TENNIS, CRICKET,
FOOT-BALL, AND CHESS CLUBS, ORNITHO-
LOGICAL SOCIETY, MASONIC LODGES.

URGAN COLLEGE is beautifully situated in extensive grounds off the Lough Road. It was founded
under the will of the late Samuel Watts, dated
August 3rd, 1847. He devised to trustees all his
property, subject to an annuity of £300 to his widow, to erect
and support an English classical and agricultural school for the
education of boys resident within half a mile of the town, with a
special proviso that none of the trustees or governors, or masters
shall be in Holy Orders. Mr. Watts died in 1850, and his
widow is now also deceased. The property was sold, and the
money invested until the interest reached £4,000. The college
was built in 1873, on 2 acres 2 roods of land, leased by Lord
Lurgan for 1,000 years at £20 a year. The Governors are
William, Baron Lurgan, Messrs. James Malcolm, D.L., John
Johnston, J.P.; George Greer, J.P. and Samuel W. M'Bride, J.P.
Mr. Wm. J. Fleming is secretary, and Mr. W. T. Kirkpatrick,
Head master. At present there is a clear income of nearly £400
a year to pay the expenses.

The Lurgan Musical Society was established about 4 years
ago. It has between 50 and 60 members, who pay a subscription of 10s. each per season, October to March. Rehearsals are
held every Thursday evening. Mr. A. H. Livock, organist of
the parish, Church of Ireland, is conductor, Mr. George Greer,
J.P., treasurer, and Messrs. James B. Hanna, and Richard G.
Chism, secretaries.

In 1885 the Lurgan Musical and Dramatic Society was
established. It has about 40 members paying a monthly subscription of 1s. The entrance fee is 5s. Rev. A. J. Finnigan,
P.P., is President, Mr. John Kennedy, secretary, Mr. Ml.
Rocks, treasurer, and Mr. David M'Gibbon, conductor.

Thanks to the great energy displayed by Mr. William White,
editor of *The Lurgan Times*, annual sports are held in Lord
Lurgan's demesne. In 1887 over £100 was distributed in prizes,
and more than 4,000 people attended. On Easter Tuesday a
programme of amusement, also in the demesne, was carried out
under Mr. White's management. It included trotting, horse-
jumping, and driving. Between £70 and £80 in prizes was
expended. There were over 70 entries for the different " events."

The attendance exceeded 10,000. Encouraged by the great success, Mr. White got up a mid-summer horse-jumping and driving competition, in connection with which there was a flower show. After paying expenses, the proceeds were to be given to the Coal Fund for the poor. The weather unfortunately proved unfavorable.

The Lurgan Tennis Club was established about eight years ago. It has three grass courts in Lord Lurgan's demesne. Mr. Thomas Watson is secretary, and Mr. Courtney Johnston, treasurer. There are 40 members. Gentlemen pay a subscription of 10s. each, and ladies 5s. each.

A Chess Club, of which Dr. S. Agnew is secretary, meets at the Mechanics' Institute. It has been in existence over ten years, and has a dozen members.

The Lurgan Demesne Cricket Club was established over 30 years ago. It has 40 members paying 10s. a year each. Mr. W. J. Allen is secretary, Mr. W. R. Ross, assistant secretary, and Mr. Richard Allan, treasurer. There are several good all-round players in the club, which was in the Northern Cricket Union for 1888.

In 1876 the Lurgan Foot-ball Club was established (Rugby). It has 30 members paying 5s. a year each. The Excelsior Foot-ball Club (Juniors) was established in 1888. It has 40 members. The Lurgan College has a first-rate Foot-ball Club.

Bicycling is popular, but there is no club.

The Lurgan Ornithological Society was established in 1880. It has 140 members paying from 5s. upward, each per annum. The last show of poultry, pigeons and cage-birds was held in the Town Hall, December 26 and 27, 1887. Mr. Joseph S. Watson is president, Mr. James Dickson, and Mr. Robert Mathers, jun., secretaries, and Mr. James Dickson, treasurer.

Freemasonry in Lurgan dates from 1743. There are two lodges at present : 134 and 24. Both meet at the Mechanics' Institute.

MANUFACTURING INTERESTS, THE OLD DIAPER HALL.

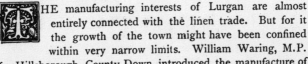

THE manufacturing interests of Lurgan are almost entirely connected with the linen trade. But for it the growth of the town might have been confined within very narrow limits. William Waring, M.P. for Hillsborough, County Down, introduced the manufacture of diapers here, and at Waringstown about the same time, shortly

Samuel W. McBride,

MANUFACTURER OF

Linux and ————

Cambric Handkerchiefs

PLAIN AND EMBROIDERED.

MANUFACTORY:

SHANKILL HILL, LURGAN.

OFFICE AND WAREHOUSE:

20 & 22 LINEN HALL ST., BELFAST.

AGENCIES:

London—13 GUTTER LANE.

Manchester—4a PORTLAND ST.

New York—84 FRANKLIN ST.

TELEGRAPHIC ADDRESS—" **SAMMAC, BELFAST.**"

after the accession of Queen Anne, 1702. The people of Lurgan and district showed an intelligent appreciation of his kindness, and made substantial progress in acquiring the knowledge which he imparted. When the training had proved effective the sale of webs began to be a feature of the weekly market. It was then held on Friday, in accordance with the patent granted to Mr. Brownlow by William III. Linen merchants stood in the open street, and made purchases, paying for and receiving the goods afterward at the hotels. At the beginning of the present century a Linen Hall was built by subscription. It was thronged every Friday by hand-loom weavers, who exposed their webbs on long tables provided for the purpose. In 1825 the weekly sales averaged from £2,500 to £3,000. The hall had a railing round it, and occupied a space which is now included in Church Place. Eventually the merchants changed their modes of dealing with the weavers to such an extent that the hall was abolished in 1865. The first power-loom weaving factory was built by the father of Mr. James Malcolm, D.L., in 1855. Up to the present his example has not been followed by half a dozen out of the large number of manufacturers whose names are recorded alphabetically at page 377. Lurgan manufacturers make handkerchiefs, plain and embroidered, a great feature. Basing a calculation upon the statements made to me by each manufacturer personally, or through his manager, I find that almost 18,000 hand-loom weavers are employed in the furtherance of enterprises wholly or partly directed from Lurgan. The weavers nearly all live in Armagh, Down, Antrim, and Tyrone, and the yarns are given out to them at offices in Lurgan and at central points in the other counties. The same manufacturers give out embroidery work to thousands of women throughout the province of Ulster. Nearly 2,500 people are employed as inside workers in the power-loom factories and preparing departments of the manufacturers by hand-loom. Since 1866, when the first hem-stitching factory was erected, this branch has increased until it now provides inside employment for about 2,400 people.

Fifty years ago, two breweries and a distillery, consuming 15,000 tons of grain annually, were flourishing. So also were two tobacco factories. One of the breweries, Mr. James Johnston's, started over a hundred years ago, still exists. The other, the distillery, and the tobacco works have been replaced by mineral water factories. Brick-making is carried on to a considerable extent.

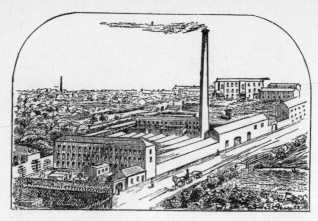

POWER-LOOM WEAVING FACTORY.

HEMMING AND VEINING FACTORY.

JAMES MALCOLM,
LURGAN.

MR. JAMES MALCOLM'S ENTERPRISES.

THE Malcolms have been for a great many years prominently identified with the manufacturing interests of Lurgan. Mr. James Malcolm, father of Mr. James Malcolm, D.L., J.P., during the palmy days of handloom weaving, was extensively engaged in the manufacture of cambric. He introduced power looms in this part of the country, erecting a factory for the purpose in 1855. The commotion created among the handloom weavers was so great, that they collected in a body, two years later, apparently with the intention of forcing him to abandon the enterprise. A public meeting of the residents of the town, called for the purpose, under the chairmanship of the seneschal, Mr. John Hancock, J.P., soon afterward, passed a series of resolutions in the highest degree complimentary to Mr. Malcolm, and they were handsomely engrossed and presented to him. At his death in 1864, the present proprietor succeeded. He had already been in active association with his father in the management of the concern, and soon began to make important structural alterations and extensions, increasing the number of power looms largely. The manufactures are confined to cambric and cambric handkerchiefs—employment being provided for about 500 people in this department. In 1866 Mr. Malcolm purchased the patents taken out by Mr. Joseph B. Robertson, and established the first factory in the United Kingdom for hemstitching by machinery. This is situated in Union Street, and gives employment to about 350 people. At first it worked in conjunction with the weaving factory only, but it is now also used in the interest of other manufacturers, and of merchants of Lurgan and Belfast. The buildings and premises, including those of the weaving factory off High Street, and the Union Street factory, extend over an area of ten acres, in the heart of the town. Steam is the motive power at both factories. Mr. Malcolm is also an extensive stock owner in and director of the New Northern Spinning and Weaving Company, Limited, Belfast.

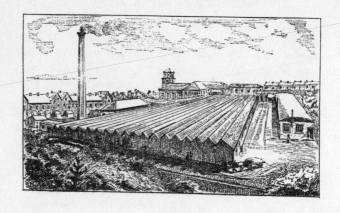

THE
LURGAN WEAVING COMPANY,

LIMITED,

Power-Loom Manufacturers

OF

LINENS, CAMBRICS AND HANDKERCHIEFS,

LURGAN.

THE LURGAN WEAVING CO., LIMITED.

BROWNLOW Terrace is a part of the town which strikes the eye of the stranger on entering Lurgan by rail from Belfast. It contains the handsome buildings and grounds belonging to the Model School, and a number of comfortable dwellings erected for work-people by the Lurgan Weaving Co., Limited. At the back of these houses the tall chimney-shaft of the Company's power loom weaving factory appears prominently in the view. The property of the Company has a frontage at Brownlow Terrace of 326 feet, and a depth of 394 feet. Nearly all of this is occupied by buildings. There are in the factory 472 looms, driven by a 200 horse compound horizontal condensing engine. Brick and glass are the chief materials in the construction of the bays. The manufactures include the weaving of cambric and cambric handkerchiefs of the finest quality, and the finest linen for shirting and under-clothing. Sale is made of the goods in the unbleached state to the manufacturers and merchants of Lurgan, Belfast, and generally of the North of Ireland. The Lurgan Weaving Company, Limited, was organized in 1881, with the object of purchasing the interest in the present concern from Messrs. William and James Macoun, who had been for about twenty years engaged in the manufacture of cambric and cambric handkerchiefs. Messrs. Macoun had 376 looms running, and the Lurgan Weaving Company, Limited, added 96 to this number, and replaced about half the old machinery by new, containing the latest improvements. Thirty houses for work-people, situated in Mary Street and Brownlow Terrace, were built by the Company, and factory alterations and extensions were made which required a considerable outlay. The directors are—Mr. Samuel A. Bell, J.P., Belle Vue, Lurgan, chairman; Mr. Fredk. W. Bell, Belle Vue, Lurgan; Mr. Thomas A. Dickson, M.P., Dublin; Mr. W. J. Hurst, J.P., Drumaness, Co. Down; Mr. James Brown, J.P., Donaghmore, Co. Tyrone; Mr. Alexander Hannah, Glasgow; and Mr. H. G. MacGeagh, Derry Lodge, Lurgan, the managing director.

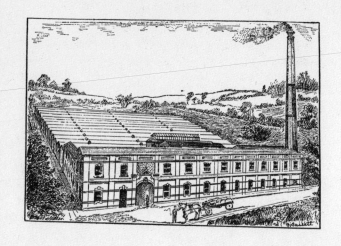

JOHNSTON, ALLEN & CO.,

Linen and Cambric

Handkerchief

Manufacturers,

LURGAN.

Telegraphic Address—"ALLENTON," LURGAN.

MESSRS. JOHNSTON, ALLEN & CO.

MESSRS. JOHNSTON, ALLEN & CO. occupy a prominent position among the manufacturers of Lurgan. The firm was established in 1867 for the manufacture of linen and cambric handkerchiefs by handloom, and a beginning was made by giving out yarns to about 500 cottage weavers. Within ten years this number had been increased to 1,000. The cloth was all sold in the brown state. Arrangements were then made for a bleaching and finishing department, and for the erection of a hemstitching factory by machine power, which gave additional employment to 300 inside workers. The enterprises enumerated are all carried out in premises consisting of about a statute acre, fronting William Street, and extending to Ulster Street.

Early in 1888 the firm decided to erect the power loom factory illustrated on the opposite page. Messrs. Young and MacKenzie, the eminent Belfast architects, supplied the design, and by a very important economical improvement, they have effected a great saving of space in the interior of the factory. The building, which fronts Victoria street, occupies with the premises, three acres. The chief materials of the structure are brick and glass. Capacity is afforded for more than 500 looms, driven by a Coates compound tandem engine, 180 horse power indicated. The chimney shaft is 150 feet high, with a centre cylinder about 60 feet. By the erection of the Victoria street factory a further addition of 500 has been made to the total number of workpeople. The manufactures consist of the finest linen cambric handkerchiefs, and the finest clear lawn cambric. Mr. James Johnston and Mr. Joseph Allen constitute the firm of Johnston, Allen and Co.

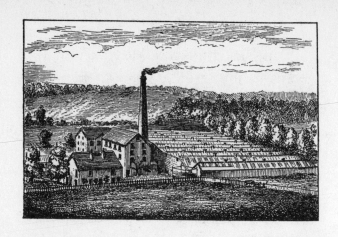

JOHN S. BROWN & SONS,

MANUFACTURERS OF

Table Linen, Diapers, Sheeting,

CAMBRIC HANDKERCHIEFS, SHIRTING LINEN, &c.

Power Loom Factory,	Hand = Loom Factory,
ST. ELLEN'S, CO. DOWN.	LURGAN.

WAREHOUSES.

BELFAST—12 Bedford Street.   LONDON—26 Gresham Street (E.C.)

NEW YORK—116 & 118 Franklin Street.

Telegraphic Addresses—"DAMASK," BELFAST and LONDON
"AVOWAL," NEW YORK.

MESSRS. JOHN S. BROWN & SONS.

ESSRS. JOHN S. BROWN & SONS, as manufacturers, have a world-wide reputation. Mr. James Brown laid the foundation of their business at Lurgan in 1795, making linens and damasks special features. The late Mr. John Shaw Brown, his nephew, succeeded Mr. James Brown in 1843. Soon afterward a partnership was formed between Mr. Brown, Mr. James Magee, and Mr. W. Liddell, and the same line of work continued at Lurgan until 1860, when Mr. Magee retired. The style of the firm then became Brown and Liddell, and head-quarters were at Belfast. Six years later this partnership was dissolved. Mr. Brown then took up the work entirely on his own account. He built the factory at St. Ellen's, County Down, a view of which appears on the opposite page. It is situated within four and a half miles of Belfast, and has 380 looms engaged in the weaving of damasks, linens, hucks, and towels. The driving power is provided by steam and water, and the buildings and premises embrace about five acres. In 1872 Messrs. John, William K., and George Herbert Brown, sons, were taken into partnership. Mr. John Brown retired in 1883, and in 1887 Mr. John Shaw Brown died, leaving the business to Messrs. William K. and George Herbert Brown, the present proprietors. Not long after the death of Mr. Brown, Mr. Thomas H. Magee also died, and the business was purchased by Messrs. John S. Brown & Sons, who continue to carry it on at Lurgan, under the style of Thomas H. Magee & Co. Employment is given just now by Messrs. John S. Brown & Sons to about 580 people at St. Ellen's, 1,500 handloom weavers of Armagh, Down, Antrim and Tyrone, and to over 3,000 wives and daughters of small farmers at hand embroidery. Messrs. Brown make a speciality of the weaving of monograms, crests, coats of arms, and flags on linen supplied to families, steamship companies, yacht clubs, hotels, etc. They are manufacturers to the Queen, the Prince of Wales, and all the Members of the Royal Family ; have contracts for supplying damasks to the Admiralty ; manufacture all the linen for the House of Commons restaurant, the Midland and London and North Western Railways, the Grand, Metropole, 1st Avenue, Langham, Inns of Court, and Charing Cross Hotels, London ; the principal clubs of the United Kingdom ; the Windsor, 5th Avenue, and St. James's Hotels, and Hoffman House, New York ; and the Grand Pacific Hotel, Chicago. Prize Medals for superior merit were obtained for their goods at the following Exhibitions : London, 1851, 1862, and 1870; Dublin, 1865 and 1872 ; Belfast, 1870; Paris—Gold—1867 ; and Philadelphia, 1876.

HARRISON BROTHERS,

Manufacturers of Table Linen,

Birdeye Diaper, Sheetings, Linen and Cambric
Handkerchiefs,

YARN BLEACHERS, &c., &c.,

ULSTER STREET, LURGAN,

COOLSALLAGH AND DROMORE, CO. DOWN,

BELFAST WAREHOUSE,

18 HOWARD STREET.

TELEGRAPHIC ADDRESS—"Looms, Belfast."

THOMAS JORDAN & SONS,

LINEN & CAMBRIC HANDKERCHIEF

MANUFACTURERS,

Plain and Embroidered,

Bleachers, Finishers, &c.,

EDWARD STREET,

LURGAN.

LURGAN DIRECTORY.

—o—

BUSINESS BRANCHES, PROFESSIONS, PUBLIC BODIES, &c

—o—

[Arranged alphabetically. Institutions, etc., not mentioned here should be sought in the Lurgan Alphabetical Directory, and in the County Directory, page 53.]

—o—

AUCTIONEERS.
Cherry, Andrew, Market st
Thompson, Rt., William st

BABY LINEN.
Ballance, Miss S., High st
Brown, Miss S., High st
Byrne, Mrs. M., William st
Collins, Mrs. Dd., Edward st
Dillon, Mrs. E., Edward st
Hill, Mrs. J., Union st
Hunter, Mrs. A., Market st
Thompson, Mrs. Sl., Market st
Ward, Miss C., Edward st

BAKERS.
Casey, Thos., Edward st
Cunningham, Thos., Edward st
Filbin, Wm., Edward st
Finch, Mrs. Mt., North st
Kennedy, Jas., 30 High st
M'Carson, Thos., Edward st
M'Climond & Sons, Hight st
Northern Baking Co., William st
Taylor, Samuel, Edward st
Turkington, George, Church pl

BANKS.
Belfast : High street, Hugh M'Donnell, mgr. ; Rd. G. Chism, cashr. ; Chas. E. Taylor, acct.

Northern : High street, Henry Megarry, mgr. ; W. J. M'Clatchie, cashr. ; Johnston Weatherup, acct.

Ulster : Market st., Rt. Patton, mgr. ; W. R. Ringland, cashr. ; N. G. Leeper, acct.

BANN (UPPER) NAVIGATION.
Fred. W. Magahan, secretary, Court house, William st

BEEHIVES.
Lonsdale, Wm., Av. road

BLACKSMITHS.
Gallagher, Henry, Castle le
Haughey, John, Edward st
Hurson, Patk., Market st
Kilpatrick, Wm., Edward st
Somerville, John, High st
Somerville, J., Market st

BOAT CLUB.
House, Kinnego.
Jas. H. Clendinning, secretary ;
Patrick M'Geown, treasurer

BOOTMAKERS
who have shops.
Black, Thos., 56 Church pl
Ferguson, Edward, 39 Market st
M'Kee, Alex. H., Market st
Moffet, Thos., William st
Northampton Boot Co., Castle le
Tyler, J., & Sons, 59 Market st
Walsh, John, 33 Church st

BOX MANUFACTURERS.
Trotter, Wm. & Co., Market st

2 A

BREWER AND MALTSTER.
Johnston, James, Market st
BRICK MANUFACTURERS.
Campbell, James, Market st
Mathers, Wm., Edward st
Menary, Thomas, Hill st
Moore, John, High st
BUILDERS & CARPENTERS.
†Carpenters only.
Archer, Dd., Church pl
Archer, D., Watson's lane
Baird, Charles, Union st
Harkin, Charles, William st
M'Cann, Ml., William st
M'Connell, Robert, North st
†Martin, Wm. J., Union st

BURIAL BOARD.
Town Commissioners
BURIAL PLACES.
Friends', High st
New Cemetery, Monbrief, one mile from town
Presbyterian, 1st Church, High st
Roman Catholic, Old Chapel
Shankill, Shankill st
CABINET MAKERS.
Hanna, William, William st
Turkington, Samuel, High st

CHANGE RINGERS, LURGAN.
Society of
William Neill, Conductor
CHINA, GLASS, &c.
See Glass, China, &c.

CHURCHES, MEETING HOUSES, &c.
Baptist — Mission, Union st., Rev. F. J. Ryan
Christians—Union st
Church of Ireland—Church pl., Very Rev. Theophilus Campbell, Dean, Rector ; Rev. Robt. Forde, Curate ; Rev. Joseph S. Carolin, Curate ; A. H. Livock, Organist
Friends'—High st
Methodist—High st., Rev. Thomas Pearson, Rev. E. DeCourcy ; Queen st., Rev. William Maguire

Presbyterian — 1st, High st., Rev. Thomas M'Afee Hamill
Presbyterian — 2nd, Hill st., Rev. C. W. Kennedy
Roman Catholic—St. Peter's, North st., Rev. Arthur J. Finnigan, P.P., Rev. Michael B. M'Conville, C.C., Rev. Peter Campbell, C.C.
St. Vincent De Paul, Church place—Rev. Emile Piché, Rev. Daniel F. Desmond
Salvation Army — Union st., Johnston Skillen, Captain
CLOTHES BROKERS.
Boston, Francis, 32 High st
Bunting, David, 82 High st
CLOTHIERS.
See also Drapers.
Fleming, John, Market st
Thompson, Maxl., 27 Market st
CLUBS.
See Lurgan descriptive.
COACH BUILDERS.
Greer, James, 19 High st
Harold, Robert, Market st
Mullen, Henry, Market st
COAL MERCHANTS.
Donnelly, A. & Co., Church pl
Fleming, John, Market st
Freeburn, John, Union st
Green, William J., Kinnego
Hewitt, Adam, Edward st
Kennedy, Richard, 54 Edward st
M'Clure, W. W., 14 High st
Mathers, R. & Co., Market st
Matthews, William, Edward st
Murray, D., 50 High st
CONFECTIONERS.
Dickson, James, Church pl
Imrie, Miss Jane, 44 High st.
Thompson, R., High st & Market st
CONFECTIONS.
Murray, Richard, Church pl
CONSTITUTIONAL ASSOCIATION.
Meets Shankill Buildings.
James Malcolm, D.L., Chairman; Hugh Hayes, solicitor, Sec. ; Robert Mathers, J.P., Treasurer

CONSULAR AGENT (U.S.)
Magahan, Fredk. W., William st

COOPERS.
Hamill John, Edward st
M'Kenna, Neal, Castle lane

DAIRY.
Greer, George, Woodville

DAMASK MACHINE MANU-
FACTURERS.
Allen, James, Avenue rd
Boyce, William H., Union st

DISPENSARY.
Union st., Dr. Samuel Agnew,
M.D. Attendance, Tuesday,
Thursday, and Saturday
Committee meets third Thurs-
day every month at 9 30 a.m.
Members of Committee:—Right
Hon. Lord Lurgan ; Colonel
Waring, D.L.; Samuel J. Bell,
J.P. ; James Malcolm, D.L. ; Jas.
Fforde, J.P. ; Joseph Murphy, J.P.;
John Jonston, J.P. ; George Greer,
J.P. ; Dr. Magennis, J.P. ; Claude
Brownlow, J.P. ; Francis Watson,
J.P. ; John M'Nally, J.P. ; Wm.
J. Allen, John Macoun, George R.
Carrick, J.P. ; Saml. W. M'Bride,
J.P. ; Nelson Ruddell, Christopher
Stevensqn, Thomas Reburn, Geo.
Robinson, John Fleming, Robert
M'Caw, Sinton Pedlow, Joseph
Coulter, Thomas Ruddell, Walter
T. K. Ruddell, James Clendinning,
Wm. H. Stevenson, Robert Ma-
thers, J.P. ; Joseph Murray
Wardens — Richard Kennedy,
Edward st. ; Thomas Menary,
Hill st. : Nath. Turkington, Der-
ryloist ; David H. Uprichard, Kil-
more ; Thomas Morrison, High st.;
Mathew Hazley, James st

DRAPERS.
Armstrong & Mathers, Market st
Brown, Miss S., 2½ High st
Collins, Miss M., 4 Edward st
Cullenan, B. & Co., Market st
Duncan, Geo. & Sons, Market st
Fitzsimons & Co., 59 Market st
Gilchrist, John, 51 Market st

Hunter, Mrs. A., 37 Market st
Livingston & Co., 47 Market st
Lurgan Drapery & Hf. Co., Wm st
Maguire, Charles, 34 Church pl
Mawhirt, Ezekiel, Edward st
Murphy & Co., 4 Market st
Reburn & Co., Market st
Tavener, A. J., 40 Market st
Toner, Bd., 10 High st

DRUGGISTS, DISPENSING.
Allan, Richard, Market st
Calvert, J. & Co., Market st
Houston, William, Church pl
Moore, James M., High st

EDUCATION.
COLLEGE, LURGAN.
Lough Road.
Head Master—William T. Kirk-
patrick
INDUSTRIAL SCHOOL,
St. Joseph's Convent, Edward st
LADIES' SCHOOLS.
High st—The Misses Murphy
St. Joseph's Convent — Mrs.
O'Hagan, superioress
MODEL.
Brownlow terrace — Solomon
Spears, Miss Eliza Collins, Mrs.
Gray
NATIONAL SCHOOLS.
Charles Wm. Dougan, Inspector
George st.—Wm. Shields, Miss
Pollock
High st.—Robert A. Shields, Mrs.
Eliza Cooney
North st.—Richard Howell, Miss
H. Evans
Queen st. (Ragged)—Mrs. Mary
A. Marshall
St Joseph's Nunnery, Edward st
St. Peter's, North st. — John
McConville
ST. VINCENT DE PAUL.
Patronage House, Church place
High School—Very Rev. Emile
Piché, Rev. D. F. Desmond, A.
Murphy.
Evening Schools—A. Murphy
EMIGRATION AGENTS.
Cherry, Andrew, Market st

Emerson, William, Church st
White, William, High st

ESTATE OFFICES.

Market Street.

Claude Brownlow, J.P., agent;
William J. Fleming, under agent;
James Ussher, solicitor.

FANCY GOODS WARE-
HOUSES.

Ballance, Miss S., High st
Bowden, Mrs. A., High st
Kennedy, Hugh, Church pl
McGeown, Mirs L. A., Church pl

FIRE DEPARTMENT.

Engine House, Town Hall.
John Long, superintendent; Jas.
Dunwoody, deputy.

FRIENDLY SOCIETY,
LURGAN.

Very Rev. T. Campbell, Pres.;
Rev. T. M. Hamill, V.P.; Dr.
Richard Howell, Sec.; Dr. J. J.
Moore, Med. officer

FRUITERERS.

Cherry, A., Market st
Dickson, Jas., Shankill Bgs.
Murray, Richard, Church pl

GAS WORKS.

William st.—The Lurgan Gas
Light & Chemical Co., Limited:
Samuel A. Bell, J.P., Chairman;
Frederick W. Magahan, secretary;
Thomas Tallentire, manager and
engineer; 3s. 11d. per 1,000 feet.

GLASS, CHINA & DELF.

See also grocers.

Bratty, Jno., High st
Murray, Daniel, High st
Parkes, John, Edward st

GRAIN MERCHANTS.

Anderson, George, Market st
Donnelly, A., Church pl
Ellis, William, North st
Ireland Bros., Church pl
McClimond, Robert, North st

GROCERS.

Marked thus [*] retail spirits, [†]
hardware, [‡] delf, &c.
Allen, James, Queen st
Barr, Alexander, Edward st

Belfast Co-op. Tea Co., Church pl
Bunting, David, 82 High st
Campbell, James, Market st
Capper, Joseph, 3 Church pl
Caulfield, William, Queen st
Crozier, Mrs. J., Union st
Dickson, William, North st
*Dobson, John, Queen st
†Donnelly, A., & Co., Church pl
*Donnelly, Miss S. J., Church pl
Duke, Jos., Union st
*Emerson, Thos., 2 Church pl
English Thomas, William st
*Esdale, Mrs. E. A., 57 Market st
Filbin, William, 76 Edward st
Finch, Mrs. M., North st
†*Fleming, John, Market st
*Gallagher, Mrs. M., Edward st
Gibson, Robert, Queen st
Graham Bros., Church pl
Green, Wm. J., Kinnego
Hall, James L., 36 Market st
†Halliday, Edward, High st
Harrison, Mrs. A., Queen st
Holland, Robert, Union st
Holland, Samuel, Union st
Holland, Thomas, Union st
Hopps, John, Union st
Hopps, Thomas, Hill st
*Ireland, Bros., Church pl
Jennings, W., 29 Church place
Kelly, Henry, North st
Kennedy, Jas., 30 High st
Kennedy, Rd., 54 Edward st
London & Co.'s Tea Co., Market st
McCaughley, Chas., 64 Edward st
McClimond & Sons, Market st
McClure, W. W., 14 High st
McCormick, Jas., Union st
McGeown, Robt., Hill st
*McMullan, Jas., 25 Market st
Magee, Mrs. A., North st
Malcolm, Saml., Victoria st
†Malcolmson, David, Market st
†Malcolmson, Jno., 3 Market st
Matthews, Wm., Edward st
Mawhirt, Ezekiel, Edward st
Murray, Rd., 47 Church pl
Nicholson, Robt., 12 Edward st
Northern Baking Co., William st

W. H. BOYCE,
DAMASK MACHINE MAKER,
(JACQUARD)
65 UNION STREET,
Lurgan.

JOHN LONG,
PLUMBER, STEAM & GAS-FITTER,
WILLIAM STREET,
LURGAN.

Hot-water Apparatus and Electric Bells Fitted up in Town & Country.
☞ Estimates and full particulars free on application.

DAVID ARCHER,
BUILDING CONTRACTOR,
CHURCH PLACE, LURGAN.

☞ Estimates given free, and Contracts taken anywhere in Ulster.
Experienced Workmen sent out in Town or Country, for jobbing
purposes, under special supervision.

JAMES GREER,
Coach=builder & General Jobbing Smith,
19 HIGH STREET,
LURGAN.

☞ All kinds of Vehicles built and repaired.

Oliver, David, Union st
‡Parkes, John, 26 Church pl
Sibit, John, Hill st
*Smyth, Mrs. M., Edward st
Soye, John, Charles st
‡Sullivan, Wm., Queen st
Taylor, James, Market st
Taylor, Saml., Edward st
Toner, Michael, North st
Turkington, Geo., Church pl
‡Uprichard, Robt., Union st
*Ward, George, Castle lane
Ward, Hugh, Edward st
†Watson, Jas., 3 High st
Whiteside, Thomas, Edward st
†Wiley, Richd., 42 Church p
Wilson, Henry, Union st

JAMES CAMPBELL,

Family grocer, Irish and American
hams and bacon, flour, meal, bran,
and pollard, steam saw mills, timber, slate, and tile merchant, 15 &
17 Market street

GEORGE WARD,

Family grocer, wine and spirit merchant, flour, meal, bran, Irish and
American bacon, jams, jellies, spices,
tobacco, &c., 7 Castle lane

HANDKERCHIEF MANU-
FACTURERS.
See Manufactures.

HARDWARE.
Donnelly, A. & Co., Church pl
Fleming, John, Market st
Graham, Bros., Church pl
Halliday, Edw., High st
Kennedy, Rd., 54 Edward st
McClure, Wm. W., 14 High st
Watson, Jas., 3 High st

HEMSTITCHING
See Manufactures.

HOTELKEEPERS.
Marked thus * are licensed.
Dickson, Jas., **SHANKILL**
BUILDINGS
McDowell, Mrs., William st
*McLarnon, Mrs., William st
*Moffitt, Miss M., **BROWN-**
LOW ARMS, Market st
*O'Brien, Mrs. E. Church pl

LINEN MANUFACTURERS.
See Manufactures.
LOAN OFFICES.
Baird, Jas., Hill st
Doak, Wm., Kinnego
Hanna, Jas., Edward st
LOUGH NEAGH DRAINAGE
C. S. Obré, Secy.; W. J. O'Neill,
C.E., District Surveyor

MANUFACTURES.

DAMASK MANUFACTURERS
Allen, James, Avenue rd
Bell, Thos. & Co., Belle vue
Bessbrook Spinning Co., Ld., Wm. st
Brown, John S. & Sons, Queen st
Harrison Bros., Ulster st
Magee, Thos. H. & Co., Queen st
Murphy, Joseph & Son, William st

H'DKERCHIEF FINISHERS.
Duke, Joseph, Union st
McConnell, Wm., Watson's le
McMullan, Robt., Hill st
Wetherall, Mrs. R., George st

HANDKERCHIEF MANU-
FACTURERS.
Cambric, Linen, &c.
Bell, Thos. & Co., Belle vue
Brown, John S. & Sons, Queen st
Bullick, Isaac, & Co., Mark st
Clendinning, Jas., High st
Douglas, Henry, North st
Douglas, John & Sons, William st
Duke, Thomas, Union st
Elliott, John & Co., Charles st
Fairley, Wm., William st
Glass, Jas. & Co., William st
Hanna & Co., William st
Hanna, Jas. B., William st
Hardy, Thos. L. & Co., Queen st
Harrison, Bros., Ulster st
Johnston, Allen & Co., Victoria st
  and William st
Jordan, Thos. & Sons, Edward st
Lurgan Weaving Co., Ltd., Brown-
  low ter
Lyons & Woods, William st
McBride, Samuel W., Shankill hill
McCaughey & Co., Church place
McCaw, Robert, Teghnevan
McConnell, Wm., Watson's lane

McMullan, Robert, Union street
Macoun, J. R. & Co., Moyraverty
Malcolm, James, High street
Matier, Henry & Co., High st
Mathers and Bunting, Mary st
Mercer and Brown, Union st
Murphy and Stevenson, High st
Nelson, W. R. & Co., William st
Stewart, Wm. & Sons, William st
Watson, Rt. & Sons, The Flush

HEMSTITCHERS (MACHINE) AND FINISHERS.

Crawford, Geo. A., Victoria st
Faloon & Co., William street
Hanna & Co., William street
Hanna, James B., William street
Lurgan Hemstitching Co., Mark st
Malcolm, James, Union street
Maxwell, John & Co., Market st
Mercer and Brown, Union street
Mercer and Magill, Lough road
Johnston, Allen & Co., Victoria st
Ross, John & Co., High street

LINEN AND CAMBRIC MANUFACTURERS.

Marked thus [*] linen only.
† Cambric only

Bell, Thomas & Co., Belle vue
Bessbrook Spinning Co..Ld.,Wm.st
Brown, J. S. & Sons, Queen st
Harrison Brothers, Ulster street
† Lurgan Weaving Co., Ltd., Brownlow terrace
† Malcolm, James, High street
Murphy, Joseph & Son, William st

PRINTERS (Handkerchief.)

Bullick, Isaac & Co., Mark street
Clendinning, James, High street

MARINE STORE.

McCartney, P., 1 Arthur st
Murray, Daniel, 50 High street

MARKET, Thursday.

MECHANICS' INSTITUTE.

Lord Lurgan, President ; James Malcolm, D.L., Vice-President ; James Johnston, Chairman of Committee ; Dr. Samuel Agnew, Sec. Courtney Johnston, Treas.

MERCHANT TAILOR.
(See also Drapers.)
Plenderleith, P., 34 Market stree

MILLERS.
Wheatmeal and Oatmeal.
McClimond, Robert, North street

MILLINERY.
Anderson, Mrs. Geo., 53 Market st

MINERAL WATER MANUFACTURERS
and Bottlers.
Crawford, Wm. H., & Co.,Wm. st.
Robertson, Joseph B., Union st
Thompson, Robt., 66 & 68 High st

MUSICAL SOCIETY, LURGAN.
James B. Hanna, Richard G. Chism, Secretaries ; George Greer,. J.P., Treas.; A. H. Livock, Conductor

MUSICAL AND DRAMATIC SOCIETY, LURGAN.
Hall, Church Place
Rev. A. J. Finnegan, P.P., President ; John Kennedy, Secretary ; Michael Rocks, Treasurer ; David McGibbon, Conductor

NEWSAGENTS.
(See also Stationers.)
Black, Thomas, Church place

NEWSPAPER.
Lurgan Times. Saturday, 1d.
Wm. White, Proprietor. Office,. High street

ORNITHOLOGICAL SOCIETY.
Joseph S. Watson, President ; James Dickson and Robt. Mathers, jun., Secretaries ; James Dickson,. Treasurer

PAINTERS AND GLAZIERS.
Bryans, William, High street
Maguire, William, Market street
Murray, Alexander, Church place
Robinson Brothers, William street
Young, James, Church place

PAWNBROKERS.
Culley, Samuel, 39 Church pl
Gamble, Thompson, William st
Hazelton, Robert, Market st

Hewitt, Holt M., Edward st
Moore, John, 9 High st
PETTY SESSIONS.
Court house, William st
1st and 3rd Tuesday of every
month
Clerk—Fredk. W. Magahan
PHYSICIANS.
Adamson, J. G. (J.P.), High st
Agnew, Samuel, High st
Darling, John S., Market st
Magennis, Edw. (J.P.), Church pl
Moore, James M., High st
PLUMBERS.
Long, John, William st
Menaul, Chas., William st
POSTING CAR OWNERS.
Berwick, Edward, Queen st
Brownlow Arms Hotel proprietor,
Market st
Collins, Joseph, Knocknashean
Gracey, Wm., Church pl
Hall Bros., Market st
Kennedy, John, Taghrane
M'Mullan, Rt., Union st
M'Quillan, Alex., Edward st
Magee, John, Union st
Mitchell, John, Hill st
O'Brien, Mrs. E., Church pl
Osborne, Wm., Market st
Speers, Htn., 26 William st
Speers, James, Market st
Thompson, Rt., High st
POST OFFICE
Market st
Mrs. Dora Lindsay, P.M.
James Neill, chief clerk
POULTERER.
Stothers, Thomas, Union st
PRINTERS.
Reid, Wm., Edward st
White, William, High st
PROCESS SERVER.
Hugh English
RAILWAY STATION.
Toll Collector—James Wilson
REED MAKERS.
Bunton, Queen st
Thompson, Robert, William st
Thompson, Wm. J., Church pl

RIFLE ASSOCIATION.
Range, Woodville.
George Greer, President ; James
Johnston, V.P. ; Thomas Watson,
Secretary; Thomas Faloon, Treas.
R. I. CONSTABULARY.
Barracks—Union st, Edward st
Queen st, High st
Wm. Bigley, D.I., Church pl
Ml. Greene, H.C., Union st
SADDLERS.
Brown, Wm., William st
Reynolds, Edward, High st
SAW MILLS.
See Timber Merchants.
SCHOOLS.
See Education.
SEED MERCHANTS.
Anderson, George, 53 Market st
Hall, James L., 36 Market st
SHUTTLE MAKERS.
Bullick, John, 21 Queen st
Duke, Wm., High st
SOLICITORS.
Hayes, Hugh, High st
Mackay, Samuel A., High st
Menary, Thos. J., Market st
Moore, W. H. D., High st
O'Reilly, John C., Church pl
Ussher & Mahaffy, William st
SPIRIT RETAILERS.
See also Grocers.
Berwick, Ed., 28 Queen st
Blayney, James, Church place
Dobson John, Queen street
Doyle, Patrick, 31 Market street
Gilmore, William, 21 Market st
Gracey, Robert, Queen street
Gracey, William, 143 Church place
Hand, William, 39 William st
McGeown, Patk., 65 Church place
Magee, Hugh, William street
Magee, John, Union street
Magee, Thomas, Edward street
Maguire, Charles, 9 Edward st
Pedlow, Saml., 104 Edward st
Sloan, Mrs. A. J., 63 Church place
STATIONERS.
Bowden. Mrs. A., 27 High street
Cowdy, L. & L. & Co., High st.

J. A. THOMPSON, M.R.C.V.S,

VETERINARY ESTABLISHMENT,

CHURCH PLACE, LURGAN,

AND

PORTADOWN.

PATRICK McGEOWN,

SPIRIT MERCHANT,

CHURCH PLACE,

LURGAN.

Speciality.—John Jameson's 6 years old Whiskey. Sandeman's Ports; bottler of Guinness's XX Stout, Bass's and Allsopp's Pale Ales.

CHARLES BAIRD,

CARPENTER AND CONTRACTOR,

UNION STREET, LURGAN.

☞ JOB WORK A SPECIAL FEATURE.

Ezekiel Mawhirt,

Family Grocer, Provision Dealer, Pork Curer and General Draper,

114 EDWARD STREET,

LURGAN.

Fleming, John, 28 Market street
McKeown, Ed. J., 46 Church pl
Pollock, George, 8 High street
Toner, Michael, North street
White, William, *Times* Office,
High street

TIMBER MERCHANTS.
*Saw Mills.

*Campbell, James, Market street
*Mathers, Rt. & Co., Market st

TINSMITHS.
French, Thos., Castle lane
Halfpenny, Wm., Castle lane
McGrevy, Hugh, Castle lane
O'Hare, James, Castle lane

TOBACCONIST.
(See also Grocers.)

Dynes, Danl. 54 Church place

TOWN COMMISSIONERS
Office—Town Hall

Chairman : Thomas Reburn ;
James Malcolm, D.L., J.P., Ex-
Chairman ; John Gilchrist ; Joseph
P. Mathers ; James Campbell ;
Alexander H. McKee ; Robert
McConnell ; Robert Mathers, J.P.;
Robert Hazelton ; James Johnston;
William H. Crawford ; John
McCaughey ; Holt M. Hewitt ;
William Livingston ; Claude
Brownwlow, J.P.

Thomas Lutton, Clerk ; Wm. J.
O'Neill, C.E., Town Surveyor ;
Dr. S. Agnew, Medical Officer of
Health ; James Dunwoody, Town
Constable and Sanitary Sub-Officer;
Robert Jones, Rate Collector.

TOWN HALL,
Union Street.

James Dunwoody, Caretaker.

UNDERTAKERS.
Donnelly, A. & Co., Church place
Gracey, William, Church place
Thompson, Robert, High street
Turkington, Samuel, High street

UNION WORKHOUSE,
Union Street and John Street

Guardians meet every Thursday
at 11 a.m.

Magistrates who are *ex-officio*
members of the Board. For
addresses see County Directory :
Lord Lurgan ; Colonel Waring,
D.L., Waringstown ; Thomas
Shillington ; George Greer ; Wm.
Liddell ; James Malcolm, D.L.;
James Fforde ; Charles Johnston ;
John Johnston ; Thos. Armstrong,
Eden hall, Lurgan ; Augustus E.
Brush, Drumabreeze house, Lurgan;
John Collen ; John C. Fulton ;
Samuel A. Bell ; Robert Mathers ;
Joseph Murphy ; John McNally,
William J. Paul; Francis Watson;
Robert Waddell, Maralin ; Claude
Brownlow ; Edward Magennis ;
Averell Shillington ; Lancelot
Turtle, Aghalee ; James L. Douie,
Moira ; Samuel W. M'Bride.

Elected Guardians and Divisions :
James Downing, Aghagallon ;
Stafford Gorman, Aghalee ; Thos.
Carroll, Ballinderry ; William
Taylor, Ballyleney ; John Crocket,
Breagh ; Nelson Ruddell, Brown-
lowsderry ; James Magennis,
Carrowbrack ; William John
Allen, Cornakinegar ; Joseph
Macoun, Donacloney ; John
Sinnamon, Drumcree ; John
Macoun, Kernan ; John Macoun,
Kilmore ; George R. Carrick, J.P.,
Lurgan ; James Johnston, Lurgan;
F. Langtry, Moira ; Wm. Bateman,
Moira ; Christopher Stevenson,
Moyntaghs ; William Hall, Port-
adown ; William Orr, Portadown ;
John Malcolmson, Portadown ;
John M'Clelland, Tartaraghan ;
John M'Clure, Tartaraghan; Wm.
H. Bingham, Tullylish ; Thomas
Bleakley, Tullylish ; Thomas
B. Brown, Waringstown.

Chairman—John Johnston, J.P.
Vice-Chairman—John Macoun
Deputy V.-C.—William Hall

Jas. Donaldson, Clerk and Re-
turning Officer ; R. Taylor, Master ;
Mrs. Lizzie Taylor, Matron; John
J. Adamson (J.P.), Medical Officer

Chaplains — Very Reverend Theophilus Campbell, C.I.; Rev. Emile H. Piché, R.C.; Rev. C. W. Kennedy, Presbyterian

Vet. Inspector—John A. Thompson, V.S.

Relieving Officers—Jas. Calvert, Market st., Lurgan; J. Alexander, Woodhouse st., Portadown

L. G. B. Officers—R. T. Hamilton, Inspect.; Col. R. M. Studdert, Auditor

VETERINARY SURGEON.

Thompson, J. A., Church pl

VICTUALLERS.

Byrne, Arthur, William st
Casey, Edw., Church pl
Castles, Wesley, 43½ Church pl
Clark, W., Market st
Livingston, Wm., 1 Market st
McCusker, Patk., Church pl
McGeown, Rd., Edward st
McGuigan, Bd., 40 Church pl

Magee, Robt. C., 1 High st
O'Neill, Jas., Market st
Ward, Hugh, Edward st

WATCHMAKERS.

Charles, Samuel, High st
Cousins, Jas., 41 Market st
Smith, Robt., Church pl
Wilson, Mrs. Mt., High st

YARN MERCHANTS.

Johnston & Allen, High st
Murphy, Jos. & Son, William st
Ross & Irwin, Church pl

YOUNG MEN'S RECREATION ROOM.

North street.

J. Chiney, Secretary

YOUNG MEN'S SOCIETY,

Shankill Buildings.

James Malcolm, D.L., President: Hugh Livingston and Charles W. Neill, Secretaries; Robt. Mathers, J.P., Treasurer

LURGAN ALPHABETICAL DIRECTORY.

—:o:—

FARMERS AND RESIDENTS.

—:o:—

For names not found here, see Lurgan Business Branches, &c., and Lurgan Sub-Post Offices.

Abraham, David, Kilvergan
Abraham, Robt., Derrymacash
Alexander, Mrs., Corso lodge
Allen, Joseph, Lough road
Allen, Sl., Derrylisnahavill
Allen, Wm., William st
Allen, W. J., Donagreagh
Anderson, John, Drumgor
Anderson, Wm., Tullygally
Armstrong, Mrs., William st
Bannister, John, Shankhill
Baxter, George, Drumnakeon
Bell, Mrs., Union st
Bell, Samuel A. (J.P.), Bellevue
Best, Jno., sen., Moyraverty
Bigley, Wm. (D.I.), Church pl
Bingham, Clement, Castle le
Black, John, High st
Black, John, Hill st

Blakley, John, Tubberhuny
Blayney, Patrick, Ballynamoney
Boyce, R., jun., Tannaghmore N
Bridgett, J. H., Monbrief
Brown, Charles, Donagreagh
Brown, Miss, High st
Brown, Mrs., 47 Queen st
Brown, Wm., Queen st
Brownlow, Claude (J.P.), Manor ho
Bullick, Isaac, Hill st
Bullick, Mrs. J., William st
Bunting, Thos., Drumnakern
Bullick, Wm., William st
Bunting, Alex., Clanrolla
Bunting, Anthony, North st
Calvert, Leonard, Brownlow ter
Campbell, Samuel, Union st
Canavan, John, William st
Carrick, Geo. R. (J.P.), High st

Carter, George, Tannaghmore N
Carville, Henry, Kinnego
Clarke, George, William st
Clarke, Mrs., High st
Clendinning, James, Aughnacloy
Clendinning, James H., 95 Hill st
Clendinning, John, Sunnyside
Clifford, R., Kilvergan
Cordner, James, Drumnakern
Cordner, William, Drumgask
Corner, John, Drumnamo
Corner, Mrs., Hill st
Coulter, Joseph, jun., Tullygally
Cowdy, Anthony, High st
Craig, Mrs., 88 Queen st
Crawford, George A., Sunnyside
Crawford, William, Woodside
Crawford, W. H., William st
Crowe, Mrs., High st
Crozier, William J., Queen st
Cumberton, Mrs. A., Market st
Cummings, Is., Mourne view ter
Cummins, Moses, Moyraverty
Cummins, William, Tullygally
Davidson, Robert L., William st
Davis, A., Knocknashane
Davis, A., Tubberhuny
Davis, Thomas, Kinnego
Davis, Thomas, Tobberhuny
Dollaghan, William J., Queen st
Doak, William, Kinnego
Donnelly, Miss M., 44 Market st
Dougan, Charles W., Florence villa
Douglas, George, William st
Douglas, Henry, Kinnego
Douglas, William, High st
Duke, Thomas, Union st
Eccles, Mrs., Turmoyra house
Faloon, James, William st
Faloon, Thos., Shankhill buildgs
Fforde, Jas. (J.P.) Raughlan
Finlay, J. D., Brownlow Arms
  hotel
Finlay, M. C., Sunnyside
Fitzsimons, J. W., 59 Market st
Fitzsimons, Robert, Moyraverty
Fleming Richard, Ballynamoney
Fleming, W. J., Mourne view ho
Flynn, Patrick, Kilvergan
Gaskin, James, Kilvergan

Gilpin, William, Moyraverty
Gordon, James, Turmoyra
Gorman, James, William st
Gorman, Mrs., The Flush
Gracey, Edward, Boconnell
Gracey, John, Drumgor
Graham, William, 58 Church pl
Green, William J., Turmoyra
Greene, William, Turmoyra
Greer Geo. (B.L., J.P.) Woodville
Greer, Mrs., The Wilderness
Halliday, James, Drumgask
Halliday, John, Moyraverty
Halliday, Mrs., 6 Edward st
Hamilton, John, Kilmoriarty
Hanna, Mrs. William, William st
Hanna, Thomas, Queen st
Harrison, Robert, Victoria st
Harrison, Valentine, 59 Market st
Heaney, Bd., Cornakinegar
Henderson, Thomas, Liscurran
Henderson, William, Liscurran
Hopps, Richard, Legacurry
Hunter, Henry, Legacurry
Hutchinson, William, Legacurry
Irwin, Thomas, Church pl
Irwin, William, Carn
Irwin, Wilson, Carn
Jackson, James, Tubberhuny
Jeffers, William, Union st
Johnston, Daniel, Cornakinegar
Johnston, James, 43 High st
Johnston, John, J.P., Hill st
Johnston, Miss, High st
Jones, James, Drumgor
Jones, Robert, Drumgor
Jones, Samuel, Moyraverty
Jones, Thomas, Moyraverty
Kane, Bd., Turmoyra
Kane, John, Ballinary
Kearns, James, Ballynamoney
Kearns, Robert, Drumnakern
Keatley, W. J., Sunnyside
Kennedy, Hugh, Church pl
Kerr, John, Tullygally
Kirk, James, Monbrief
Knox, George, Liscurran
Larkin, John, Tannaghmore N
Lattimer, John, Brownlow ter
Lavery, Henry, Kilvergan

2 B

Lavery, John, Kilvergan
Lavery, Johnston, Ballyblough
Livingston, J. R., Union st
Livingston, Mrs., Silverwood
Livingston, R. H., Av road
Lockhart, John G., High st
Lockhart, Misses, High st
Lonsdale, Rt. G., Queen st
Lunn, Wm., Clankilworiff
Lurgan, Lord, Brownlow ho
Lutton, Thomas, 5 Union st
Lutton, Toler, Moyraverty
Lynass, Joseph, Cairn
Lynass, Robert, Cairn
M'Alinden, Hugh, jun., Tannagh-more W
M'Alindon, Arthur, Annaloist
M'Cahilly, Ptk., Turmoyra
M'Cann, Charles, Donagreagh
M'Cann, John (P.M.), Kilvergan
M'Caughey, John, Church pl
M'Caughley, Wm., Annaloist
M'Caw, Robert, Tegnavin
M'Clean, Hugh, Monbrief
M'Climond, Robert, Dougher
M'Collum, Andrew, Kilvergan
M'Conaghey, Bd., Legacurry
M'Conn, John, Drumgor
M'Connell, Henry, Tubberhuny
M'Connell, Wm., Tubberhuny
M'Conville, Bd., Cornakinegar
M'Conville, James, Ballymoney
M'Conville, John, Drumgor
M'Corry, Henry, Turmoyra
M'Corry, John, Lurgantarry
M'Court, W., Donegreagh
M'Cready, Jos., Aghacommon
M'Gaffin, Hugh, 6 High st
MacGeagh, H. G., Derry lodge
M'Geown, Mrs. M. A., Kilvergan
M'Glynn, B. (J.P.), 4 Market st
M'Ilduff, Ter., Derrymacash
M'Ilwain, Soln., Hill st
M'Ivor, Joseph, William st
M'Kinstry, Samuel, Ballymoney
M'Kinstry, Wm., Tullygally
M'Mullen, Miss, Queen st
M'Mullan, Rt., Union st
M'Murtagh, Henry, Aughcommon
M'Murtagh, Henry, Kilvergan

M'Murtagh, James, Ballynamoney
M'Nab, James, Drumgor
M'Nabb, Thomas, Drumgor
M'Nally, John (J.P.), Av. rd
M'Stay, Wm. J., Tannaghmore N
Macoun, Abraham, Drumgor
Macoun, John, Kilmore
Macoun, John, Moyraverty
Macoun, Miss, Adelaide ter
Magahan, Fredk. W., Hill st
Magee, John, Killaghy
Maguire, Alex., Tobberhuny
Magill, Charles, Springhill
Magowan, James, Drumgor
Mahaffy, William, Lough rd
Malcolm, James (D.L.), High st
Malcomson, Jos., Lisnamintry
Martin, Henry, Kilvergan
Mathers, Robt. (J.P.), Market st
Mathers, Robt., jun., High st
Matthews, John, Tegnavin
Maxwell, Joseph, High st
Maxwell, Mrs., High st
Mercer, James, Queen st
Mercer, Robert, Lough rd
Midgley, Mrs., William st
Millar, Robert J., Kinnego
Moore, Miss, 9 High st
Morrow, Wm., Clanrolla
Mulholland, Wm., Killaghy
Murphy, Joseph (J.P.), William st
Murphy, Miss, High st
Murtagh, John, Ballynamoney
Murray, A., Turmoyra
Murray, Denis, Killaghy
Nettleton, Miss, Queen st
Nicholson, Thomas, Legacurry
Noble, John, Ballyblough
O'Hara, Wm., Dougher
O'Neill, Wm. J. (C.E.), Sunnyside
Parkes, John, William st
Pegg, Matthew, Tersogue
Pickering, Wm., Monbrief
Reburn, Thos. (C.T.C.), Market st
Robinson, Wm., 134 Hill st
Ross, John, 27 Church pl
Ross, Mrs., High st
Ross, Wm., High st
Ruddell, David, Ballinacorr
Ruddell, Nelson, Aughcommon

Ruddell, Thos., jun., Knockramer
Ruddell, Walter T. K., Turmoyra
Russell, Alexander, jun., Drumgor
Russell, Alexander, sen., Drumgor
Russell, William, Drumgor
Searight, James, Tobberhuny
Seaton, George, Knocknashane
Simenton, Wm., Knockmenagh
Stevenson, A. W., High street
Stevenson, Richard, Monbrief
Stevenson, Robert, Annaloist
Tate, William, Aughcommon
Taylor, Mrs., Market street
Taylor, W., Clanrolla
Turkington, Fr., Annaloist
Twinem, William, Moyraverty
Uprichard, Charles, Clankilrooriff
Uprichard, Dd., Tannaghmore
Uprichard, Samuel, Legacurry
Uprichard, Thomas, Donagreagh
Ussher, Jas,, Solr., Florence villa

Waite, Henry, Tegnavin
Wallace, John, Moyraverty
Warren, M., Monbrief
Watson, Francis, Lake view
Watson, Joseph, Lake view
Watson, Misses, High street
Watson, Misses, Lake view
Watson, Thomas, Lake view
Wells, James, Legacurry
Wells, Miss, 90 High street
Whitfield, Mrs., Union street
Williams, George, Tullygally
Williams, Thomas, Silverwood
Williamson, John, Drumnagoon
Wilson, J. B., Glenavon place
Wilson, Mrs., Derry lodge
Wilson, Mrs., High street
Wilson, Robert, 10 High street
Woodhouse, Wm., Tamnafiglasson
Woods, M., Hill street
Wright, James, Clanrolla

SUB-POST OFFICES
IN THE LURGAN DISTRICT.

LETTERS addressed to residents of a sub-postal district should bear the name of the head office, thus : Kilvergan, Lurgan. Kilvergan is a rural post-office, 3 miles from Lurgan. The names of its principal farmers and residents will be found included in the alphabetical list of Residents and Farmers of Lurgan, at page 384.

DERRYADD.

DERRYADD is a rural post office, 4 miles north-west of Lurgan. Lord Lurgan and Mr. J. Fforde are the landlords of the district. Oats and potatoes are the chief crops.

Blacksmith : John Bullock
Churches, C. I. : Rev. T. P. Harper ; Presbyterian, Rev. John Hutchinson
Grocers : Rt. Abraham, Edward Castles, Edward M'Caughley, Rt. Robinson, Sarah Stephenson
Post M. : James Castles
School, Natl. : Elizabeth Lutton

Spirit Retailer : Isabella Henon
Farmers & Residents
(See also Lurgan Alphabetical.)
Abraham, Hy., Ardmore, D'add
Abraham, Rt., Derryadd
Burns, John, Derryadd
Castles, Edward, Derryadd
Castles, Thos. D., Derryadd
Doyle, Hh., Derrytagh

Emmerson, Fr., Ardmore
Hendron, Joseph, Derrycorr
Humphreys, T. sen., Derryadd
Kearns, James, Ballinary
Lennon, John, Derrycorr
M'Aleese, John, Ardmore
M'Cann, Edward, Derryadd
M'Conville, Hugh, Derrycorr
M'Geown, Henry, Ballinary
M'Geown, James, Ballinary
M'Geown, Patrick, Derrycorr

M'Ilduff, M., D'macash
M'Kerr, John, Ballinary
M'Shane, J., Ballinary
Mulholland, J., D'cash
Parks, John, Ardmore
Pickering, R., Ardmore
Robinson, John, Ardmore
Robinson, Robert, Derryadd
Stephenson, R., Ardmore
Stevenson, W. H., Derryadd

DERRYTRASNA.

ERRYTRASNA is a rural post office in a boggy district, 6 miles from Lurgan. Lord Lurgan is the landlord. Potatoes and a little oats are the crops.

Churches, C. I. : Rev. Edward
Harpur ; Presbyterian, Rev. John
Hutchinson ; R. C., Rev. James
O'Hare, P.P.
  Grocers : Samuel Adamson, Chr.
Stevenson, Jos. Stevenson, Thos.
Tighe, Oliver Turkington
  Post M. : John Stevenson
  Spirit Retailer : James M'Corry
  Schools, Natl. : Miss Teresa
Carden, Charles M'Grath
Farmers & Residents
  (See also Lurgan Alphabetical.)
Abraham, George, Derryadd
Abraham, Hrsn., Derryloist
Abraham, Robert, Derryloist
Austin, Patrick, Derrytrasna
Breen, Mrs. J., Derryloist
Burns, Charles, Derrytagh S
Cairns, Daniel, Derrytagh S
Cairns, Wm., Derrytagh S
Cordner, Wm. J., Derryloist
Falloon, John, Derrytrasna
Haughain, Jos., Derrytrasna
Heaney, Bernard, Derrytagh S
Heaney, John, Derrytagh S
Hendron, John, Derryloist

M'Cann, John, Ballinary
M'Corry, James, Derryinver
M'Geown, John, Derryloist
M'Kinney, Sol., Derryinver
Mathers, John, Derrytrasna
Murray, Wm., Derryloist
Murray, Wm., Derrytrasna
Richardson, Ml., Derryniver
Stephenson, Chr., Derryloist
Stephenson, Chr., Derrytrasna
Stephenson, J., sen., Derrytrasna
Stephenson, Rd., Derryniver
Stevenson, Edward, Derrytrasna
Stevenson, John, Derrytrasna
Stevenson, Joseph, Derrytrasna
Stevenson, Mrs. E., Derrytrasna
Tighe, Chas., Derrytagh S
Turkington, Dd., Derryloist
Turkington, James, Derryloist
Turkington, Joseph, Derryinver
Turkington, Nl., Derryloist
Turkington, Oliver, Derryinver
Turkington, S., Derryloist
Turkington, S., Derrytrasna
Turkington, Wm., Derrytagh S
Turkington, W., jun., Derryloist
Wilson, J., sen., Derryinver

FAIRS OF COUNTY ARMAGH.

[The compiler of this list, although having exhausted the sources of information, does not hold himself responsible for its accuracy.]

Armagh, 1st Thursday every month.

Ballsmill, 26th May.

Ballybot, 1st Monday every month.

Camlough, 3rd Monday every month.

Crossmaglen, 1st Friday in every month.

Forkhill, 1st May, 1st Aug., 29th Sept., 8th Dec.

Hamiltonsbawn, 26th May, 26th Nov.

Keady, 2nd Friday every month, and 28th Oct.

Killylea, last Friday every month.

Lurgan, 2nd Thursday every month, 5th Aug., 22nd Nov.

Markethill, 3rd Friday every month.

Newtownhamilton, last Saturday every month.

Portadown, 3rd Saturday every month.

Poyntzpass, 1st Saturday every month. If the month begins on Saturday, fair is held on following Saturday.

THE

BUSHMILLS OLD DISTILLERY CO.,

LIMITED,

MALT WHISKEY DISTILLERS.

OFFICES:

1 HILL STREET,
BELFAST.

☞ TELEGRAMS—"BUSH, BELFAST."

[See page 392.]

INDEX.

TOWNS, VILLAGES AND RURAL POST-OFFICES.

	PAGE		PAGE
Ahorey	318	Hamiltonsbawn	161
Allistragh	143	Hockley (see Woodview)	213
Altnamachin	248	Jerretspass	243
Annaghmore	319	Jonesborough	243
Armagh	59	Keady	165
Ballsmill	222	Killeavy	245
Ballybot	235	Killylea	175
Ballynacorr	315	Kilmore	177
Battlehill	315	Kilvergan	387
Belleek	249	Laurelvale	231
Benburb	214	Lislea, Castleblayney	260
Bessbrook	236	Lislea, Armagh	179
Birches, The	322	Lisnadill	180
Blackwatertown	215	Loughgall	183
Caledon	151	Loughgilly	182
Camlough	250	Lurgan	324
Carnagh	257	Madden	188
Castleblayney	248	Maghery	217
Charlemont	216	Markethill	191
Cladymilltown	149	Meigh	245
Clare	231	Middletown	197
Clenroll	315	Milford	143
Clontigora	242	Milltown (see The Birches)	213
Collone	150	Mountnorris	200
Crabtree Lane	315	Mowhan	196
Crossmaglen	253	Moy	214
Cullyhanna	258	Mullaghbawn	223
Darkley	154	Mullantine	315
Derryadd	387	Newry	235
Derryanville	315	Newtownhamilton	261
Derryhale Corner	315	Portadown	265
Derryhaw	210-11	Poyntzpass	245
Derrynoose	155	Richhill	201
Derrytrasna	388	Scotchstreet	315
Diamond	320	Scarva	321
Drumachee	156	Silverbridge	224
Drumannon	160	Tandragee	225
Drumantee	242	Tartaraghan	207
Edenderry	305	Tassagh	208
Eleven Lane Ends	234	The Birches	322
Fathom	235	Tullyrone	218
Flurrybridge	243	Tynan	209
Forkhill	221	Vernersbridge	219
Gilford	317	Whitecross	212
Glenanne	157	Woodview	213

THE BUSHMILLS DISTILLERY.

[*From the* BOOK OF ANTRIM, BY GEORGE HENRY BASSETT.]

THE distillation of whiskey at Bushmills is the only industry which has continued during a period of over a century. It dates from 1784, and its matured brands have ever since been known and appreciated in various parts of the world for sterling medicinal qualities. The premises occupy a conspicuous site at the head of the village, comprising between four and five acres. In 1885 the buildings were destroyed by fire, and all those seen in the illustration are new. The machinery and stills are also new. In fact there is nothing old about the place except the whiskey and the methods—pot stills, etc.—employed to sustain its reputation for purity and excellence. To guard against another burning, electricity is used for lighting purposes in every department. The stream which supplies the distillery is a small tributary of the Bush, rising about five miles to the south-east, and flowing through peat bogs, in this way contributing the special flavor to the spirit that Mr. Edmund Yates considered worthy of reference in his " Recollections and Experiences," and of the following paragraph in the *World* of December 22nd, 1886 :—" Mention made in certain ' Reminiscences ' of mine of a pleasant and wholesome alcoholic stimulant called ' Bushmills Whiskey,' has led the propietors of the famous distillery near Belfast to assure me that their alcohol is still extant in its pristine excellence   *   *   ' All taps,' we are told by Mr. Stiggins, is ' wanity,' but I am glad to find that a favourite ' wanity ' of my youth is as mellow and innocuous as when first introduced to my notice by my old friend, Capt. Mayne Reid." The medicinal qualities of " Bushmills " are referred to by ¿Dr. Sheridan Muspratt, F.R.S.E., M.R.I.A., F.C.S., in his treatise on Alcohol, 1860 :—" Before concluding the article on Malt Whiskey," says the writer, " a short account of the *Bushmills* may prove interesting, as this spirit is said by many to claim pre-eminence over all others in the same manner that genuine Hollands is considered superior to any gins made in this country." A first prize medal was awarded to the Bushmills Old Distillery Co., Limited, at the Cork Exhibition, 1883, a gold medal at the Liverpool Exhibition, 1886, and a diploma of honor at the Paris Exhibition, 1886 ; also the highest award, viz. : First Order of Merit at Adelaide Exhibition, 1887. The head offices of The Bushmills Old Distillery Co., Limited, are at 1 Hill Street, Belfast.

INDEX.—GENERAL.

[*For Alphabetical Index to Towns and Villages, see page 391.*]

	PAGE
Abbeys, by St. Patrick	. 81
St. Aidan's	. 177
Tynan	. 209
Angling, rivers and lakes	. 41
Apparitions	. 267
Archery	. 51
Argial, Principality of	. 13
Assizes	. 53
Antiquities	. 27
Bells. Bronze trumpet	. 27
Cairns	. 31
Caves	. 31
Druidic Circles	. 31
Emania	27-117
Fort leveling	. 31
Lisnadill "Find"	. 180
Navan Fort	. 117
Ogham stone, Pillow "Find"	31
Ornaments, Gold, silver, brass and bronze	. 27
Rath dwellings	. 29
Tassagh "Find".	. 208
ARMAGH CITY.	
Archery and lawn tennis	. 105
Banks	. 113
Blind Asylum	. 111
Building Improvements	. 109
Cathedral, Ancient	. 75
Cathedral, R.C.	. 97
Catholic Reading Room	. 107
Charter of James I.	. 69
Christian Brothers	. 103
Christians	. 97
City burned	63, 67
Clubs	. 103
College, St. Patrick's	. 101
Congregational Church	. 97
Convent	. 101
Court House	. 115
Crosses, Ancient	. 83
De Lacy, Hugh, visit to	65
Directory	. 131
Drelincourt School	. 111
Emania	. 117
Fairs	. 75
Fire Brigade	. 73

	PAGE
Folly	. 93
Football	. 105
Gaol	. 115
Gas Works	. 113
Governmental system	. 69
Hills of	. 59
James II.	. 69
Library, Public	. 85
Mall	. 91
Markets, History of	. 73
Masonic Hall	. 109
Methodist Churches	. 95
Natural History. & P.S.	. 103
Obelisk	. 91
Observatory	. 89
Ornithological Society	. 107
Palace of Primate	. 89
Parliamentary Reprs.	. 69
Philharmonic Society	. 105
Presbyterian Churches	. 95
Property owners	. 109
Protestant M.I. Society	. 107
Protestant Orphans	. 107
Royal School	. 85
St. Bride's Well	. 91
St. Mark's Church	. 93
Sewerage system	. 71
Sheil's Institution	. 111
Tontine Buildings	. 113
Union Workhouse	. 113
Water supply	. 71
Bagnall, Sir Henry	. 67
Baronies of County	. 19
Barony Cess Collectors	. 53
Battle Yellow Ford	. 67
"Bawn," meaning of	. 239
Bicycling	. 51
"Book of Armagh"	. 87
Brian Boru, visit to Armagh	65
Bruce, Edw., King of Ireland	15
"Buried Alive?"	. 226
Canals	. 23
Castles, Ancient	. 33
Cattle in County	. 39
Church of Ireland	. 53
Coal in County	. 21

	PAGE
Collas, The . . .	13
Emania destroyed by	119
Conmael, King, Grave	180
Commissioners, Oaths, &c.	53
Coroners . .	54
County, area . .	11
County Court .	54
County Directory .	53
County History .	11
County Infirmary .	111
County, when formed	13
Co. Surveyor and Assts	54
Course Lodge .	203
Coursing . .	47
Cricket . .	51
Crimes Department .	54
Crop statistics .	39
Crown office . .	54
Dairying in County .	37
Danes, Arrival of .	13
Burnings by .	15
In Armagh city .	63
De Courcey, Sir John	15
Visit to Armagh .	65
Deputy Lieutenants .	54
Diamond, Battle of .	320
Dogs, well-bred .	49
Collies . .	49
Donkeys, Number of	39
Duel, Campbell-Boyd	115
Electric Railway .	23, 237
Emania of the Kings	117
English in County .	10
Fairs . .	41, 389
Farming . .	37
Fergus, King, overthrown	13
Fishing, Net .	41
Foot-ball . .	51
Foreigners in County	10
Fowling places .	43
Fruit Growing .	37
Geology . .	19
Goats in County .	39
Grand Jury officers .	54
Granite . .	19
"Heating" the bog .	322
Horses in County .	39
Horse-finishing .	49
Hunting, History of .	45

	PAGE
County Harriers .	45
Wolves . .	47
Industries . .	23
Inscription, curious .	193
Ireland, Legislative and Judicial Independence .	19
Sir Capel Molyneux, and .	19
Kings of Ulster, Palace	117
James II., Revolution	17
Lurgan destroyed	327
Lakes of Armagh .	43
Camlough .	250
Crossmaglen .	253
Lawn tennis .	51
Lead mines .	19
Limestone .	21
Loughgilly, 16th century	200
Lough Neagh	
Area in Armagh .	43
Medicinal character of Waters .	345
Lunatic Asylum, County	113
Lunatic Asylums, Private	
Course Lodge .	203
Retreat, The .	129
LURGAN.	
Athletic sports .	355
Baptist church .	351
Boat Club .	345
Brownlow House and demesne .	343
Burial places .	335
Change Bell Ringers	347
Chess club .	357
Church of Ireland .	345
C. I. Y. M. Society	349
College .	355
Convent . .	353
Cricket club .	357
Directory .	369
Fire Department .	333
Flower show .	357
Football . .	357
Friends, Society of .	353
Gas Works .	341
Girls Friendly Society	349
Horse jumping & driving	355
James II. destroys town .	327
Linen Hall .	359

	PAGE
Lurgan, Lord and estate .	343
Manufactures . .	357
Market and street scheme	335
Masonic lodges .	357
Mechanics Institute .	339
Methodist churches .	351
Millar Monument .	349
Musical Society .	355
Musical and Dramatic Sy.	355
Navigation . .	343
Ornithological Society .	357
Presbyterian churches .	349
Rifle Association . .	345
R.˙ C. church . .	353
R. I. Constabulary .	341
St. Vincent's Patronage .	353
Salvation Temple .	353
Settlers, original . .	325
Sewerage system . .	329
Talking Figure . .	351
Tennis club . .	357
Town destroyed . .	327
Town Government .	327
Town Hall . .	339
Union Workhouse .	341
War of 1641 . .	327
Waring, William, M.P. .	327
Water "schemes" .	331
William III. . .	327
Y. M. C. A. . .	349
Macha, Queen . .	117
Magistrates . . .	54
Magistrates Resident : Latest	
appointments : Thomas	
D. Gibson, Norman L.	
Townsend . .	
Manufactures . .	23
Marble . . .	19
Markets . . .	41
Marriages, District Registrars	57
Military Head-Quarters .	57
Militia . . .	57
Mountains . . .	21
Obelisks	
In Primate's demesne .	91
Near Castle Dillon .	19
O'Donnell, Tyrone's ally, at	
Belleek . .	249
Leaves Ireland . .	17

	PAGE
Old People	
Jenkinson, John . .	156
Locke, Ml. . .	222
Sheals, Patk. . .	183
O'Neill, Hugh, Rebellion .	15
Battle, Moyre Pass .	17
Battle of Yellow Ford	17, 67
Ditches at Poyntzpass .	246
Leaves for Rome .	17
O'Neill, Owen Roe . .	17
Catholic Army Command	17
O'Neill, Shane, Rebellion of	65
O'Neill, Sir Phelim . .	17
At Armagh City . .	67
Charlemont Castle, seizure of	17
Lurgan destroyed .	327
Scenes at Portadown .	267
Trial and execution .	17
Orchards in County . .	37
Ornithological Societies .	39
Ossian & Slieve Gullion .	222
Parliament, Members .	57
Peep-o'-Day-Boys . .	320
Pigeon shooting . .	43
Mandeville Gun Club .	43
Pigs, Number of . .	39
Plantation of Ulster . .	17
Polling places . .	57
Poor Law Unions . .	57
Population, County . .	11
Population from '41 . .	57
PORTADOWN.	
Apparitions at Bridge .	267
Athletic Club . .	285
Bann Drainage . .	279
Boundary . .	269
Burial Places . .	291
Carrying trade . .	279
Christians . .	291
Church of Ireland .	285
Convent . .	291
Cricket . .	285
Directory . .	299
Fairs . .	273
Fire Brigade , .	275
Gas Works . .	275
Lawn tennis . .	283
Library . .	283
Manufacturers . .	277

	PAGE			PAGE
Markets .	. 271	St. Patrick		
Methodist Church	. 287	Arrival in Armagh	.	61
Musical Society .	. 283	Abbey, founded by	.	81
Obins mansion .	. 267	School founded by	.	83
Park -	. 281	Scenery, County .	.	10
Presbyterian Churches	. 289	Scotch in County .	.	10
Rowing Club .	. 285	Sheep in County .	.	39
R. C. Church .	. 291	Sheriffs .	.	59
R.C.Y.M.A. .	. 283	Slate quarries .	.	19
Settlers, Original .	. 267	Social Experiments		
Sewerage system .	. 275	Bessbrook .	.	236
Town Hall .	. 281	Loughgall .	.	183
Town Government	. 269	Swift, Dean		
Water supply .	. 275	Hamilton's Bawn .	.	162
Y. M. Institute .	. 281	Markethill .	.	192
Poultry, Number of .	. 39	Talking Figure .	.	351
Poyntz, Lieut. .	. 246	Tricycling .	.	51
Prison, H. M. .	. 115	United Irishmen, Rebellion .		19
Probate Registry .	. 57	Valuation, County .	.	10
Racing . .	. 49	Volunteers .	.	19
Railways . .	. 21	Charlemont, Lord, and .		19
Great Northern .	. 57	Convention .	.	19
Red Branch Knights	. 119	Why disbanded .	.	69
Retreat, The .	. 129	War of 1641 .	.	17
Rifle shooting .	. 45	Welsh in County .	.	10
Roads in County .	. 23	William of Orange & James II	17
Roman Catholic Church	59	Wolves in Armagh .	.	47
R.I. Constabulary .	. 59	Last in Ireland .	.	47
Sir O. St. John's Skull	. 226	Yellow Ford, Battle .	.	17

INDEX.

MANUFACTURERS MERCHANTS, TRADERS, &c., &c., OF THE COUNTY ARMAGH.

[*See also Index to Manufacturers, Merchants, &c., not in County, p.* 399]

Acheson, D., Armagh	. 110	Armstrong, Geo., Markethill .	191
Acheson, J. & J. & Acheson,		Bailie, John, Keady	. 166
J. & J. & Co. Portadown	. 268	Baird, Chas., Lurgan	. 382
Addey, W. H. & Co., Armagh	126	Balfour, Henry, Portadown	. 290
Aiken, Jas. & Co., Armagh	. 108	Begley, Jas., Crossmaglen	. 253
Albert Hotel, Portadown	. 302	Bell, M. A., Armagh	. 104
Allen, Alex. D., The Retreat	. 128	Bell, Thos. & Co., Lurgan	. 356
Allen, James, Lurgan	. 374	Beresford Arms Hotel, Armagh	62
Anderson, Joseph, Armagh 52,	116	Bessbrook Spinning Co., Ld. .	238
Anderson, W., Portadown	. 308	Biggart, Wm., Armagh	. 40
Archer, David, Lurgan	. 376	Bleakley, Wm., Killylea	. 175
Armagh Guardian	. 114	Bourke, Mrs. M., Armagh	. 130
Armstrong & Mathers, Lurgan	334	Bowden, Mrs. A., Lurgan	. 378

	PAGE
Boyce, W. H., Lurgan	. 376
Boyd, & Co., Armagh	. 90
Boyd, Mrs. Wm. C., Armagh	108
Boyle, Jas., Portadown	. 272
Brice's Medical Hall, Armagh	78
Brown, John S., & Sons, Lurgan	366
Brownlow Arms Hotel, Lurgan	378
Bullick, Isaac & Co., Lurgan	. 348
Burke, A., Middletown	. 199
Burnett, A. J., Portadown	. 290
Calvert, J. & Co., Lurgan	. 324
Campbell, James, Lurgan	. 377
Campbell, J. W., Keady	. 164
Campbell, Peter, Keady	. 164
Canavan, Ml., Poyntzpass	. 246
Carragher, B., Silverbridge	. 224
Carson, S. E., Armagh	. 106
Carter, Wm., Armagh	. 108
CharlemontArmsHotel,Armagh	80
Cinnamon, Bros., Bessbrook	. 241
Clendinning, Jas., Lurgan	. 346
Clow, Jas. & Co., Portadown	. 284
Collen, T. & Son, Armagh	. 66
Collins, J. & A., Armagh	. 134
Collins, James, Armagh	. 134
Compton, John, Armagh	. 124
Connell, H., Cullyhanna	. 258
Corr, Peter, Middletown	. 197
Course Lodge, Richhill	. 202
Courtney, Clement, Portadown	286
Cowdy, Wm., Portadown	. 280
Crawford, W. H. & Co., Lurgan	338
Crozier, Hh., N'townhamilton	261
Cuming & Son, Markethill	. 190
Dawson, Thos., Portadown	. 294
Deighan, Bros., Whitecross	. 212
Deighan, Jas., Middletown	. 197
Dickson, Jas., Lurgan	. 330
Dickson, Mrs. W., Portadown	296
Dickson, Wm., Portadown	. 296
Donnelly & Somerville, Armagh	76
Donnelly, Ml., Armagh	. 106
Donnelly, Miss S. J., Lurgan	332
Douglas, Henry, Lurgan	. 370
Douglas, Jos., Portadown	. 274
Duke, Thos., Lurgan	. 372
Dymond, J. J., Newry	. 34
Dynes, Daniel, Lurgan	. 344
Edwards, Geo. A., Armagh	. 60

	PAGE
Elliott, Wm., Armagh	. 104
Fairley, Wm., Lurgan	. 374
Fegan, E., Keady	. 172
Fitzsimons & Co., Lurgan	. 342
Fleming, Jno., Lurgan	. 330
Fleming, Jos., Portadown	. 270
Fleming, Wm. J., Lurgan	. 374
Frazer, Henry (M.D.), Armagh	92
Frizell's Cabinet Wks., Armagh	84
Gilchrist, John, Lurgan	. 378
Gilpin, J., Verner's Bridge	. 219
Glass, Jas. & Co., Lurgan	. 354
Graham, Bros., Lurgan	. 336
Graham D. & Co., Portadown	292
Gray, David, Portadown	. 308
Gray, Geo., & Sons, Glenanne	158
Gray, Wm. & Co., Armagh	. 96
Greer, Arthur, Armagh	. 112
Greer, George, Lurgan	. 36
Greer, James, Lurgan	. 376
Grew, Jas. & Co., Portadown	280
Haire, Thos., ElevenLaneEnds	234
Hanna, Wm. M'Clure, Armagh	134
Harrison, Bros., Lurgan	. 368
Hawthorn, J., N'townhamilton	261
Hewitt, Adam, Lurgan	. 336
Hewton, Thos. W., Armagh	132
Hillock, Henry, Armagh	. 70
Hillock, James, Armagh (5th page from cover)	
Houston, Wm., Lurgan	. 332
Imperial Hotel, Portadown	. 298
Jackson, Jno., Richhill	. 206
Jenkinson, W. J., Portadown	302
Johnston, Allen & Co., Lurgan	364
Johnston, James, Lurgan	. 328
Jordan, T. & Sons, Lurgan	. 368
Kennedy, Rd., Lurgan	. 380
Kilpatrick, Wm., Tandragee	225
Kirk, W. M. & Partners, A'vale	168
Lamb, Bros., Richhill	. 206
Leeman, H. G. & Co., Armagh	88
Lennon, Henry, Crossmagien	252
Lennox, W. J., Armagh	. 72
Livingston, J. G., Portadown	302
Locke, Geo., Portadown	. 302
Locke, Wm. John, Portadown	302
Lockhart, Wm., Armagh	. 118
Logan, Hy. & Son, Portadown	272

	PAGE
Long, John, Lurgan	376
Loudan, B. M., Armagh 106,	110
Lurgan Times	374
Lurgan Weaving Co., Ld.	362
Lutton, A. J. & Son, Portadown	278
Lyons & Woods, Lurgan	352
M'Aleavy, T., Drumantee	242
M'Ardle, Owen, Crossmaglen	252
M'Ardle, Philip, Crossmaglen	254
M'Bride, Sl. W., Lurgan	358
M'Cammon & Sprott, P'down	288
M'Cann, Stephen, Lislea	260
M'Caughey & Co., Lurgan	372
M'Clelland, Geo., Tullyrone	218
M'Clure, Wm. W., Lurgan	378
M'Connell, Javanna, Armagh	98
M'Connell, Wm., Lurgan	372
M'Conville, J. & Co., C'maglen	253
M'Conville, Jno., Portadown	308
M'Cormick, A. & W. F., Keady	164
M'Cormick, W. F., House and Land Agent, Keady	164
M'Creesh, John, Armagh	110
M'Crum, Rt. & Co., Armagh	122
M'Garity, P. J., Armagh	112
M'Geown, Patrick, Lurgan	382
M'Gredy, S. & Son, Portadown	297
M'Ilveen, W. J., Portadown	280
M'Kell, Jas., Portadown	288
M'Kelvey, G. W., Poyntzpass	246
M'Kenney, Jas., Keady	164
M'Lorinan, P., Armagh	58
M'Loughlin, R. J., Armagh	108
M'Mahon, Armagh	104
M'Namee, Jas., Forkhill	220
M'Shane, L., Keady	166
M'Watters, Rt. P., Armagh	106
Macoun, J. R. & Co., Lurgan	372
Magee, Hugh, Lurgan	340
Magee, John, Lurgan	340
Magee, R. C., Lurgan	380
Magee, Thos., Lurgan	340
Magowan, J. T., Armagh	110
Magowan, W. C., Armagh	106
Malcolm, James, Lurgan	360
Mallagh, Jos., Markethill	190
Martin, D. P. & Co., Armagh	130
Massey, Francis A., Armagh	100
Mathers & Bunting, Lurgan	370
	PAGE
Mawhirt, Ezekiel, Lurgan	382
Maxwell, J. & Co., Lurgan	372
Maxwell, Jas., Armagh	110
Milligan, E., Portadown	302
Montgomery, J. & Sons, P'down	280
Monypeny & Watson, P'down	276
Moore, Thos. & Co., Armagh	94
Morrison, T., Portadown	272
Murphy, Jos. & Son, Lurgan	370
Murray, Jas., Armagh	114
Murray, Richard, Lurgan	374
Nelson, Arthur, Armagh	74
Nelson, W. R. & Co., Lurgan	350
Nugent, J. & Co., Keady	166
Orr, J. & W., Richhill	202
Orr, Jos. & Sons, Cranagill	184
Palmer, Thos., The Birches	322
Paul, Wm. & Son, Portadown (3rd page from cover) and	266
Peel, Josiah, Armagh and Portadown	96, 300
Portadown & Lurgan News	299
Qua, Miss M. R., Markethill	190
Queen's Hotel, Portadown	284
Reburn & Co., Lurgan	326
Redmond, W. J., Portadown	298
Reid, Rt. & Son, Portadown	280
Retreat, Armagh	128
Reilly, Henry, Armagh	100
Rodden, Edw., Tandragee	225
Roleston, R. H., Keady	166
Rolston, Andrew, Armagh	68
Ross & Irwin, Lurgan	372
Ross, J. H., Portadown	286
Short, Francis, Crossmaglen	254
Sinton, Thos., Tandragee	228
Sinton, W. F., Hamiltonsbawn	161
Sloane, Sl. C., Armagh	149
Slowey, P., Portadown	302
Small, A. & S., Keady	166
Small, Robt., Markethill	190
Smith, James, Forkhill	220
Smyth, Rt., Armagh	120
Somers, Jas., Armagh	112
Tavener, A. J., Lurgan	338
Taylor, Bros., Armagh	86
Taylor, James, Lurgan	380
The Northern Baking Co.	380
Thompson, A. G., Portadown	272

	PAGE		PAGE
Thompson, J. A., Lurgan	382	Wallace, Rt. & Co., Armagh	82
Thompson, Max, Lurgan	380	Walsh, Jas., Portadown	300
Thompson, Robt., Lurgan	16	Ward, Geo., Lurgan	377
Towell, Jos. Richhill	206	Watson, Jas. Alex., Armagh	104
Turkington, S., Lurgan	380	Watters & Smyth, Keady	164
Turner, Rt. & Co., Armagh	102	White, Samuel, Armagh	100
Turtle, Wm. J., Tandragee	230	Whitsitt, Bros., Armagh	64
Ulster Gazette, Armagh	130	Williamson, S., Armagh	114
Vogan, Rt., Armagh	110	Willis, James, Armagh	134
Waddell, Robt., Keady	164	Wilson, Jas., Armagh	112
Wallace, A., grocer Armagh	118, 132	Wilson, Jno., Bessbrook	241
		Wilson, Sl., Portadown	284
Wallace, A., hardware, Armagh	98	Woods, B. & T., Keady	172
		Woods, Hy. G., Mowhan	196
Wallace, Hugh, Portadown	282	Wright, Jos., Portadown	296
Wallace, Miss M., Armagh	130	Wynne, Thos. & Co., Armagh	178

INDEX.—MANUFACTURERS, MERCHANTS, ETC., NOT IN COUNTY ARMAGH.

Anderson, D. & Son, Belfast (4th page from cover)		Kirker & Co., Belfast	26
		Kirker, Thomas, Belfast	42
Anderson, Jas., Belfast	26	King, Fredk. & Co. (facing inside back cover)	
Belfast Steamship Co. (back of map)			
		Leahy, Kelly & Leahy, Belfast (inside first cover)	
Brown & Polson	20		
Bushmills (see Old Bushmills)		Maclean & Co., Newry	42
Butterick's Patterns	20	Mellin, G.	30
Byrne, Edward A., Newry	28	Mercier, W. & S., Moyallon	316
Cantrell & Cochrane, Belfast (1st page from cover)		Neill, Sharman D., Belfast (inside back cover)	
Cathcart, Jos. & Co., Newry	10	Northern Assurance Co.	18
Chamberlin, James, & Smith	46	Old Bushmills Distillery Co. Ld. (facing 1st & 2nd pages Index and at 260)	
Connor, Dr. Sl., Newry	38		
Creeth, James, Belfast	32		
Culley, Wm. J., Newry	22	Robson, John, Belfast (2nd page from cover)	
Cunningham, Bros., Newry	50		
Doyle, Mark J., Newry	32	Ross & Co., Belfast (facing map)	
Dymond, J. J. Newry	34		
Edinburgh Life Assurance Co.	74	Sealy, Bryers & Walker	32
Electric Appliance Co., Ld.	14	Sherrard, Smith & Co., Caledon	152
Fleming, S., Newry	34	Thompson, James, Newry	24, 389
Harper A. & Co., Belfast	44	Thompson, John, Newry	34
Inglis, Jas. & Co., Belfast	12	Wightman, David, Belfast	38
Johnson, Thos. & Sons, Belfast	48	Wilson, Wm., Belfast	48
Johnston, Henry, Belfast	28	Worth, Jos., Belfast	16

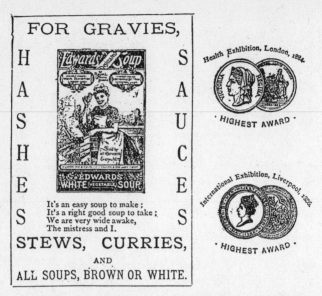